CRIMINOLOGY

PATTERSON SMITH

REPRINT SERIES IN

CRIMINOLOGY, LAW ENFORCEMENT,
AND SOCIAL PROBLEMS

———

PUBLICATIONS

PUBLICATION No. 12: PATTERSON SMITH REPRINT SERIES IN CRIMINOLOGY, LAW ENFORCEMENT, AND SOCIAL PROBLEMS

Criminology

BY

BARON RAFFAELE ₋GAROFALO

Procurator General at the Court of Appeals of Venice and Senator of the Kingdom of Italy

Translated by

ROBERT WYNESS MILLAR

Lecturer in Northwestern University Law School

WITH AN INTRODUCTION BY

E. RAY STEVENS

Judge of the Circuit Court, Madison, Wis., Member of Executive Board of American Institute of Criminal Law and Criminology

Montclair, New Jersey

PATTERSON SMITH

1968

GENERAL INTRODUCTION TO THE MODERN CRIMINAL SCIENCE SERIES.

AT the National Conference of Criminal Law and Criminology, held in Chicago, at Northwestern University, in June, 1909, the American Institute of Criminal Law and Criminology was organized; and, as a part of its work, the following resolution was passed:

"*Whereas*, it is exceedingly desirable that important treatises on criminology in foreign languages be made readily accessible in the English language, *Resolved*, that the president appoint a committee of five with power to select such treatises as in their judgment should be translated, and to arrange for their publication."

The Committee appointed under this Resolution has made careful investigation of the literature of the subject, and has consulted by frequent correspondence. It has selected several works from among the mass of material. It has arranged with publisher, with authors, and with translators, for the immediate undertaking and rapid progress of the task. It realizes the necessity of educating the professions and the public by the wide diffusion of information on this subject. It desires here to explain the considerations which have moved it in seeking to select the treatises best adapted to the purpose.

For the community at large, it is important to recognize that criminal science is a larger thing than criminal law. The legal profession in particular has a duty to familiarize itself with the principles of that science, as the sole means for intelligent and systematic improvement of the criminal law.

Two centuries ago, while modern medical science was still young, medical practitioners proceeded upon two general assumptions: one as to the cause of disease, the other as to its treatment. As to the cause of disease, — disease was sent by the inscrutable will of God. No man could fathom that will, nor its arbitrary operation. As to the treatment of disease, there were believed to be a few remedial agents of universal efficacy. Calomel and blood-letting, for example, were two of the principal ones. A larger or smaller dose of calomel, a greater or less quantity of bloodletting, — this blindly indiscriminate mode of treatment was regarded as orthodox for all common varieties of ailment. And so his calomel pill and his bloodletting lancet were carried everywhere with him by the doctor.

Nowadays, all this is past, in medical science. As to the causes of disease, we know that they are facts of nature, — various, but distinguishable by diagnosis and research, and more or less capable of prevention or control or counteraction. As to the treatment, we now know that there are various specific modes of treatment for specific causes or symptoms, and that the treatment must be adapted to the cause. In short, the individualization of disease, in cause and in treatment, is the dominant truth of modern medical science.

The same truth is now known about crime; but the understanding and the application of it are just opening upon us. The old and still dominant thought is, as to cause, that a crime is caused by the inscrutable moral free will of the human being, doing or not doing the crime, just as it pleases; absolutely free in advance, at any moment of time, to choose or not to choose the criminal act, and therefore in itself the sole and ultimate cause of crime. As to treatment, there still are just two traditional measures, used in varying doses for all kinds of crime and all kinds of persons, — jail, or a fine (for death is now employed in rare cases only). But modern science, here as in medicine, recognizes that crime also (like disease) has natural causes. It need not be asserted for one moment that crime is a disease. But it does have natural causes, — that is, circumstances which work to produce it in a given case. And as to treatment, modern science recognizes that penal or remedial treatment cannot possibly be indiscriminate and machine-like, but must be adapted to the causes, and to the man as affected by those causes. Common sense and logic alike require, inevitably, that the moment we predicate a specific cause for an undesirable effect, the remedial treatment must be specifically adapted to that cause.

Thus the great truth of the present and the future, for criminal science, is the individualization of penal treatment, — for that man, and for the cause of that man's crime.

Now this truth opens up a vast field for re-examination. It means that we must study all the possible data that can be causes of crime, — the man's heredity, the man's physical and moral make-up, his emotional temperament, the surroundings of his youth, his present home, and other conditions, — all the influencing circumstances. And it means that the effect of different methods of treatment, old or new, for different kinds of men and of causes, must be studied, experimented, and compared. Only in this way can accurate knowledge be reached, and new efficient measures be adopted.

All this has been going on in Europe for forty years past, and in limited fields in this country. All the branches of science that can help have been working, — anthropology, medicine, psychology, economics, sociology, philanthropy, penology. The law alone has abstained. The science of law is the one to be served by all this. But the public in general and the legal profession in particular have remained either ignorant of the entire subject or indifferent to the entire scientific movement. And this ignorance or indifference has blocked the way to progress in administration.

The Institute therefore takes upon itself, as one of its aims, to inculcate the study of modern criminal science, as a pressing duty for the legal profession and for the thoughtful community at large. One of its principal modes of stimulating and aiding this study is to make available in the English language the most useful treatises now extant in the Continental languages. Our country has started late. There is much to catch up with, in the results reached elsewhere. We shall, to be sure, profit by the long period of argument and theorizing and experimentation which European thinkers and workers have passed through. But to reap that profit, the results of their experience must be made accessible in the English language.

The effort, in selecting this series of translations, has been to choose those works which best represent the various schools of thought in criminal science, the general results reached, the points of contact or of controversy, and the contrasts of method — having always in view that class of works which have a more than local value and could best be serviceable to criminal science in our country. As the science has various aspects and emphases — the anthropological, psychological, sociological, legal, statistical, economic, pathological — due regard was paid, in the selection, to a representation of all these aspects. And as the several Continental countries have contributed in different ways to these various aspects, — France, Germany, Italy, most abundantly, but the others each its share, — the effort was made also to recognize the different contributions as far as feasible.

The selection made by the Committee, then, represents its judgment of the works that are most useful and most instructive for the purpose of translation. It is its conviction that this Series, when completed, will furnish the American student of criminal science a systematic and sufficient acquaintance with the controlling doctrines and methods that now hold the stage of thought in Continental Europe.

Which of the various principles and methods will prove best adapted to help our problems can only be told after our students and workers have tested them in our own experience. But it is certain that we must first acquaint ourselves with these results of a generation of European thought.

In closing, the Committee thinks it desirable to refer the members of the Institute, for purposes of further investigation of the literature, to the " Preliminary Bibliography of Modern Criminal Law and Criminology " (Bulletin No. 1 of the Gary Library of Law of Northwestern University), already issued to members of the Conference. The Committee believes that some of the Anglo-American works listed therein will be found useful.

COMMITTEE ON TRANSLATIONS.

Chairman, JOHN H. WIGMORE,
> Dean of Northwestern University School of Law, Chicago.

ERNST FREUND,
> Professor of Law in the University of Chicago.

EDWARD LINDSEY,
> Associate Editor of the Journal of the American Institute of Criminal Law and Criminology, Warren, Penn.

MAURICE PARMELEE,
> Associate Professor of Sociology in the University of Missouri, Columbia, Missouri.

ROSCOE POUND,
> Professor of Law in Harvard Law School, Cambridge, Mass.

WILLIAM W. SMITHERS,
> Secretary of the Comparative Law Bureau of the American Bar Association, Philadelphia, Penn.

TRANSLATOR'S PREFACE

NONE of the Continental writers who deal with crime and the criminal seems destined to a larger audience among English-speaking peoples than the author of the work here translated. His teachings, in the main, are characterized by a simplicity and directness that should have a special appeal to the Anglo-Saxon mind. They contain "no anointings for broken bones, no fine theories 'de finibus,' no arguments to persuade men out of their senses." And, indeed, Anglo-Saxon influences have not been without their part in the groundwork of his system. Here Darwin, Spencer, and Bagehot have all contributed to shape his thought and color his ideas. But whatever of indebtedness thus exists on his part has been repaid with usury. Few of us, perhaps, would be willing to accept all the applications of his principles, fewer, perhaps, to regard the system of procedure for which he contends as the last word in the mechanics of the criminal law; but, none the less, he offers much that England and America, without departing from their traditions, may lay hold of to advantage in building for the future.

Baron RAFFAELE GAROFALO, a member of an Italian noble family of Spanish origin, was born in the city of Naples in 1852. He was educated for the law, and at the conclusion of his university studies entered what in Italy, as elsewhere on the Continent, is really a profession by itself, namely, the magistracy. Passing from grade to grade, he attained high place at a comparatively early age. Among the important offices which he has held are those of President of the Civil Tribunal of Pisa, Substitute Procurator-General at the Court of Cassation in Rome, and President of Division ("Sezione") in the Court of Appeal of Naples. At present he is Procurator-

General at the Court of Appeal of Venice. Added to this, he
is a Senator of the Kingdom of Italy and Adjunct Professor
of Criminal Law and Procedure in the University of Naples,
with personal distinctions including membership in the governing body of the Heraldic Council, the rank of Officer in the
Order of Saint Maurice and Saint Lazarus, and that of "Com-
mendatore" in the Royal Order of the Crown of Italy.

At the time of his appointment to the Senate, he had already
a long record of usefulness in connection with legislation for
the betterment of the criminal law. A notable achievement
in this field was the preparation, in 1903, at the instance of the
Minister of Justice, of the draft of a code for the reformation
of criminal procedure in the Italian courts. Political reasons,
unfortunately, forced the Government to lay this project aside.

He has been a member of the Royal Academy of Naples,
as also of the International Institute of Sociology, which has
its headquarters at Paris. As President of the last-mentioned
organization, he was Chairman of the Congress held at Berne
in 1909, whose subject of discussion was "Solidarity." Some
time ago he was elected to the Presidency of the Italian Society
of Sociology, which office he still holds. He is the author of
many articles on legal, sociologic, and economic topics, and
of numerous papers read before societies for the advancement
of related studies, in particular that of crime and its treatment.
Other writings of his are: "Criminal Attempt by Insufficient
Means;"[1] "The True Manner of Trial and Sentence;"[2] "Indemnification of Persons Injured by Crime;"[3] "The Socialist
Superstition;"[4] and "International Solidarity in the Repression of Crime."[5]

But it is upon his "Criminology" that Garofalo's title to
international renown principally rests. Its doctrines, varying

[1] "Il tentativo criminoso con mezzi inidonei" (Turin, Loescher, 1882).

[2] "Ciò che dovrebbe essere un giudizio penale" (Turin, Loescher, 1882).

[3] "Riparazione alle vittime del delitto" (Turin, Bocca, 1887).

[4] Tr. Dietrich, "La Superstition socialiste" (Paris, F. Alcan, 1895).

[5] "De la solidarité des nations dans la lutte contre la criminalité" (Paris,
Giard et Brière, 1909).

markedly from those of Lombroso and Ferri, but attaching the same value to experimental and inductive methods,
have ranked him as one of the three protagonists of the Italian
positive school, and earned him commanding place among
the leaders of criminal science. As explained in his own preface, this book was the outgrowth of a brochure which he
published in 1880: "Concerning a Positive Criterion of
Punishment." The first Italian edition of the "Criminology"
appeared at Naples in 1885, the second at Turin in 1891. To
ensure a wider public, a French version was prepared by the
author personally. This has gone through five editions, in
the last of which, brought out in 1905, he took occasion to
effect a complete recasting of the work. Translations have
also been made into Spanish and Portuguese, the former by
P. Dorado y Montero, the latter by J. De Mattos.

Conformably to the wishes of the author, the present version is taken from the French edition of 1905. The translator,
however, has kept the second Italian edition constantly before him, and has found it of much service. Indeed, the interests of the English version have at times seemed to require
that the Italian edition be laid under direct contribution.
It is thus responsible for verbal deviations, here and there,
from the French text, for some amplification of statements
of fact in relation to criminal cases referred to by the author
(containing, as a rule, a fuller account of such cases), and for
slight additions to the foot-notes. So, also, it has considerably influenced the matter of quotations from Italian
writers.

In the work of translation, closeness of rendition has not
been looked upon as an inflexible canon. The aim has been
to say what Garofalo has said, but to say it as an Englishman
or American would have said it. Where literalness would have
interfered with naturalness, literalness has been freely sacri-
ficed. Pursuant to the ideas of the Editorial Committee,
titles have been given to the sections (these, save in a few
instances, being without superscription in the original) and

italic side-headings introduced where they appeared of advantage. Some re-arrangement of subdivisions has likewise been found advisable. Except in the case of the material for an international penal code, comprising Part IV, such re-arrangements are indicated by a foot-note at the outset of the chapter wherein they occur. It also seemed more in keeping with our ideas of book-making that the matter contained in the appendices should follow Part IV, instead of preceding it. One or two minor inadvertencies of the author have been corrected without comment.

A certain amount of hesitation was experienced as to the proper rendition of "probité," the term used by the author to designate the second of the elementary altruistic instincts, that is to say, the sentiment of respect for the property of others. It was a question whether it should not be translated as "honesty," in view of the specific meaning which this word usually carries in modern English, unlike its corresponding forms in French and Italian. But for one thing, the wider meaning of "honesty" is not altogether extinct: we still speak of the "honest" man as the opposite of the criminal, without necessarily referring to the thievish or mendacious criminal. Then again, there is little difference in meaning between "probity" on the one hand, and the French "probité" and the Italian "probità" on the other. The objection to the use of "probity" in the present connection is that it implies a high degree of respect, or a superior kind of respect, for what belongs to others — a maximum, rather than otherwise, of the moral quality sought to be denoted. But the same thing unquestionably holds true of the French and Italian words. Speaking of "probità," in his second Italian edition, Garofalo himself owns to its lack of precision, and emphasizes the fact that it has only been adopted in default of an apter term.[1] These considerations, together with the further advantage of preserving the identity of the author's terminology, dictated the employment of "probity" as the nearest equivalent.

[1] P. 32 (Turin, Bocca, 1891).

It is to be sure inexact, but in this it merely reproduces the acknowledged inexactness of its original.

Some notes have been added by the translator, chiefly with reference to the meaning of legal terms. In this regard (as well as for guidance to specific renderings) Sir James Fitzjames Stephen's "History of the Criminal Law of England" has been repeatedly drawn upon. For the general explanation, however, which would have been a desirable pendant of Garofalo's chapter on procedure, the reader is directly referred to the illuminating account of French criminal procedure (with which the Italian substantially accords) contained in Stephen's first volume. On this head, too, the collection of entertaining sketches translated and edited by Gerald P. Moriarty under the title of "The Paris Law Courts" [1] will be found to yield much serious information. The paper by Alfred Le Poittevin, in Barrows' "Penal Codes of France, Germany, Belgium, and Japan," [2] may likewise be consulted with profit. A number of articles in English and American legal periodicals also deal with the subject, of which should be mentioned: "The Trial of Crime in France," by Thomas Barclay, 10 Harvard Law Review, 46–48, "Criminal Procedure in France and England," by Léon de Montluc, 12 Journal of Comparative Legislation (N. s.), 157–174; "The French Judicial System," by C. A. Hereshoff Bartlett, Part II, "Criminal," 38 Law Magazine and Review, 428–446; and (by all means) Judge Lawson's interesting notes on his recent study of the French courts, appearing in the current volume of the American Law Review (Vol. 47, 143–152, 300–312, 458–469).

As a final word, the translator would record his indebtedness to the Chairman of the Editorial Committee, whose counsel has smoothed out numerous difficulties and whose encouragement has lent an added agreeableness to the task.

CHICAGO, October 10, 1913.

[1] New York, Scribner, 1894.
[2] Pp. 43–80 (Washington, Government Printing Office, 1901).

INTRODUCTION TO THE ENGLISH VERSION

By E. Ray Stevens [1]

BEGINNING with the days when the accused was without counsel, without witnesses, without even the right to testify in his own behalf, the attention of society was long engrossed with the protection of the accused before conviction. His rights have been made so secure by bills of rights and other constitutional limitations as to protect, often, the guilty as well as the innocent from punishment. We cling so tenaciously to the old methods of protecting the accused that Baron Garofalo justly says that the dominant theory today is to protect the criminal against society rather than to protect society against the criminal.

Were it not for our worship of these old rules that have long since ceased to be applicable to the administration of modern criminal justice, we would compel the defendant to take the stand in criminal as well as in civil actions, because, of all men, he knows most about his guilt or innocence. The object of the trial of a criminal action should be to find the truth, — not to shield a guilty person from a just conviction. Adherence to these archaic rules is one of the chief causes for the existing dissatisfaction with the administration of criminal justice, because the accused is allowed to play his game with loaded dice, while justice travels with leaden heel.[2] This

---

[1] Judge of the Ninth Judicial Circuit, Madison, Wisconsin; member of the Executive Board of the American Institute of Criminal Law and Criminology.

[2] Chief Justice Winslow, in *Hack* v. *State*, 141 Wis. 346, 352.

condition was tolerated because society considered punishment as a substitute for private vengeance and still looked
upon the trial as a kind of warfare in which the end—acquittal
— justified the means.

Up to recent times society as a whole felt that it had done
its full duty to itself and to the accused when it protected
him at every step up to his conviction. Upon his conviction
the individual ceased to be of interest to society, at least until,
his sentence past, he emerged from prison and was again
featured in the newspapers in some new crime. Up to very
recent times society has failed to recognize the fact that the
great problems connected with the administration of criminal justice begin when the guilt of the accused has been
determined.

Happily we have discovered the large part which juvenile
courts, indeterminate sentences, probation, and parole can
play in the administration of our criminal justice. But we
need to have shed on our path of progress such light as is
thrown by Baron Garofalo's practical and sane book on Criminology, which gives the conclusions formed in a life spent
in the administration of the criminal law as lawyer,
prosecuting officer, and judge. As one reads this enlight-
ening work, he is impressed again and again by the fact that
the men with whom the author dealt were actuated by the
same motives and were in need of the same treatment as
those who appear in the criminal courts of our English-
speaking countries.

Proceeding upon the theory that punishment at the hands
of the public is a substitute for private vengenace, society has
attempted to measure punishment by the harm done to society;
so that the quantum of punishment inflicted on the offender
should weigh as heavily on one side of the scales of justice as
the harm done by the accused does upon the other. This
theory overlooks entirely the fact that the object of punishment is not to replace private vengeance, but that it should
be to protect society from future harm from the offender by

so changing the *motives* that guide his action that he will no longer remain a menace. As the author puts it: "Our efforts . . . are to be directed, not to measuring the quantum of harm to be inflicted on the criminal, but to determining the kind of restraint best fitted to the peculiarities of his nature" (p. 299).

We have given too much consideration to the offense, too little to the offender. We must give more consideration to the individual, less to the chapter and verse of the written law that declares the punishment. for each offense. If the offense be burglary, we have been prone to impose the same punishment whether the defendant be a recidivist or a first offender. We have given altogether too little consideration to the personal history and characteristics of the individual in determining what shall be done to protect society against future harm. As the author so ably demonstrates, the only way of protecting society from the recidivist is to eliminate him. At present, we confine him for the prescribed orthodox period and then give him liberty, with no better equipment for becoming a desirable member of society than the reputation of being a convict and the inherent aptitude to commit another crime, which may in fact be his only means of securing even the barest necessities of continued physical existence. Such men are as much in need of treatment and care as if suffering from a physical ailment.

One great obstacle in the way of giving to each offender the individual treatment which Baron Garofalo would have him receive is that the law imposes on the trial judge the impossible task of determining in advance the punishment best suited to the needs of each individual offender. That determination must be made in most cases after the most limited opportunity to observe the defendant. In the great majority of cases he enters a plea of guilty without trial; frequently he is practically unknown in the community. Yet under such circumstances the trial judge is expected to play the part of the wise physician, to determine to the day the length of treatment that the defendant must undergo for his reform or cure and for the protection of society. No physician, even the most able and experienced, can treat his patients without oppor-- tunity to observe them from day to day that he may adapt his treatment to their needs. The trial judge is not wiser than the physician.

Far too many sentences imposed in our criminal courts today are leaps in the dark. The needs of society and of the prisoner can be determined only by an investigation of the personal history of the individual, of his physical condition and his mental characteristics, of his companions and his environment, and above all other things, of the motives that prompted the defendant to commit the crime. Often the trial judge cannot make this investigation. In many cases it must be continued for a considerable period while the defendant is undergoing punishment. As a rule the older the defendant the more skilful he is in concealing these essential facts and in playing the part of a first offender. The writer of this introduction has sentenced more than one defendant believing each to be a first offender, after investigating the case, only to be informed by the prison officials that an investigation of the records in other states showed him to be a confirmed criminal. Yet after completing comparatively short terms these men have gone forth to prey on society, emboldened perhaps by their success in escaping with short terms.

These experiences, as well as the impossibility of determining in advance the punishment that should be given to each offender, lead one to suggest that, at least in all the more serious offenses, the functions of the court should cease with the determination of the guilt or innocence of the accused. The punishment to be imposed should be determined by those especially qualified to judge of the need of the individual and of society, who can investigate the history of the prisoner and observe his progress from day to day as does the physician, with power to change the treatment, within certain prescribed limits, as the needs of the individual may require.

Among the chief contributions made by the author is the development of the thought that the *motive* that moved the offender to commit the crime is one of the most important elements to be considered in determining what shall be done to protect society from future harm from the same offender. Discover the motive and give such treatment as will tend to change that motive, and the first step has been taken toward so changing the offender that he shall no longer be a menace to society.

The defects of our present method of punishment become apparent as we read the author's discussion of the means of punishment that should be employed with different classes of offenders. If the prisoner has taken the property of another, let a part of his punishment consist of a restoration of the property, voluntarily if he will, at hard penal labor if he will not or cannot restore it otherwise. If he deserts his family, let him be compelled to support them by building roads or performing other labor found by the proper officers, instead of condemning him to a life of idleness in some jail where he may play cards and smoke with other gentlemen of leisure like himself and eat his three meals a day at the expense of the same taxpayers who are compelled to aid in the support of the deserted family.

Society will find much greater protection under our criminal law when we recognize the truth of Baron Garofalo's teachings that punishment should have the single aim of disarming an enemy of society, by adapting the quantum and kind of punishment to the needs of each individual offender, so that none shall suffer more than his individual needs shall warrant in order that he shall cease to offend against society, — which is the end that should be achieved by all punishment. The habitual criminal should be eliminated from society. The offender who can be adapted to an upright life among his fellowmen should be given the aid to that better life which it is the duty of society to give to those whom it can restore to good citizenship.

The author takes an eminently sane view of criminology. He is wholly free from false sentiment. He approaches the subject from the point of view which will mark the next step in advance in a modern and enlightened criminal science.

MADISON, WISCONSIN,
September, 1913.

AUTHOR'S PREFACE TO THIS EDITION

I

FROM the earliest period of my legal studies, the question had begun to present itself to my mind: How has the lawmaker arrived at an exact knowledge of the kind and degree of punishment appropriate to each of the various criminal offenses? By what means has he reached the conviction, for example, that five years in the penitentiary is the proper punishment for one kind of larceny, while for another, two years of a milder form of imprisonment will suffice? What steps has he taken to weigh this or that aggravating or extenuating circumstance with such exactness as to warrant an increase or diminution in the punishment of six months, one year, five years, ten years, as the case may be? Where has he found his criterion, his thread of guidance in this labyrinth?

My first impression was the ingenuous one that he had proceeded by experiment. But after having had my curiosity and admiration thus aroused, I discovered this notion to be wholly without foundation. I learned that in establishing his rules, the legislator had not taken the slightest pains to test their efficacy. To seek *remedies* for crime, this social disease which assumes such different forms and exhibits such variations with the individual — such, one would think, ought to have been the course pursued. Clearly, without the employment of this method no physician would venture to announce a discovery. But it has not been followed by the law-maker. He has left us wholly in the dark as to how much or how little any given punishment, in its kind, duration, or relation to the nature of the crime or the criminal, has contributed either to social defense or the reformation of the offender.

The progress of the social sciences during the past quarter of a century, it is true, has been such as to compel some recognition from the legal world. Hence, in that quarter the alliance of law with sociology, psychology, and anthropology has been in terms admitted. This admission, however, has remained wholly a matter of theory: it has been followed by no modification of the legal systems. The lawyers have contented themselves with abstract pronouncements, such as that "the object of punishment is to reëstablish the juridical order of which crime is an infraction and, therefore, a disturbance," or again that "every punishment should have for its primary object the reformation of the offender," or else that "the punishment should secure society against a repetition of the crime." They have nevertheless wholly failed to furnish us with any proof of the fitness of the repressive measures which on their recommendation have been embodied in the codes. In every other department of science at the present day, the experimental method is dominant. The science of criminal law, although preëminently a social science, stands alone in refusing to acknowledge its supremacy.

The chief purpose of this book, — first published many years ago and now for the first time made accessible to the English reader, — is the introduction of the experimental method into that science which, in its study of the criminal phenomenon, ought to seek the means best adapted to its extirpation. This aim of criminology ought to be equally that of criminal law. Before we can speak of reforming criminals, we must first consider whether criminals as a class or as individuals are susceptible of reformation, and examine the means necessary to effect such reformation. And if we would speak of securing society against criminal attack, we must begin by ascertaining whether there are punishments capable of disarming the criminal, and determining in what manner these are to be employed. To save theory from a useless labor it must be preceded by experience.

II

A further purpose of the present work is to harmonize judicial logic with the social interest. It cannot be gainsaid that from the moral standpoint individual responsibility is much lessened by bad examples at an impressionable age, by the contagion of the social environment, by traditions of race or family, by ingrained evil habits, by the violence of the passions, by the temperament, etc. But according to the juridical theories, every lessening of responsibility is an element of excuse for the criminal; punishments ought to vary in proportion to the greater or less importance attached to such element, and, when it is possible to establish the extreme force of the criminal impulse, ought to be reduced to an insignificant minimum.

Now, there are but few cases in which the offender is without some extenuating circumstances of this kind. In fact, there is no crime in which it is not easy to discover them. It requires but a slight investigation and they swarm on all sides. In short, the only criminals who appear to us to be without excuse, are those for whom we have not taken the trouble to find it. It may be answered that after all it is simply a question of evil inclinations, and that the free will is always bound to assert itself. But, the question arises, how are we to distinguish the part played by these evil inclinations from that which is played by the free will? What, moreover, shall we say to the data of anthropology, which demonstrate that the most dangerous criminals almost all exhibit a psycho-physical abnormality of organization? To make punishment depend on the moral responsibility would insure the acquittal of the most ferocious type of murderer. Once establish his extreme natural brutality or the irresistibility of his criminal impulses, and no shred of moral responsibility remains. The outcome in every case would be the proportionate diminution of punishment, according as the causes of the evil inclinations became better known and more evident.

Thus repression in its exercise would operate in a relation wholly inverse to the perversity and incorrigibility of the criminal.   It is idle to say that we are needlessly alarmed, and that the stage of declaring the impunity of crime will never be reached.   The philosophic views of an epoch exert an irresistible influence even upon the most unwilling subjects. This principle is exemplified in the present condition of criminal justice, constantly invaded as it is by a current of erroneous ideas to which it offers but a flimsy barrier.   It is useless to protest against verdicts of acquittal or the leniency of judges.   What we see is, after all, the triumph of judicial logic, but a triumph which is at the expense of social security and morality.   For this condition, the sole remedy is the adoption of a different criterion of punishment, — the substitution of the principle of social necessity for that of the moral responsibility of the individual.

The spectacle of crime in a civilized society is much more grievous than in a barbarous tribe or in a group of savages. Its victim appeals much more strongly to our commiseration, because, relying upon the protection of the laws, accustomed to the peaceful adjustment of personal differences, surrounded, in a word, by the amenities of civilization, he has omitted those precautions for the defense of life and property, which in an uncivilized environment he assuredly would have adopted. The forms of brutal crime which persist in our day — murder, rape, arson, robbery, cruelties practised upon women and children, attacks of all sorts upon individual liberty — are the disgrace of contemporary civilization.

Neither for the victim of crime nor the prevention of future crimes does society show sufficient concern.   The fact that in civilized communities many thousands of persons annually lose their lives by direct murder or by murder as an incident to robbery,[1] — that vast sums of money become the booty of

---

[1] This is not an exaggeration.   In European Russia alone, the number of homicide cases coming to the attention of the judges of instruction during the year 1901 was 15,236; in France the average annual number from 1896 to 1900 was nearly 1200; in Italy, during the year 1899, 3587 cases of the same

criminal activity, — to my mind presents a question infinitely more serious than almost any of the much debated topics of parliamentary discussion. Murder and robbery are facts the more hideous as existence becomes more peaceful and life less uncertain. Yet, sanguinary anachronisms as they are, we are content to regard them as deplorable but exceptional instances, — seldom viewing the actuality with our own eyes, we persist in believing that the danger of its repetition is exceedingly remote.

But here statistical science steps in. Adding the figures, combining the scattered sums of human misery produced by human wickedness, it unrolls to us the scenes in a world-appalling tragedy. It shows us a field of battle littered with the remains of frightful carnage; it joins in a single heart-rending cry the groans of the wounded, the lamentations of their kindred; it causes to file before us legions of the maimed, of orphans, and of paupers; it blinds us with the light of a vast incendiary conflagration devouring forests and homes; it deafens us with the yells of an army of pirates. And in sinister climax, it reveals to us the author of these scenes of desolation — an enemy mysterious, unrecognized by history; — we call him the CRIMINAL.

The State does but little for our protection. Since, thanks to the legalists, criminal law is one thing and the measures necessary against malefactors another, action of the State has been rendered almost ineffective. It is an absurd thing that thousands of professional thieves are able to ply their calling in spite of the exertions of the police. It is equally

crime were reported to the police. The average annual number of *convictions* for various forms of homicide (including infanticide) may be estimated as almost 10,000, if we combine the figures for the following countries: Spain, France, Italy, Austria, Hungary, Germany, Great Britain and Ireland, Belgium, Holland, Sweden, Norway, Denmark, and Russia (excepting, in the case of the last-mentioned country, Poland and the Caucasus). The statistics of the other European countries are not accessible. See, further, the table in Appendix B of this volume (*post*, p. 437) and what is said in connection therewith (*post*, pp. 438, 439). It is to be noted, moreover, that the number of convictions represent but a little more than one-third of the total number of criminals.

absurd that the only punishments which need be feared
have at best a merely conventional value and none whatever
in the case of professional criminals. Indeed, in certain cases
these punishments represent a positive advantage to the criminal. After having been lodged, fed, warmed, and clothed,
at public expense, he emerges a free citizen, and none has the
right to remind him of his crimes. It is supposed that he has
expiated his offenses, that he has *paid* to society what he
owed and that henceforth he must be regarded as an *honest*
man. All this is sheer rhetoric. The truth is that the criminal
has paid nothing: the public, on the other hand, has defrayed
the expenses of his maintenance; a new burden has been
imposed on the taxpayer, and the damage which society had
already suffered from the offense has been resultingly increased. The criminal has not undergone a moral reformation;
the prison works no such wonders, — far from it. He is not
intimidated, because our penitentiary systems have become
so mild as to lose every intimidatory effect. Even if he has
suffered from his imprisonment, he will soon forget; for the
memory of physical sufferings is quickly effaced. The liberated convict, then, comes out of prison the same man who
went in, and, moreover, is replaced in the environment from
which he was taken, there to find the same temptations and
encounter the same occasions which impelled him to a career
of crime.

What I have just said applies in general to the penitentiary
systems of Europe. There are however exceptions. In
France, especially, the question of criminality has been the
subject of much attention. By means of laws directed against
recidivists an effort has been made to check the activity of
the habitual offender. Although of too restricted an application, the benefit of these laws has been manifest from the
outset. Since their adoption criminality, especially in its
more serious forms, has perceptibly diminished. It may be
justly said that France is perhaps the only country of continental Europe where the juridical theories concerning pun-

ishment do not hold absolute sway. The principle of defense against the natural enemies of society is much better understood than elsewhere, and to this all other principles have often been tacitly subordinated in the French legislation. Moreover, at the instance of Prins and Liszt, there has been organized an association — the "Union Internationale de Droit Pénal," whose membership is composed of lawyers and judges who have broken away from the old metaphysical notions of punishment — for the experimental study of crime and criminals. From the new direction given by this association to study of these subjects have resulted, in many European countries, laws, or proposed laws, relating to the repression of recidivism, the treatment of first offenders and juvenile delinquents, and the individualization of punishment.

The time has come to proclaim warfare on crime in the name of civilization as the watchword of penal science. We are dealing with a distinctly social function, — and one which ought not to be trammeled by the narrow views and faulty reasoning of the juridical school.

In the popular view, the substantive law, procedure, and the judicial power itself too often seem to work in combination for the protection of the criminal against society rather than society against the criminal. To remove this impression and to justify the sacrifice of the many millions annually expended in the struggle against crime [1] — a struggle which, up to the present time, has failed to yield adequate results, — this is the duty incumbent upon those directing the destinies of the State.

In the great inventions which have changed the face of the world, the nineteenth century found its crowning achieve-

---

[1] It has been computed that seven European nations (France, Germany, England, Austria-Hungary, Italy, Russia, and Spain) alone expend 221,481,174 francs annually merely for the maintenance of prisoners and administration of prison establishments. The total receipts from prison labor represent but a ninth part of that sum — 25,893,232 francs. If to the disbursement in question we add the expense of maintaining the police, our figures will assume immense proportions.

ment. The task of the twentieth century is to eradicate those traces of primitive barbarity which we know as criminality.

III

The present work has often been classed as belonging to the school of criminal anthropology.[1] If it be granted that of this science criminal psychology is the most important chapter, then I am quite willing to be considered a "rational anthropologist" ("anthropologiste raisonnable") as Leveillé has called me.

[1] For the features which especially characterize my system, see *Frassati*, "La nuova scuola penale in Italia" (Turin, 1891); *Dorado Montero*, introduction to my work: "Indemnización á las victimas del delito" (Madrid, 1893): *Van Kan*, "Les causes économiques de la criminalité" (Paris, 1903). See further, G. *Tarde*, "La criminalité comparée"; "La philosophie du droit pénal" [American edition: "Penal Philosophy" (Criminal Science Series, Boston, Little, Brown & Co., 1912)]; *Prins*, "Science pénale et droit positif" (Brussels, 1899); *Saleilles*, "L'Individualisation des peines" (Paris, 1898) [American edition: "The Individualization of Punishment" (Criminal Science Series, Boston, Little, Brown & Co., 1911)]; *J. de Mattos*, preface to the Portuguese translation of the present work (São Paulo, 1893); *J. De Aramburu*, "La nueva ciencia penal" (Madrid, 1887); *Lozano*, "La escuela antropologica y sociologica criminal" (La Plata, 1889); *Proal*, "Le crime et la peine" (Paris, 1891); *Puglia*, "Prolegomeni al diritto repressivo" (1883); *Viveiros de Castro*, "A nova escola penal" (Rio de Janeiro, 1894); *A. Marucci*, "La nuova filosofia del diritto criminale" (Rome, 1904); *Mendes Martins*, "Sociologia criminal" (Lisbon, 1903); and *Havelock Ellis*, "The Criminal" (London, 1890).

The principle of enforced reparation ("indemnisation") in lieu of punishment, which in certain classes of offenses and in the case of certain offenders, I have advocated for the past twenty-five years and defended before many gatherings of scholars, particularly in the Penitentiary Congress of Rome, 1885, the Congress of "L'Union Internationale de Droit Pénal," at Brussels, 1889, and Paris, 1893, and the International Penitentiary Congress of Brussels, 1900 (see Appendix A, *post*, pp. 419–435), has made great advances since the appearance of the last French edition of the present work, and I am informed that even now (1911) it is under consideration by the French Minister of Justice.

Much the same may be said of the theory of individualization of punishment which I suggested and outlined in a general way. It has been subsequently worked out in detail by others, notably by Saleilles in his interesting work which is cited above. This theory progresses steadily. Especially in the matter of juvenile criminality has it impressed itself upon legislation. The conditional sentence and those improvements in penal science which have reached their highest development in the United States, namely, the juvenile court, the probation system, and the indeterminate sentence, all bear witness to its practical value.

No success, it is true, has attended the effort to obtain an accurate external description which will enable us to distinguish the criminal from other men. But this in no way trenches upon the proposition that there exists in criminals a psychic anomaly differentiating them from the generality of men. By some physiologists this proposition has been regarded as destitute of scientific value. Yet the very writers who refuse to recognize, as of any value whatsoever, certain physical signs apparently found in criminals, at the same time distinctly assert that a correlation necessarily exists between the moral character and the physical constitution of the individual. They do not believe in the possibility of defining the differences in this respect between individuals, because such differences must be sought in the histologic organization, in the composition of the blood and the nerve-fibre, and in the functioning of the organs. "The physiologic actions," it is said, "are largely the result of molecular phenomena, and we are very far from possessing an anatomy of molecules." It is plain, however, that this argument in nowise contradicts the idea of criminal anomaly: it means only that the substratum of this moral anomaly is unknown to us.

The physiologist has no reason for refusing to align himself with the new school. Since we do not reject the hypothesis of a correlation between the criminal's instincts, impulses, defect of moral sense, and the constitution (albeit impossible to ascertain) of his nerve-cells, there is nothing in our doctrines which the physiologist may not freely accept.

The charge of fatalism which has been brought against our school is wholly without foundation. It will be seen in the sequel that we believe in utilizing for the moral progress of society all the new discoveries of experimental science. This accusation is due to the placing of a wrong construction upon our ideas. It has been thought that we believe man, and consequently the criminal, to be incapable of transformation and never to act except in a determined direction. No such

error has at any time found place in our views. What experience has demonstrated is that the individual acts always
in the same direction, so long as his intellectual and moral
conditions remain unchanged and he finds himself in the same
external circumstances. This is why we deem it the height
of folly to hope for the reformation of the criminal by imprisonment or any other kind of punishment, if, as soon as
it is ended, he is remitted to the same environment and the
same conditions of existence as before. But by no means do
we believe it impossible *to transform the activity of the offender.*
And this will be brought about when his environment has
been changed, when his new conditions of existence convince him of the necessity of honest labor, and when, finally,
he sees that the predatory life has lost for him all attraction
and profit.

It is rather our opponents who deserve this imputation.
For, while recognizing the inefficacy of the prevailing penal
systems, they decline to admit that there is anything to be
changed. According to them, crime has always existed and
must always be endured as one of the evils which afflict
society. Holding such views, clearly it is not for them
to call fatalistic a school whose aim is to discover the surest
and most effective means of removing this blot from civilization.

Our opponents are equally open to the other charge which
has been laid at our doors, that of materialism. For it is
they who have made a tariff of crimes, and are responsible for
a system of laws in which the objective fact is alone considered,
and the nature of the criminal counts for nothing. It is they
who have materialized criminal law. The positivism which we
advocate, on the contrary, is purely a question of means. It
signifies no philosophic system but simply the experimental
method.

We take fully into account the influences of the physical
and moral environment, and this is exactly why we are unable

to understand a theory which leaves the offender exposed to these — the very influences which have contributed to his degeneration. But the contention that, in lieu of punishing, we should aim to modify the environment and thus suppress the causes of crime, is not one entitled to serious regard. The law-maker cannot accomplish that which is the work of time alone.

What manner of legislation could effect the abolition of misery and ignorance, the disappearance of temptations, the suppression of cupidity, ambition, vanity, and all the other passions which agitate mankind? It is impossible for the State to entrust everything to the slow and sometimes intermittent progress of civilization. And furthermore, would not this same progress be violently interrupted if repression were to cease or be relented? We leave to Tolstoi his dreams. We admire him as a philanthropist and writer, but his theory of non-resistance to evil, we cannot even admit as a topic of discussion. The unconditional pardoning of all offenses means nothing else than the oppression of the honest citizen by the vicious and criminal. The struggle against crime ought not to cease for a single instant. In this lies the first duty of the State, for the first right of the citizen — I would say, even the principal reason for society's existence — is that he be guaranteed his physical integrity, his freedom of action, and the enjoyment of his lawful property. Far from allowing itself to be disarmed, the State in this warfare must constantly aim at the employment of more and more perfect weapons, from time to time discarding those which experience has shown to be unavailing.

But to fight with any hope of success we must know our enemy. The enemy which we are called upon to face is unknown to the followers of the juridical school. Knowledge of him comes only from long-continued observation in prisons, penitentiaries and penal colonies. To those who have studied him under such conditions will the future commit the task of making criminal law responsive to social necessities.

IV

My conviction that the principles of the prevailing criminal law were far from being at one with its true object, led me to publish, in 1876–78, some essays which later became my first book: "Di un criterio positivo della penalità."[1] The plan there outlined was later completed in my "Criminologia."[2] This latter I personally translated into French, since, on account of the changes which I wished to make, it would have been impossible to entrust the work to another. For its indulgence in overlooking my presumption, as well as for many encouragements received at its hands, my cordial thanks are due to the French public.

When the question of an English version arose, I expressly requested that it be made from the most recent French edition — that of 1905, — rather than from the last Italian edition. Inasmuch as the French translation was my own work, no possible objection could exist to this course. My decision was prompted by the thorough revision — in fact, the almost entire recasting — which the book had undergone since its last appearance in Italian. For one thing, it contained the answer to a number of objections which had been urged against my views.[3] Again, the many changes supervening in European criminality had to be taken into account. And finally, my own ideas could not help experiencing some modifications. Accordingly, some statements of too absolute a nature were eliminated, and while the basis of my work was preserved intact, my expression in other instances was given a different form. Time may frequently show to an author the inadequacy or obscurity of a passage which at the moment of writing appeared best to represent his

[1] (Naples, 1880).

[2] (Turin, 1885).

[3] That all my critics were not answered is due to the purely physical reason that it would have been a matter of dealing with hundreds of books, pamphlets, and articles in which my theories came under consideration. In particular, I left unanswered such criticisms as attacked the experimental method which I had endeavored to follow.

thought.   It may often convince him of the existence of matter quite irrelevant or, indeed, disclose the presence in some portion of his work of a wholly unsuspected confusion.

But there are some ideas which neither the most learned criticism nor my own later examination, has influenced me in the slightest degree to modify.   Such is the idea of "natural crime" as opposed to crime which is merely legal or conventional.   I might concede the possibility of it being clothed in a different form of words, but I believe the fundamental notion of "natural crime" has come to stay.   It has been the subject of discussion for twenty years and is still a living topic.   It will not be lost, because it exists in the universal consciousness.   It will furnish the means of establishing an international penal code — an undertaking which is awaited by the civilized world.[1]   An international code of this description will be a manifestation of that universal solidarity which demands the mutual aid of the nations in the struggle against crime.

[1] The outlines of such a code will be found in Part IV of this work (*post,* p. 403).

CONTENTS

PART I

CRIME

CHAPTER I

THE NATURAL CRIME

CHAPTER II

THE LEGAL NOTION OF CRIME

PART II

THE CRIMINAL

CHAPTER I

CRIMINAL ANOMALY

CONTENTS

CHAPTER II

Social Influences

CHAPTER III

Influence of the Laws

PART III

REPRESSION

CHAPTER I

The Law of Adaptation

CHAPTER II

The Existing Theories of Criminal Law

CHAPTER III

DEFECTS OF THE EXISTING CRIMINAL PROCEDURE

CHAPTER IV

THE RATIONAL SYSTEM OF PUNISHMENT

PART IV

OUTLINE OF PRINCIPLES

SUGGESTED AS A BASIS FOR AN INTERNATIONAL PENAL CODE

APPENDICES

PART I

CRIME

CRIMINOLOGY

CHAPTER I

THE NATURAL CRIME

§ 1. The Need of a Sociologic Notion of Crime

The Lack of a Sociologic Definition of Crime. — Toward the close of the 1800s the study of the criminal from the point of view of the natural sciences began to engage marked attention. As a result, his anthropologic and psychologic descriptions have been noted; he has been presented as a type, as a variety of the "genus homo." But when we come to consider how this theory may be applied to legislation, serious difficulties are encountered. By no means every person who is an offender according to legal standards answers the description of the naturalists' criminal man — a circumstance which has thrown doubt upon the practical value of such studies. Nor could the case be otherwise, from the very fact that although the naturalists speak of the *criminal*, they have omitted to tell us what they understand by the word *crime*. This task of definition they have left to the jurists, without

---

[1] [In this chapter, §§ 1 and 2 = § I of original; §§ 3, 4, and 5 = §§ II, III, and IV, respectively; § 7 = note, original, pp. 49-52; and § 8 = § II, c. II. — TRANSL.]

attempting to say whether or not criminality from the legal standpoint is coterminous with criminality from the sociologic point of view. It is this lack of definition which has hitherto rendered the naturalists' study of crime a thing apart and caused it to be regarded as a matter of purely scientific interest with which legislation has nothing to do.

Crime not properly a Juridical Notion. — To my mind, then, the initial step in our investigation should be the attainment of the sociologic notion of crime. It will not do to say that we are dealing with a legal notion and that consequently its definition belongs to the jurists alone. We are here concerned not with a technical term, but with a word which expresses an idea accessible to every one, irrespective of his knowledge of the law. The law-maker has not created this term, but has borrowed it from the popular language. He has not even defined it. All that he has done is to group a certain number of acts and call them crimes. This is why, at the same period of time and often within the confines of a single nation, we find a given act in one locality treated as a crime and in another not punished at all. It follows that the legal classification can in no way foreclose sociologic investigation. For the solution of his doubts regarding the boundaries of criminality, the sociologist cannot turn to the man of law, as he would to the chemist to learn the nature of salts or acid, or to the physicist to be informed of the notion of light or electricity. This notion of crime he must seek for himself. Only when he will have taken the pains to tell us what he understands by crime, shall we know what criminals he is talking about. In a word, we must arrive at the notion of the *natural crime*. In this expression, be it noted, the word "natural" is given the meaning of that which is not conventional, of that which exists in a human society independently of the circumstances and exigencies of a given epoch or the particular views of the law-maker. I employ the phrase "natural crime," because I believe it to be the clearest and least inexact — I do not say the most exact — form of words

to designate those acts which no civilized society can refuse to recognize as criminal and repress by means of
punishment.

§ 2. Method of Attaining the Sociologic Notion

Analysis of Facts Inadequate. — The first question to which
we must address ourselves is whether it is possible to assemble
a group of acts which at all times and in all places have been
regarded as crimes. The inquiry is not whether all that which
is crime at the present day and in modern society has always
and everywhere been so regarded. Such a question almost
answers itself. Is it not familiar learning that by the customs
of many peoples murder to avenge murder was not only
tolerated, but enjoined as the most sacred of filial duties, —
that in the course of history the duel, at one time, has been
visited with heavy penalties, at another, has been so legalized
as to become the principal form of legal procedure, — that
heresy, witchcraft, and sacrilege, once considered crimes of a
most detestable character, have today disappeared from the
statute-books of all civilized nations, — that the pillage of
foreign vessels driven ashore by stress of weather was in some
countries at one time authorized by law, — that, for centuries,
many peoples who are now civilized, employed brigandage
and piracy as their principal means of livelihood, — and that
finally, quite apart from the matter of savage customs, we
have but to go outside of the European races to find semi-
civilized societies where infanticide and the sale of infants
are authorized, where prostitution is an honorable calling,
and adultery has even become an established institution?
Is it not equally true that in civilized Europe, within a comparatively recent period, to differ in political opinion from
those in control of the State was esteemed a crime of the greatest magnitude? Is it not a fact of history that the death penalty has been inflicted for the cornering of breadstuffs or their
sale at prices in excess of the maximum fixed by law? Such
matters are too well known to need dwelling upon. The sole

point of inquiry is whether, among the crimes and offenses
recognized by existing laws, there are any which, at all times
and in all places, have been recognized as punishable acts.
When we think of certain hideous crimes, such as parricide,
assassination, murder for the sake of robbery, murder from
sheer brutality, . . . the question would seem to require an
affirmative answer. But a slight investigation serves to dispel
this idea. From the descriptions of savage customs furnished
by ancient and modern explorers, we learn that among many
tribes parricide has been dictated by religious custom. A
sentiment of filial duty impelled the Massagetæ, the Sardi,
and the Slavs and Scandinavians of prehistoric times, to kill
their parents when the latter had become helpless from sick-
ness or extreme old age. It is said that the Fuegians, the
Fijians, the Battas of Sumatra, the Chukchi, the Kamcha-
dales, and the aborigines of New Caledonia, all followed this
atrocious practice. Murder from sheer brutality is still
frequently practised by the chiefs of numerous savage tribes,
especially in Central Africa. It is even allowable for a warrior
to kill a man for the purpose of exhibiting his strength or
dexterity, or to exercise his arm, or to try his weapon; the
public conscience is not in the slightest degree disturbed.
We have stories of cannibal feasts from Tahiti and elsewhere.
Finally, murder for the purpose of robbery has been constantly
practised by the members of one savage tribe upon those of
another.

Analysis of Sentiments the True Method. — But if we thus
are compelled to relinquish the idea of collecting a group of
facts universally hated and punished, it by no means follows
that the notion of the natural crime is impossible of achievement. To attain it, however, we must change method:
we must lay aside the analysis of *facts* and undertake that of
sentiments. Crime, in reality, is always a harmful action,
but, at the same time, an action which wounds some one of
the sentiments which, by common consent, are called the moral
sense of a human aggregation. Now, the moral sense has

developed but slowly: it has varied and continues to vary according to circumstances of race and time. Each of the sentiments of which it is composed has from time to time undergone perceptible augmentation or diminution of strength. Hence it is that there exist wide differences in ideas of morality, and as a necessary result, differences not less considerable in this species of immorality without which no harmful action can ever be regarded as a crime. We must endeavor, then, to ascertain whether, in spite of the lack of uniformity in the emotions excited by acts differently appreciated by different aggregations, there is not a constant character in the emotions aroused by acts which are appreciated in an identical manner, — in other words, whether the difference is not one of form rather than of substance. Reference to the evolution of the moral sense can alone throw light on this question.

The origin of the moral sense is attributed by Darwin to instinctive sympathy for our fellow beings, by Spencer to the mental process which, impressing upon our ancestors the necessity of obeying certain precepts of conduct, has become a habit of mind hereditarily transmitted to posterity and transformed into an instinct. These fundamental moral intuitions, then, appear to be. "the results of accumulated experiences of Utility, gradually organized and inherited" so that "they have come to be quite independent of conscious experience. . . . The experiences of utility organized and consolidated through all past generations of the human race, have been producing corresponding nervous modifications, which, by continued transmission and accumulation, have become in us certain faculties of moral intuition — certain emotions responding to right and wrong conduct, which have no apparent basis in the individual experiences of utility. . . . Preferences or aversions are rendered organic by inheritance of the effects of pleasurable and painful experiences in progenitors." [1] Whatever may be thought of this hypothesis or of Darwin's theory of instinctive sympathy, it is certain that every race

[1] *Herbert Spencer*, "The Data of Ethics," c. VII.

today possesses a sum of moral instincts which are not due to individual reasoning, but are the inheritance of the individual quite as much as is the physical type of his race.   Some of these instincts may be noticed in the child, not before the intellectual development begins to reveal itself, to be sure, but certainly before he is capable of the difficult mental process necessary to convince him of the indirect individual utility of altruism.   Likewise, the existence of the moral sense alone can explain the solitary and obscure sacrifices which men are sometimes led to make of their most vital interests in order not to violate what seems to be their duty.   Say as we will, that altruism is only enlightened egoism, it is nevertheless true that in frequent instances egoism would be much the more useful to us, would spare us many an ill or enable us to attain what we most keenly desire, with nothing to fear either for the present or the future.   The knowledge that a man will suffer an evil or reject a benefit, with no thought of the utility of his sacrifice, compels us to recognize the existence of a sentiment which depends on no power of reasoning, although, according to the hypothesis above mentioned, such sentiment, inherited by us and for which we deserve no credit, may have had a utilitarian origin in our remote ancestors.   As before indicated, Darwin himself, without the aid of this hypothesis, comes to the same conclusion.   "Although," says he, "man, as he now exists, has few special instincts, having lost any which his progenitors may have possessed, this is no reason why he should not have retained from an extremely remote period some degree of instinctive love and sympathy for his fellows. . . . At last man comes to feel, through acquired and perhaps inherited habit, that it is best for him to obey his most persistent impulses.   The imperious word *ought* seems merely to imply the consciousness of the existence of a rule of conduct, however it may have originated." [1]

Moreover, if morality were simply the product of *individual* reasoning, plainly the most intelligent persons would be the

[1] *Darwin*, "The Descent of Man," Part I, c. IV.

most honest. The higher the intelligence, the easier would it be to attain the idea of altruism — the conception of the highest morality which, according to the positivists, consists in the completest possible fusion of egoism and altruism. We do not say that the opposite is true, but assuredly instances are not lacking of highly intelligent men who at the same time are thoroughly dishonest. On the other hand, we often encounter persons of very limited intelligence who set their faces against the least departure from the severest standards of moral conduct. And why so? Clearly not from any understanding on their part of the indirect utility of what they do, but solely because they *feel obliged* to respect the moral precepts, and this even where religion and the law of the land are silent.

We must take as established, then, the existence of the moral sense of a race of people, created, like all the other sentiments, by evolution, and transmitted from generation to generation, either as the effect of psychologic heredity alone, or as the effect of such heredity combined with the imitative faculties of the child, and the influence of family traditions. But since the moral sense is a psychic activity, it may be subject to change and infirmity, may become diseased, may even become entirely lost. It may be wanting from birth as a result of some psychic monstrosity which, like other monstrosities to be found in the human organism, we are compelled, in the absence of a better explanation, to attribute to atavism. Innumerable gradations exist "between the highest energy of a well-fashioned will and the complete absence of moral sense." [1]

It is not a matter for astonishment, therefore, if, in a race morally advanced, we find a number, more or less great, of individuals who exhibit an utter absence of morality. These are psychic anomalies — exceptions similar to physical monstrosities.

The question is rather in what measure does this moral

---

[1] *Maudsley,* "Responsibility in Mental Disease," c. I.

sense vary through time and space, — what it is at the present day among the European races and the civilized peoples of other races, what it has been in the past, and what it will be in the future. It is further to be inquired what part, if any, of this moral sense is to be detected in the oldest human aggregations, what were the moral instincts which held sway in the age of an inferior civilization, and what the instincts which, scarcely embryonic in that day, have since developed into the basis of public morality.

Prehistoric man need not detain us. In the present respect we know nothing about him. Savage tribes which are either degenerate or insusceptible of development we may equally pass over, since, properly considered, they are anomalies of the human species. Our inquiry is directed to putting in distinct relief the moral sentiments which the civilized part of mankind may be said definitely to possess — the sentiments absolutely exacted by the necessity of social coexistence, which form the true contemporaneous morality, susceptible not of loss but of ever-increasing development. The result will not be precisely the "recta ratio" of Cicero, "naturæ congruens, diffusa in omnes, constans, sempiterna," but it will be the "recta ratio" of the higher races of mankind in their present stage of civilization — a stage which has raised to a nearly equal level all peoples whose dominant activities are those of peace.

§ 3. The Moral Sense in General

Absolute Morality. — Our attention, be it noted, is to be confined to the average moral sense of the whole community. There are always persons morally superior to the social average, just as there are those who do not reach it. The former are such as have by their own efforts attained absolute morality, — according to Spencer, that ideal of conduct attainable by society as a whole, in which there exists a complete fusion of the sentiments of a rational egoism with those of an enlightened altruism. Of such idealists, however, we find but few; and they cannot do much to advance their times or accelerate evolutionary progress. As has been remarked by a learned author, the establishment and spread of the religious and moral idealism of Christianity, by which the human race is conceived as a single family under God, became possible only when Rome, maintaining relations with all the known world, had united nearly all the civilized peoples in a single empire — this Rome which, in the words of the poet,

> " . . . græmio victos . . . sola recepit,
> Humanumque genus communi nomine fovit."

"Without this condition, the ethics of Christianity would perhaps have failed to find a soil favorable to their development and permanence. . . . The moral ideas of a people have never emanated as a whole from a given philosophic system, any more than have the by-laws of a corporation." [1]

Relative Morality. — This capital of moral ideas is the elaborated product of the past centuries, transmitted to us by heredity with the aid of tradition. This is why in every age there has existed a relative morality, consisting in the adaptation of the individual to society. A morality still more relative exists in every section of the country and in every social class: this is what we term "social usage " ("mœurs "). As long as the individual has conformed to the principles of conduct generally received in the people, the tribe, or the caste, to which he belongs, he cannot be said to have acted immorally, however much his conduct may fall short of absolute morality. Thus, slavery, for example, judged by ideal standards, is an immoral institution; in a perfect human society, there can be no such thing as ownership of one man by another. But does this give us the right to conclude that the slave-owners of the ancient world were immoral? The tendency of that day to an ideal morality manifested itself in the sentiment which impelled the most humane masters to emancipate such of their slaves as had shown marked zeal and fidelity, or by reason of their intelligence, attainments, and special aptitudes,

---

[1] *Schaeffle,* "Structure et vie du corps social," c. v, ii.

were capable of making their own way and assuming a better position in society.

Variations in Morality. — Of the wide differences existing in many respects between the morality of different peoples, or of the same people at different periods, it would be unprofit‑ able to multiply illustrations. Savage tribes and barbarous nations furnish examples of usages which to our eyes seem of incredible immorality. Although modesty appears to be an absolutely natural instinct, yet we read of human aggregations in which complete nudity is the fashion, and where custom prescribes that the consummation of marriage take place in public. Captain Cook, the discoverer of the Sandwich Islands, describes an incident of this character which he there wit‑ nessed — a circumstance which elicited no astonishment from a contemporary jurist, since, as the latter pertinently sug‑ gested, marriage ought to be celebrated by public act. Xeno‑ phon speaks of a similar custom among the Mosynœci.[1] We read also of the Spartan maidens wrestling naked in the gymnasia. Even at the present day, the Japanese lady makes no scruple of receiving visits during her bath, while her humbler sister may be seen taking her plunge in a barrel set in the middle of the public street.

Although, in the kind and degree of its civilization, the classic world was not far removed from our own, we find there prevailing usages which were the complete negation of modesty, — witness the celebration of certain mysteries of nature; the cult of the god Priapus and the processions in his honor; the religious prostitution of Cyprus and Lydia; the transfer of wives, instances of which occurred in Rome; the adultery which was permitted by the customs of Sparta and encouraged by the husband, when the marriage had failed to result in offspring; those strange attachments which the Greek writers speak of as a thing not only tolerated, but even looked upon with approbation;[2] and the practice of incestu‑

---

[1] *Xenophon,* "Anabasis," V, 19.

[2] Owing to what he considered its honorable character, Solon prohibited this relation to any but freemen. (*Plutarch,* Life of Solon.)

ous marriage followed in the Pharaonic families, as well as
by their Greek successors, the Ptolemies.

Superficial Rules of Conduct. — But leaving history,
let us turn to contemporary society. Here, at the outset,
we discover certain precepts of conduct constituting what is
known as usage. Of these, some are common to all the
strata of society, some peculiar to separate classes, associations, and groups. Everything is the subject of regulation,
from the most solemn ceremonial to the matter of personal
salutation and individual dress. Not only is it decreed
what phrases are proper under given circumstances, but the
manner of expression and the inflection to be lent to particular words are equally prescribed by usage. Those who
do not conform to such rules are called, sometimes eccentric,
sometimes ignorant or ill-bred; they excite our mirth or pity,
sometimes our contempt.

Many things permitted in one class or association are elsewhere strictly forbidden. The season, the place, the hour, the
object of a gathering, each has its influence upon the rules of
conduct. Thus, a lady must appear décolletée at a dinner or
an evening party, while in making an afternoon call such a
costume would be entirely inappropriate. So, a gentleman
who has just been presented to a lady at a ball, is acting in
conformity with social usage, when, asking her to dance,
he clasps her waist to lead her through a waltz, — although
on any other occasion, except in the intimacy of love, such
an action would be deemed an unpardonable familiarity.
Each of our movements is dictated by an established usage; —
scarcely any of our actions but is subject to some rule. Tradition, education, and continual example oblige us unquestion-
ingly to follow these precepts.

Morality Proper. — But above all transitory and special
laws of this character, we find others of a much more general
nature, and, like the solar ray which traverses all the liquid
strata of a pool of water, of a force which reaches through all
the social classes. And just as the ray of sunlight undergoes a

different refraction, according to the difference in density of the medium through which it passes, so these general principles of conduct are subject to important variations in the different strata of society. In these principles (whose sum is properly called morality) time works change, but so gradually, that in order to find true contrasts we must resort to peoples who have preceded us, or to those below us in the scale of civilization. It is indisputable, however, that, at the same period and in a single nation, there exist principles universally obeyed. Still, these principles do not operate with the same force and the same expression in every stratum of society. "If men differ in anything," says Bagehot, "they differ in the fineness and delicacy of their moral intuitions, however we may suppose those feelings to have been acquired. We need not go as far as savages to learn that lesson; we need only talk with the English poor or to our own servants, and we shall be taught it very completely. The lower classes in civilized countries, like all classes in uncivilized countries, are clearly wanting in the nicer part of those feelings which, taken together, we call the *sense* of morality." [1] We must be careful not to mistake the meaning of this passage. The author remarks in the lower classes only the absence of the nicer part of the moral sense. In other words, there exists, although perhaps in rough outline, an all-pervading moral sense. Taken as a whole and viewed with respect to the majority of its members, even the lowest stratum of society has in point of morality something in common with the highest. The reason is apparent. If it be admitted that morality is purely a product of evolution, it is necessarily less refined, less perfect, in those classes of society which, not having been able to keep abreast of the others, exhibit an inferior degree of psychic development. Nevertheless, the same instincts exist in a rudimentary state throughout all classes. And for the same reason, they exist in such barbarous tribes as are inferior in development to the lowest stratum of our society, but here their existence is

[1] "Physics and Politics," No. IV: "Nation-making."

merely embryonic. As a result, it is possible in every moral
sentiment to distinguish superposed layers which tend to an
increasing niceness. If, then, we separate the superficial
parts from their underlying structure, we shall have in the
latter the really substantial moral sense which is identical in
all peoples whose psychic evolution and progress in civilization
closely resemble our own. And so, while discarding the idea
that morality is universal, it will nevertheless be possible for
us to ascertain the identity of certain sentiments in a very
wide field of human existence. It will also become clear
to us that crime consists in acts which violate these same
sentiments.

§ 4. The Constituent Instincts of the Moral Sense — their Analysis

Certain Sentiments to be distinguished as Non-Elementary. —
The subject of our inquiry, then, is the elementary moral
sentiments — such sentiments as are recognized and enforced
in a human society which has emerged from infancy and by
the preponderance of the intellectual life is differentiated
from the brute creation. But first it is necessary to clear
the way. There are some sentiments regarded as essential to
individual morality, without the acts which they inhibit being
regarded as criminal, because not anti-social, or, in other
words, because they do not attack the primordial conditions
of human coexistence. Although immoral and subject to
the censure of public opinion, such acts are really harmful
only to the authors themselves, their families or the State,
not to society as a whole.

The *love of country* is a sentiment of undoubted nobility,
but nowadays an act contrary to the interests of the State
does not of itself make the agent a criminal. One does not
commit crime by the sole fact of preferring a foreign country
to his own, or by failing to be moved to tears at the sight of
the national emblem. If a man disobeys an established government, if he accepts employment at the hands of a foreign

nation, inconsistent with his duty to the State, he may deserve to be called a bad citizen but not a bad man. Now,
what we are dealing with is the immorality of the individual
considered as a member of the human race, not his immorality
as a member of a particular aggregation. It is the possibility
of drawing this distinction — a possibility existing neither in
Sparta nor in Rome — which demonstrates the present separation between national sentiment and individual morality.

The same is equally true of the *religious sentiment*.
Throughout all the countries subject to the European race,
governments have long since ceased to impose upon the citizen the rules of a particular creed. With the ancients, the
sentiment of religion was intimately connected with that of
patriotism, because it was believed that upon the worship
of the divinity depended the safety of the country. The same
prejudice still obtains at the present day in many barbarous
tribes. In the Middle Ages the idea that the Christians
were the family of God, rendered them implacable enemies
of all infidels. Blasphemy, heresy, sacrilege, witchcraft, even
scientific teachings contradictory of dogma, were crimes of the
most serious character. But today the precepts of religion are
distinguished from those of social conduct, it being nevertheless true that the Gospel, in favoring the development of
altruism, is in part the basis of contemporary morality.

It is recognized, moreover, that goodness and rectitude are
not inconsistent with the absence of faith. Religion is the
source of much happiness; he who is without it is perhaps
to be pitied, but in no sense can he be looked upon as an
enemy of society.

We come now to *chastity*. The presence of this sentiment,
which we admire as the paramount feminine virtue, is, none
the less, quite unessential to the well-being of a human society.
In those countries where the hospitality due to a guest includes the offer of the host's wife for the night (Greenland,
Ceylon, Tahiti at the time of the discovery), it is wholly
unknown. It is equally unknown where one wife belongs in

common to a number of brothers (Todas and Tottiyars of India),[1] or where the woman engages her fidelity for five or six days of the week only (certain African tribes). In our own society, indeed, polyandry is of frequent enough existence, substantially the only difference being the hypocritical effort which is made to hide it. The progress of civilization has no appreciable effect in its diminution, perhaps even tends to its spread throughout the social classes. The figure of the beautiful and elegant woman of fashion who bestows her affections upon a lover chosen by her inclinations as well as upon the husband of her legal choice is by no means unknown in our social centers. And the fact that other women of the same class have a reputation for chastity may often argue nothing more than their better success in concealing similar frailties. She whom Juvenal sought in vain — the " unico gaudens mulier marito " — is not always and everywhere found today. The assertion that polyandry has disappeared from our social usages is one of those conventional lies which are the subject of Max Nordau's satirical analysis.

The unmarried woman has more apparent reserve, at least in the Latin races; elsewhere she is allowed more liberty and governed with much less strictness. Still, and in spite of the fact that we are merciless toward her faults, must it not be admitted that the case of a working girl who has reached the age of eighteen or twenty years, without lapse from virtue, is the exception rather than the rule ? And what of the upper classes, whose daughters are the subject of constant watchfulness? Instances are frequent where girls brought up in the best principles and in the most austere family surroundings have suddenly succumbed to the influence of passion or the arts of the seducer.

What free-love runs counter to is oftenest the special situation of the individual — almost always some personal or family interest. In other cases of rarer occurrence it offends the purity of the religious sentiment.

[1] *Sir John Lubbock* (*Lord Avebury*), "The Origin of Civilization," c. III.

There is finally the sentiment of *honor*. A few words will here suffice, since it is apparent that of all the sentiments, this is the least definite. Every association, every social class, every family, has its own standards of honor. The same may be said of almost every individual. In the name of honor are done all manner of acts, good and evil. It is this sentiment which guides the dagger of the assassin, which inspires the soldier to throw himself upon the enemy's works, and which in the duel obliges the mild and peace-loving citizen to serve as target for the pistol of his adversary. In the lowest classes of society, in the most degraded human associations, in criminal organizations, among transported convicts, there exists a point of honor which sometimes causes the perpetration of the most brutal crimes of vengeance. What is honor in one aggregation is dishonor in another. The murderer's point of honor is not to be considered a thief; that of the vagabond is to respect the property of his benefactor; the most vicious criminals pride themselves upon the cleverness or boldness of their crimes.

Sometimes the sentiment of honor signifies but the existence and predominance of a part only of the elementary moral instincts. Sometimes it represents nothing more than a residuum, the wreckage of what was once a moral sense. Again, by a singular inversion, it sometimes serves to render more conspicuous the total absence of a moral sense. Oftenest it consists merely of an exaggerated form of self-esteem limited, however, to a particular kind of activity. In fine, it is ordinarily but the external and most salient expression of the qualities and defects of the individual character, intermingled with singular and irrational prejudices of class, caste, profession, or sect. Nothing, therefore, can be more elastic and changeable than this sentiment of honor — a sentiment which Spencer classes as ego-altruistic, because other persons come within its scope only so far as it enables us to evoke their admiration and applause.

It is scarcely true today in our better classes that the ques-

tion of honor turns principally upon the maintenance of a
high standard of probity. But where it does, the sentiment
of honor assumes an enhanced importance and falls into the
category now to engage our attention.

The Altruistic Sentiments. — The only sentiments which
at the present day are of true importance for social morality
are those termed altruistic, that is to say, such sentiments as
have for their direct object the interest of others, although
indirectly their exercise may redound to our own advantage.
These altruistic sentiments are found in a very different degree
of development in different peoples and in different classes
of the same people. Nevertheless, they are encountered
everywhere, except possibly in a very few savage tribes.
They may be reduced to two distinct types: the sentiment
of *benevolence* and the sentiment of *justice.*

In ·tracing these sentiments to their origin, it is true, we
may become convinced that they are merely a development
or after-growth of egoistic sentiments. The instinct of individual conservation expands first to include the family
and then extends to the tribe. From it there becomes slowly
detached a feeling of sympathy for our fellow-beings. The
circle of fellow-beings at first embraces those of the same tribe,
then those of the same country and tongue, next all men of
the same race and color, and in the end, comprises all mankind irrespective of race.

The Sentiment of Benevolence. — Thus the sentiment of
love or benevolence for our fellows begins as an egoistic
sentiment under the form of love for our own children, who
are almost a part of ourselves. It then extends to the other
members of our family, but becomes altruistic only when
no longer determined by ties of blood. At this period, it is
determined by the physical or moral resemblance of persons
belonging to the same caste, the same nation, or the same
race, and expressing themselves in an almost identical fashion, — because we are unable to entertain sympathy for persons who totally differ from us and with whose feelings we

are entirely unacquainted. For this reason, as Darwin has very clearly pointed out, the difference of race, and therefore of appearance and customs, is one of the principal obstacles to the universality of the sentiment of benevolence.[1] Only by slow degrees is man able to reach the point at which he looks upon the men of all countries and races as his fellow creatures. Lastly, sympathy for animals is a moral acquisition of tardy growth. Even at the present day it prevails only among men of the highest moral refinement, as is abundantly testified by the existence of the chase and the slaughter-house.

But in order to distinguish the different degrees of this instinct of benevolence and to discover how much of it is really an essential of morality and to a certain extent universal, we must proceed somewhat further with our analysis.

We find, first of all, a small number of persons whose sole interest is the well-being of others, and whose entire lives are devoted to the relief of poverty and suffering, without thought of recompense, — who act from no promptings of ambition, but, on the contrary, seek to keep their good deeds from being known, — persons who deprive themselves not only of luxuries but even of necessities, for the good of others. Such people are philanthropists in the true acceptation of the term. Next, we have a larger number of persons who do not make service to others the principal object of their existence, but who, nevertheless, eagerly avail themselves of the opportunity to render such service, when occasion presents. They do not seek such occasions, but they do not shun them. The chance to do something for others affords them pleasure. This class of persons may be designated as the beneficent or generous. The mass, however, is composed of persons who neither make any effort nor submit to any sacrifice to increase the happiness or lessen the misfortunes of others, but who yet do not willingly inflict suffering upon their neighbors. In such persons exists the ability to repress every voluntary act productive of pain to their fellows.

---

[1] *Darwin*, "The Descent of Man," Part I, c. IV.

This resistance to the impulses which, unchecked, would result in the infliction of suffering on others, arises from the sentiment of pity or humanity, that is to say, repugnance to cruelty. In origin this last-mentioned sentiment is not absolutely altruistic. Just as the pleasure that we experience in representing to ourselves the pleasure of others gives rise to the generous action, so, as Herbert Spencer has said, pity is derived from the personal pain felt in representing to ourselves the pain of others, which we thus feel as if it were our own. It originates, therefore, in egoism, but its egoism has become transformed into an unreasoning instinct of which our fellows are the direct object. It is in this sense, then, that we may term altruistic a sentiment which grows out of sympathy for suffering, and hence from the fear of experiencing a painful emotion at the sight of suffering of which we have been the cause.

"Sympathy with pain, produces in conduct modifications of several kinds. In the first place, it puts a check on the intentional infliction of pain. Various degrees of this effect are observable. Supposing no animosity is felt, the hurting another by accident arouses a genuine feeling of regret in all adults save the very brutal: representation of the physical pain produced, is sufficiently vivid in nearly all civilized persons to make them avoid producing it. Where there exists a higher degree of representative power, there is a reluctance to inflict emotional pain. The disagreeable state of mind that would be excited in another by a sharp word or harsh act, is imagined with such clearness that the imagination serves partially or wholly as a deterrent. . . . In another class of cases, pity modifies conduct by prompting efforts to assuage pain that is already being borne — pain arising from disease, or from accident, or from the cruelty of enemies, or even from the anger of the pitying person himself. . . . If his imagination is vivid, and if he also sees that the suffering can be diminished by his aid, then he cannot escape from his disagreeable consciousness by going away; since the represented pain continues with him, impelling him to return and assist." [1]

It follows, therefore, that the sentiment of benevolence exhibits many degrees of development: the pity which restrains us from causing physical suffering, the pity which hinders us from causing moral suffering, the pity which leads us to help our neighbor whom we see in distress, and those higher types of the same sentiment, namely, beneficence, generosity, and philanthropy, by which pleasure is derived from aiding others, not only with the view of relieving their present sufferings, but also with that of rendering their future less burdensome. The first two manifestations are negative, that is to say, they consist in the abstention from certain acts; the others, on the contrary, are positive, implying not omissions but acts. And just here, we see the fallacy of the theory which supposes an act or omission to be criminal whenever it assumes the two-fold aspect of immorality and injury to the community. As a matter of fact, this double aspect distinctly appears in any action characterized by the want of that positive kind of pity which impels us to lend a hand to others. The refusal to give alms to a deserving subject of charity or to do what one can to assist the poor and needy, may work an injury to the community, at the same time arguing a lack of proper development of the altruistic sentiments. Still, ungenerous as such conduct may be, public opinion nowhere regards it as crime. To associate an act with the idea of crime it is not enough that it be immoral, not enough that it wounds the altruistic sentiments as they exist in their superior stages of development, in that refined degree which characterizes a few exceptional persons; the act must be such as wounds these sentiments as they exist in the lowest phase of this development, in what we may call their rudimentary stage. This explains why we find the sentiment of pity almost universal among the higher races of mankind and those who

[1] *Herbert Spencer*, "Principles of Psychology," II, Part IX: "Corollaries," c. VIII.

are on the road to civilization, but only in its negative forms. As a result, the abnormal fact to which we attach the idea of crime necessarily involves the violation of the sentiment which prevents us from being the voluntary cause of suffering.

The Sentiment of Pity. — It is then only the first degree of pity which has become nearly universal — namely, repugnance to acts which produce physical pain. As to those which cause moral suffering, a distinction is required. There are some acts whose effect depends chiefly upon the sensibility of the person aimed at. The identical injury which produces suffering in a cultured man, may leave a boor almost untouched. In this case the general representative power is insufficient to feel the pain. Hence it is that harsh words and vulgar epithets are of such common occurrence among the lower classes, taking the place which in the higher ranks of society is occupied by the biting jest and the polished sarcasm. In neither case do we consider how much suffering is inflicted upon the person whose refinement is superior to that of his environment: no wound is sustained by the common sense of morality.

Nor is it necessary to consider those sorts of moral suffering which may eventuate in disease or death. The effect varies too much with different natures, the intention of the wounding person is too uncertain a matter, for the moral sense to revolt. If it does revolt, it can do no more than deplore the fact, since it has no means of definitely attributing the result to any given act. For this reason, the moral homicide which some authors speak of, has no practical interest for criminology. Being insusceptible of exact determination, it can have no place in the category of crime.

But a very different situation is presented when the moral suffering is complicated with a physical element, as in the case of forcible restraint of the person or an offense against chastity committed by violence. A difference also exists when to the moral suffering there is added an injury to the social position of the person attacked. Such is the case, for example, in defamation ("diffamation"), false accusation ("calomnie"), [1] enticement to prostitution, and seduction before the age of consent. Acts of this description are calculated to produce irreparable injury: they may result in reducing the victim to the uttermost degradation. By the prevision of such consequences the universal sentiment becomes aroused and stamps the authors of such acts as criminal.

What has been said in the present connection, shows us

---

[1] [The Continental law of criminal defamation differs widely from our own. Apart from the defamation of public officers, three principal categories are recognized in the French and Italian systems:

(a) *False accusation* ("dénonciation calomnieuse; " " calunnia ").

"Dénonciation calomnieuse" (Art. 373 of the French Code): malicious false accusation of a punishable fact made in writing and to the authorities. ("Calomnie," formerly recognized in the French Code, was a distinct offense. It existed when one imputed to another in a specified public manner [otherwise than by the written accusation essential in " dénonciation calomnieuse"] facts exposing him to prosecution or to public hatred or contempt. The provision with reference to it [Art. 367] was, however, repealed in 1819, and the wrongful act now constitutes either "diffamation" or "injure" according to the facts of the case; see *Garraud*, "Traité de droit pénal français," V, p. 325.)

"Calunnia" (Art. 212, Italian Code): false accusation of a punishable offense made to the authorities against a person whom the wrong-doer knows to be innocent; or the fabrication of evidence tending to inculpate an innocent person.

(b) *Defamation* (" diffamation; " " diffamazione ").

"Diffamation" (Law of 29 July, 1881, Art. 29, § 1) is the "allegation or imputation *of a fact* attacking the honor or good standing ('considération') of the person to whom, or body to which the fact is imputed," made in a specified public manner. Truth is no defense (*Garraud, loc. cit.*).

"Diffamazione" (Art. 393, Italian Code) exists when the wrong-doer "in communication with more than one person, separately or together, attributes to another a *determinate fact* such as to expose him to contempt or to public hatred or to offend his honor or reputation." Truth is not a defense except under special circumstances (Art. 394).

(c) *Insulting language* ("injure; " " ingiuria ").

"Injure" (Law of 29 July, 1881, Art. 29, § 2). "Every expression outraging the feelings, every term of contempt ('mépris') or invective, *not imputing a fact*, is an 'injure.'" If public, the offense is a "délit," otherwise it is a "contravention" (*Garraud, loc. cit.; see post*, p. 59, note 1).

"Ingiuria" (Art. 395, Italian Code) consists in words "offending, in any manner whatsoever, the honor, the reputation, or the dignity ('decoro') of another." Unless the offense is committed in the presence of the injured person, or by means of a writing addressed to him, there must be, as in "diffamazione," communication to more than one person, separately or together. — TRANSL.]

clearly that there has hitherto existed an altruistic sentiment which in the rudimentary stage of its development is all-pervading, at least throughout the higher races of mankind and such peoples as have emerged from savagery — the sentiment of benevolence toward our fellows, or pity, at least in its negative form. In the case of races which have attained a certain degree of development, this would appear, therefore, to be a fixed and immutable sentiment. And except for certain tribes of a retarded development which, as compared with the rest of humanity, represent but an insignificant minority, it may properly be said to be *universal*.

It has been suggested that this result is in conflict with the theory of evolution. "If morality is the product of evolution," says one writer, "why should its variations be other than uniform? And if, up to a given point of time, it has undergone uniform variation, why should the procession of changes be arrested and not continue 'ad infinitum'?" [1] The answer is furnished by the following words of Spencer: "To infer that no settled sentiments can ever be generated by the process described, is to assume that there are no settled conditions to social welfare. Clearly if the temporary forms of conduct needful, initiate temporary ideas of right and wrong with responsive excitements of the sentiments, it is to be inferred that the permanent forms of conduct needful, will initiate permanent ideas of right and wrong with responsive excitements of the sentiments; and hence to question the genesis of these sentiments is to doubt the existence of these forms. That there are such permanent forms of conduct, no one can deny who compares the law-books of all races which have outgrown the purely-predatory life. This variability of sentiment is but the concomitant of the transition from the aboriginal type of society fitted for destructive activities, to the civilized type of society fitted for peaceful activities." [2] Although the great

---

[1] *De Aramburu,* "La nueva ciencia penal," p. 101 (Madrid, 1887).
[2] *Herbert Spencer,* "Principles of Psychology," II, Part IX: "Corollaries," c. VIII.

contemporary philosopher was not here dealing with the theory of crime, the concluding words of this passage serve completely to refute the objection in question.

But, it may be urged, the conclusion that benevolence is a sentiment or instinct of the human race is contradicted by many facts of history: piracy, for example; the pillage of wrecks, traces of which have survived in Europe to a comparatively recent date; the sale of children, tolerated in China; the institution of human slavery, not long since existing in America; the barbarous forms of punishment practised in the Middle Ages; and the numberless cruelties inflicted by Christians upon the heretics and the Moors, by the Spaniards upon the natives of the New World. How, moreover, are we to explain the attitude of mind which could enable the old chronicler to recount the cannibal feast of Richard Cœur de Lion,[1] not only without a shudder, but without in the least abating his enthusiasm for the chivalric character of the hero?

This contradiction, however, is only apparent. The explanation is not far to seek. The objects of the sentiment of pity have already been indicated: we have shown that its scope is restricted to those who are our fellow-beings. As already seen, man has begun by regarding as his fellows only the members of his own tribe; he has next included in this category all men of the same country, later all those united by one faith, one language, or a common origin, — and not before our own day perhaps, all men without respect to race or religion.

Pity existed from the beginning, but was far from being cosmopolitan in its scope. It still falls far short of that, whatever may be said to the contrary. The proof is furnished by the cruelties inflicted by European armies not many years

---

[1] "His people kill a young Saracen, fresh and tender; they cook him and salt him; the king eats of the dish and finds it very good. . . . He causes thirty of the most noble Saracens to be beheaded, orders his cook to boil the heads and serve one to each ambassador, and eats his with good relish" (*Taine,* "De la littérature anglaise," I, c. II, § 7).

ago upon the Tonkinese and Chinese, in total disregard of the humanitarian laws of modern warfare.[1] Here we may see why, in a less enlightened age, the Spaniards did not look upon the Indian races as men. We may see also why, some centuries before, the Moors, the Saracens, non-Christians of every description, the Albigenses and all other manner of heretics, deserved pity no more than mad dogs. They were not the fellow-beings of the .Catholics; they differed from the latter as much as the host of Satan from that of the Archangel Michael; they were the enemies of Christ, and must be destroyed, root and branch. The cause was not any deficiency in the sentiment of pity; it lay in the failure to see the resemblance between men without which sympathy, the origin of pity, could not exist.

It required the 1800s to evoke from Victor Hugo that triumphant but exaggerated cry of cosmopolitanism: "The hero is naught but a variety of murderer." To appreciate the changes which evolution may effect in a moral sentiment, it is only necessary to ask if we could imagine any monarch of the present day ordering the engraving of an inscription like that of Assur-nazir-pal, in which it is related how the King, upon taking a hostile city, caused a number of the principal men to be flayed, others to be buried alive, and still others to be crucified and impaled.[2] In the expansion of this sentiment of pity the progress has been immense. Restricted in prehistoric times to members of the family, it now recognizes no other limits than those of mankind. The tendency, indeed, is even to transcend these limits by the cultivation of zoöphily, that is to say, pity for the lower animals.

And yet this sentiment whose circle of objects has thus been ever widening, has always existed, since the earliest formation of the savage group, since the moment when man first saw his fellows around him. The contradiction suggested above is therefore non-existent.

[1] On this subject, see an admirable passage in *Tarde's* "Criminalité comparée," pp. 188, 189 (Paris, Felix Alcan).

[2] *Maspero*, "Histoire ancienne des peuples de l' Orient," c. IX.

There are, however, some facts which do not admit of the same explanation, viz., religious parricide, human sacrifice, the sale of children, and authorized infanticide. Here we must adopt a different point of view.

Do we not all number among our acquaintances persons whose profession is surgery and who, in the performance of operations, are in the habit of inflicting pain, heedless of the outcries and unaffected by the anguished shuddering of their patients? Still these persons are not wicked men. For the performance of these very operations they receive pecuniary compensation, praise, and gratitude. Clearly, here is no proof that pity is not a moral sentiment, not a fundamental sentiment of human nature. The reason is simply this, that since the purpose of the painful operation is not to work harm, but, on the contrary, to benefit the health of the patient, it would be an absurd and irrational sort of pity that would stay the surgeon's hand. For the true pity, the present and transitory suffering of the patient is outshadowed by the representation of his future suffering or of his certain death in the absence of the operation.

From this point of view, then, are to be judged the atrocious customs existing among primitive peoples and still in some measure encountered in savage tribes, which have given rise to the facts above referred to. Sometimes the determining motive was the welfare of the aggregation: this was true of human sacrifices. Sometimes it was the victim's own good, as in the case of aged or infirm parents publicly slain by their children. Superstition repressed every tendency to rebel at such practices; individual repugnance was obliged to yield before the demands of social, religious, or filial duty. Similar reasons account for the existence of funeral sacrifices in Dahomey today, as in Peru in the times of the Incas. Like reasons prompted Agamemnon and Jephthah to sacrifice their daughters. Patriotic or religious prejudices, usages explicable only by the necessity of selection or the prevention of too great an increase in the population have given rise to the toleration of infanticide in China, Australia, Paraguay, and South Africa, as well as the practice of abortion in many Polynesian tribes. The operation of the same causes produced the law of Lycurgus, under which all weak and deformed children were exposed. Here, then, the question of individual cruelty is not involved: the question is one of social institutions against which the individual is powerless. It is the element of harmfulness which makes cruelty obnoxious to altruism. Where such practices prevailed it was the *not doing* of these acts of supposedly necessary cruelty that would have been looked upon as harmful.

Among the inhuman practices authorized by the laws of the peoples of whom we have spoken, there remain to be accounted for: cannibalism; the right of chiefs and warriors to kill from pure caprice, or from a desire to exhibit their dexterity or to test their weapons; and lastly, such cruel acts as are not due to religious or patriotic prejudices or to institutions having an economic or social end and can only be explained by the total absence of the sentiment of pity. Customs of this sort are in fact found among certain barbarous peoples, or at least existed among them at the time of their discovery by civilized man. Such are or were the Fijians, the Maoris of New Zealand, the Australian aborigines, and some tribes of the interior of Africa. But these are exceptions which prove the rule. They are social anomalies which, in relation to the human species, correspond to individual anomalies in relation to a race or nation.

Sufficient has been said on this subject to warrant the positive assertion that there exists a rudimentary sentiment of benevolence or pity possessed by the whole species (with probably some exceptions) in a negative form, that is to say, a sentiment which prompts abstention from cruelty useless to a community, and further, that public opinion has always treated violations of this sentiment as crimes. It is apparent, moreover, that today the scope of this sentiment has become greatly enlarged by the progress of human sympathy and the gradual disappearance of religious and political prejudices and superstitious beliefs.

The Sentiment of Justice. — We pass now to the most signifi-- cant form of altruism, to the sentiment which stands out most prominently among the ego-altruistic instincts — the senti- ment of *justice.* "This sentiment," Spencer tells us, "evi- dently does not consist of representations of simple pleasures or pains experienced by others; but it consists of represen- tations of those emotions which others feel, when actually or prospectively allowed or forbidden the activities by which pleasures are to be gained or pains escaped. The sentiment of justice is thus constituted by representation of a feeling that is itself highly re-representative. . . . The limit toward which this highest altruistic sentiment advances, is tolerably clear. . . . The advance is towards a state in which, while each citizen will tolerate no other restriction on his freedom, he will tolerate that restriction on it which the like claims of fellow-citizens involve. Nay more — he will not simply tolerate this restriction, but will spontaneously recognize it and assert it — will be sympathetically anxious for each other citizen's due sphere of action as for his own; and will defend it against invasion while he refrains from invading it himself." [1] For the sentiment of justice in this refined degree, the term "delicacy" ("délicatesse") has been adopted. It will be readily understood that a sentiment so complex in character can be possessed in full measure by only a select few. Although the idea of justice is well developed in children and in the lower classes, it is seldom that they act in conform- ity to this idea, when it would interfere with their personal interest. The child and the savage are perfectly able to dis- tinguish what belongs to them from what belongs to another, yet they constantly endeavor to seize whatever is placed within their reach. This proves that it is the sentiment and not the idea of justice which they lack. So far as the adult

---

[1] *Herbert Spencer,* "Principles of Psychology," II, Part IX: "Corollaries," c. VIII.

persons of a civilized race are concerned, they possess *generally*, as a result of heredity and tradition, a certain instinct which restrains them from taking by fraud or violence that which does not belong to them. In this we have an altruistic sentiment corresponding to the egoistic sentiment of property, which an Italian writer has accurately described as "a secondary form of the sentiment of individual conservation." [1]

The Sentiment of Probity. — The only word which we find to designate this last-mentioned altruistic sentiment is "probity" — a term expressive of respect for all that which belongs to others.

It is evident that the *average* moral sense of a society cannot comprise all the gradations of the sentiment of justice. An exquisite niceness in this sentiment would, for example, prevent us from accepting mere praise which we know is not our due. But feelings of this sort belong only to a select minority. Before the moral sense of the community is violated, it is necessary that some nearly universal sentiment be the subject of attack. And the only sentiment of this description to be met with is that elementary probity which, as has been said, consists in respecting the property of others.[2]

From this point of view, mere pretended insolvency ("simple insolvabilité simulée") would be a crime. In reality, it wounds the moral sense quite as much as any species of fraud now recognized as criminal. It is not improbable that we shall arrive at this point. Perhaps we shall go even farther: the time may come when we shall consider as criminal all those tricks and sharp practices ("tromperies auxquels on donne

---

[1] *Sergi*, "Elementi di psicologia," pp. 590, 591 (Messina, 1879).

[2] Frassati questions the definite possession of this sentiment. He suggests that, owing to the influences of socialism, respect for the property of others is at a low ebb, and is liable entirely to disappear in the event of a reorganization of society on a collectivist basis. But if this change should come about, the honest man will respect the collective property. The ownership of the principal mass of property by the community will not effect the disappearance of probity or improbity. The only difference will be that they will then relate to the community property instead of to the property of individuals.

le nom de simulations") occurring in the conduct of civil cases, by which one party obtains an undue advantage at the expense of the other. But the effort to bring this about might not be unattended with danger. In the first place, it is a matter of great difficulty to expose the bad faith which may lurk in the legal subleties of a civil case. Then again, if real property rights are involved, the mere presence of the disputed property has a reassuring effect. Frauds of this kind, therefore, do not seriously alarm society and consequently are not classed among the harmful actions.

Finally, it is to be remembered that probity is a sentiment not nearly so deep-rooted as sympathy, much more detached than this latter from our organism, much less instinctive, and much more variable according to our respective methods of reasoning and individual ideas. It is derived, in a much less degree than pity, from natural heredity, in a much greater degree than pity, from education and example. Hence, it is a matter of the utmost difficulty to trace any line of demarcation between common probity and the superior sort of probity, that delicacy of feeling which constitutes the ideal sentiment of justice outlined above.

When one considers to what extent society tolerates the use of false marks and labels in manufactured goods, the employment of false statements and representations in the sale of horses, objects of art, and the like, and the various other sources of improper gain from which a very numerous class derives its principal income, he is sometimes tempted to doubt whether this sentiment of probity has any existence at all in the majority of men. Dissimulation, breach of trust, and disregard for the finer feelings of honesty are so common as to render a reciprocal tolerance indispensable. As a result, the stigma of improbity, by an arbitrary limitation, attaches only to the grossest and most apparent forms of attack on property, whereas it should apply to all manner of attacks upon property, and this whether the property be tangible or intangible. For example, the laws provide severe punishment in the case of but one species of counterfeiting, namely, that of money, yet the moral sense is not less offended by the spurious imitation of some manufactured product, even although, being sold at a cheaper price than the original, its effect might be to benefit every one but the manufacturer of the genuine article. Undoubtedly the presence of an infinitely greater social danger in the former case is not without its influence, but nevertheless public opinion recognizes the same character of improbity in both these species of counterfeiting, although one is punished by penal servitude and the other merely by a fine. On the other hand, in spite of any amount of reasoning on the subject, we can never be induced to feel the same repugnance for the smuggler or for one who accepts the benefits of his offense, as we entertain for the thief or the receiver of stolen goods. The difference is simply this, that in the first case the offender merely evades the payment of a tax — refuses to give his own money to the State. Plainly, the refusal to contribute to another's enrichment is quite a different thing from stealing what is already his. If there chanced to come to the hands of even the most honest of men, a box of Havanas which had escaped the payment of customs duty, it would be very singular if this fact interfered with his enjoyment of the contents, however much he might be inclined to condemn the practice of smuggling.

§ 5. Rationale of the Natural Crime

Injury to Pity or Probity the Essential Element. — From what has been said in § 4, we may conclude that the element of immorality requisite before a harmful act can be regarded as criminal by public opinion, is the injury to so much of the moral sense as is represented by one or the other of the elementary altruistic sentiments of *pity* and *probity*. Moreover, the injury must wound these sentiments not in their superior and finer degrees, but in the average measure in which they are possessed by a community — a measure which is indispensable for the adaptation of the individual

to society. Given such a violation of either of these sentiments, and we have what may properly be called *natural
crime*. The foregoing, I concede, is not a complete definition,
but it furnishes a determinant which I believe to be of the
highest importance. I have sought to show the futility of
saying in the usual fashion that crime is an act at once immoral and harmful. It is something more: it is a determinate
species of immorality. Hundreds of deeds might be mentioned
which are both harmful and immoral and still not considered
as crimes. And this is so, because the element of immorality
which they contain is neither cruelty nor improbity. If, for
example, immorality *in general* be spoken of, we are obliged
to recognize that this element in some degree exists in every
voluntary disobedience to law. But it is nevertheless true
that there is a host of acts which are misdemeanors and even
crimes in the eye of the law and yet do not tend to lower
their authors in the estimation of their friends.

Beyond question, every disobedience to law should be attended with a penal sanction, whether such disobedience
does or does not wound the altruistic sentiments. What
then is the practical object of your distinction? — some one
may inquire. This we shall presently explain, but first, to
complete our analysis, we must show why certain violations
of a different order of sentiments have been excluded from our
category of criminality.

Distinctions : Acts wounding Modesty and Chastity. — The
result of our discussion of the subject of modesty sufficiently justifies the exclusion of all acts which wound this
sentiment alone. Offenses against chastity are rendered
criminal by the interference with individual liberty — the
violation of the sentiment of benevolence or pity, — and this
even if the offense is accomplished by seduction unattended
with force, because of the moral suffering, shame, and other
harmful consequences suffered by the victim. But when the
woman has submitted of her own free will and no element of
seduction is involved, the unchaste act of itself is a matter of

indifference. The same reason equally prevents us from classing as crimes certain acts of sexual perversion, although the
laws of some countries still endeavor to repress such offenses
by means of physical punishments ("peines afflictives" [1]).
Civilized society does insist on the observance of public decorum: it will not tolerate complete nudity or the commerce
of the sexes in public; — spectacles of this sort would excite
mirth or disgust, or, especially among parents, the keenest
sense of indignation. But even the last would hardly demand
the death of the offenders; they would protest, not against
crime, but against indecency. Manifestly, in these cases
the only thing that needs to be changed is a modality, namely,
the place, and there is nothing to complain of. For this reason,
such facts have been, according to the period, visited with the
lash, minor restrictions of liberty, or fines, just as the case
of drunkenness, but no more than in the last-mentioned
case, has it ever been thought proper to invoke the punishments which are set apart for crimes. The public conscience is unable to discover crime in that which becomes a
breach of decorum ("inconvenance") only by the single external circumstance of publicity. The seriousness of the
breach of decorum, it may be added, depends upon how
public the place in question is. This explains why public
opinion in these instances can see only police offenses ("contraventions de police"), however they may be classed by
the positive law.

Acts wounding Sentiments of Family. — Let us turn now
to another class of sentiments which at one time possessed
great importance, viz., the sentiments of family. We know
that the family was the nucleus of the tribe and hence of the
nation, and that the moral sense first appeared under the form
of love for one's children, — this being a sentiment not yet
altruistic, but purely ego-altruistic. The progress of altruism
has greatly diminished the importance of the family group,
morality having first passed beyond the limits of the family,

---

[1] [See *post*, p. 59, note 1. — TRANSL.]

to transcend in later stages those of the tribe, the caste, and the people, and, ultimately, to recognize no other boundaries than those of mankind.

But in spite of this constant progression, the family has continued to exist, with its natural rules of obedience, fidelity, and mutual assistance on the part of its members. What then of the violation of such sentiments? Does it always constitute a natural crime? By no means, unless there exists at the same time a violation of one or both of the elementary altruistic sentiments discussed above. Suppose that a son maltreats his parents, a mother abandons her offspring, what sentiment is really wounded here? Is it the sentiment of family — of the family regarded as an aggregation, an organism — or is it not rather the sentiment of pity, — which, it may be noted, is generally more vivid when its objects are related to us by blood?

It is this same universality of pity within the family which renders criminal certain acts in relation to our parents and children, which if committed against outsiders would not be given a criminal character. On the other hand, the idea of the family community — a traditional idea which persists in spite of the laws — denies a criminal character to certain attacks upon property within the family circle, as, for example, larceny between father and son, husband and wife, or brother and sister. And this is not because the sentiment of probity is overborne by the sentiment of family, but simply because the idea of a common ownership diminishes the degree of improbity or renders its existence doubtful.

Disobedience to the paternal authority has long since ceased to be classed as a crime, but adultery continues to be so regarded. That adultery is harmful to the family order, and from this point of view is immoral, cannot admit of the slightest doubt. Nevertheless, save in some exceptional cases, it does not directly wound the elementary altruistic sentiments. It is merely the breach of a duty, the violation of a contract, and, as in the case of other contractual relations,

its legal consequences should be limited to the giving rise to a
right to rescind on the part of the aggrieved party. We have
not yet come to this, but history shows us a progressive
diminution in the punishment of adultery. The Israelitish
stoning, the Teutonic fustigation, the pillory and other forms
of corporal punishment which obtained in the Middle Ages,
have all given way to the few months of correctional imprisonment [1] by which the offense is punished at the present day.
In brief, that which is nothing more than the violation of a
right, and wounds neither the sentiment of pity nor that of
probity cannot be deemed a crime by public opinion. On the
other hand, the criminal character of bigamy, for example,
where the second spouse is unaware of the prior marriage
("bigamie frauduleuse"), is easily recognized. The same is
true of the false pretenses ("fausses qualités") under which
an adventurer insinuates himself into a respectable family
and effects a marriage with one of its members. Although
this last-mentioned fact has yet no place in the code, it cannot
be gainsaid that a marriage procured by fraud excites public
indignation to a much greater degree than the fault of adultery.

In some measure adultery is the political crime of the family.
To it may be applied many of the considerations now to be
mentioned in relation to political crimes in general.

Political Crimes. — The subject of political crimes presents
difficulties of a most serious character. How are we to contend that conspiracy or rebellion against a lawful government is not a true crime ? Can there be anything more dangerous to the particular society? Does it not attack the public
peace in the directest manner possible? And yet, how else
can we explain the sympathy that political offenders often
inspire in their bitterest enemies, as opposed to the repugnance which every honest man feels for thieves, swindlers,
forgers, and men of that stripe? There is here a clear-cut
distinction. One may, to be sure, speak of *political crime*,
but the word " crime," standing alone, has nothing to do

---

[1] [As to correctional imprisonment, see *post*, p. 59, note 1. — TRANSL.]

with the present class of acts. This difference is one which the public conscience never fails to recognize. As an example may be cited its expression by that most philosophic of novelists, Balzac, in " The Magic Skin." The speakers are young men of the literary Bohemia:

"'Oh, well,' resumes the first, 'there is still left to us . . .'

" 'What?' inquires another.

" ' Crime . . .'

" ' There 's a word which has all the height of the gallows and all the depth of the Seine,' replies Raphael.

"'Oh! You don't understand me. I mean political crime.'"

In reality, egoism is often alien to political crimes. They are explained, not by the default of moral sense, but rather by a revolutionary ingenuousness which feels capable of making over the world.

Still, there are certain crimes commonly called political which, nevertheless, properly come under our definition. Such, for example, are attacks upon the life of the head of the State or other public officers, the use of bombs and dynamite to further revolutionary propaganda, and similar acts of violence. In these cases it is of little moment what the political object may be, if the sentiment of humanity is wounded. Has there been killing or an attempt to kill, not in the course of war or in the exercise of lawful self-defense? If so, the author, by that fact alone, is a criminal. His degree of criminality may be greater or less, according to the intent and the surrounding circumstances — a matter to which we shall later refer. But if crime arises from the single fact of a serious violation of pity, there must be at least an attempt to commit it. This is so, because we cannot admit that any crime exists before some step has been taken in its accomplishment, even if the design has been fully formed in the author's mind. It may be that public policy, in cases of this character, will treat as a punishable attempt that which is not an attempt in the ordinary sense; here we have a true political crime. The cases to which we have reference, however, are those in which

there has been murder, incendiarism, or dynamiting, actual
or attempted. In such cases the crime exists independently
of the passion which has provoked it. It exists because of the
wilful intent to destroy human lives. Only when the act of
the fanatic or revolutionary exhibits no such cruelty or
carelessness of human life can we distinguish the true political
crime, and say that it inherently differs from the natural
crime. But the act which is normally a political crime may become a natural crime when a society suddenly returns to a
condition in which the collective existence is threatened.
War, a state resembling that of the predatory life, relegates
the sentiments developed by pacific activity to a subordinate
station. Let independence once become the principal concern
of a people, and the attempt of a citizen to betray his country
to the enemy assumes the worst aspects of immorality.
Under such circumstances every citizen must be considered
as a soldier; martial law reigns supreme; the laws of peace
have disappeared. Treason, desertion, espionage are then
true crimes, because tending to national destruction. But at
the present day the state of war is a crisis of short duration.
As pacific activity succeeds to the predatory activity, the
morality of the state of peace succeeds to that of war, and the
offense which was esteemed a crime only in relation to that
state of war, becomes a political crime or no crime at all;
at all events, it ceases to be numbered among the natural
crimes. Thus desertion becomes no more than voluntary
expatriation; conspiracy and revolt no longer threaten the
national life, but only the form of government. As for espionage, it is no more than the revealing of State secrets, which,
like many other acts of a similar character, may still be culpable if it involves the selling for money or other object a
secret which one is in honor bound to keep. In this case the
element of improbity is present, the moral sense is in consequence wounded, and the act continues to be a natural crime.

Non-Political Local Offenses menacing Public Peace. — There
are other offenses which are not political, but which

from a local point of view are a menace to public peace. Such, for example, are attempts to subvert a particular governmental institution, disobedience to the constituted authorities, and the refusal of a citizen to perform a public duty legally incumbent upon him. So far as these are concerned, we need only repeat that for public opinion there can be neither crime nor criminal in the absence of injury to the universal moral sense.

§ 6. The Delimitation of Criminality

And now as to our delimitation of criminality. For us, all crime falls into two extensive categories, according as offense is principally occasioned to the one or the other of the two primordial altruistic sentiments. So far as this distribution is concerned, it is of no consequence what rights may be attacked or how the offense may be classified in the codes.

(1) *Offense to the Sentiment of Pity.* — The first category — offense to the sentiment of pity or humanity — therefore includes: (*a*) attacks upon human life and all manner of acts tending to produce physical harm to human beings, such as the deliberate infliction of physical torture ("sévices"), mayhem ("mutilations"), the maltreatment of the weak and infirm, the voluntary causing of illness, the imposition upon children of excessive labor or such work as tends to injure their health or stunt their physical development; [1] (*b*) physical acts which produce suffering at once physical and moral, such as the violation of personal liberty in an egoistic end, whether for carnal pleasure or pecuniary gain: — abduction of a female or kidnapping for ransom may be cited as types; and (*c*) acts which directly produce moral suffering. Defamation ("diffamation"), false accusation ("calomnie"), and seduction under promise of marriage are of this last character.

(2) *Offense to the Sentiment of Probity.* — In the second cate-

---

[1] These last are not yet recognized by the codes, or at most are classed as police offenses ("contraventions").

gory — offense to the elementary sentiment of probity — are comprised: (*a*) attacks upon property involving violence, viz.: robbery, extortion by threats, malicious mischief ("dévastation"), arson, and the like; (*b*) attacks unaccompanied by violence, but involving breach of trust: obtaining money by false pretenses; embezzlement; the conveyance of property in fraud of creditors ("insolvabilité volontaire"), bankruptcy occurring through negligence or fraud ("banqueroute"),[1] the revelation of professional secrets,[2] the misappropriation of literary property ("plagiat"), and all the various forms of counterfeiting tending to injure the rights of inventors and manufacturers; and (*c*) all indirect injuries to a person's property or civil rights occasioned by false statements or entries made in some formal or solemn manner, among which may be mentioned perjury, the forgery or spoliation of official documents and records ("faux dans les actes authentiques"), the substitution of children, and the suppression of civil status ("suppression d'état civil").[3]

Offenses excluded. — It will be noted that we thus exclude from the field of criminality: (*a*) acts which menace the State

[1] ["Banqueroute" (unlike our term "bankruptcy") signifies a criminal offense, viz., the failure ("faillite") of a trader under circumstances of which the criminal law takes cognizance. There are two varieties of this offense: *simple* and *fraudulent*. (*a*) The general theory of "simple bankruptcy" is that the insolvent has been guilty of negligent acts or omissions in dealing with his estate. It "consists 'in those omissions of diligence or violations of special duties, imposed by law on the trader, which have contributed to his failure or aggravated its consequences'" ("Digesto Italiano," V, 173). (*b*) "Fraudulent bankruptcy" exists where there has been actual fraud, such as the making away with books of account or the concealment of assets. — TRANSL.]

[2] [Art. 378 of the French Penal Code provides that "Physicians, surgeons, and all other officers of health, as well as pharmacists, midwives, and all other persons entrusted with secrets in virtue of their status or profession, who reveal such secrets (except where compelled to testify in a court of justice) will be punished by imprisonment of from one to six months and by a fine of from one hundred to five hundred francs." A similar provision is to be found in Art. 163 of the present Italian Code. — TRANSL.]

[3] ["Suppression d'état civil" = a criminal act operating to deprive an individual of the evidence of his civil status, such as the failure to make or the false making of declarations of birth, or the forgery, spoliation, or destruction of certificates of birth ("actes de naissance"). — TRANSL.]

as a governmental organization. Of this type are such deeds as may involve one nation in hostilities with another, unauthorized military enlistments, political rioting, meetings to conspire against the government, the utterance of seditious outcries, seditious offenses of the press, affiliation with revolutionary sects or anti-constitutional parties, inciting to civil war, etc. (*b*) Acts which attack the social power but without a political object. Among these would be: resistance to officers of the law (except when involving murder or the infliction of bodily injury), the usurpation of titles, dignities, or public functions, without purpose of unlawful pecuniary gain, the refusal to perform a service owed to the State, smuggling, etc.; (*c*) acts resulting in injury to the public peace, the political rights of citizens, or the respect due to religion, or causing offense to public decency. In this division would fall the unlawful invasion of private dwellings ("violation de domicile"),[1] the exercise of a right by force instead of by legal means, the spreading of false news tending to alarm the public, the act of aiding or abetting the escape of prisoners, election intrigues, offenses against religion or worship, illegal arrests, acts of sexual perversion of which no innocent person has been made the victim; and (*d*) acts which contravene the local or special legislation of a given country, *e. g.*, gambling, the unlawful carrying of arms, clandestine prostitution, and infringements of laws relating to railroads, telegraphs, sanitation, the customs, hunting, fishing, forests, and water-courses, and the civil status of citizens, as well as violations of many kinds of municipal regulations, etc.

Certain Objections Considered. — With respect to the foregoing classification, De Aramburu,[2] followed by Lozano,[3]

---

[1] ["Violation de domicile" is of two kinds. One comprises unlawful domiciliary visitations by the police or other public officers. The other consists of the act of a private person in effecting an entrance to a dwelling house, against the will of the owner, by the use of force or threats, and for an unlawful purpose, not necessarily that of theft. — TRANSL.]

[2] *De Aramburu, op. cit.*, p. 102.

[3] *Lozano*, "La escuela antropologica y sociologica criminal," p. 98 (La Plata, 1889).

contends that it would be easily demonstrable that the crimes of one category might with equal propriety be assigned to the other, since, they say, that which is unjust is cruel, and that which is cruel is unjust. On the contrary, I am firmly convinced that the two sentiments are entirely distinct, and that one may be wounded without the other being affected, although it may frequently happen that both are wounded by a single act. Is there, for example, any cruelty in robbing a rich man's house which has been shut up for the summer, or in embezzling a few thousand francs from a metropolitan bank? Clearly, improbity alone is involved. On the other hand, what element of improbity exists in a murder for revenge, occurring solely as the exaggerated reaction against a wrong done to the murderer or his kindred? True, it may be said that it is always wicked to harm any one in any way whatsoever. But wickedness and injustice are not synonymous terms, and in any event, the element of wickedness inherent in the last example is not a violation of the sentiment of justice heretofore designated as " probity."

The further objection has been raised that the altruistic sentiments possess little uniformity and that the boundaries of the field of crime are constantly expanding.[1] We, of course, fully admit that the altruistic sentiments, at a former period and in a different state of society, had by no means attained their present degree of development. This, in fact, was our point of departure in speaking of the progression of these sentiments abreast of civilization. Moreover, it is to be borne in mind that the present-day morality is based on altruism, whereas the morality of other peoples and other ages was based on sentiments of a different nature — patriotism, religion, loyalty to the sovereign, the respect due to caste, the point of honor, and the like. The purpose of our investigation, then, is to discover what are the true crimes of contemporary society, — to ascertain what constitutes a crime

---

[1] *Colajanni,* "La sociologia criminale," pp. 54, 55; *De Aramburu, op. cit.,* pp. 102–104.

in our eyes — in the eyes of Europeans of the present century. There is nothing in this to contradict the possibility of a still further development of altruism, or that acts which today are not considered as crimes may one day acquire that character. Progress, assuredly, will tend more and more to the enrichment of the moral sense. "If the moral sense becomes augmented," says Fouillée, "the displeasing things of today will become the odious things of the future. . . . Our sympathy embraces a continually increasing number of objects; it extends not only to humanity, but to the whole of nature; and, for this reason, it is nowadays much more easily wounded than formerly, especially in its moral force." [1]

Thus, it will very probably ensue that many facts today regarded as indifferent will come to be viewed as immoral, and that others simply immoral will be vested with a criminal character. Of the latter class might be instanced the abandonment of illegitimate children, the failure on the part of parents properly to care for their children, or to give them an adequate education, or again, vivisection, artificial fattening, and other forms of cruelty to animals, which in recent years have aroused the just indignation of zoöphilist societies. The advance will equally affect the sentiment of probity. All those non-punishable acts of chicane which occur in the conduct of civil cases will come to take their place — unless the practical difficulties are insurmountable — beside the other species of frauds which are today punishable, so that the two will become indistinguishable. So, too, a criminal character will come to be given to the abandonment of such persons as already have, or may be awarded by future laws, the right to assistance and support — parents, children, and aged or infirm domestics or workmen, without means of existence.

It is easily understood, however, that the sentiments wounded by the crimes of the future will be the same sentiments with which we have dealt, but these sentiments in

[1] *Alfred Fouillée* in Revue des Deux Mondes, 15 March, 1888.

their higher and more refined development — a state which the efflux of time will have rendered much more common than at the present day. It is wholly impossible to suppose crimes of a different character, or to suppose that offenses to other sentiments can ever become crimes. As we have already noticed, the tendency is quite the opposite. Offenses not involving injury to the sentiments in question, are treated less and less as crimes in proportion as civilization increases.

So much for the future. Does not this glance at it furnish new proof of the validity of our concept of crime?

The offenses which have no place in our scheme, do not come within the scope of the sociologic study of crime. They are relative to the special conditions of particular countries. They do not reveal in their authors, anomaly — the default of that part of the moral sense which evolution has rendered almost universal. The law-maker, no doubt, ought to adopt measures looking to their chastisement, but from our point of view it is the true crime alone which, in demanding investigation of its natural causes and social remedies, is capable of interesting true science. The excluded offenses often consist merely of violations of prejudice or contraventions of custom, or in any event simply run counter to the laws of a determinate society — laws varying with different countries and unnecessary to the social coexistence. In these cases investigation of biologic causes is unnecessary, and as for remedy, none other is needed than chastisement depending in severity upon the degree of intimidation required.

§ 7. Criticisms of the Theory of Natural Crime

Objections of De Aramburu et al. — Since 1885, when first appeared my definition of *natural crime*, criticism has been unceasing. Some of the objections which have been urged are due to a misapprehension. It is said, for example, that there can be no such thing as natural crime, because in nature the fact of a crime is neither good nor bad: it is an action like every other and becomes criminal only in the social state.[1] But inasmuch as our treatment has been from a sociologic standpoint, it is very plain that the *nature* with which we are concerned is none other than *social nature*.

The commonest objection is that many crimes remain outside the boundaries which I have assigned to criminality.[2] There is here no room for argument, since this is precisely what I have aimed at. My investigations have been limited to one section of punishable facts, interrelated by a common character, — for it is these alone which possess interest for science.

Views of Vaccaro. — Another writer is willing to concede me this right, but asserts that my investigations lack practical value, because, he says, if the acts which I have treated as natural crimes are now regarded in law as punishable, then my discovery comes too late; if, on the other hand, such acts are not now punishable by law, the discovery is useless, because the social power will recognize in them a criminal character only in so far as it has an interest affected and is in position to protect that interest.[3] This criticism, however, confuses the aim of arriving at a distinction whose object is purely scientific, with that of ascertaining for the guidance of the law-maker what actions should be the subject of punishment — something which is not at all within my design. The sole object of my concept of crime is to distinguish among the punishable facts, those which are governed by the same natural laws, because revealing certain individual anomalies, principally the lack of a part of the moral sense or, in other words, a deficiency in the sentiments which, as the basis of morality, are constantly undergoing development in the progress of civilized nations. Assuming that my observations are accurate, can it be gainsaid that such an in-

---

[1] *De Aramburu,* "La nueva ciencia penal," p. 98 (Madrid, 1887); Lucchini, "Semplicisti"; *Colajanni,* "La sociologia criminale."

[2] *De Aramburu, Lucchini, Colajanni, ut sup.*

[3] *Vaccaro,* "Genesi e funzione delle leggi penali," p. 176 (Rome, 1889).

vestigation possesses scientific interest? And if everything that is scientific is not at the same time practical, I venture to add that with regard to determining means of repression and prevention my concept of crime is far from fruitless, as will appear, I hope, in the sequel.

The same author maintains that the criminalist of the positive school cannot conceive crime except as "an act forbidden under a penalty." "In reality," says he, "to the sociologist who can admit no freedom of choice in the human aggregation, search for the natural crime is absurd, because this would be something independent of positive laws. Just as the explosion of a cannon obeys certain laws of chemistry, of physics, and of mechanics, so the constituted authority, in forbidding certain acts and permitting others, is merely obeying the natural laws of society. Every act prohibited under a penalty is therefore a natural crime. I would go even further and say that the only existing natural crime is that which the laws consider as such." It seems to me that this criticism confuses the meaning of words. Unquestionably, for the positivist, every violation of law is a natural fact, neither more nor less than the promulgation of the laws themselves and the penal sanctions which they contain. But is my concept in any way inconsistent with this notion? What I have done has been to select from among all these natural facts, a certain class of offenses which exhibit the distinctive character of a special immorality, and these I have termed "natural crimes," to denote that, at the present day, they are universally such, irrespective of laws and governments. This objection, therefore, seems rather a play upon words than serious criticism.

Of those who disagree with my views, Vaccaro alone is disposed to scoff at altruism. He takes this to be a word void of meaning or at least of no social importance. In answer, I venture to quote this notable passage from Fouillée: "Contemporary philosophy, far from deriding the moral instinct, tends more and more to its justification, for it finds in that instinct an almost infallible intuition of the deepest-seated laws of life. Instead of looking upon pity as an illusion, it sees in it the foremost and most effectual means of dispelling the illusion of the isolated and self-sufficing Ego." [1]

Vaccaro further asserts that the moral sense cannot be made a directive criterion in the matter of criminality, since the moral sense itself is in great part owed to the fear and the effect of punishment. This being so, he continues, to look to the moral sense in order to ascertain what acts ought to be punished, would be arguing in a circle.[2] But what this author overlooks is that acts which offend the interest or the morality of an aggregation in a serious measure, have, precisely because of this, invariably been followed by a movement of social reaction. It is to be admitted that punishments in their turn have contributed to the reinforcement of the moral sense, since the recollection of penal sanctions transmitted by inheritance from generation to generation, has converted into an instinct that which, at one time, was solely the effect of fear or of a process of reasoning. But it is none the less true that punishment alone has never succeeded in carrying conviction of the criminal character of actions which have not been considered as crimes by public opinion, such as dueling, adultery, political offenses, or freedom of thought in respect of religion. It is well known that facts of this description have been visited by punishments exceeding in severity those applied to any other crime. Why, then, do they not equally come under the ban of morality?

Colajanni on the Average Moral Sentiments. — Colajanni, the distinguished sociologist, is of opinion that the adoption of the average moral sentiments of the superior races as the criterion by which to distinguish crimes, would involve the

---

[1] *A. Fouillée,* "Les transformations de l'idée morale " (Revue des Deux Mondes, 15 September, 1889).

[2] *Vaccaro, op. cit.,* pp. 176–180. My thanks are due to Scipio Sighele for his brilliant article in support of my theory, written in reply to the criticism of Vaccaro. See Archivio di psichiatria, scienze penali etc., Vol. X, pp. 410, 411 (1889).

risk of authorizing crime itself. For example, he writes, the average moral sentiment gives rise to lynching in the United States; it exacts murder for revenge in Albania and Montenegro, as formerly in Corsica and Sicily. It will be noted, however, that I have not spoken unqualifiedly of the superior races: I have added "of the civilized world." Albania and Montenegro, like all the Balkan countries, are still in a state of semi-barbarism. So far as Corsica and Sicily are concerned, as the author himself admits, the vendetta no longer meets with the approval of the better classes, and in general persists only in the lower classes, which are necessarily the most backward portion of the population. And as to lynching, this is merely a species of summary justice and wholly irrelevant to the present question.

Moreover, whatever may have been the manner of its formation, the moral sense today, beyond peradventure, exists independently of punishment. It is for this reason that I have deemed it possible to seek out from among the harmful facts which it is necessary to suppress, those which must be attributed to an inferior degree of individual morality. The latter are such as wound the most elementary altruistic instincts; here, and not elsewhere, do we find crime. In reality it is impossible at the present day to conceive as crime any fact whatsoever from which this condition is absent.

I have suggested that although facts of this description may be less disturbing to the public peace than certain other acts of a different character, the public conscience nevertheless looks upon them as much more serious. A distinction thus exists, as I have indicated, between two classes of harmful acts: on the one hand, acts which place their author in a condition of social inferiority, and are known in the popular language as crimes; and on the other, acts which are characterized by revolt against the State or disobedience to the laws, without any implication that the agent is lacking in the elements of morality which contemporary society deems essential.

Dragu's Theory of Crime. — Dragu, in his recent work,[1] admits that from the moral and social point of view, the murderer is an abnormal individual,[2] that he differs in his psychic make-up from honest men, and that in the case of murder, the objective gravity of the crime corresponds to the nature of the criminal, the act being irreparable and the man unreformable.[3] For Dragu the word "crime" designates only such acts as aim at the destruction of human life — a thing which cannot be replaced and admits of no equivalent, — as distinguished from attacks upon all other things ("tout autre bien") which may be replaced or made the subject of compensation. One might well entertain doubts as to this reparability of all criminal acts other than murder. But although this writer has thus limited the meaning of "crime," it is apparent that he comes very close to my conception of "natural crime." For, basically, the conclusion which results from his theory is that it is impossible for a morally normal man to be a murderer. Although the author is unwilling to admit it, the principle is identical. What I further maintain is, that not only is it impossible for a normal man to be a murderer, but it is equally impossible for him to be an incendiary, forger, swindler, or thief.

§ 8. The Same: Views of Tarde

Here too it may be appropriate to consider an observation made by Tarde which, perhaps, has been called forth by the expression of my views. "Can an act be criminal," he asks, "from the sole fact that it offends the average sentiment of pity or justice? Clearly not, unless it is deemed criminal by public opinion. The sight of the dead on a field of battle produces keener feelings of horror than the sight of a single murdered man. Our sympathies more readily go out to the victim despoiled by the raid of a hostile army, than to the victim of an ordinary theft. And yet the commander responsible

---

[1] "L'infraction, phénomène social" (Paris, 1903).
[2] *Op. cit.*, p. 129.   [3] *Ibid.*, p. 158.

for the taking of life in the one case, for the taking of property in the other, is not a criminal. The lawful or unlawful character of a given act — for example, homicide in lawful self-defense, murder for revenge, the seizure of property as an act of war or an act of piracy — is determined by the received opinion dominating in the social group to which one belongs. Moreover, the act which is forbidden by public opinion when it aims at a member of this group, or even of a larger group, becomes permitted by that same opinion when it strikes outside of the group limits." [1] True enough, nor have we forgotten this last fact in speaking of the progressive expansion of the moral sense, which, as we have explained, from first embracing only the family, finally came to include all mankind. But why distinguish the average moral sentiment from public opinion? From what is this opinion derived if not from the average measure in which the moral sentiments are possessed? The point is devoid of merit.

War and Capital Punishment. — The question why a commander who is responsible for voluntarily causing the death of many men is not a criminal admits of easy solution. As has already been seen, before we can speak of a criminal, we must have the notion of crime. And for this notion, it is not enough that the act in question be cruel or unjust: it must, in addition, be *harmful to society.* War, manifestly, is not a crime. It always has at least the appearance of social necessity: its object is not to injure the nation, but to preserve its interests or save it from destruction. In one way the case is identical with that of capital punishment. Taking life upon the battle-field is the nation's defense against external enemies; taking life upon the scaffold is its defense against internal enemies.

But, it may be objected, this very self-defense necessarily involves offense to the sentiment of pity. Assuming this to be true, offense to the sentiment of pity is an element common

---

[1] *Tarde,* "La criminalité comparée" (Paris, F. Alcan, 1890).

both to crimes and to acts which are non-criminal, and hence cannot of itself serve as a criterion. In our opinion, however, there is no such identity of element. The reader who has taken the pains to follow us so far, will see the force of this suggestion. It has been indicated how the sentiment of pity, in its common or average measure, is derived from that of sympathy, and how sympathy itself arises from the faculty of representing to ourselves the feelings of our fellows.[1] So, when we are shown a criminal totally destitute of moral instincts and therefore totally differing from us morally, we cannot see in him our fellow-being, and consequently cannot feel for him that sympathy which renders pity possible. This is because of the great importance which the psychic life has for men. While the lower animals expel from the community individuals of their kind whose physical deformity is offensive, men are tolerant and even sympathetic toward physical defects. Psychic anomaly alone loses for a man the sympathy of those about him, since for them he is not a fellow-being. Thus we prefer the society of a faithful dog to that of a brutalized man. The moral qualities of the former place him more nearly on our own level. He resembles us morally much more than the murderer resembles us physically. Man insists above all on the moral resemblance. And this seems to explain why benevolent-minded persons — even those of the opposite sex whose sensibilities are in general more delicate than our own — never experience the desire of saving from the gallows one who has been sentenced to death for a cold-blooded murder. The accomplishment of the ends of justice even affords them a certain inward satisfaction. The representative power with which they have been endowed makes them feel the full horror of the crime, and the fineness of their moral instincts prevents them from yielding to its author any place within the range of their sympathy. And without sympathy no pity can exist.

For these reasons, although an analogy exists between the

[1] *A. Espinas*, "Les sociétés animales," Conclusion, § 1.

two *facts* of crime and capital punishment, there is none between the *sentiments* which these facts respectively provoke.[1]

In the case of war the element of necessity is more emphatically present. But apart from this, the case admits of similar explanation to that of capital punishment. We feel no pity toward the enemy, for precisely the same reason which restrains our pity from the criminal: we cannot feel for him this sympathy from which pity arises. In this case, however, the absence of sympathy is not due to a refined sensibility, but, on the contrary, to a sort of historical retrogression, to the backward flight of our sentiments to their stage at the period of the predatory life, when man considered as his fellow-beings none but members of the same clan or horde. The stages of development which in the course of centuries the sentiment of benevolence has slowly achieved are recrossed at a single bound; the sound of the cannon suffices to bring back the primitive hatreds of race and tribe and to drive forth the love of humanity — this moral instinct so toilsomely acquired through the evolution of centuries.

---

[1] De Aramburu takes issue with me on this point, asserting that in Spain every death sentence is the signal for pronounced agitation against its infliction, and that every effort is made to procure a pardon for the offender. ("La nueva ciencia penal," pp. 238, 239. — Madrid, 1887.) All I have to say is that, in other countries not less civilized, the very opposite is true. Witness the wide-spread movement in Belgium in the case of the brothers Peltzer; the petition for the carrying out of the death sentence which had been passed upon them bore hundreds of thousands of respectable signatures. In France the clemency of President Grévy earned for him the popular nickname of "the father of murderers" ("le père des assassins"), and was the subject of severe censure on the part of the press. Our readers will also recall the riot at Cincinnati (U. S. A.), in March, 1884, which was the culmination of a long-standing popular feeling against leniency shown to criminals, but which was immediately provoked by the inadequate verdicts in the cases of Berner and Palmer, both guilty of murder. An effort was made by the rioters to storm the county jail for the purpose of lynching the prisoners. As a result of the disturbance, which lasted three days, the court house was burned down, 45 persons were killed and 145 injured. — See *Martinez*, "El derecho penal ante la ciencia," p. 59 (Buenos Ayres, 1892).

CHAPTER II

THE LEGAL NOTION OF CRIME

§ 1. Inadequacy of the Legal Notion.
§ 2. The Need of Direct Study of the Criminal.[1]

§ 1. Inadequacy of the Legal Notion

IN modern society the science of crimes is treated as merely a branch of the science of law; punishment has been vested with a juridical character; the function of the lawyer extends not only to the making of the criminal laws, but to their application. One and the same class of public officers delivers judgment in matters both civil and criminal; the court-rooms present almost the same scene, — black-robed judges on the bench, court-clerks busy with pen and paper, advocates presenting their causes. . . . And yet the observer cannot but feel that there is no real relation between the two classes of cases, — that between these two court-rooms whose entrances are but a few feet apart, the moral distance is immeasurably wide.

The jurists have taken possession of the science of criminality. They have been allowed to do so, and this, it seems to me, has been a mistake. The assertion may appear somewhat strange, but I hope in the course of this work to convince the reader of its truth.

Objective Character of Juristic Study of Crime. — For the present, however, let us consider how the juridical school approaches the criminal phenomenon. In the first place,

---

[1] [§ 2 = § III of original. § II of original appears *ante* as § 8, c. I of the present version. — TRANSL.]

what does criminality mean for the jurist? He hardly knows
the word. He troubles himself not at all about the natural
causes of crime. Knowledge of such matters is for him, at
most, a species of academic learning. He looks upon the
criminal, not as a psychically abnormal man, but as a man
differing from other men only in the fact that he has committed a forbidden and punishable act. The jurist studies
crime only in its external form; he makes no analysis from
the standpoint of experimental psychology; the derivation
of crime does not enter into his calculations. What concerns him is the ascertainment of the *external* characteristics
of the different felonies and misdemeanors — the classification of facts according to the rights which they infringe —
the quest for the punishment which, proportionally and "in
abstracto," is a just punishment, not for the punishment
which experience has proved efficacious for the diminution
of crime in general.

Absence of Accurate Definition. — We might at least expect
to find an accurate definition of just what the jurist understands by "crime." But here too we are disappointed.
The old utilitarian school never got beyond the notion that
crime was "an act which it is deemed necessary to forbid,
because of the harm which it produces or tends to produce," [1]
or merely "an act forbidden by law," [2] or else "some act
which is detrimental to the public good." [3] The vagueness of
such definitions is at once apparent. They might fit almost
any sort of act — certainly every act which in any aspect
could be deemed harmful to society.

Since then, an attempt has been made to introduce a moral
element — that of injustice. Thus we are told by a distinguished Italian writer that crime is the "voluntary act of a
person of sound mind ("di persona intelligente e libera"),
harmful to others and at the same time unjust." [4] Similarly,

---

[1] *Bentham*, "Traité de législation pénale," c. i.
[2] *Filangieri*, "Scienza della legislazione," Book I, c. xxxvii.
[3] *Beccaria*, "Dei delitti e delle pene," § VI.
[4] *Romagnosi*, "Genesi del diritto penale," § 554 *et seq.*

the founder of the modern French school maintains that "the only thing which the social power can regard as crime is the violation of such duties toward society and individuals as contribute to the maintenance of the social order and are capable of absolute legal enforcement" ("exigibles en soi").[1]

Although this notion has been everywhere accepted, it is plainly defective in treating social utility as merely one of the conditions which render punishable an immoral act. Nor can it be other than loose, in positing as the concomitant condition the idea of injustice in general, without specifying its kind or character. The latter fault is exemplified in the following passage from a standard French work on criminal law: "Every disturbance inflicted upon the social order is a moral crime, since such disturbance is the violation of a duty — that of man to society. Hence, the acts with which punitive justice has to deal with are of two kinds: (1) those which bear the imprint of an intrinsic immorality, and (2) those which are intrinsically free from immorality, but assume an immoral character because involving a breach of duty. In these two cases social crime exists. In the one case the element of criminality is intrinsic; in the other it is relative. For the greater part, police offenses ("contraventions matérielles") fall under the second head." [2] In other words, when one does an act forbidden by lawful authority, immorality exists because of the disobedience to the law. What then is the use of singling out the moral element and insisting upon it as an indispensable condition of crime? If obedience to law is a moral duty, we might just as well fall back upon the definitions of the older school and say point blank that crime is an act forbidden by law.

For the theory of Rossi, Franck proposes to substitute its correlative. The one speaks of the violation of a duty,

[1] *Rossi*, "Traité du droit pénal," Book II, c. i. Among others who have followed this definition are: Ortolan, Trébutien, Guizot and Bertault in France, Haus in Belgium, and Mittermaier in Germany.

[2] *Chauveau* and *Hélie*, "Théorie du code pénal," c. XVII.

the other of a violation of a right: "No act can be made the subject of prosecution and punishment, on the part of society, unless it consists of the violation, not of a duty, but of a right — a right either individual or collective and founded like society itself upon the moral law." [1] The question here introduced is perhaps only one of words, notwithstanding the author's efforts to show the existence of a substantial distinction. In criticism of Rossi's definition, Franck brings forward a number of instances of duties owed to society, violations of which, though harmful, can in no sense be regarded as meriting prosecution or repression at the hands of society. Such is the duty of "devoting to our country's service all our strength of body and mind." Such, too, are the virtue-duties which conscience enjoins upon us in relation to our fellows, as, for example, the practice of charity and the forgiveness of injuries. It will be noted, however, that Franck has here overlooked the concluding portion of Rossi's definition, in which distinctly appears the qualification that the duties contemplated must be absolutely enforcible by law ("exigibles en soi"). Since the examples cited by Franck exhibit no instance of duties thus enforcible, the scope of the two definitions is precisely the same. Inasmuch as right and duty are correlative terms and no right can exist without a corresponding duty, no other result would be admissible. Nor is the definition of Franck any less vague than its predecessors. He gains nothing by adding restrictions, by introducing qualifications, by saying, for example, that the only rights whose violation constitutes crime are such as are susceptible of exact determination, or, because their enforcement is absolutely essential to the fulfillment of the duties with which they respectively correspond, enforcible by legal means. Equally useless is his further suggestion that the violation of one of these circumscribed rights does not always or alone suffice to constitute crime, and that in addition it is necessary that the penal sanction be possible, efficacious, and not of such

---

[1] *Adolphe Franck*, "Philosophie du droit pénal," p. 96 (Paris, 1880).

a nature as to offend public decorum.[1]   In spite of the evident
care bestowed upon this definition, it is still much too broad.
For example, a debtor who fails to pay what he owes, violates
a right fully determinate and enforcible by law.   Suppose
the failure to pay is due to his insolvency, can we call him a
criminal?   Not according to existing laws, even where his
apparent insolvency has resulted from a fraudulent conveyance of his property.   And still another example: A father
has a right to the custody of his children.   If they leave home
he may take them back by force.   Yet no one for an instant
could suppose that the violation of his right to their custody
is a crime on the part of the children.

Moreover, according to the definition under discussion,
every transgression of law— in fact, every disobedience to a
lawful order of the public authorities,— would be a social
crime.   Thus we always come back to our starting point.
The argument is simply a vicious circle.   The attempt to
show us what the law views as a crime, ends in our being
told that crime, in the eyes of the law, is the doing of that
which the law itself forbids.

Notion of Natural Crime the only Solution. — The conception of the criminal act is therefore just as uncertain as before.
Certainty will only be attained with the determination of the
particular kind of immorality, which must exist before public
opinion can say that a crime has been committed.

It is not sufficient to say with Jhering that crime is the
ascertained jeopardizing of the conditions of social life
("constatirte Gefährdung der Lebensbedingungen der Gesell-
schaft").   For one thing, it ought to be specified just what
acts are of this character.   Exactness of description is important, if we are not to confuse the necessary conditions of the
evolved social life with the conditions necessary to the security of the State at a given period.   Then again, the

---

[1] " Thus," he says, "a wife who refuses to her husband the right of cohabitation would have complete impunity.   From the standpoint of public
decency, any measures which society might adopt in this case would be
more harmful than the action complained of."   (p. 101.)

danger or harmfulness of an act does not necessarily render it criminal.

It may be urged that our analysis will result in dropping from the criminal code a large number of offenses now punishable and which in the interests of social security ought to remain punishable. But what is to prevent the existence, side by side with the criminal code, of a separate code of disobediences ("révoltes"), the one dealing with natural criminality, the other with all mere transgressions of law which public policy finds it necessary to repress with measures of severity? Differentiation is one of the characteristics of progress. The rules of criminal and civil law, intermingled in the codes of Manu and Moses, underwent separation at the hands of the European law-makers. Later, a distinction came to be made between different classes of crimes, as on the Continent, between "crimes," "délits," and "contraventions,"[1] and in the English law, between felonies and

---

[1] [This is the classification of the French Penal Code, "*crimes* answering very roughly to felonies, *délits* to indictable misdemeanors and *contraventions* to police offenses punishable on summary conviction." (*Stephen*, "History of the Criminal Law of England," II, pp. 193, 194.) The distinction is based upon the nature of the punishment: an offense is a "crime," "délit," or "contravention," according as it calls for criminal, correctional, or police punishment. For non-political offenses, criminal punishments are always "peines afflictives et infamantes," that is to say, punishments which affect the body of the offender, and at the same time render him infamous by entailing his civic degradation. They include death, penal servitude ("travaux forcés"), and penitentiary imprisonment ("réclusion"). Correctional punishments ("peines correctionelles") comprise imprisonments intended to be of a reformatory character, in duration from 6 days to 5 years, and fines of from 16 francs upward. Police punishments ("peines de police") are such as involve imprisonment of from 1 to 5 days or fine of from 1 to 15 francs. — Civic degradation, it will be noticed, is always an accessary punishment in the case of "crimes." Where the conviction is for a "délit," there may be a suspension, in whole or in part, of certain "civil, civic, and family rights," but, unlike civic degradation, this is complementary and not accessary: in other words, it must be ordered in the judgment of conviction. A considerable number of other incapacities and disabilities exist, depending upon, and varying with the principal punishment. — "Relégation" (*i. e.*, life internment in a colony beyond seas), as fixed by a law of 1885, is not included in the foregoing division; it is a complementary punishment to be undergone by certain recidivists following the termination of a principal punishment, which may be either criminal or correctional. (See *Garçon*, "Code pénal annoté,"

misdemeanors. The formation of a code of natural crimes uniform throughout all civilized countries, as opposed to the special repressive laws of the several nations, would only be the logical outcome of this process.

The necessities of scientific study have required us to isolate the natural crime. No such study would be possible if we were obliged to deal with all the punishable acts heterogeneously assembled in the codes. So, too, the legal notion of crime must be laid aside as valueless for our purposes. Consequently our first step has been to disregard all facts not wounding the altruistic sentiments; such facts it is absolutely impossible to conceive as crimes. Next, we have reduced the altruistic sentiments to two distinct types. And lastly, we have fixed the average measure in which these sentiments are possessed by civilized mankind; their nicer development, being present only in a small minority, does not enter into the question.

In a word, it is not upon the violation of rights but upon the violation of sentiments that the concept of natural crime must be based. In this, the principle for which we contend is totally different from that of the jurists. Nor is there any reason to fear that this principle will tend to bring into the field of criminality acts which merely reveal immoral inclinations, and which have never been and never will be of a punishable character. Our fixation of the necessary measure of the altruistic sentiments stands in the way. With this as a criterion we are effectually prevented from regarding as crimes, acts which, despite their harmfulness, cannot properly be made the subject of punishment.

I, p. 40 *et seq.; Le Sueur* in "La grande encyclopédie," XXVI, pp. 235, 236, XXVIII, p. 333; and *post*, pp. 212, 328 of the present work).

The same classification of offenses was followed by the former Italian Code, which dealt with the three groups of "crimini," "delitti," and "contravvenzioni." But by the Penal Code of 1889, this tripartite classification was discarded in favor of the bipartite division of "delitti" and "contravvenzioni." The distinction between these two classes is based, not upon the character of the punishment, but upon the intrinsic nature of the offense. — Garofalo, however, speaks throughout in terms of the tripartite classification. — TRANSL.]

§ 2. The Need of Direct Study of the Criminal

The Criminal an Individual Incompatible with Society. — The importance of fixing the notion of crime in the manner we have outlined, will more fully appear in the course of our study. Since crime consists in an act which is at once harmful to society and violative of one or both of the most elementary sentiments of pity and probity, the criminal is necessarily a man in whom there is an absence, eclipse or weakness of these sentiments, one or both. This is evident, because if he had possessed the elementary altruistic sentiments in a sufficient degree, any *real* violation of them on his part would have been impossible. Possession of them is perhaps not inconsistent with an *apparent* violation, but in this case the crime is not really a crime.

The sentiments in question being the substratum of all morality, their absence renders the deficient person incompatible with society. If average and relative morality consists in the individual's adaptation to society, this adaptation becomes impossible when the sentiments lacking are precisely those which the environment regards as indispensable. The same thing happens in a narrower circle where a higher sense of morality is requisite, and where refinement, the maintenance of a high standard of honor, and extreme politeness are the rule. There the absence of these qualities implies the inadaptability of the individual to his environment. Thus, in those associations whose morality is based upon sentiments of religion or patriotism, violation of these sentiments is a mortal offense. Society at large is contented with little: it demands that the individual refrain from offending the slender measure of morality of which we have spoken, — it insists on keeping inviolate that most elementary and least refined degree of morality which is vital to its existence. Only when this is trampled under foot does society protest that a crime has been committed.

Method of Study. — It is now plain what classes of crimes are to engage our attention. To these classes, as we shall find, there correspond, beyond question, two psychic varieties of the race, two distinct types — on the one hand, men devoid of the sentiment of pity in its average measure, on the other, men devoid of the average sentiment of probity. These we must study directly, and ascertain the cases in which, because of the criminal's insusceptibility to the sentiment which he has violated, the anomaly is irreducible. This insusceptibility will depend, as a contemporary writer has excellently put it, "upon the existence in the mental organization of lacunæ (corresponding to the loss of a physical member or a physical function) whereby these beings are completely dehumanized." [1] Other cases exist in which the anomaly may perhaps be lessened, because there is not a total absence, but merely a weakness, of the moral sense. Here the defect renders impossible the adaptation of the criminal so long as his surroundings remain unchanged, but permits such adaptation when he is withdrawn from his deleterious surroundings and subjected to new conditions of existence.

[1] *Th. Ribot* in his opening lecture at the Sorbonne (Revue politique elt littéraire, No. 25, 19 December, 1885). See also *Q. Newmann*, "Notas sueltas sobre la pena de muerte" (Santiago de Chile, 1896).

PART II

THE CRIMINAL

CHAPTER I

CRIMINAL ANOMALY

§ 1. Anthropologic Data

As was said at the close of the preceding chapter, the notion of crime for which we contend naturally involves the idea of the criminal's moral anomaly. It may be objected that this is sheer assertion,— that the mere fact of the criminal's violation of a moral sentiment gives us no right to conclude that his psychic organization is different from that of other men,— that, with equal propriety, it may be inferred that he is a normal man capable of repentance, who has temporarily deviated from the rules of moral conduct. There is no proof, we may be told, that the act reflects the nature of the agent or establishes his insusceptibility to the sentiment which he has violated. Moreover, — so might run the argument — even admitting the theory of the naturalists, according to which the will is a resultant, still (to quote a contemporary psychologist) "the voluntary act presupposes the participation of a whole group of conscious or subconscious states which constitute the Ego at a given moment." Is it not, then, possible for these states so to vary as to produce new voluntary acts entirely the opposite of former acts? May not the criminal of

---

[1] [§ 7 appears in original as a note to the present chapter, pp. 143–145.— TRANSL.]

today be the honest man of tomorrow? What proof is there
of the total absence or organic defect of the moral sense, or
even of the weakness of either of the elementary altruistic
sentiments? Is it not sufficient to say that the force of certain
motives may be such at a given moment as to overcome the
resistance of the moral sense, without going the length of
supposing the existence in some men of an anomalous psychic
organization?

Such doubts are met by the decisive answer, that our knowledge of the criminal is not limited to what we learn from his
acts. We are in possession of a whole series of anthropologic
and psychologic data, which demonstrate the coherence of an
act of this sort with certain special characteristics of the agent,
and point to the conclusion that the act is not an isolated
phenomenon but the symptom of moral anomaly. A brief
summary of such data therefore becomes inportant.

Anthropologic Theories; Views of Lombroso. — Although
efforts had been made from the very earliest times to establish a correlation between certain forms of perversity and
certain external physical signs, it may properly be said that the
conception of the criminal as an abnormal being is wholly
modern, in fact, contemporary. Gall's theory was quite
different from that of the present-day anthropologists. As is
well known, he assigned to each human propensity a separate
portion of the brain, the development of the particular propensity being recognizable by the conformation of the skull
at the corresponding place. According to this theory, each
passion, each propensity, good or bad, had its particular
"bump." Gall, however, never dreamed of describing
the criminal as a degenerate. This is an idea of recent origin
due to the researches of Lauvergne, Ferrus, Lucas, Morel,
Despine, Thomson, Nicolson, Virgilio, and others. As for
Lombroso, his belief was that the presence of certain physical
characteristics frequently found in criminals, afforded ground
for treating the criminal as an *anthropologic type*. Of the
characteristics which he has thus noted, the principal are:

asymmetry of the cranium or of the face, submicrocephaly, anomaly in the shape of the ears, the absence of beard, nervous contractions of the facial muscles, prognathism (*i. e.* the elongation, prominence, or obliquity of the jaw-bones), inequality in the size of the pupils, flat or misshapen nose, retreating forehead, extreme length of the face, exaggerated development of the zygomata, and the neutral tint of the eyes and hair.[1] None of these characteristics is constant, but comparison of criminals with non-criminals justifies the assertion that their occurrence is more frequent among the former.

Lombroso's conclusions, in whole or in part, have been attacked or confirmed by a number of subsequent writers, notably Benedikt, Ferri, Marro, and Corre. It seems, however, to be generally admitted that in criminals, the occipital region exhibits a much greater development than the frontal region. According to Corre, this characteristic signifies the predominance of the occipital activity — that which is in probable alliance with the impulsive sensitivity — over the frontal activity, which is today recognized as an activity of a purely intellectual and reflective nature.[2]

Still, the authorities are very far from being at one on this point, as shown in the various Congresses of Criminal Anthropology, held at Rome, Paris, Brussels, and Geneva. Indeed, the characteristics described by some writers as peculiar to criminals, are said by other observers to be found in larger proportion among the non-criminal. It must, however, be conceded, as Marro has said, "that all who deal with the physical study of the criminal are forced to the conclusion

---

[1] *Lombroso*, "L'uomo delinquente," p. 284 (4th Ital. ed., Turin, Bocca, 1889), and French translation: "L'homme criminel" (Paris, F. Alcan, 1895). Among other characteristics studied by this author and his pupils is especially worthy of attention one indicated by Ottolenghi, viz., the scarcity of gray hair and baldness among criminals, as among epileptics and crétins — a condition which in his opinion is in keeping with their lesser degree of sensibility and emotional reaction. (Appendix to "L'uomo delinquente," Vol. II, p. 470.)

[2] *Corre*, "Les criminels," p. 37 (Paris, 1889).

that he is a being apart." Few who have ever visited a prison
or penitentiary will maintain the contrary. Without undertaking to examine all the works which have appeared on this
subject, I propose briefly to indicate some of the characteristics which, by reason of their frequent occurrence, have
particularly impressed students of the criminal.

Physical Anomalies. — With respect to anomalies of a regressive character, Virgilio, as the result of an examination of
living criminals, found 28% who had retreating foreheads.
Post-mortem examination by Bordier of criminals who had
suffered capital punishment, showed a slightly larger proportion — 33% — of the same characteristic. This anomaly, it
should be noted, attains a proportion of but 4% among persons
who have never been convicted of crime. The difference in
percentage between the criminals examined by Virgilio and
the post-mortem cases of Bordier, is unquestionably due to
the fact that the latter necessarily included a larger number
of true criminals — a fact which we may fairly assume from
the very circumstance that in these cases the full penalty
of the law was exacted. It is of course probable that even
among the executed offenders, some were lesser criminals
or mere "révoltés." Prognathism is still more frequent.
Penta's observation of 500 convicts disclosed the existence of
this anomaly in the proportion of 45%. Again, Lombroso
notes the undue development of the lower part of the forehead,
which he describes as prominence of the supra-orbital ridges
and the frontal sinuses, in 66.9 cases out of each 100 criminal
skulls examined.[1] The figures of Bordier approach this
closely, the proportion observed by him being 60%. Marro,
however, found but 23% among inmates of prisons and 18%
among the non-criminal.[2] According to Lombroso, euryg-
nathism (exaggerated distance between the zygomata) is
present to the extent of 36%.[3] The same anomaly to an ex-

[1] "L'uomo delinquente," pp. 173, 174 (3d. ed. 1885).
[2] "Caratteri dei delinquenti," pp. 156, 157 (1887).
[3] "L'uomo delinquente," p. 176.

treme degree was noticed by Marro in 5 criminals out of 141, without a single case being discovered among the non-criminal.[1] The last observer assures us that in 13.9 cases out of 100, he verified the complete absence of beard; among the non-criminal this trait shows a proportion of only 1.5%.[2] He also noted low and narrow foreheads ("fronts petits") in the proportion of 41% among criminals, as opposed to 15% among the non-criminal.[3] Lombroso found many cases of microcephaly and a large number of cases of submicrocephaly among criminals. These anomalies, we know, are quite rare among normal persons.[4] In the prisons of Waldheim, out of 1,214 inmates, 579 exhibited physical deviations from the normal type (Knecht, 1883). Of 400 persons presumably honest, but one had the typical physiognomy of the extreme criminals (Lombroso).

As for the cranial deformations which may be called teratologic or atypic, such as plagiocephaly, scaphocephaly, and oxycephaly, Marro found them present in almost equal numbers among prison inmates and persons reputed honest.

It has, however, been observed that the presence of a group of many anomalies, whether degenerative or teratologic, occurs more frequently in a single criminal subject than in any single non-criminal individual. In fact, Ferri's comparison of 711 soldiers with 699 prison inmates showed 37% of the soldiers as against 10% of the prisoners to be without anomaly. Irregular characteristics to the number of three or four were remarked in individual soldiers, the proportion of such individuals being 11%. Of the prisoners 33% showed similar groups of anomalies in individuals, but, whereas among the soldiers the number of anomalies was never in excess of three or four to the individual, the individual prisoner showed as many as six or seven or even more.[5]

[1] "Caratteri dei delinquenti," p. 128.   [2] *Ibid.*, p. 149.

[3] *Ibid.*, pp. 125, 126.

[4] "L'uomo delinquente," pp. 232, 233, 240.

[5] "L'omicidio," p. 211 (Turin, 1895). It is a mistake to criticize Ferri's comparison on the ground that soldiers are especially healthy and robust

But assuming the accuracy of all these observations to be beyond dispute, they still do not give us an anthropologic type of the criminal. It has not been possible to fix a single *constant* external characteristic which will enable us to distinguish him from the normal man. One fact alone seems to have been definitely established, namely, that among criminals certain characteristics are found oftener in one class than another. The murderer ("assassin"), for example, as Lombroso says, almost always "has a cold and glassy look, sometimes bloodshot eyes, always a large nose which is frequently aquiline or hooked, long ears, heavy jaws, widely-spaced zygomata, crisp and abundant hair, strongly developed canine teeth, and thin lips; he often suffers from nervous contractions and twitchings confined to one side of the face, the effect of which is to lay bare the canine teeth and seemingly impart to the countenance an expression of sardonic menace." [1]

Some observers add that there is less physical resemblance in a given section of the country between murderers generally and the rest of the population, than between the latter and the inhabitants of other sections, even where these are ethnographically different. Thus the murderers of Southern Italy would seem to differ more from the soldiers of the same provinces, than the latter from the soldiers of Northern Italy, in respect of the frontal diameter, frontal index, mandibular diameter, and development of the face.[2]

Except for the immobility of the eye, the vagueness of the look, and thinness of the lips, the same characteristics are very often observable in the whole class of homicidal criminals ("meurtriers"). In this class there is a very marked predominance of strongly-developed supra-orbital ridges, of widely-separated zygomata (a characteristic common to certain in-

---

men. The comparison is limited to the matter of cranial anomalies. An anomaly of this character, it is to be borne in mind, seldom represents a physical infirmity sufficient to cause the rejection of a recruit.

[1] *Lombroso*, "L'uomo delinquente" p. 232 (4th ed., Turin, 1889).

[2] *Ferri*, "L'omicidio," p. 206 (Turin, 1895).

ferior races, such as the Malays),[1] and contracted foreheads,[2] but especially noticeable are the excessive length of the face in relation to the cranium,[3] and the undue size of the mandibles. No observer questions this last-mentioned characteristic; it is an unmistakable sign of brutality or violence. Its derivation, however, is the subject of discussion, some attributing it to degeneracy (Lauvergne), some to atavism (Ferri and Delaunay), and still others simply believing it always to exist in individuals of a retarded evolutionary development (Manouvrier).

However this may be, it is recognized that "among mankind as a whole, as in our own race, the smallness of the forehead and the relatively excessive size of the jaw, coincide with homicidal tendency" (Foley). Emile Gautier, who underwent a term of imprisonment for political reasons, declared that after the lapse of many years, his mind still retains the composite photograph of the criminal type, especially vivid being the impression of its heavy jaws.[4] It suffices to glance at a group of photographs of homicidal criminals to be convinced of the frequency of this characteristic. The same thing is noticeable among rapists — a circumstance easily explicable if one remembers that rape is a result of the same violent instincts which impel attack on human life.

Thieves, on the other hand, appear very often to be characterized by cranial anomalies of the sort that may be called atypic, such as submicrocephaly, oxycephaly, scaphocephaly, and trococephaly. Their physiognomy, too, is recognizable by the mobility of the countenance, the small size and vivacity of the eyes, the thickness of the eyebrows (which often meet), their small and retreating foreheads, their long, twisted, or

[1] *Topinard,* "Anthropologie," p. 492 (Paris, 1879).

[2] *E. Ferri, op. cit.*

[3] Sometimes it is the opposite type which occurs: brachyprosopy, or extreme smallness of the face. This I have observed in some murderers, accompanied by a frontal diameter very short in relation to the bizygomatic diameter.

[4] *E. Gautier,* "Le monde des prisons" (Archives de l'anthropologie criminelle, 15 December, 1888, — Lyons).

misshapen noses, and the pallor of their complexion coupled
with an inability to blush (Lombroso).

Without attaching undue importance to this description,
I am compelled to admit that it has very often been confirmed
by my own direct observation. In visiting prisons and penitentiaries and observing the inmates, I have frequently been
enabled to distinguish those under sentence for homicide from
others whose offense was theft or obtaining money by false
pretenses, although I knew nothing of their previous history.
On these occasions, as appears from my notes, I came to
the wrong conclusion not more than seven or eight times
out of a hundred.

But attempt at description does not stop here. Marro,
in the work before cited, assigns distinctive characteristics
to no less than eleven classes of criminals. It must, however,
be said, that the most marked of these distinctive features are
not all physical, but are for the most part drawn from their
propensities, habits, and covetousnesses, as well as from their
degree of intelligence and education.

Physiognomic Types. — One thing, however, seems clear.
The three classes which I have just indicated are especially
distinguishable by a peculiar expression of their physiognomy.
So that if we cannot arrive at an anthropologic type of criminal, it may at least be affirmed that we have these *physiognomic types*, viz., (1) *the murderer*, (2) *the violent criminal*,
and (3) *the thief*.

It has been said that comparison of the inmates of penal
institutions with persons at liberty, shows that many of the
characteristics just noted are more frequently found in the
former than in the latter. Still, even among prisoners, the
proportion of anomalies is but 45 or 50%, and the larger
number of criminals would therefore seem to be without them.
In this lies the weakness of criminal anthropology. "How
are we to speak of a criminal type when 60 out of every 100
criminals show no vestige of its characteristics?"

Such an objection, however, would not really be serious if

we could regard it as settled that there exists a greater proportion of congenital anomalies in a given number of convicts
than in an equal number of non-convicts. Unfortunately,
this has not been established. If we were in possession of such
proof, I would not hesitate to regard it as a definite gain for
criminal anthropology, notwithstanding that only 60% of
the convicts might answer the typical description, and that
the same description might apply to 20% of the non-convicts.
For it is clear that the latter class cannot all be honest men:
it is bound to contain many individuals whose criminal propensities but await the opportunity to reveal themselves.
The fact is well known that not the half of those guilty of
established crimes are brought to justice. Moreover, these
established crimes represent but a small part of the total
number of crimes committed, most of which are not discovered,
or else are not reported to the police. Finally, there are social
classes in which the criminal instincts reveal themselves under
other forms, keeping clear of the criminal code: "Encouragement to perilous adventures is preferred to slaying with the
knife, cheating at play supplants highway robbery, seduction
and subsequent desertion take the place of rape." [1]

"Through cowardice or stupidity," adds Corre, "we persist
in closing our eyes to the fact that under the arrogance and
brilliant externals of high political and financial life, lurk
murder, theft, and crime of every description. Crime seems
to become minimized so as almost to lose the character of
crime, in proportion as it assumes a wider significance and
becomes more deserving of chastisement and reprobation by
the standards of social conventions. It is a truth as commonplace as lamentable that the man who holds cheap the rights
of his neighbors is not always found behind prison walls:
in very considerable number he poses as a virtuous personage
in the ranks of the rich and respected. This is what will
make it difficult to apply anthropologic principles to the
study of the criminal. . . . Many a supposedly honest man

[1] *E. Ferri, op. cit.*

is more deserving of the ball and chain than the humbler law-breaker upon whom he has aided in fastening them." [1]

In short, to compare the convicted with the non-convicted would be a serious mistake. Instead, for terms of comparison we must take, on the one hand, the true criminals, on the other, the really honest men. This latter class is undoubtedly the harder to recognize with certainty, but difficulty is also presented by the former, since it is by no means as numerous as that of the convicted. Our two terms are therefore (1) a class in which honest men are in majority and (2) a class in which criminals are in majority. In view of this, we need not be astonished by the fact that if criminality has a physical stamp, that stamp does not appear on all the inmates of prisons. Moreover, if it be true that these stigmata are more often found among the convicted, clearly this fact would have an important significance.

In that case the objection referred to would be unfounded. But what criminal anthropology really lacks, as I have heretofore had occasion to suggest, is convincing proof that a given character of the skull or skeleton is found more often among criminals than among persons presumably honest.

We must then be content with the physiognomic characteristics or rather physiognomic expressions of which mention has been made. These do not constitute true anthropologic types. The case is the same as that of the international dissimilarities existing between members of a single race. We speak, for example, of the different European types, but can anyone say just what are the exact features which distinguish them? Stress can be laid on nothing in particular. The difference consists of something in the features taken as a whole — something which gives to the face an almost indefinable character, but nevertheless enables us to distinguish any group, however small, of Germans from an equal number of French or Slavs or Italians.

Although Tarde, in a brilliant chapter of his "Criminalité

[1] *Corre,* "Les criminels," Introduction (Paris, 1889).

comparée," has raised many questions touching the anthropologic characteristics of criminals, he nevertheless concludes
by admitting the reality of the type. But instead of seeking
to distinguish this type from that of the normal man, he op-
poses it to the respective types of the scholarly man, the religious man, the artistic man, and the virtuous man. This is
an idea which is perhaps destined to meet ultimate acceptance,
but the lack of relative data forbids its present discussion.

All that can be said is that the contrast between certain
characteristics common enough in criminals, and the ordinary
characteristics of persons not suspected of crime, would become much more pronounced if it were possible to compare the
criminals with their exact opposites, that is to say, virtuous
men. But we are obliged to content ourselves with the observations which, up to the present time, it has been possible
to make.[1]

For Tarde, however, as well as for Colajanni and Prins,
the criminal type is not an anthropologic type, such as that
of the Chinese or the negro, the Anglo-Saxon or the Latin,
but merely a professional or social type formed by the subjection of individuals to identical conditions of existence. Under such circumstances they assume "a uniform imprint."
Imitation, the exercise of the one trade or profession, the one
kind of mental exertion, the repetition of the same movements
whether in a drawing-room or a coal-mine, are all factors
in the acquisition of common muscular and nervous habitudes,
which are reflected in the bearing, the facial expression, the
character, and even in the physical aspect of the persons affected . . . "We can all tell a sailor from an artist. In my
younger days there existed a type then easily recognizable,

---

[1] Lombroso maintains that Italian criminals resemble French and German
criminals much more than any one of these groups resembles its national
type. Heger, on the contrary, declares that his observations have yielded an
opposite result. It must be kept in mind, however, that Heger's observations
were limited to craniology, and were not concerned with physiognomic traits.
For my own part, I have not been able to make any direct observations on
the subject.

but now extinct — the republican of '48. . . . . Among work-
ingmen, notice the quarry-man, the glass-blower, the coal-
miner, the brickmaker. . . . There is also a type of habitual
criminal. . . . To recognize it one needs but visit a prison.
. . . Experience makes it easy to distinguish the recidivist,
and even the particular kind of recidivist. . . . There is a
still more special type of thief who may be readily distinguished and recognized — an ill figure ("individu dé-
hanché"), low of forehead, with an air of impudence and
mockery, who represents the pickpocket." [1] Without passing
judgment on this suggestion, which doubtless is not without
a basis of fact, we are inclined to question the relevancy of
the low forehead, which can hardly be the result of imitation.
A further fact which is difficult to explain otherwise than
anthropologically should be marked, viz., that the frequency
of the regressive anomalies, noted above, shows much increase
among the extreme criminals [2] — those responsible for the
most frightful crimes committed under the most atrocious
circumstances. For example, murderers for the sake of robbery seldom fail to show some of the salient characteristics
which approximate them to the inferior races, such as prognathism, narrow and retreating forehead, prominent supra-
orbital ridges, etc. It is evident that this can be established
only by cumulative proof, but such proof, in fact, is abundantly
found in works on anthropology and in the accounts of
celebrated cases.

My own experience has always been in the affirmative.
On one occasion, for instance, I selected a number of notorious

---

[1] *Prins*, "Les doctrines nouvelles de droit pénal " (Brussels, 1895).

[2] "The anatomic signs occur more frequently among notorious figures
in the criminal world than among its ordinary rank and file," said Benedikt
in his notable address to the Congress of Phreniatry, held at Antwerp, in
September, 1885. This is why, as I have before indicated, certain absolutely
degenerative cranial anomalies such as retreating forehead and prognathism,
have been found in larger proportion among criminals who had suffered capital
punishment than among living prisoners. Since the former had met the extreme penalty, they must have been all, or nearly all, extreme criminals, while
the living prisoners must have included a larger number of lesser criminals
or mere "révoltés."

murderers whom I had never seen, but with the details of whose crimes I had become acquainted from reading the documents on file in their cases. Visiting them in prison, I reached the conviction that not one of them was exempt from some very striking degenerative or regressive characteristics.[1]

Still, these characteristics are not always the same: sometimes it is one which is present, sometimes another. The murderer type cannot be described anthropologically. It is no wonder, then, that physical anomalies are still less pronounced and constant in the lesser criminals. In the first place, we cannot be sure that all those who are authors of crime in the eye of the law are true criminals according to the psychologic acceptation which we have assigned to the term. Again, it would be strange if anomalies of the same importance were observed in ordinary criminals. It is natural that the latter are physically less distinguishable from the normal man; for the same reason, they are morally less remote from him. Their crimes while revolting to us, do not appear absolutely contrary to human nature. It is even possible for us to imagine, not without a sense of fear, that under certain circumstances, we ourselves might be driven to do something of the same kind. This idea, which flits through our mind, we reject with terror — terror which is wholly unnecessary, because, our character being fixed, we are in no danger of experiencing that dreaded volitive movement. Nevertheless, the fact of having entertained even for an instant the idea of this possibility proves to us that there are criminals whom we can understand, who are beings not wholly alien to our moral nature. That even physically these individuals do not show marked traits of degeneracy is therefore not at all remarkable. But although the anomaly is less, this does not mean that it is imperceptible. That evil facial expression, that indefinable but sinister appearance which we associate with the term "gallows-bird," is very common among the inmates of

[1] See my "Contribution à l'étude du type criminel," published in the bulletins of the "Société de Psychologie physiologique" (Paris, 1880).

prisons. Scarcely ever do we meet with regular features or a
pleasant expression. Ugliness, extreme and repulsive, not,
however, amounting to true deformity, is very common in
these establishments, and, strange to say, especially among the
women. I remember visiting a prison for women, where, out
of 163 inmates, I found but three or four with regular features
and only one who could be called pretty; all the rest, old and
young, were more or less of an ugly and repulsive appearance.
It will be granted that no such proportion of ugly women
exists in any race or in any other environment.

The same thing is noted by Tarde. "It is certain," says
he, "that the beautiful classic head, with its straight brow
and nose, its small and gracefully curved mouth, its rounded
cheek, its small ear set close to the temples, affords a perfect
contrast to the head of the criminal, the ugliness of which is
its most pronounced characteristic. Out of 275 photographs
of criminals, I found but one attractive face, and this of a
woman; the majority of the others were repulsive, and monstrous faces were not lacking." [1]

Speaking of his fellow-prisoners, Dostoieffsky says: "Sirot-
kin was the only one of the convicts who was really handsome.
As for his companions of the special section (that of the life
prisoners) — to the number of fifteen — they were frightful
to behold with their hideous, disgusting physiognomies." [2]

What then is the conclusion? From the anthropologic
point of view, as has been seen, the type is very far from being
fixed, and it is doubtful whether further observations will
succeed in establishing it. The only thing which has been
clearly ascertained is that there exist certain physiognomic
characteristics, or rather physiognomic expressions, which
enable the observer readily to distinguish one group from
another — to distinguish murderers from thieves, and from

---

[1] *Tarde,* "La criminalité comparée," p. 16 (Paris, F. Alcan, 1886).

[2] "House of the Dead," Part I, c. IV, p. 54. [This and the passages from
Dostoieffsky's work subsequently occurring are taken from the English ver-
sion in Everyman's Library (London, J. M. Dent & Sons, Ltd., and New
York, E. P. Dutton & Co.). — TRANSL.]

both of these the violent or impulsive criminal.[1] In my own opinion, however, as will be developed in the sequel, the criminal, in a non-barbarous society, is an abnormal being, since he differs from the majority of his contemporaries and fellow-citizens by the want of certain sentiments and certain repugnances, this want being associated with a peculiar temperament or a deficiency in moral energy. The question whether this want is organic, or, in other words, whether the moral anomaly has always a physiologic substratum, unfortunately must remain unanswered. The substratum might be found in an imperceptible deviation of the organs or the nervous system or in the molecular formation, but these are matters which the insufficiency of our means of observation makes it impossible to take into account.[2]

We shall therefore leave the anatomic aspect of the subject and direct our attention to the criminal's psychic anomaly, without admitting or denying that this latter may have a purely physical source.

§ 2. Psychic Anomaly

Extreme Cases. — We must first look at criminality in its most serious forms. Take murderers of the most brutal sort — who strangle old women, who, like Papavoine, cut the throats of children, who commit crimes like those of Jack the Ripper — can any one doubt their moral insensibility? This lack of moral sensibility is even more striking in the case of young offenders, — for instance, the sixteen-year-old boy (referred to in my communication to the "Société de Psychologie physiologique") who early one morning got out of bed, went to the stable where a beggar child against whom he had some grievance, had taken shelter for the night, wakened the little fellow and told him he was about to throw

---

[1] "Physiognomy and psychologic character are the most important criteria of the born criminal." *Forel* in Actes du Congrès de Genève, 1897.

[2] To use the apt expression of *Benedikt,* "We are very far from possessing an anatomy of molecules."

him in the well — a purpose which he carried out in spite of his victim's tears and entreaties, — or the twelve-year-old girl convicted in Berlin, who, coveting the earrings of a child of four, snatched them away from her and seizing the infant in her arms, tossed her out of a second-story window, all of which the prisoner confessed at her trial without the least symptom of feeling, adding that her intention was to sell the earrings and buy sweets with the money, and that she had killed the child to prevent the theft being found out.

Since the moral anomaly in these cases is too manifest to be doubted, the whole question comes to this: Is such anomaly of a pathologic nature? Is it the same thing as insanity? Should it be regarded as a new nosologic form — the "moral insanity" of the English writers? The existence of this form of alienation is questionable, to say the least. In spite of the utmost efforts to discover traces of insanity, one is often obliged to admit that the individual under examination possesses an intelligence which leaves nothing to be desired, that he exhibits no nosologic symptom, unless it be the absence of the moral sense, and that, to quote a French physician, whatever may be the subject's unity of mind, "the psychic key-board has one false note and only one." [1]

But I shall presently revert to this topic. In the meantime, I wish to make it clear that individuals such as those of whom I have just spoken are in respect of their psychic nature beings apart, — every one feels it. Still, these dangerous criminals, these children born with ferocious instincts, are only the most salient cases. In descending the scale of criminality, it is quite natural that the anomaly becomes less pronounced, but it nevertheless exists down to the very bottom. "Natura non facit saltum." What we have is a decreasing series whose lowest terms approximate so very closely to the normal state that it becomes difficult to distinguish them. For our purposes, therefore, an examination of the foot of the scale will be of

[1] See *V. du Bled*, "Les aliénés en France et à l'étranger" (Revue des Deux Mondes, 1 November, 1886).

little value; we must fix our attention on the classes which constitute the intermediate degrees.

Intermediate Cases. — Let us take, first of all, the inmates of penitentiaries. Complete descriptions of their sentiments are at hand. We are told of their impassibility, of the instability of their emotions, of their tastes, of their unbridled passion for gambling, drink, and debauchery. Imprudence and lack of foresight are two characteristics which especially distinguish them, as was pointed out by Despine many years ago. Their frivolity and changeableness have also been noted. To these traits may be added, says Lombroso, "the exaggeration of that tendency to mockery and foolish jest, which has long since been recognized as one of the surest signs of wickedness or of limited intelligence ('Risus abundat in ore stultorum'; 'Guardati da chi ride troppo!') — a tendency which especially reveals itself in the need of turning into ridicule and loading with absurd and obscene names the things which are holiest and most dear." This flippancy serves to explain at the same time the propensity of criminals in general and thieves in particular, for purposeless and almost unconscious lying, as well as the habitual inexactness of statement which proves a lack of precision in their perceptions and memory.[1] Their moral insensibility appears from the brazenness of their public confessions. Murderers who confess do not hesitate to describe the most horrible details of their crimes; they exhibit complete indifference to the shame and grief which they bring upon their families. "On the night of 21–22 September, 1846," relates the Abbé Moreau, "Mme. Dackle, residing at No. 10, Rue de Moineaux, was the victim of an unprovoked murder. Extended search by the police culminated in the arrest of the guilty persons, among them a woman named Dubos. When asked why she had taken part in the murder, her sole answer was: 'So that I could have pretty hats.' . . . An old man, one Cornu, . . . meeting some young thieves who were warm admirers of his prowess,

[1] *Lombroso, op. cit.,* p. 446.

was asked by them: 'Well, Père Cornu, what are you doing now?' 'Still the "grande soulasse," boys, still the "grande soulasse,"' was the cheerful reply. — The 'grande soulasse' is murder coupled with robbery. . . . To one of his jailers, who asked him why he had killed Adèle Blondin, Prévost answered: 'What else could I do? She was a millstone around my neck, and there was no other way to get rid of her.'" [1]

Examples might be multiplied indefinitely. Drago tells us of Ruiz Castruccio, who poisoned a man and then choked him to death. In referring to his crime, the murderer said with no trace of emotion, "I killed him as Othello killed Desdemona." The notorious Castro Rodriguez reënacted before his judges the murder of his wife and ten-year-old daughter — a crime which he had committed under circumstances of peculiar atrocity, — even going so far as to burlesque the actions of his victims. At the conclusion of his interrogatory, he requested the officials not to withdraw a sum of money which he had on deposit in a bank, so that he might not lose the interest! [2] I myself heard the confession of one Tufano in which he related that he had strangled his wife in order to marry another woman who would bring him a dowry, and told of the horrible manner of his victim's death, which did not ensue until after half an hour of agony. [3]

Criminal Sentiments. — Such men are wholly incapable of remorse, not only of that genuine remorse which, as said by Lévy-Bruhl, [4] is no longer the fear of punishment, but its hope and desire, and leads to an inconsolable brooding over the harm one has inflicted, but incapable even of a passing regret or the slightest betrayal of emotion at the mention of their victim's name.

Observations reported by those unfamiliar with the life

---

[1] *Abbé Moreau*, "Le monde des prisons," pp. 25, 26 (Paris, 1887).
[2] *Drago*, "Los hombres de presa," pp. 65, 66 (2d. ed. Buenos Ayres, 1888).
[3] See my "Contributions," above cited.
[4] *Lévy-Bruhl*, "L'idée de responsabilité," p. 89 (Paris, 1884).

of the offender may perhaps be open to question, but we are obliged to lend credence to details coming from persons who have lived within the four walls of a prison. The Abbé Moreau, who was chaplain of the Grande Roquette, thus describes his charges: "When you see them at close range, you wonder if they have souls. The impression which they give, of insensibility, heartlessness, and naturally ferocious instincts, is so great that they almost seem to you animals with human faces, rather than men of our own race. . . . It is a bitter thing to say, but nothing can imbue these creatures with ideas of honesty, be it religion or their own interests or the thought of the harm which they have wrought; they are absolutely proof against even momentary good instincts; nothing touches them; nothing will stay their hand. . . . They have a different vision from ours. Their brain has lesions which incapacitate it from transmitting certain messages. It responds only to the call of ignoble passions." [1]

Nor can we doubt the accuracy of the description furnished us by a distinguished man of letters who spent many years of his life in a Siberian prison. Dostoieffsky, in his "House of the Dead," has given to the world a literary masterpiece which contains our most complete account of the psychology of the criminal. The astonishing thing is the perfect resemblance between the picture of the Slavic criminal confined in a Siberian prison and that of the Italian criminal described by Lombroso. "This strange family," says Dostoieffsky, "had a general likeness so pronounced that it could be recognized at a glance. . . . All the convicts were morose, envious, frightfully vain, presumptuous, susceptible, and excessively ceremonious. . . . Vanity was always their salient quality. . . . Not the least sign of shame or of repentance.[2] . . . During many years I never remarked the least sign of repentance, not even the slightest uneasiness with regard to the crime committed. . . . Certainly vanity, evil examples, deceitful-

[1] *Abbé Moreau*, "Le monde des prisons " (Paris, 1887).
[2] "House of the Dead," Part I, c. II, pp. 13, 14.

ness, and false shame were responsible for much. . . . It would seem all the same, that during so many years I ought to have been able to notice some indication, even the most fugitive, of some regret, some moral suffering. I positively saw nothing of the kind. . . . In spite of different opinions, every one will acknowledge, that there are crimes which everywhere, always, under no matter what legislation, are beyond discussion crimes, and should be regarded as such as long as man is man. It is only at the convict prison that I have heard related with a childish, unrestrained laugh, the strangest, most atrocious offenses. I shall never forget a certain parricide, formerly a nobleman and a public functionary. He had given great grief to his father — a true prodigal son. The old man endeavored in vain to restrain him by remonstrance on the fatal slope down which he was sliding. As he was loaded with debts, and his father was suspected of having, besides an estate, a sum of ready money, he killed him in order to enter more quickly into his inheritance. This crime was not discovered until a month afterwards. During all this time the murderer, who meanwhile had informed the police of his father's disappearance, continued his debauches. At last, during his absence, the police discovered the old man's corpse in a drain. The gray head was severed from the trunk, but replaced in its original position. The body was entirely dressed. Beneath, as if by derision, the assassin had placed a cushion. — The young man confessed nothing. He was degraded, deprived of his nobiliary privileges, and condemned to twenty years' hard labour. As long as I knew him I always found him to be careless of his position. He was the most light-minded, inconsiderate man that I ever met, although he was far from being a fool. I never observed in him any great tendency to cruelty. The other convicts despised him, not on account of his crime, of which there was never any question, but because he was without dignity. He sometimes spoke of his father. One day for instance, boasting of the hereditary good health of his family, he said: 'My father, for example,

until his death was never ill.' — Animal insensibility carried
to such a point is most remarkable — it is, indeed, phenomenal.
There must have been in this case an organic defect in the man,
some physical and moral monstrosity unknown hitherto to
science, and not simply crime. I naturally did not believe
in so atrocious a crime; but people of the same town as himself, who knew all the details of his history, related it to me.
The facts were so clear that it would have been madness
not to accept them. The prisoners once heard him cry out
during his sleep: 'Hold him! hold him! Cut his head off,
his head, his head!' — Nearly all the convicts dreamed aloud,
or were delirious in their sleep. Insults, words of slang,
knives, hatchets, seemed constantly present in their dreams.
'We are crushed ' they would say; 'we are without entrails;
that is why we shriek in the night.'" [1]

This inability to feel remorse or repentance, and the exhibi-
tion of vanity are characteristics well known to all observers.
Lombroso has suggested that in these the criminal is akin to
the savage. But there are some still more striking characteristics which complete the resemblance to the savage and at
the same time are common to children. "On holidays the
dandies of the prison put on their Sunday best. They were
worth seeing as they strutted about their part of the barracks.
The pleasure of feeling themselves well dressed amounted
with them to childishness; indeed, in many things convicts
are only children. Their fine clothes disappeared very soon,
often the evening of the very day on which they had been
bought. Their owners pledged them or sold them again for a
trifle. — The feasts were generally held at fixed times. They
coincided with religious festivals, or with the name's day of the
drunken convict. On getting up in the morning he would
place a wax taper before the holy image, then he said his
prayer, dressed, and ordered his dinner. He had bought
beforehand meat, fish, and little patties; then he gorged like
an ox, almost always alone. It was very rare to see a convict

---

[1] *Op. cit.*, Part I, c. II, pp. 16, 18.

invite another convict to share his repast. At dinner the vodka was produced. The convict would suck it up like the sole of a boot, and then walk through the barracks swaggering and tottering. It was his desire to show all his companions that he was drunk, that he was carrying on, and thus obtain their particular esteem." [1]

Further on, we find another childish characteristic, the impossibility of repressing a desire: "Reason has no power on people like Petroff unless they are spurred on by will. When they desire something there are no obstacles in their way. . . . People like him are born with one idea, which, without being aware of it, pursues them all their life. They wander until they meet with some object which apparently excites their desire, and then they do not mind risking their head. . . . More than once I was astonished to see that he (Petroff) was robbing me in spite of his affection for me; but he did so from time to time. Thus he stole my Bible, which I had asked him to carry to its place. He had only a few steps to go; but on his way he met with a purchaser, to whom he sold the book, at once spending the money he had received on vodka. Probably he felt that day a violent desire for drink, and when he desired something it was necessary that he should have it. A man like Petroff will assassinate any one for twenty-five kopecks, simply to get himself a pint of vodka. On any other occasion he will disdain hundreds and thousands of roubles. He told me the same evening of the theft he had committed, but without showing the least sign of repentance or confusion, in a perfectly indifferent tone, as though he were speaking of an ordinary incident. I endeavoured to reprove him as he deserved, for I regretted the loss of my Bible. He listened to me without hesitation very calmly. He agreed that the Bible was a very useful book, and sincerely regretted that I had it no longer; but he was not for one moment sorry, though he had stolen it. He looked at me with such assurance that I gave up scolding him. He bore my reproaches because he thought

[1] *Op. cit.*, Part I, c. IV, pp. 46, 47.

that I could not do otherwise than I was doing. He knew that he ought to be punished for such an action, and consequently thought I ought to abuse him for my own satisfaction, and to console myself for my loss. But in his inner heart he considered that it was all nonsense, to which a serious man ought to be ashamed to descend." [1]

The same utter carelessness as to their life and future: 'A convict will marry, have children, live for five years in the same place, then all of a sudden he will disappear one fine morning, abandoning wife and children, to the stupefaction of his family and the whole neighborhood." [2]

No Moral Anomaly, No Natural Crime. — Curiously enough, Dostoieffsky tells us of two or three convicts who were men of excellent character, of substantial qualities, devoted friends, incapable of hatred. . . . However, if we turn to the account of what brought them to the penitentiary, we shall find that their faults were not true crimes, in our sense of the word. He relates first the story of an "Old Believer" [3] of Starodoub [4] who was entrusted with the convicts' savings, which they found it necessary to conceal. This man, says our author, "was about sixty years old, thin, and getting very gray. He excited my curiosity the first time I saw him, for he was not like any of the others; his look was so tranquil and mild, and I always saw with pleasure his clear and limpid eyes, surrounded by a number of little wrinkles. I often talked

---

[1] *Op. cit.*, Part I, c. vIII, pp. 121, 122, 123.

[2] *Op. cit.*, Part II, c. v, p. 266.

[3] [Old Believers ("Starovyeri") or Old Ritualists ("Staroöbryadtsi"): a sect of Russian dissenters. In the 1700s occurred the "Raskol" or Great Schism, as a result of the reforms introduced into the Orthodox Church under the Patriarch Nikon in the reign of Alexis, father of Peter the Great. The schismatics of that day later split into two main divisions: the Old Believers and the Priestless People. The Priestless People has since become subdivided into a great number of independent sects, while the Old Believers "have remained a compact body little troubled by differences of opinion . . . Of all the sects, the Old Ritualists stand nearest to the official church. They hold the same dogmas, practise the same rites, and differ only in trifling ceremonial matters, which few people consider essential." (*Wallace*, "Russia," c. xvIII.) — TRANSL.]

[4] Government of Tchernigoff.

with him, and rarely have I met with so kind, so benevolent
a being. He had been consigned to hard labour for a serious
crime. A certain number of the 'Old Believers' at Staroudoub
had been converted to the orthodox religion. The Government had done everything to encourage them and, at the same
time, to convert the other dissenters. The old man and some
other fanatics had resolved to 'defend the faith.' When the
orthodox church was being constructed in their town they set
fire to the building. This offense had brought upon its author
the sentence of deportation. This well-to-do shopkeeper — he
was in trade — had left a wife and family whom he loved,
and had gone off courageously into exile, believing in his
blindness that he was 'suffering for the faith.' — When one
had lived some time by the side of this kind old man, one
could not help asking the question, how could he have rebelled? I spoke to him several times about his faith. He
gave up none of his convictions, but in his answers I never
noticed the slightest hatred; and yet he had destroyed a
church, and was far from denying it. In his view, the offense
he had committed and his martyrdom were things to be proud
of. — There were other 'Old Believers' among the convicts —
Siberians for the most part — men of well-developed intelligence, and as cunning as all peasants. Dialecticians in their
way, they followed blindly their law, and delighted in discussing it. But they had great faults; they were haughty,
proud, and very intolerant. The old man in no way resembled
them. With full more belief in religious exposition than
others of the same faith, he avoided all controversy. As he
was of a gay and expansive disposition he often laughed —
not with the coarse cynical laugh of the other convicts, but
with a laugh of clearness and simplicity, in which there was
something of the child, and which harmonised perfectly with
his gray head. I may perhaps be in error, but it seems to me
that a man may be known by his laugh alone. If the laugh
of a man you are acquainted with inspires you with sympathy,
be assured that he is an honest man. — The old man had

acquired the respect of all the prisoners without exception; but he was not proud of it. The convicts called him grandfather, and he took no offense. I then understood what an influence he must have exercised on his co-religionists. — In spite of the firmness with which he supported the prison life, one felt that he was tormented by a profound, incurable melancholy. I slept in the same barrack with him. One night, towards three o'clock in the morning, I woke up; I heard a slow, stifling sob. The old man was sitting upon the stove . . . and was reading from his manuscript prayer-book. As he wept I heard him repeating: 'Lord, do not forsake me. Master, strengthen me. My poor little children, my dear little children, we shall never see one another again.' I cannot say how much this moved me." [1]

Now, if we analyze the "crime" of this man, it becomes plain that Dostoieffsky has no right to be astonished at his good qualities. The case is simply one of a man who defended the religion of his country against the invasion of a new belief — an act which may be likened to a political crime. This "Old Believer" was merely a "révolté": he was not a criminal. "And yet he had destroyed a church!" exclaims our author. True, but without taking human life, without the slightest idea of doing harm to any one in the world. What elementary altruistic sentiment had he violated? Freedom of religious faith is not such a sentiment. It is a sentiment too highly refined, the product of an intellectual development which we can hardly expect to find in the average morality of a people. From our view-point, the burning of the church at Starodoub could not be a natural crime. It belongs to the class of facts which, though punishable by law, fall outside the boundaries of criminality which we have attempted to trace. And in this non-criminal incendiary, we find one of the rare exceptions noted by the writer to the moral degradation which surrounded him.

A second exception appears in the saintly figure of one Ali,

---

[1] *Op. cit.*, Part I, c. IV, pp. 44, 45.

a Tartar of Daghestan, who had been sentenced for taking part in an act of brigandage. But the following were the circumstances of his offense: "One day his eldest brother . . . had ordered him to take his yataghan, to get on horseback, and follow him. The respect of the mountaineers for their elders is so great that young Ali did not dare to ask the object of the expedition. He probably knew nothing about it, nor did his brothers consider it necessary to tell him." [1] All he could do was to obey. He could not argue, could not question, because he had no right. Manifestly, this youth was not a criminal. Dostoieffsky, on the contrary, calls him "an exceptional being" — one of those "natures so spontaneously good and endowed by God with such great qualities that the idea of their getting perverted seems absurd." [2]

There is finally the portrait of Akim Akimitch — a man of the utmost honesty, ready to serve, exact, of small intelligence, but "as argumentative and as particular about details as a German." The author presents him as an original character of much simplicity. "When he quarreled with the convicts, he reproached them with being thieves, and exhorted them in all sincerity to steal no more." Again, "it was sufficient for him that there was injustice, to interfere in an affair which did not concern him." Nor was this man a criminal. "He had served as a sub-lieutenant in the Caucasus. I made friends with him the first day, and he related to me his 'affair.' He had begun as a cadet in a Line regiment. After waiting some time to be appointed to his commission as sub-lieutenant, he at last received it, and was sent into the mountains to command a small fort. A small tributary prince in the neighborhood set fire to the fort, and made a night attack, which had no success. — Akimitch was very cunning, and pretended not to know that he was the author of the attack, which he attributed to some insurgents wandering about the mountains. After a month he invited the prince, in a friendly way, to come and see him. The prince arrived on horseback, without

[1] *Op. cit.*, Part I, c. v, p. 72.   [2] *Ibid.*, p. 73.

suspecting anything. Akimitch drew up his garrison in line
of battle, and exposed to the soldiers the treason and villainy
of his visitor. He reproached him with his conduct; proved
to him that to set fire to the fort was a shameful crime; explained to him minutely the duties of a tributary prince;
and then, by way of peroration to his harangue, had him shot.
He at once informed his superior officers of this execution,
with all the details necessary. Thereupon Akimitch was
brought to trial. He appeared before a court-martial, and
was condemned to death; but his sentence was commuted,
and he was sent to Siberia as a convict of the second class —
condemned, that is to say, to twelve years hard labour and
imprisonment in a fortress. He admitted willingly that he had
acted illegally, and that the prince ought to have been tried
in a civil court, and not by a court-martial. Nevertheless,
he could not understand that his action was a crime. — 'He
had burned my fort; what was I to do? Was I to thank
him for it? ' he answered to my objections." [1]

Akimitch was right; he had exercised the law of war in
punishing treason with death; the execution was deserved.
But his ignorance made him believe that he was authorized
to hold a council of war, to try and regularly condemn a
brigand. A council of war convened according to law would
probably have done the same thing which he, unable to understand the limits of his authority, had done illegally, and the
minor prince would have met precisely the same fate.

If I am not mistaken, these three are the only examples of
good and honest men whom Dostoieffsky encountered in his
years of imprisonment — the only ones who did not inspire
him with disgust, who became his friends, who had nothing of
the cynicism or the conspicuous immorality of the rest.
They had none of the characteristics of criminals, simply
because they were not criminals. They had merely disobeyed
the law without being in anywise guilty of that which, from
our standpoint, constitutes true crime. We therefore see

[1] *Op. cit.*, Part I, c. III, pp. 33, 34.

how these exceptions confirm the rule and what support they give to our views in relation to natural crime and the criminal type.

§ 3. Hereditary Transmission of Criminal Propensities

We shall not stop to consider symptoms of a psycho-psychical order, such as obtuseness of the general sensibility, analgesia, and imperfect vascular reaction. Study of this phase of our subject is still in its beginnings, and but few observations have been made. Although such observations have already yielded satisfactory results, it will be necessary to await further investigation before we can draw on them in support of our theory. It is, however, to be noted that a lower degree of sensibility to physical pain seems to be demonstrated by the readiness with which prisoners submit to the operation of tattooing.

Evidentiary Data. — Passing then to heredity, we find in this a fact established by unimpeachable evidence. The world has been made acquainted with some startling genealogies — that of Lemaire or of Chrétien for example, or that of the "Juke" family. In the last, the descendants of one Max, a drunkard, included in the course of seventy-five years, 200 murderers and thieves, 288 diseased persons, and 90 harlots.

Out of 109 convicts, Thomson found 50 who were related to each other, and among these 8 members of a single family descended from a convicted recidivist. Virgilio, out of 266 criminals, found 195 afflicted with diseases common in degenerate families, such as scrofula, caries, necrosis, and phthisis, mostly hereditary. But what is more important in the latter's observations is the fact of transmission of crime by heredity, either direct or collateral, in the case of 32.24% of the convicts examined.

If we take into consideration the number of cases which must lie outside our knowledge, either because the facts have been forgotten or else because of the difficulties attending investigation in the matter of collateral heredity and the impossibility which nearly always exists of carrying such investigations back of the grandfather, these figures ought sufficiently to prove the law of the hereditary transmission of crime. But this is not all. The author last cited has shown that out of 48 recidivists (who most often are true criminals), 42 exhibited characteristics of congenital degeneracy.

Some very curious observations have been contributed by Marro. Among non-criminals he found 24%, among criminals, 32%, children of parents advanced in years. In this respect, murderers viewed apart, attained the remarkable figure of 52%, homicidal criminals in general showed 40%, swindlers, 37%, while thieves and authors of indecent offenses ("attentats aux mœurs") fell below the average. He attributes this disproportionate result to the psychic changes of old age, increasing egoism, the spirit of calculation, avarice, all of which are necessarily reflected in the children, predisposing them to evil propensities. This is why the percentage is so high in the case of murderers and homicidal criminals—who are deficient in the affective sentiments,—and in that of swindlers—whose operations require circumspection and craft, — while theft, on the other hand, shows much lower figures, because this vice is derived from the inclination for pleasure, for idleness, for debauch — characteristics of the age at which the passions dominate.

The same author found among criminals an average of 41% who were sons of drunkards, as opposed to 16% among non-criminals. The criminals showed 16% whose brothers had undergone criminal conviction, the non-criminals but 1%. Future investigation in this direction, we may be sure, will yield proof of an increasingly convincing character. It is difficult to see how it can be otherwise, if we stop to think what a common thing is the transmission of degenerative characteristics. Moreover, even the opponents of positivism are forced to recognize that "heredity exhibits itself more actively according as the phenomena are more closely related to the organism, that it is stronger in the reflex acts, in the case of unconscious cerebration, in the impressions, the instincts, decreasing and becoming vaguer in the phenomena of higher sensibility." [1] Within these limitations, criminal heredity finds its well-defined place. If we are right in supposing crime to be a want of that part of the moral sense which is the least refined, the least pure, the least delicate, the most akin to the organism, then the propensity or predisposition to crime must be hereditarily transmissible like all other phenomena of the same description. It is not a question of a phenomenon of the higher sensibility, but of one depending on the commonest sort of moral sensibility, a sensibility which is necessarily absent in the children of those who are destitute of it. If exceptions can be imagined to a biologic law which embraces all mankind, it is most assuredly not here that one can find them.

Antiquity, which did not possess a science of statistics, had nevertheless the intuition of the great natural laws. Wiser than the present day, it knew how to utilize this intuition. Whole families were declared impure, and proscribed. This subject calls for an observation which may appear somewhat singular. Cases will be remembered of Biblical curses extending even to the fifth generation. Modern science justifies this limitation, since it teaches that a marked character for good or evil does not persist beyond the fifth generation. It is this fact, moreover, which accounts in part for the decay of all aristocracies.[2]

Recidivism an Effect of Heredity. — In view of the congenital and hereditary nature of criminal propensities, which appears thus established, we need not wonder at the proportions attained by recidivism. The correctionalist school credulously attributed the existence of recidivism to the bad condition of the prisons and the defective organization of the peniten-

[1] *Caro,* "Essais de psychologie sociale" (Revue de Deux Mondes, 15 April, 1883).
[2] *Ribot,* "L'hérédité psychologique" (Paris, F. Alcan, 1882).

tiary system. Subsequent experience has shown the error of
this view: improvement of the system has had scarcely any
effect in the diminution of recidivists. Recidivism is the rule,
reform of the criminal the exception. The official figures
do not give us the whole truth, for a number of reasons.
For one thing, the professional offender has become more expert in keeping out of the clutches of the police. Then too,
when arrested he is very often able to conceal his name.
Moreover, the recidivism of the codes is much narrower than
recidivism proper. It is limited to particular cases, sometimes
to special recidivism, and again to recidivism occurring after
a sentence of not less than one year in prison, or after a
criminal as distinguished from a correctional conviction.[1]
And yet, in spite of these limitations, legal recidivism reaches
a proportion of 46% in France, 49% in Belgium, and 45%
in Austria. "It is the same individuals," as one author
has justly observed, "who always commit the same crimes."

§ 4. The Distinction between Moral Anomaly and Pathologic Anomaly

Casual Offender Non-existent. — Few scientists today absolutely deny the existence of innate criminal impulses. There
are many, however, who regard such propensities as reducible
to a limited number of pathologic cases. For them, the great
majority of offenders is composed of normal men who, suffering from a neglected moral education, have been impelled to
crime by external causes. Without doubt, external causes
such as tradition, prejudices, bad examples, climate, alcoholic
liquors, and the like are not without an important influence.
But in our opinion, there is always present in the instincts
of the true criminal, a specific element which is congenital
or inherited, or else acquired in early infancy and become
inseparable from his psychic organism. There is no such thing
as the *casual* offender, — if by the use of this term we grant

[1] [*I. e.*, conviction for a "crime" as distinguished from a "délit." See
ante, p. 59, note 1. — TRANSL.]

the possibility of a morally well-organized man committing a crime solely by the force of external circumstances. If, out of a hundred persons who are subjected to the same conditions, but one is thereby actuated to commit crime, it must be admitted that this individual has felt differently from the others the influence of these conditions, — that he possesses something which the others are without, a peculiar diathesis or manner of being. This is a conclusive answer to the argument which attributes certain kinds of crime to the misery of the poorer classes. For these classes, notwithstanding the uniform prevalence of misery, are by no means composed of criminals; — criminals, on the contrary, represent there but a small minority. Perhaps, as has been often said, the conditions surrounding these classes are the bouillon most favorable to the development of the microbe, but the microbe, that is to say, the criminal, is not their necessary product. In a different environment his criminality would probably remain latent, but would nevertheless exist. Criminals therefore cannot be separated into the two distinct classes of normal and abnormal beings; they can be classed only according to the greater or less degree of their anomaly. In born or instinctive criminals and criminals who are termed casual or occasional, there is an equal lack of repugnance to crime.

The Question Stated; Certain Objections Considered. — It now becomes important to distinguish between, on the one hand, certain pathologic conditions associated with criminal impulses, such as imbecility, insanity, hysteria, and epilepsy — conditions which may be either congenital or acquired — and, on the other, the exclusively moral anomaly which is characterized by perversity or the absence of the elementary moral instincts, and which is not a disease.

On the subject of this distinction many doubts have arisen. Arrayed against us are, in the first place, those writers who decline to admit that the will can be the slave of propensities and instincts, who are unable to understand how the human soul can be led to evil through the peculiarity of the individual organization, unless the intelligence is affected or some disease interferes with the subjection of the acts to the will. Discussion of the question of free will would be here out of place. Nor is it at all necessary, since, suffice it to say, a correct understanding of our views will not attribute to us the idea that every criminal propensity necessarily impels to action. We believe, on the contrary, that the manifestation of such propensities can be repressed by the favorable concurrence of a multitude of external circumstances, even in the case of individuals whose perversity is innate. Whether the will is the resultant of many forces or whether it is an initial psychic movement, it is certain that the criminal impulses can always be paralyzed by an external motive, such as terror of the death penalty or the fear of losing advantages greater than those to be gained by the crime. The absence of the moral sense, it must be added, is merely the favorable condition which enables the crime to be accomplished at a given moment. Many persons who suffer from a predisposition of this sort never become criminals, simply because they can satisfy their greatest desires without in the slightest degree injuring others. It is thus that individuals with latent criminal instincts pass for honest men all their lives: the moment has never arrived at which crime would be useful to them. The merit of their regular conduct is not then to be ascribed to their character, but to the situation in which it has been their good fortune to find themselves.

We turn to an objection of a diametrically opposite nature. By many authors criminal anomaly is classed as a form of alienation under the name of "moral insanity." In our opinion, this term is erroneous and should be expunged from the scientific vocabulary. In the first place, its use engenders many misunderstandings. In fact, it is because of this term that the positive school has been criticized for making criminality a chapter of insanity. Again, the word "insanity" is synonymous with "mental alienation." Now, although reason and sentiment both reside in the nervous system, it cannot

be disputed that these are activities of a very different nature,
and that it is possible for one of them — the faculty of ideation — to be perfectly regular, although the other — the
faculty of emotion — may be abnormal. And finally, the
word " insanity " or " alienation " implies the idea of disease,
since the non-pathologic insanity of Despine is no longer admitted. The term, therefore, is wholly inapplicable, since our
instinctive criminals are not diseased persons. It will be in
place to give some attention to this point.

Criminal Instinct not Disease. — When the criminal's
anomaly consists only in a moral deviation, when it is revealed only by maliciousness, cruelty, or heartlessness, without the least disturbance of the faculties of ideation or any
evidence of a different kind of neurosis, such as hysteria or
epilepsy, how is it possible to say that a pathologic condition
is present? The only way in which we can here predicate a
pathologic condition is by regarding the words "disease"
and "anomaly" as identical in meaning. But if we did, there
would no longer be any difference between a physiologic
condition and a pathologic condition, since every atypic
variation, every irregularity of the body, every eccentricity
of character, every peculiarity of temperament would be a
morbid form. . . . Inasmuch as there are almost no individuals who do not exhibit some physical or moral peculiarity,
the condition of health would become impossible to find:
the word would lose all practical significance. Yet there is a
condition of physical health and a condition of mental health.
There is again an intermediate zone between each of these
conditions and that of disease. Hence it is, that although we
have never been furnished with an adequate definition of
alienation, we can none the less, in the particular case, distinguish the lunatic from the man of sane mind.[1]

[1] *Taylor*, "Principles and Practice of Medical Jurisprudence," 3d ed., c. 89.
Fioretti, in his interesting monograph "Genio e follia" (Naples, 1902),
takes a resolute stand in favor of this idea. "To get the notion what a lunatic
is," says he, "it is necessary to resort, not to the physician, but to the common
and vulgar opinion which regards certain individuals as lunatics and others

The distinction between anomaly and disease is by no means new. For example, the Digest with reference to rescission of the sale of a slave, distinguishes "vitium" from "morbus": "Utputa si quis balbus sit, nam hunc vitiosum magis esse quam morbosum." The mute, adds Sabinus, is diseased, but not he who speaks difficultly and with little intelligibility. "He who lacks a tooth," says Paulus, "is not a diseased man."[1] We may say, likewise, that he who is destitute of certain instincts is an abnormal man ("vitiosus"), — but not a diseased man ("morbosus").

Disease a Deviation from the Species — Moral Anomaly from the Civilized Type. — It may be urged that, everything considered, to quote from an Italian alienist, "disease is nothing but life under abnormal conditions, and that from this point of view there is no absolute antithesis between health and disease."[2] But what warrant has science for annulling the meaning of words which for ages man has deemed indispensable? The word "disease" or "infirmity" always signifies something which tends to the destruction of the organism or the part thereof which is attacked. If there is no process of destruction, there is a process of cure — never a condition of stability as is the case in many kinds of anomaly. But even supposing that the meaning of the word could be extended so as to include every abnormal condition of life, our position remains unchanged. To know what is meant by abnormal

as not. The lunatic is he who is without the aptitudes necessary to the social coexistence. Insanity, like criminality, is a form of inadaptability of the individual to the social life. . . . Really, it is a strange thing that we should seek from the physician the notion and definition of insanity, when these can only be given by the social environment. . . . The fact that the notion of insanity has always varied shows how true this is. . . . In my opinion, it is a serious error to declare a man insane, simply because an objective diagnosis discloses the presence of certain phenomena. . . . No one could be sure of escaping this diagnosis. . . . The criminal, like the lunatic, is an abnormal. In this lies the only resemblance between them. It is just as if we would say that a sphere and a triangle are alike, because they both differ from a straight line."

[1] Dig., Lib. XXI, Tit. I. See *Fioretti*, "Polemica in difesa della scuola criminale positiva," p. 254 (1886).

[2] *Virgilio*, "La fisiologia e la patologia della mente" (Caserta, 1883).

conditions, we must first be certain what are the normal
conditions of life. Do we mean the normal life conditions of a
people, a race, or of mankind in general? Plainly, the expressions "physiologic conditions" and "pathologic conditions" must have reference to mankind as a whole, independently of race variations. Woolly hair, prognathism, and flat
noses are anomalies in our race, to be sure, but they cannot
be assigned a pathologic character, for the obvious reason
that they are not deviations from the human type. Indeed,
in certain inferior races, they are race characteristics. They
do not disturb or change the organic functions in the slightest
degree. Why should not the same thing be true of the psychic
variations? Moral insensibility, lack of prevision, cruelty,
are not today characteristics of our race, but in other races
they are very common. Consequently they do not constitute
anomaly in relation to the "genus homo": their anomaly
exists only in relation to the *perfected type* represented by civilized peoples. To put this distinction in a clearer light, let
us contrast the anomaly of innate perversity with other species of psychic anomaly, such as want of the faculty of co-
ordinating ideas, lack of memory, aphasia, or the inability
of the psychic process to respond to any external excitation.
In these we have true cases of disease, because they represent
anomalies in relation to the species. The faculty of ideation
which is affected in such instances, is not the heritage of a
particular race, nor does it make its first appearance at any
given stage of moral evolution: its existence is coeval with
the existence of mankind. What a difference is presented
by the case of instinctive perversity or absence of the moral
sense! Here no organic function is dissolved or disturbed;
the physiologic conditions necessary to the life of the species
remain the same. The only result is the incompatibility
of the subject with his environment, provided that this environment consists of an aggregation of families, for so long
as it consists of but a single family, the egoistic sentiments
suffice.

And still, for this incompatibility to exist, the aggregation must be to some extent removed from the savage state. It will be recollected that there are today, or have been within recent times, tribes in which the most unbridled cruelty and lust appear almost normal. The Maoris and Fijians, who killed for the pleasure of killing, were destitute of the instinct of pity, or rather, this instinct did not cross the limits of their families. Yet they were not diseased men, any more than is the African negro who steals whenever occasion presents. It is very clear that neither anatomic characteristics, which are anomalies only in relation to race, nor the signs of an arrested psychic development common to some savage tribes and to the typical criminal, can cause us to look upon the latter as the victim of disease, if the former, with the same physical and moral deficiencies, are to be regarded as men in perfect health.

It counts for little in this regard that the altruistic sentiments today prevail nearly everywhere. There was a time when they existed only in an embryonic state, when they scarcely transcended the boundaries of the family, rarely that of the tribe. But if the men of these remote times were in sound health, why should it be otherwise with the criminals of our own day, who resemble these savage men and, by some mysterious atavism perhaps, have inherited from their prehistoric ancestors the characteristics which now constitute moral anomaly? To regard as disease the absence of the moral sense would necessarily lead to this strange result: that upon the degree of social advancement would depend the degree of seriousness and even the eventual disappearance of one and the same disease. So that under precisely the same state of facts, a man might be gravely ill in the civilized countries, of a rather doubtful condition of health among half savage peoples, and wholly free from disease in the Fiji Islands, New Zealand, and Dahomey.[1]

---

[1] *Drago* ("Los hombres de presa," pp. 75, 76, — Buenos Ayres, 1888) thinks this suggestion somewhat misleading. Meeting me on my own ground,

This, of course, is absurd. When we speak of pathologic conditions, we do not inquire if the subject is modern, or if he belongs to the stone age, or whether he is a Malay, a Polynesian, or an Anglo-Saxon. Irrespective of period or race, the essential conditions of life remain the same.

It therefore follows that the existence of non-pathologic anomalies, and, among these, the absence of the moral sense, must be taken as established. In our opinion, however, as before suggested, the expression "moral insanity" is utterly indefensible. Without doubt, there are instances of extreme perversity of a true pathologic character, but in these cases the perversity is nothing more than the most prominent symptom of some serious neurosis, such as epilepsy or hysteria, or of some form of alienation, such as melancholia, progressive paralysis, or idiocy. On the other hand, when no derangement of the physiologic functions can be detected, the case is not one of disease, however great may be the incompatibility of the individual with the social environment.

Different Effect of External Impressions in Insanity and Moral Anomaly. — The following considerations, it seems to me, are completely decisive of the question under discussion: In the lunatic or idiot, perceptions of the external world produce exaggerated impressions; they give rise to a psychic process which is not in accord with the external cause; hence, there follows an incoherence between this cause and the reaction of the subject. In this fact lies the explanation of the many atrocious murders committed solely to get rid of a disagreeable sensation, — of the annoyance caused by the victim's presence. One Grandi, a semi-idiot, disturbed by the noise of his neighbors' children playing in front of his workshop,

he objects that a native of Tierra del Fuego would consider in sound health a civilized man afflicted with aphasia, that is to say, unable to articulate words distinctly, because the Fuegian language is composed of inarticulate sounds. My answer would be that if this is true of the Fuegian language, it has not been shown that the natives are incapable of learning to articulate the words of another language — a task which would be impossible for a European suffering from aphasia. *Dellepiane* ("Las causas del delito," — Buenos Ayres, 1892) adopts my views on this point.

enticed them one by one into the premises, put them under lock and key, and, after night-fall, buried them alive — to the number of ten. He believed that he thus would be enabled to work in peace. This was his sole motive. Edgar Allan Poe's madman in "The Tell-tale Heart" takes the life of the old man, so that he may not have to bear the sight of his victim's "vulture eye." In other cases, a pathologic pleasure is the determining motive, as in that of the lunatic cited by Maudsley, who dismembered a little girl, entering in a diary which he kept: "Killed a little girl: it was fine and hot." [1]

In the born criminal, on the other hand, the psychic process is in accord with the impressions of the external world. If the motive is revenge, there is always a real wrong or injury. If it is the hope of an advantage, the advantage contemplated is such as would be a real advantage in the eyes of any other person. If pleasure, it is a pleasure in no way abnormal. It is not the end in itself, but the criminal method employed to encompass it, which reveals the moral anomaly. There are, it is true, certain crimes, which the absence of the moral sense alone does not always suffice to explain. This absence, however, is sometimes accompanied by an exaggerated self-esteem, as a result of which a fancied or trivial grievance is more keenly felt than would otherwise be the case. Thus, one T, becoming enraged because his domestic had left his service, lay in wait for the latter and shot him dead. The victim's conduct would have been merely a trivial vexation for another, but for this man it was an affront which could only be requited with the offender's life. In such cases it is said that there is a disproportion between cause and effect. This expression is philosophically absurd. Proportion must always exist. But the cause here is not alone that which we suppose it to be, for this would be insufficient. There is further present the absence of moral sense, coupled with exaggerated self-esteem, immoderate vanity, and extreme susceptibility —

[1] *Maudsley,* "Responsibility in Mental Disease," c. v.

characteristics which, as has been seen, are very frequently found among criminals.

Tarde, accepting my views as to the difference between the so-called "moral insanity" and criminal instinct—a difference which he considers of capital importance, rounds them out in this notable passage: "For the lunatic himself, crime is indeed, if we choose so to call it, a means of pleasure, since as Maudsley observes, the accomplishment of a homicide procures for the agent who has acted through an irresistible criminal impulse, a true solacing effect. But it is the abnormal nature of this pleasure and the fact that no other is sought in committing the crime, which distinguish the lunatic from the criminal. The criminal, it is true, also shows certain anomalies of the affective sentiments ("anomalies affectives"), but they consist in his being more or less incapable of certain sympathetic sufferings, of certain repugnances which in the honest man are sufficiently strong to restrain him on the brink of certain acts. Another thing is the presence of a morbid attraction, which impels him to action even where there is no provocation from without. Still another is the absence of any internal repulsion which could prevent him from yielding to external temptations."

Criminal anomaly is therefore a deviation from the type of civilized man; in this it differs from disease, which is an anomaly in relation to the human species as a whole, and not in relation to the particular condition of moral superiority — a condition which, moreover, is itself the result of a series of imperceptible organic individual modifications.

The Death Penalty Justified. — In thus granting the possibility of a somatic substratum in anomaly as well as in disease, we by no means convert the question into one of words. The difference means much from the standpoint of penal science; it furnishes the possibility of justifying the death penalty. If criminals were to be regarded as suffering beings who, by that very fact, had the right to our sympathy or even to our pity, — their crimes being but an accident of disease and not

the effect of their character or temperament, — the infliction
of the death penalty would wear the aspect of intolerable
cruelty.　In the lines of Shakespeare:

> "Hamlet is of the faction that is wrong'd;
> His madness is poor Hamlet's enemy."[1]

The character, the temperament, on the contrary, go to make
up the moral physiognomy of the individual: they constitute
the Ego.　If the criminal lacks moral sense, this defect is not
for him a cause of suffering;　it only renders him an inferior
being from the social standpoint.　It is for this reason that
we have deemed it important to lay stress on the danger
attending the use of the term "moral insanity" and to em-
phasize the clear-cut distinction which exists between the
criminal destitute of moral sense and the insane criminal.

§ 5. Hypotheses as to the Source of Moral Anomaly

Since, therefore, the existence of criminal anomaly is no
longer open to doubt, what is the explanation of this phenomenon?　It cannot always be attributed to direct heredity.
Are we then to regard it as a case of atavism or a case of
degeneracy?

The Theory of Atavism. — Because of the marked resemblance between the typical criminal and the savage considered
as a representative of prehistoric man, Lombroso held to the
theory of atavism.　Certain characteristics of prehistoric
skulls found upon comparison with the skulls of criminals
confirmed him in this view.　In addition, his psychologic
studies of infancy, — which reproduces in miniature the first
stages of human development, — resulted in the discovery of many characteristics also observable in savages and
criminals.

In his later writings the same author contended that epilepsy
is always to be found in the born criminal.　This theory
I shall not stop to discuss since the fact is far from being

---

[1] "Hamlet," Act V, Scene II, 249, 250.

established. Moreover, it is flatly contradictory of the theory of atavism, despite Lombroso's efforts to reconcile the two theories. It seems hardly possible to conceive our first parents as unhappy epileptics.

On the contrary, although we do not know prehistoric man, it may easily be believed that he could not have possessed altruistic instincts. The almost isolated life which he led with his progeny, — although the period in which such life was led by man could not have been of long duration, — renders this highly probable. Such a moral state, it is important to notice, depends solely on the absence of the conditions of social life. We see altruism begin to develop as soon as a tribe is formed; we see it later extending to the whole of a people or nation. In the criminal, on the other hand, the altruistic sentiments do not exist, in spite of the social environment into which he is born.

If, then, we take as a term of comparison, not the man of the forests and marshes whose sole society was that of his mate and offspring, but the member of the oldest social aggregations, we are compelled to agree with Tarde "that the baseness, cruelty, heartlessness, cowardice, sloth, and bad faith observable among criminals cannot proceed from the majority of our common ancestors, since they are incompatible with the age-long existence of a well-ordered society." [1]

Féré's observation is equally in point. He suggests "that the traces of degeneracy such as vesanic or neuropathic manifestations, scrofula, etc., so often met with in criminals, have nothing to do with atavism; being incompatible with a regular process of generation, they even seem to exclude the idea of atavism." [2]

Still, facts are not lacking which seem to lend justification to Lombroso's earlier theory. In the first place, there is the matter of anatomic characteristics. Among these, the fact

[1] *Tarde*, "L'atavisme moral" (Archives d'anthropologie criminelle, 15 May, 1889).
[2] *Féré*, "Dégénerescence et criminalité," p. 67 (Paris, F. Alcan, 1888).

most worthy of attention is the extreme prognathism which characterizes certain skulls belonging to the ages of the mammoth and the reindeer. But these few facts, as Topinard points out, afford no basis for any conclusion. The proofs are insufficient. And yet there can be no doubt of the regressive character of prognathism, in view of the fact that elongation and prominence of the jaws are the rule in the black races of Africa and Oceanica, and exceptional in the races of Europe.[1] Moreover, "using the word in its ordinary and current meaning, we may say that the white races are never prognathous, while the yellow and black races are prognathous in varying degrees."[2] And it is further to be noted that the peoples who are classed among the most degenerate of mankind, such as the Hottentots (Bushmen and Namas) attain the highest degree of prognathism known "in all mankind."[3]

It would seem therefore reasonable to suppose that our first ancestors were still more prognathous than the savages. And granting that the skulls of Canstadt and Cro-Magnon[4] may have been exceptions in the race contemporary with the mammoth, it is fair to assume, as does Topinard,[5] that they were the last representatives of a race, then almost extinct, which dated back to the pliocene or miocene age. "'The same thing unquestionably accounts for the extraordinary prognathism of the celebrated Namas of the Museum. . . . They were, in all probability, the survivors of an early African race, long since extinct."

Aside from the matter of anatomic characteristics, prehistoric man must have had many points of resemblance to the

---

[1] *Topinard,* "Anthropologie," pp. 451, 452 (3d ed., Paris, 1879).

[2] *Ibid.,* p. 284.　　　　　[3] *Ibid.,* p. 390.

[4] [Canstadt is a village in the neighborhood of Stuttgart. The skull to which it gives the name is a portion of a cranial vault found in 1700, during the excavation of a Roman "oppidum" by Duke Eberhard Ludwig of Wurtemberg, and brought to the attention of the scientific world by Jaeger in 1835. (*Quatrefages,* "The Human Species," p. 302.) The Cro-Magnon skulls are "the numerous remains found by Lartet, Christy and others in the cave of that name at Eyzies, Tayac district, Périgord (Dordogne)." (*Keane,* "Ethnology," p. 149). — TRANSL.]

[5] *Topinard, op. cit.,* pp. 289, 290.

modern savage. But a distinction is here necessary. There are hundreds of different savage races of varying degrees of social advancement. Unquestionably, none of these races is a perfect exemplar of prehistoric man. Bagehot has thrown a valuable light on this point. Although, he says, it may be well believed that in certain respects prehistoric man "was identical with a modern savage, in another respect there is equal or greater reason to suppose that he was most unlike a modern savage. A modern savage is anything but the simple being which philosophers of the eighteenth century imagined him to be; on the contrary, his life is twisted into a thousand curious habits; his reason is darkened by a thousand strange prejudices; his feelings are frightened by a thousand cruel superstitions." [1] These early ancestors of ours " were ' savages without the fixed habits of savages '; that is, like savages, they had strong passions and weak reason ; like savages, they preferred short spasms of greedy pleasure to mild and equable enjoyment; like savages, they could not postpone the present to the future; like savages, their in-grained sense of morality was, to say the best of it, rudiment-ary and defective." [2]

Are not these last the very characteristics which our analy-sis disclosed in criminals? But we find other traits in which the two have nothing in common. Obviously, prehistoric man must have had physical and moral strength. Only the posses-sion of courage could have enabled him to combat ferocious beasts, naked as he was and without arms; only a love of labor could have led him to force a way through the trackless forest, to build the first rude houses, to protect his offspring against a variety of perils. "Often," says Tarde, "he must have been a hero." Without such qualities the human species would have been at a stand-still. It would have remained in that state in which certain exceptionally backward peoples are found today: the Malays of the islands, for example,

[1] *Bagehot,* "Physics and Politics," No. IV: "Nation-making."
[2] *Ibid.*

whose huts are built upon posts set in the middle of lakes, and whose only method of traversing the virgin forests which surround them is by leaping like apes from branch to branch.

The resemblances to be noted between the instincts of the savage and the criminal, or between the instincts of the modern savage and the primitive savage, fall very short of establishing their identity. For that matter, certain points of resemblance, such as egoism and the lack of moral sense, appear in the characteristics of criminals and children. But this is hardly a reason for saying that children are criminals in miniature: there is here the wide difference which exists between a development not yet commenced and a development which a defective moral organization has rendered impossible. The only conclusion which we are justified in forming is that criminals have regressive characteristics — characteristics which indicate a degree of advancement lower than that of their neighbors. There is nothing astonishing in the resemblance between criminals and the inferior and primitive races of mankind. It is certain that criminals have the primitive instincts — the instincts of the predatory life, coupled with total lack of the sentiment of justice and the absence of any inward restraint upon the passions. What wonder, then, that we find such instincts so combined with physical and especially physiognomic characteristics which recall those of the most barbarous races, as to result in a correspondence of the moral and physical character.

Moreover, many criminals exhibit traits which cannot be attributed to atavism, and which are really atypic. For this reason, I am constrained to agree with that part of Tarde's conclusions in which he says that the criminal is "a monster who, like many other monsters, exhibits characteristics of regression to the past of the race or species. But he combines them in a different way, and we must take care not to judge our ancestors by this example."

The Theory of Moral Degeneracy. — The simplest explanation is undoubtedly that of moral degeneracy, as the effect of a retrogressive selection ("sélection à rebours"), which has caused the man to lose the better qualities which he had acquired by secular evolution, and has led him back to the same degree of inferiority whence he had slowly risen. This retrogressive selection is due to the mating of the weakest and most unfit, of those who have become brutalized by alcohol or abased by extreme misery against which their apathy has prevented them from struggling. Thus are formed demoralized and outcast families whose interbreeding in time produces a true race of inferior quality.

"The degenerate, whether moral or physical," writes Tarde, "is in general the result of heredity. We need but run back one or two steps in the line of descent to find the explanation of his anomalies. Hence it is a vain thing to pass over his parents and I know not how many other generations, in order to demand of his misty ancestors the secret of his perversities or deformities." [1]

The Hypothesis of Prehuman Atavism. — But there are monstrosities which cannot be attributed to parents or ancestors. Whence could nature have derived them? To this question Sergi answers without hesitation, "From the prehuman life, from the lower animality." If this prehuman atavism can be admitted in the case of morphologic anomalies, why not in the case of the corresponding functions? This would furnish the key to certain instincts which degrade the human type to the type of the beast, — explainable biologically by the arrested development of those parts of

---

[1] What we call moral degeneracy is not necessarily accompanied by physical degeneracy. In this regard we disagree with Magnan and Féré, as with the French school in general. Their views run counter to the undeniable fact that a large proportion of criminals (and indeed of the worst criminals) enjoy perfect health and exhibit no trace of bodily degeneracy. But this does not prevent the existence in their organization, in their molecular anatomy, of some deviation, some difference which makes them moral degenerates. Such condition, however, is not a peculiarity, idiosyncracy, or disturbance capable of deranging their physiologic condition: it merely produces a moral anomaly.

certain organs which have a direct influence upon the psychic functions. It would explain that extraordinary brutality which sometimes appears in criminals — that ferocity which always and everywhere would stamp its possessor as an exceptional being. The typical criminal is much worse than the worst of savages — his regressive moral traits, at least, are much more marked; the lesser criminals, on the other hand, are in many respects better developed than many savages. In fine, the typical criminal would seem to be a psychic monster with regressive traits which place him on a level with the lower animals, while the lesser criminal would seem to possess a psychic organization whose characteristics approximate him to the savage.

It is idle to say that the hypothesis of pre-human atavism can be accepted only by those who unreservedly believe in the transformation of species. Yet the theory is not altogether free from improbabilities. Better it is to acknowledge humbly that this phenomenon, like so many others, is shrouded in mystery. But even so, the fact nevertheless remains that the typical criminal is morally a monster possessed of some characteristics in common with the savages and still others which sink him beneath the level of humanity.

§ 6. Classes of Criminals

(1) *Murderers.* — The typical criminal, as we view him, is a man in whom altruism is totally lacking. Now, when we find complete egoism, or in other words, absence of any sentiment of benevolence or pity, it is useless to look for traces of the sentiment of justice. This sentiment is later in origin than that of benevolence and presupposes a higher degree of moral evolution. Hence the same criminal will be thief or murderer as occasion arises: he will take life to satisfy his greed for money, to gain an inheritance, to rid himself of his wife that he may marry another, to put out of the way an incriminating witness, to avenge a fancied or insignificant wrong, or even to exhibit his physical dexterity, his sure eye,

his firm hand, to display his contempt for the police or his hatred for men of another class.

Such is the criminal whom we may call the murderer ("assassin"), — using the word in its general acceptation and not in the restricted sense of many of the codes. Being at the summit of the scale of criminality, he almost always presents a combination of the principal characteristics described above, — sometimes in an extreme degree. In such exaggerated cases the anomaly, I would add, is disclosed by the very circumstances of the crime. In less evident cases the nature of the criminal cannot be determined without anthropologic and psychologic examination. In dealing with the classification of the lesser criminals, therefore, science is called upon to render a more important service.

(2) *Violent Criminals:* (a) *Endemic Crimes.* — These same lesser criminals — men who neither morally nor physically are so far removed from the generality as the preceding — must now engage our attention. And here, in consequence of the distinction in criminals which corresponds to that already pointed out in natural crime, there emerge into plain view two well-defined classes — the one characterized by lack of benevolence or pity, the other by lack of probity.

The *violent criminals* comprise the first class. Under this class fall, in the first place, the authors of such crimes against the person as may be termed *endemic*, or in other words, such crimes as constitute the special criminality of a given locality. Modern examples of this sort of criminality are found in the vendettas of the Neapolitan Camorrists or the political assassinations of the Russian Nihilists.

In such cases the environment has unquestionably much influence. Prejudices of honor, of politics, and of religion figure very largely. In some countries, the general character of the population, the instinct of race, or an inferior degree of civilization or sensibility causes even trivial wrongs to result in bloodshed. Thus in various localities of the South of

Europe, to be a witness in even a civil suit is to run the risk of losing one's life, and he who supplants the tenant of a farm by offering better terms to the landlord is quite likely to die of a gunshot wound.

"At Rome," says Gabelli, . . . "the most trivial motive, a displeasing remark in the excitement of play, malicious tale-bearing, professional rivalry, a vague suspicion of the faithfulness of a fiancée or a wife, still suffices to cause murders of a character to make one shudder. . . . The general state of civilization naturally contributes to this phenomenon, but what most directly contributes is ideas and usages — ideas and usages not altogether without something generous and romantic, — which still persist in the rural districts, notwithstanding their gradual disappearance in the cities. He who pockets an insult is not a man. As late as fifteen or twenty years ago the young woman of the lower classes would hardly look at a man who had never made use of his knife,[1] or been embroiled with the police. . . . The keen-bladed, glistening knives displayed at the fairs dazzle the covetous eyes of the young 'contadino.' Picking one up from the stall, measuring it, brandishing it, making it flash in the sunlight, he finally becomes its possessor and hastens to thrust it in his pocket, whence it will one day emerge to be plunged between the ribs of a comrade or friend. It is of little moment who has the right of the quarrel. The thing is not to yield, not to allow oneself to be intimidated, not to depart without seeing the affair to an end." [2]

Almost the same ideas are found prevailing in certain localities of the North of Europe, as, for example, in the Aspö Islands [3] and among the Frisians — a fact which is evidently due to racial traditions.

As is well known, certain superstitions, such as belief in witchcraft, the casting of spells, the evil eye, certain class or

[1] In many places in the environs of Rome and Naples, a knife is still the first present from a young woman to her fiancé.

[2] A. Gabelli, "Roma e i Romani," p. 32 et seq. (Rome, 1884).

[3] See post, p. 119.

caste ideas, certain refinements of the point of honor, all
have had their influence upon criminality. In the South of
Italy there are people who believe that sexual intercourse with
a virgin is a cure for venereal disease. It is this belief which
accounts for many cases of rape. Among the lower classes
of Naples it is supposed that priests and nuns have the gift
of prophecy. Instances have occurred of their imprisonment
and torture in the attempt to make them divulge their supposed knowledge of the winning number in an approaching
lottery-drawing. One of them, Frate Ambrogio, is said to
have died from the effects of his maltreatment. In the same
classes a prejudice of honor makes it a serious offense for a
young woman to jilt her sweetheart. By way of punishment
she is slashed in the face with a razor and thus disfigured for
life. In France, within a comparatively recent period, it became quite common for women betrayed by their lovers to
have recourse to vitriol for the purposes of disfigurement — a
practice which at times seems to have assumed the proportions
of an epidemic. In Scotland, at the beginning of the 1800s,
vitriol-throwing seems likewise to have flourished, but here
its victims were employers and its perpetrators their dissatisfied workmen.[1]

It is also apparent from these facts that imitation plays a
considerable part in a multitude of crimes against life and
liberty. Must we then infer that the criminal is a normal man
and that crime is merely the effect of example? [2] If such were
the case, criminals would no longer form a small minority:

[1] *Aubry*, "La contagion du meurtre," pp. 95, 96 (Paris, F. Alcan, 1888).

[2] "We speak of the born criminal, — but all criminals are born criminals.
It is their organization which impels them to crime just as the organization
of the artist impels him to the study of the beautiful. Raphael was a born
painter. Nevertheless, occasion had much to do with his production, for
instance, of the Stanze. Moreover, without an ardent passion for art, it
would not have been possible for him to create such a number of master-
pieces in a comparatively short life. Congenital predisposition excludes the
influence of neither occasion nor passion. This is true whether the influence
is for good or for evil." (Paper read by *Benedikt* before the first Congress
of Criminal Anthropology. Actes du 1er Congrès d'Anthropologie criminelle, p. 140, — Rome, 1887.)

crime would lose the character of an exceptional fact. The people who commit the offenses just spoken of, are always destitute of some part of the sentiment of pity in the average measure possessed by the great majority of the population. Even in the races to which allusion has been made — races whose sensibility or civilization has not attained the same degree of development as our own, — murder and kindred crimes are abnormal facts. This sort of endemic criminality affects but a small number — individuals whose psychic organization lacks resisting agents of adequate strength, in whom the part of the moral sense denominated the sentiment of pity, has barely an existence. "With this defect," says Benedikt, "which is due to a congenital diminution of sensibility to mental suffering and disagreeable feelings, there is often combined a defective vulnerability," that is to say, the quality which some people possess of not feeling physical injuries, of feeling them less than others, or of having them heal rapidly. This author cites some remarkable examples, from which he draws the conclusion that such people regard themselves as privileged persons, holding the delicate and sensitive in contempt and taking a positive pleasure in inflicting pain upon what in their eyes are inferior beings.

This physical insensibility, moreover, prevents any vivid representation in their minds of the suffering which they cause to others, since they themselves either would not feel such suffering or would feel it but little. It must be admitted, however, that this lack of vulnerability, very frequent in other races, as, for example, the Chinese, is seldom found among Europeans, and is especially rare in the city populations, where even the lower social strata have acquired a certain degree of refinement.

Violent Criminals (continued): (b) Crimes of Passion. — Following this class of endemic crimes, come crimes which are committed under the influence of *passion*. This condition "may be habitual and represent the temperament of the individual" (Benedikt), or else may be the result of external causes, such as alcoholic liquors, high temperature, or even circumstances of a really extraordinary nature which are calculated to arouse the anger of any person, although not to quite the same degree. In the last case the criminal may closely approach the normal man. When, for example, there is an instantaneous reaction against a sudden and serious wrong, the shade of distinction may be almost imperceptible. Under such circumstances even homicide may lose its horrors. Given a case which justifies a violent reaction, taking the offender's life seems merely an excessive form of reaction. The difference is only one of degree, but it is just this difference which proves the existence of a minimum of moral anomaly.

In our opinion, therefore, a differential psychic element is always to be found. Let us take, for example, the case of a permanent passionate state due to the temperament. Anger is merely an elementary disorder of the psychic functions, an abnormal mode of reaction on the part of the brain against external excitations. As Virgilio says, this disorder often accompanies degenerative conditions characterized by lack of development of the cerebral organs or excessive weakness of the nervous system proceeding from an hereditary cause. The question then is — is the existence of this temperament of itself sufficient to explain an act of cruelty? In other words, is it possible for one who takes life in a fit of anger to be endowed with a sentiment of humanity in no respect inferior to that of non-criminals?

I do not think so. A man in an access of violent rage, may suffer himself to strike the person who has provoked him, but he uses his fists and not his knife. Anger merely exaggerates the character: it is the determining cause of crime, but only when the agent is lacking in the strength of moral resistance which comes from the altruistic sentiment. It goes without saying that the case of a true pathologic condition, such as a neurosis or phrenosis, of which passion is merely a symptom, must always be excepted.

A question related to the preceding is whether external agents such as alcoholic liquors or high temperature are capable of engendering such a state of passion as will impel an honest man to commit a criminal act. Comparative statistics prove drunkenness to be uncommon in the countries which show the highest percentage of homicide and, on the other hand, very common in countries where homicides seldom occur.[1] Without doubt, drunkenness easily excites the mind and is often the cause of quarrels. But in these quarrels it is only the drunkard with a criminal temperament who seeks to use the knife or revolver. The non-criminal drunkard, on the contrary, fights with his bare hands. His object is to lay his opponent prostrate, to "knock him out" as the English say. When he has succeeded, he will himself perhaps aid his fallen foe to regain his feet. In Italy a tavern brawl often results in bloodshed, in England almost never. Shall we say this is due to the difference of race, or shall we not rather ascribe it to the degree of civilization and moral evolution?

Of this question later. For the present we seem to be completely justified in saying that alcohol has but little effect upon crime of this character. Moreover, it has been my uniform experience as a criminal magistrate that men who have taken life under the influence of liquor are nearly always persons who had sustained a previous bad character or had been formerly convicted of similar crimes.

With respect to climate and variations of atmosphere and temperature, it is clear that so long as all the inhabitants of a country are equally exposed to their influence, this influence can be considered important only in the matter of comparative statistics, — as one of the causes which account for the differences in criminality between different countries. Beyond doubt, in the territory occupied by one and the same race, the localities in which a warm climate prevails, at least in Europe and America, are characterized by a larger number

[1] On this subject, see a notable monograph by *Colajanni:* "L'alcoolismo, sue consequenze morali, e sue cause " (Catanea, 1887).

of murders, while in the Northern countries, crimes against
property are the predominant form of criminality. This contrast is noticeable, for example, between Upper and Lower
Italy, Northern France and the Midi, and the Northern and
Southern States of the American Union. But in the case of
peoples who have left their racial confines, this climatologic
influence seems to lose its effect. Thus the Arabs of Egypt
are less disposed to crimes of bloodshed than many peoples
living in cooler climates. This, however, is no reason for altogether denying the influence of temperature upon the passions. Tarde himself admits that climate has something to do
with geographic contrasts in the matter of crime, and that
"high temperatures exercise an indirect influence upon the
evil passions." That this is so seems to be fully proved if,
in connection with geographic data, we take into consideration the further fact that in the same country, the maximum
number of crimes against the person occurs in the warm
months, while crimes against property attain their maximum
in winter. By a comparison of the variations in temperature
during a period of many years, with the number of offenses
against chastity which occurred during the same period,
Ferri has shown this to be a settled law.[1]

Buckle, as we know, makes much of the influence exerted
by the physical environment upon the character and predominant temperament of the people, — carries it even to
the point of exaggeration. But bound up as it is with other
elements, how are we to measure this influence? Is it in climate or in heredity that we are to seek the principal source
of what we call the character of a people? Not only does
anthropology seem to point to heredity, but history also
lends support to this view. The persistence from the earliest
antiquity of similar types of character among certain peoples,
and especially the wide differences in character between
peoples who, although living under the same isotherm and

---

[1] See, however, *Colajanni's* criticism of this theory in Archives d'anthropologie criminelle, 1886, No. 6.

sometimes even in the same locality, belong to different races, are significant facts in this regard.

To see this persistence of racial moral character strikingly exemplified, compare the Gauls as described by Cæsar, or the ancient Germans as we see them in the pages of Tacitus, with their descendants of the present day. Except for the differences due to civilization — differences, moreover, which are but superficial and do not affect the essential virtues and faults of the two peoples, — the description of the Gauls exactly fits the modern French, as does that of the first-century Germans, the Germans of the twentieth.

I am in possession of some very interesting data relating to the inhabitants of the Aspö Islands, which lie in the Baltic near the Åland group and not far from the coast of Finland. These people, both physically and morally, show a marked contrast to their blond and phlegmatic Scandinavian neighbors. They have bluish-black curly hair, black eyes, an aquiline nose; they are small but powerfully built; in short, their type is altogether Southern. Moreover, they possess an excitable temperament: in their quarrels they constantly resort to the knife. The tradition is that they are of Southern origin, Spanish or Arab. Their ancestors, it would appear, were the survivors of a shipwreck, who settled on the island many centuries ago. They took to themselves wives from the adjoining shores, and from these unions sprang an isolated community which apparently did not further intermingle with the surrounding peoples.

Corsica affords another example of the persistence of racial character. Its endemic criminality, which from time to time has been put down with an iron hand, ever tends to break out anew as soon as repression shows signs of relenting.[1] In Austria, homicides and strikings and woundings ("coups et blessures") are most frequent in the Slavic provinces of the South, such as Dalmatia and Styria. In Belgium, the same thing is true of the Flemish provinces; — impulsiveness and

[1] *Bournet,* "La criminalité en Corse" (Lyons, 1887).

irascibility of temper are well known Flemish characteristics.[1] In England, this place is occupied by the Welsh counties of Glamorgan, Montgomery, and Brecon, where the population is almost entirely of Celtic origin.

Opposing my views on this subject, Colajanni insists that the Scots of the 1700s, unlike their modern descendants, were addicted to forays and brigandage. He forgets, however, that this was true, not of the Scots as a whole, but only of certain Highland clans, who regarded themselves as belligerents. That they raided the Lowlands, that they took the lives and carried off the cattle of their Southern neighbors — these facts are wholly irrelevant, so far as the question of the country's internal criminality is concerned. There is no proof that these same Highlanders were given to theft and murder among themselves.

That civilization may operate to milden the racial character is not, after all, to be denied. But its effect becomes appreciable only after the lapse of many centuries, and there always remains at bottom something of the ancient racial instincts.

Moreover, since climate is an element inseparable from the life of an established people, its influence upon crime is as constant as that of heredity. Whether race or climate is the principal element in a people's character is a question of small moment, for the influence of both is exerted upon the people as a whole, and not upon individuals. The important thing for us is to measure the influences which mould, not *national* character, but the character of *individuals* who are comprised in a given nation. With this in view, a subsequent chapter will be devoted to a consideration of those external agencies which operate differently upon different individuals, such as, for example, traditions, family life, education, economic conditions, religion, legislation — in short, all that which goes to make up what we know as the social environment.

[1] *Bosco,* " Gli omicidii in alcuni stati " (Rome, 1889).

For the present, then, we may conclude that neither endemic criminality, nor that apparently due to variations of climate and temperature or the abuse of alcoholic liquors, can exist independently of the agent's individual anomaly. Throughout the whole class of crimes against the person, this anomaly consists in the peculiarity of a violent temperament combined with an hereditary absence of instincts of pity. This, however, does not exclude the existence in some cases of true degeneracy, in the medical sense of the term, — that is to say, pathologic conditions such as hysterical neurosis (frequently occurring in cases of false accusation ["calomnies"] and crimes characterized by cruelty and brutality), epileptic neurosis, and alcoholism (often found in the case of strikings ["coups"], woundings ["blessures"] and threats), and lastly, certain perversions of the sexual instincts (not uncommon in cases of indecent assault ["attentats à la pudeur"] and rape).

Cases are possible in which a crime of the class under discussion appears as an isolated fact in the life of the offender, and neither anthropology nor psychology can shed any light on his character. The exceptional nature of the circumstances which have impelled him to crime renders it difficult to compare him with normal men, since we are unable to say what would have been the conduct of another man in the same situation. If there were such a thing, we would have here a true case of the casual or occasional criminal. Yet even here, if the offense in question is a natural crime, it cannot be gainsaid that the offender is lacking in repugnance for violence, cruelty, or brutality. But from the very fact that nature itself deals in fine shades of distinction, we are unable to trace a line which distinctly marks off the world of criminals from that of honest men. For practical purposes, then, we may regard an intermediate zone as existing between the two. Into this zone enter the least serious violations of the sentiment of pity — all such offenses as are attributable, not to an instinctive cruelty, but rather to a certain rudeness of feeling ("rudesse"), due principally to the lack of training

or the absence of conventional restraints. Cases of offensive
words ("injures"), threats, and strikings and woundings
("coups et blessures") are sometimes of this character, as
when they occur in the course of one of those brawls which,
among the lower classes, spring up almost without warning, —
there being no intention on the part of the assailant to do
his adversary serious harm. So, too, are cases of homicide
due to negligence ("imprudence ou le manque de prévoyance")
and seduction not under promise of marriage ("sans trom-
perie"). Here we find the extreme limit of natural criminality.
In the authors of these offenses moral anomaly may or may
not be present. In any event, whatever be their psychic difference from normal man, it is often very slight. They cannot,
therefore, be looked upon as wholly inadaptable to society.[1]

In this connection, the subject of *criminal mobs* [2] also
requires some attention. Whenever crimes are committed in
the course of popular agitations or disturbances, the question
arises whether there is any individual responsibility for such
acts or whether individual responsibility is not almost wholly
merged into a collective responsibility. An excited mob, for
example, burns and kills. If we can single out the men who
actually applied the torch or fired the shots, is it just to punish
them? Some writers do not think so: they regard the suggestion of the crowd as an irresistible force; for them the

---

[1] On this point alone can I agree with Zuccarelli, respecting the existence
of the casual offender. This author (see Anomalo, June, 1889) believes
that any man is liable to commit crime under really extraordinary circumstances — an opinion which is fairly widespread. In such cases, however,
true crime often does not exist: there is nothing but the appearance of crime.
On the other hand, if crime really exists, the agent cannot be a casual offender.
The fact that circumstances are visible and the moral anomaly difficult to
discover, makes it easy to ascribe almost any sort of act to the influence of
circumstances. Circumstances, indeed, may sometimes furnish the complete
explanation of a criminal act, but only when, during a long period of time,
they have so woven themselves around the agent's being as to result in
destroying his moral sense and rendering him a degenerate. But here there
can be no question of a casual offender.

[2] See *Sighele*, "La folla delinquente" (Turin, 1891): French translation
(Paris, F. Alcan); *Gustave Le Bon*, "La psychologie des foules" (Paris, F.
Alcan); *Tarde*, in Revue des Deux Mondes, 15 November, 1893.

individual is an unconscious member of a new species of criminal — the heedless, furious mob. Other writers, while rejecting this view, contend for a diminished individual responsibility. But is there really any basis for this concept of collective crime? As Tarde has accurately pointed out, even those popular movements which appear the most spontaneous are not without their secret leaders: there is no public disturbance, however extended, which may not be traced to the activities of a few individuals. It is seldom, however, that these instigators take any actual part in the doings of the mob: they have, as we know, a fashion of prudently disappearing.

Take this raging mob which holds the street — of what elements is it composed? A sprinkling of respectable men there is, to be sure, but each moment sees its ranks augmented by swarms of sinister figures. They come, one knows not whence, the scum of the city and its environs — roughs and vagabonds scenting opportunity for plunder, professional criminals guided by an instinct which never fails. The strength of these elements in Paris in 1792–93 has been estimated at 40,000. This was the "people" of the street orators' harangues — that "people" which crowded the galleries at the sittings of the Convention, urging the most violent of the speakers to even greater extravagances and coercing the Convention itself into the adoption of measures whose injustice was only equalled by their absurdity.

The mob begins its work of destruction and pillage, becomes drunken with its own menacing outcries, — but at this stage, the people of respectability, whether attracted in the first place by curiosity or otherwise, all slip away. Of its remaining members a majority are men who have already committed criminal offenses, or at least possess a predisposition to crime. When an unfortunate police agent is seized and cast into the river, this is the work, not of the people, but of a handful of criminals. It was not the people who decapitated the Marquis du Launay after the taking of the Bastille, or inflicted upon

Bailly in front of his scaffold tortures which would have put a redskin to the blush. It was, instead, a horde of criminals, thus wreaking their revenge upon a society whose hand had ever been raised against them, — among them lunatics and degenerates of every description. Such were the men whose crimes dishonored the revolutions of 1793 and 1871.

Whenever it has been possible to identify the persons who actually participated in crimes committed by mobs, they have nearly always been found to be recidivists, habitual offenders, or vagabonds.[1]

In support of the opposite view, Le Bon cites the case of the Septembrists, who, in 1792, stormed the prisons of Paris and massacred a large number of royalist prisoners. This mob, he says, apart from a few professional ruffians ("gredins professionels") was composed of small shopkeepers and artisans of all sorts.[2] This is possible, although we are not informed as to the exact proportion of these "professional ruffians," and for all we know, these shopkeepers and artisans may have been the worst elements of their respective classes. But in any event, this case proves nothing. It is a well authenticated fact that the Septembrists were selected in advance, organized and paid by the Commune to do what they did — to effect this massacre, which, according to Danton, was to put a river of blood between the Revolution and the Royalists.[3] They constituted, in reality, a quasi-military organization, and in obeying the orders of their superiors believed that they were rendering a patriotic service. This was by no means the suddenly-gathered mob which the impulse of the moment makes criminal.

For my part, I find it impossible to believe that in such cases "a momentary current of ferocity passes through the normal mind and effects a complete change in its nature." [4] I believe, on the contrary, that excesses always cause a normal

---

[1] *Sighele, op. cit.*, p. 62.
[2] *Gustave Le Bon*, "Psychologie des foules," p. 149 (Paris, F. Alcan).
[3] *Lamartine*, "Les Girondins," III, pp. 320, 321, 382 (Paris, 1847).
[4] *Tarde*, article cited.

mind to revolt, and that as soon as they appear, the normal
man who finds himself in a mob, takes his departure as soon
as possible, — knowing that intercession on his part would be
of no avail. Far from being swayed by suggestion, the sight
of the tortures endured by the unhappy victim of the mob
causes him to shudder; nothing but fear and a sense of his
own impotence prevent him from betraying his inward
revolt. To saturate a man with petroleum and set fire to
him, to throw women out of windows, to take delight in pro-
longing the sufferings of a victim — this is the work of criminals — true criminals, who add cowardice to cruelty. If
such men constitute a mob, it needs no diminution of individual responsibility to call this a criminal mob.

There have been many instances of mobs whose "anthropologic composition," to use Sighele's expression, was not bad —
mobs which it has been possible to calm by means of reasoning
or energetic action or which in any event have stopped short
of the bloodshed to which they were incited.[1] These examples
are proof of what we have been contending. "A mob composed
of honest men may be guilty of excesses, but it can never
attain that degree of perversity which characterizes a mob in
which criminals form a majority." Belief in the all-powerfulness of suggestion is unfounded. "If it be an established
fact that hypnotic suggestion, the most powerful of all suggestion, does not go so far as to annul the human personality,
how is it possible that any species of suggestion can destroy
the personality of a man who is fully awake?"[2] There is
consequently no such thing as a collective crime. The only
criminal mob is a mob which is composed of criminals.

(3) *Criminals Deficient in Probity.* — We may next consider
criminals belonging to the other division, namely, those guilty
of *crimes against property.* Here, unquestionably, social
factors are much more influential than in the preceding classes.
But this fact does not always prevent us from detecting
in the criminal's organism an element which preëxists any

---

[1] *Sighele, op. cit.,* pp. 65, 66.　　　[2] *Ibid.,* p. 84.

effect of environmental influence. The sentiment of probity is undoubtedly less instinctive than that of pity, or to state the matter more accurately, it is not so strictly dependent upon the organism. It is a sentiment of more modern acquisition, it represents a superposed, almost superficial, stratum of the moral sense, and consequently is less susceptible of hereditary transmission than the sentiment of pity. It lacks, moreover, that peculiarly congenital nature for which education can furnish no substitute. In a civilized society this sentiment of probity is generally the effect of examples in infancy which, continually renewed, have produced an ingrained instinct which in all probability will persist for life.

Yet it may sometimes happen that the child of an honest family exhibits a thievish instinct whose existence can be attributed neither to education nor to example, since his brothers and sisters who are wholly without any such trait, have been exposed to these identical influences. From his earliest childhood, this little being, who seems born only to overwhelm his parents with shame, steals articles belonging to friends of the family or even to servants, hides them, and sometimes sells them to procure what he most wants. Such an instinct, it is clear, has nothing in common with that form of alienation which we call kleptomania. In the latter case the sole motive which actuates the thief is the pathologic pleasure of stealing. He does not seek to derive any profit from his theft; he does not even take pains to hide what he has stolen; he makes no use of it; frequently he will return it of his own accord. In the case of congenital improbity, on the other hand, the thief has often recourse to dissimulation and deceit, and to prevent discovery he is likely to accuse an innocent person of the crime. When a propensity of this kind cannot be ascribed to bad examples or direct inheritance, it can be attributed only to a remote atavism. In no other way can we account for an instinct so utterly at war with the subject's education and training and the instincts of his family.

But the case most frequently met with is that where the improbity is the result of direct inheritance from the parents, intensified and continued by the influence of bad examples. In such case the instinct is at once congenital and acquired. The external element and the organic element are so combined that it is impossible to distinguish them.

Again, apart from the family and its influence upon the formation of the instincts during early childhood, there are certain environments especially favorable to the development of rapacious instincts. The limits of such an environment need not be wide: two or three evil companions, sometimes a single intimate friend, are sufficient to lead a youth into this sort of crime. Since crimes against property are rarely justified by the prejudices or customs of a whole people, they never acquire an endemic character, as do certain crimes against the person. It is only from hereditary moral degeneracy, or by the influence of his individual environment — that immediately surrounding him — which may create an instinct as deep-rooted as if it had been hereditary, that a man becomes a thief. There are but few exceptions. As one of these might be cited brigandage, which has become endemic in certain places, such as Calabria, Greece, Servia, and Albania. But in these countries the brigand is looked upon as an insurgent ("révolté") rather than as a thief; he is in a state of open war with the social power, of which he stands in armed defiance. Continually risking his life, he presents a certain chivalrous aspect which causes him to be admired by the very people whom he harries. Entire peoples have been addicted to brigandage, such as the Normans of the Middle Ages and the Highland clans of Scotland in the 1700s. Here, then, we are not called upon to deal with criminality, but with the predatory life of a nation or tribe not yet reconciled to the activities of peace. Crime always involves the idea of an act harmful to the people of which the agent forms part. It is the more or less exceptional and censurable act of an individual, never of a whole aggregation. This distinction is too plain to need further argument.

In contemporary society, the propensity to theft is often accompanied by laziness, and desires surpassing the means at the individual's lawful disposal. Benedikt defines the psychic anomaly of such criminals as a "moral neurasthenia" combined with a "physical neurasthenia," either congenital, or acquired in early childhood. Its principal element is an "aversion to work, so great as to amount to resistance, and which is itself due to the nervous constitution of the child. . . . If, from his infancy, an individual has neither the strength to resist momentary impulses ("entraînements"), nor the power to obey generous excitations, and particularly if this moral struggle has for him the effect of something painful, then he is a moral neurasthenic. As such, in the course of time, he will avoid every moral struggle, he will think, he will feel, he will act, under the pressure of this moral neurasthenia. He will develop a complete system of philosophy and practice based upon his aversion to moral conflict."

All this, however, presupposes an individual who is capable of the moral struggle in question, — education having impressed upon him some notion of his duties. But with the majority of thieves, the case is otherwise: reared in unprincipled and brutalized families, such a conflict is something wholly foreign to their natures. While Benedikt's description for this reason is only partially true of thieves, it fits much more closely the case of the vagabond. Vagabondage, according to this author, must be attributed to a purely physical neurasthenia taken in connection with the necessity of getting the means of existence. "In the absence of complications, the vagabond never becomes guilty of crime." But if "the physical neurasthenia is combined with a keen appetite for pleasure, there results a dangerous desire of procuring at all costs the means of satisfying this appetite. If, then, the individual is also a moral neurasthenic, he will offer no resistance to this desire, and, other means failing, he will commit crime to attain it. Such a combination plays a very considerable part in the psychology of thieves, forgers, swindlers, foot-pads, and professional criminals in general. The neurasthenic criminal calculates in a perfectly normal manner the chances of success or failure of his enterprises. He soon comes to recognize the superiority of the social power. But since he is incapable of sustained effort, he is contented with transitory results, and, like most men, his hope is greater than his chances of success." To these characteristics must be added an ambition to make the most of his criminal talents, to become a master of his criminal specialty, to gain renown in the criminal world. "When a moral neurasthenic once discovers the ease with which he may turn to advantage the inattentiveness, absence of mind, credulity, and timidity of the public in general, he loses no time in improving his opportunities, he studies his art until there is no crook or turn which he has not fully explored. Success yields him not only the pleasure of its material results, but also a sense of pride in the adroitness with which he has duped his victim and a consequent belief in the superiority of his own intelligence. . . . These two elements: the desire to shine in their criminal profession, and the fascination of plots and schemes — taken in combination — constitute a motive which counts for much in the psychology of burglars, forgers, swindlers, and highwaymen."

This description enables us to perceive in its full significance the difference existing between the present class of criminals and that which is characterized by absence of the sentiment of pity. That thieves, forgers, and swindlers are very often incapable of an act of violence against the person, and that such repugnance to cruelty frequently leads convicts of this character to boast that they were sentenced for theft and not for murder, are facts which need not excite our wonder. Except in the case of the extreme murderers, who lack every vestige of moral sense, the other class of criminals shows exactly the opposite feeling. The prisoner convicted of homicide or wounding ("blessures"), where the motive of

his crime was vengeance, jealousy, or a notion of honor, or
where the crime was immediately due to a passionate temperament or the effect of alcohol, will contemptuously declare
that he has never been guilty of theft.   In fact, this sort of
criminal may possess the sentiment of probity in a marked
degree; he may be capable not only of fidelity, but even of
devotion, to his employers and benefactors; he may even
be wholly incapable of the slightest deceit.

These facts prove that in the lesser degrees of criminality,
we have to deal, not with the complete absence of the moral
sense, but merely with the absence or weakness of the one
or the other of the two elementary altruistic sentiments —
pity and probity.

(4) *Lascivious Criminals* (*"Cyniques"*). — We come now
to crimes due to sexual impulse and offenses against chastity
in general.   In many cases the authors of such crimes must be
assigned to the class of violent criminals.   But where an extreme degree of lasciviousness is the sole motive of the offense,
satyrs of this description are often found suffering from some
form of alienation.   The very considerable number of old men
who offend in the present respect shows that in their cases
the crime frequently stands in very close relation to senile
dementia.   Still, it must be admitted that there are many
non-pathologic cases of this description — cases of lecherous
offenders ("cyniques") who take indecent liberties with
little girls, or are guilty of other degrading sexual manifestations.   Such criminals look no further than the pleasure to
be experienced in committing the punishable act.   To this,
they sacrifice reputation; for this, they endure shame and
ridicule.   In general, it is a lack of moral energy rather than
absence of the sentiment of pity which explains these crimes.
For this reason, it becomes a difficult matter to class them all
among the violent criminals, although, in common with the
latter, they are characterized by total disregard of the physical
or moral pain which their acts occasion to others.

Accordingly, I have deemed it proper to assign criminals

of this kind to a separate class — the *lascivious criminals*
("cyniques"), — which completes our classification.

Summary; Concluding Observations. — It is thus apparent
that under our scheme of distribution all criminals (that
is to say, true criminals and not mere "révoltés" whose
offenses consist solely in disobedience to the law, and reveal
no moral inferiority on the part of the agent) fall into four
classes, viz.: (1) murderers, (2) violent criminals, (3) criminals deficient in probity, and (4) lascivious criminals ("cyniques"). Side by side with these types we must range the
corresponding forms of alienation or neurosis — with the
first two classes, for example, homicidal mania, pyromania,
epilepsy, hysteria; with the third, kleptomania; with the
fourth, sadism.[1] And lastly, it will be necessary in each class,
to group by themselves such youthful offenders as do not fully
understand what they do and err either from imitation or
because the environment in which they have been reared has
impeded their intellectual development.

Such a classification, based upon moral anomaly, or if one
prefers, upon a particular kind of immorality, possesses the
distinct advantage, as we shall later see, of directly suggesting
appropriate measures of repression. It could be used as the
basis for a code wherein its principles would determine the
definition and grouping of crimes. Here, in connection with
each type-description might be indicated the means of rendering the criminal inoffensive, of turning his activity into useful
channels, and of educating his moral sense where the case admits of this possibility. With respect to true crimes, this might
serve as an international code, — as the one criminal code of
the civilized world, — appropriate provision being made for
extradition and mutual police aid among the several nations.

---

[1] In addition to the works already referred to, dealing with criminal insanity and its forms, the following will be found of value: *J. de Mattos,*
"A loucura;" *Antonio d'Azevedo,* "Carceres e manicomios" and "Estudios
penitenciarios;" *Bernardo Lucas,* "A lei penal no processo Marinho de Cruz;"
E. Bonvecchiato, "Il senso morale e la follia morale;" *Ballerini,* "Le psico-
patie e la capacità giuridica" (1891); *Corre,* "Crime et suicide" (1891).

The only offenses not included in this classification are such as constitute mere acts of rebellion or legal disobediences ("révoltes, désobéissances et contraventions"), — acts in the punishment of which no regard need be paid to the psychology of the offender. In the event of the adoption of the code suggested, it would be these last mentioned offenses alone with which the local codes of the different nations would have to deal.

§ 7. The Same: Ferri's Classification

I do not propose to examine the numerous classifications of criminals which have been suggested by various writers on anthropology and psychology. But a word may not be out of place here regarding the classification which Ferri has constantly advocated. According to this, criminals are divided into the five classes of (1) born criminals, (2) habitual criminals, (3) occasional criminals, (4) passionate criminals, and (5) insane criminals.

As I pointed out at the first Congress of Criminal Anthropology, held at Rome in 1885, and have subsequently had occasion to repeat, this classification is without a scientific basis and lacks homogeneity and exactness. In fact, from the anthropologic point of view, it may be said that there is no such thing as a class of habitual offenders. If his criminal habitudes are due to inherited instincts, the habitual offender may be a born criminal. If, on the other hand, these habitudes have been acquired by the force of examples and the influence of his environment, he can only be an occasional criminal. The habitual offender is neither an anthropologic nor a pathologic variety.

The attempt to distinguish the born criminal, the habitual criminal, and the passionate criminal is equally without anthropologic justification. In the first place, all criminals are in one sense born criminals, in another, occasional criminals. All criminals possess a predisposition to crime, which is not the effect of external circumstances, but of something

residing in the individual's moral organization, in his manner
of feeling and thinking.   On the other hand, there are certain
environmental influences which retard the development of
the sentiments of civilized man and produce perverted
instincts which, although not hereditary, are none the less
ingrained.   But, in the second place, whether the criminal
is such from birth or becomes such by subsequently acquired
perverted instincts, the determining influence in his commission of a crime, unless he be insane, is always an external fact.
And if he is without a predisposition to crime, he will never
commit it, whatever be the occasion.   To suppose it possible
to glimpse the casual offender is to confuse with crime an
act which has but the appearance of crime and which morally
is not a crime.

Similar considerations apply to the passionate criminal.
If the passion which actuates him is an anti-social passion,
such as cupidity, then he falls into the class of born criminals:
if it is a pathologic passion, as in the case of sadism, then he
belongs to the class of insane criminals.   Then again, if, on
the contrary, it is a passion not abnormal, such as love,
jealousy, or the point of honor, how are we to distinguish
the passionate criminal from the casual or occasional
offender?   Moreover, passion of any kind may be the immediate cause of the born criminal's act.   Congenital predisposition, as said by Benedikt, excludes the influence of
neither occasion nor passion.   And, we may add, one or the
other of these two is always the element which determines a
criminal act.

It is therefore apparent that this scheme lacks clearly
defined class-limits; with equal propriety one and the same
offender may be assigned indifferently to any one of several
of the classes proposed.   Wholly without homogeneity, it
offers nothing tangible to the law-maker.   Since under its
terms the necessities of repression may be very different in
different cases, it precludes any possibility of a plan of repression whose measures shall answer respectively to distinct

classes of criminals. Being of no avail to legislation, it is consequently without practical interest.

Considerations of utility clearly require that any classification of criminals shall be according to a single criterion. Starting with the idea that every *true* criminal (every author, in other words, of a true *natural* crime) is morally always an inferior, it then is a question of ascertaining the special nature of his moral defect, that is to say, the sentiments and energies which he lacks and the evil instincts by which he is dominated. Such is the theory upon which proceeds my classification of offenders into (1) typical criminals or murderers, (2) violent criminals, (3) criminals deficient in probity, and (4) lascivious criminals.

CHAPTER II

SOCIAL INFLUENCES

§ 1. Civilization

To the reader who has followed us through the foregoing chapters, the conclusions which we shall seek to deduce from the theory of natural crime, already begin to be apparent. These conclusions, however, we shall reserve for a later chapter since, before developing them, it will be necessary to consider the social causes which are generally regarded as contributing to criminality.

It cannot be denied that in countries possessing a civilization in the true sense of the word ("une civilisation bien entendue"), criminality is diminishing, or at least, undergoing a transformation in which adroitness and cunning take the place of violence; the most barbarous forms of criminality, such as piracy, brigandage, murder for revenge, homicide due to notions of honor, robbery, arson, etc., are there gradually tending to disappear, as witness the countries of Northwestern Europe.

By "civilization in the true sense of the word," I mean to imply a state of moral advancement, as distinguished from what is sometimes called material civilization. The word "civilization" ought above all to signify "morality, education, respect, cordiality, activity." [1] Pains taken in the rearing of

---

[1] *Romagnosi*, "Genesi del diritto penale."

children, the dissemination of right principles of conduct
throughout all the social strata, — a work in which the higher
classes by themselves setting proper examples, are called
upon to perform an important share, — just dealing in all
departments of the government, and, finally, the energetic
repression of crime, will contribute much more effectively
than the most extended network of railways to impart to
the word this desirable meaning. And with reference to the
last of these factors, — the repression of crime, — we shall
presently have occasion to show that the mildening of punishment is by no means that mark of civil progress which some
suppose it to be. As we shall see, punishments have been made
only too mild in certain countries, and these, unfortunately,
are the very countries in which criminality not only does not
diminish, but even, under certain forms, is still epidemic,
despite the fact that in other respects they exhibit a state of
flourishing civilization. The mildening of punishments
is bound to lessen appreciation of the gravity of the crime;
leniency toward criminals cannot fail to dull the moral sense
of the people to whose knowledge it comes.

That congeries of moral principles which, during the course
of centuries, has been gradually extending its dominion
throughout all the social strata has, aided by severe penal
sanctions, culminated in the production of self-respect, probity, and repugnance for cruelty and injustice. Refractory
individuals still exist, but their number tends to grow less
when a large majority of the population has arrived at a definite acquisition of these principles of conduct. Certain social
causes may operate to retard or even to arrest moral progress. Among these, and not the least dangerous, is the propaganda of class-hatred, the preaching of revolt against all the
principles of the social and moral order — a movement for
which the communists, before turning reformists, shared the
responsibility with the anarchists. Not until these doctrines
are stripped of their violence will civilization in the true sense
of the word be enabled uninterruptedly to continue its prog-

ress. The countries of Southern Europe, where the lower
classes have not yet attained the degree of moral progress
which characterizes the North and West, are undoubtedly the
most exposed to the consequences of such teachings.

In any event, just as in a human organism which is recover-
ing from some disease of the blood, there always remains a
residuum of microbes in a state of latent activity, so in the
social organism, there will always be individuals whose nature
is criminal, there will always be moral lunatics, moral neu-
rasthenics, and cases of atavism. Others, too, there will be
of a criminal character not fully decided, and who lack
merely energy or moral resistance; but these the good example
of the majority will lead to good, just as an opposite example
would have led them to evil.

§ 2. The School

Notwithstanding the undoubted benefits conferred by
civilization as a whole, an examination of its several manifestations will disclose that, taken singly, these elements
have no appreciable effect upon criminality.

One of the most important is the knowledge of reading and
writing — an acquisition of inestimable value to the individual
in the struggle for existence. And yet, if we think to find in
literacy a counter-active of criminality, we shall meet an
unlooked for disappointment. The practical interest of the
question is the greater, inasmuch as the school and its work
are subject to the control of the State, in whose power it lies
to further or impede their progress or impart to their activities whatever direction it pleases.

It is supposed that ignorance is one of the principal causes
of criminality. If such were the case, then criminality
ought to diminish in proportion as illiteracy becomes less.
Unfortunately, this is a conclusion not borne out by statistics.
It is a matter of common knowledge that multitudes of crimes,
such as forgery, obtaining money by false pretenses, and crimi-

nal bankruptcy, are committed by men who are not illiterate. Moreover, the extreme crimes are not any more uncommon among literates than among persons absolutely ignorant. Sometimes, even persons of a liberal education appear in the Courts of Assizes to answer well-founded charges of abortion, infanticide, or murder.

In Italy, the percentage of criminality is greater at the present time than it was in 1860, when the school system was only in its beginnings. Today, in spite of the continually decreasing proportion of illiterates, the sum total of crimes increases at the rate of 3% per annum.

The situation in France is shown by D'Haussonville's conclusions from comparatively recent statistics. "In 1826," he writes, "out of 100 persons accused of crime, 61 were illiterate and 39 had received some sort of an education. Today the proportion is reversed: 70 literates (in the most modest sense of the word), as against 38 illiterates. This difference is fully accounted for by the extension of primary instruction. But in view of the fact that the total number of crimes has increased rather than diminished, the only result of such instruction is to increase the number of literate criminals, without lessening the number of crimes."[1] To the same effect is the report of the Keeper of the Seals[2] for the year 1900: "From an educational standpoint the same thing is true of individuals with criminal instincts as of the people as a whole: illiterate in the past, they are able to read and write today."

"In Spain," says Tarde, "where the illiterate count for two-thirds in the total population, they represent but one-half of the total number of criminals."

One need not be a pessimist to recognize, therefore, that the school is without direct influence in the diminution of criminality, so far at least as the total number of crimes is con-

---

[1] *D'Haussonville*, "Le combat contre le vice" (Revue des Deux Mondes, 1 April, 1887).

[2] ["Garde des sceaux": the Minister of Justice. — TRANSL.]

cerned. The influence which it has is upon the *kind* of crimes
committed, for in imparting knowledge and developing aptitudes it may be determinative of *criminal specialities.* But
this is a matter which falls outside the scope of our inquiry.
We see, then, the ineffectiveness of this supposedly powerful
weapon. The saying that for every school which opened,
a prison would close, was never anything more than pure
rhetoric. It is needless to dwell on this point. Even if we
were without the figures to prove our conclusion, ought not
simple good sense to tell us that there is no connection between grammar and morality, between an acquaintance
with the alphabet and the possession of the noble or ignoble
passions? As to the matter of higher education, we shall
see later that this has no such effect upon moral development
as is commonly believed.[1] The popularization of classical
instruction, it may be added, could only be fraught with
disastrous consequences. Classical history in particular, as
it is usually taught, is no more than a continual apology for
immoralities and misdeeds of every description.

To be sure, a high degree of culture carries with it a presumption of morality. But this presumption is due, not
to the effect of cultural education upon moral development,
but to the nature of the individual. The very attainment
of a high degree of culture is proof of an intellectual nature,
of a nature devoted to the ideal, contemning the pleasures
and interests of the vulgar. Only by unceasing efforts is
this stage of intellectual development to be realized. The type
of mind which aspires to the high places of knowledge and
has the strength and skill to surmount them, is wholly incompatible with baseness of instinct. In this sense is to be
taken the theory of Nietzsche, "that lofty spirituality itself
exists only as the ultimate product of moral qualities; that it
is a synthesis of all qualities attributed to the 'merely moral'
man . . . that lofty spirituality is precisely the spiritualizing
of justice, and the beneficent severity which knows that it

---

[1] See *post* pp. 157-158.

is authorized to maintain gradations of rank in the world, even among things — and not only among men." [1]

Study has not moralized man; it is man's spiritual nature which has moralized study.

In ordinary cases the influence of the school upon morality counts for nothing. If the school were to contribute to moral instruction, the fact would be far otherwise. But, as is well known, in the Latin countries, and especially in the secular schools, there is little or no moral instruction. Moreover, it is not by pedagogic teaching that we can hope to reform the moral character. The only education which has influence upon the child is that afforded by examples of conduct. If the child sees in his own family only examples of vice and crime, all the good teachings of the school will prove unavailing.

§ 3. Religion

The religious emotions when aroused in early childhood have an undoubted effect upon morality. However faint may grow the traces which they always leave, these never entirely disappear, even in the break-down of faith. So vivid is the impression which the mysteries of religion make upon the imagination that rules of conduct imposed in the name of the Divinity may become instinctive; and this because, as Darwin says, "a belief constantly inculcated during the early years of life, while the brain is impressible, appears to acquire almost the nature of an instinct; and the very essence of an instinct is that it is followed independently of reason." [2] "The operativeness of a code of morals," adds Spencer, "depends much more on the emotions called forth by its injunctions than on the consciousness of the utility of obeying such injunctions. The feelings drawn out during early life towards moral principles, by witnessing the social

[1] *Nietzche*, "Jenseit von Gut und Böse," § 219 [From Eng. transl. by *Helen Zimmern*, "Beyond Good and Evil" (Edinburgh and London, T. N. Foulis, 1909). — TRANSL.]

[2] *Darwin*, "The Descent of Man," Part I, c. IV.

sanction and the religious sanction they possess, influence conduct far more than the perception that conformity to such principles conduces to welfare. And in the absence of the feelings which manifestation of these sanctions arouse, the utilitarian belief is commonly inadequate to produce conformity." Even in the higher races, he further observes, for the most developed men, in whom the sympathies that have become organic, produce spontaneous conformity to altruistic precepts, " the social sanction which is in part derived from the religious sanction, is important as strengthening the influence of these precepts. And for persons endowed with less of moral sentiment, the social and religious sanctions are still more important aids to guidance." [1]

The same author recognizes a harmful influence in anti-religious or anti-theological bias. To those who believe that it is a simple matter for associated men to conform to the principles of morality, he puts the question: " How, then, can there be looked for such power of self-guidance, as in the absence of inherited authoritative rules, would require them to understand why, in the nature of things, these modes of action are injurious and those modes beneficial — would require them to pass beyond proximate results, and see clearly the involved remote results, as worked out on self, on others, and on society? " [2]

That religion, therefore, may be one of the most active of the educational forces, is something which the positivists regard as beyond question. But its efficacy in this regard depends upon two conditions: first, that its influence be exerted upon the child, and secondly, that instruction in moral conduct be the true aim of its teachings. In many of the Roman Catholic countries, the second condition is almost non-existent. This is particularly true in the rural parishes, where an ignorant clergy, with the sole object of insuring the complete obedience of its parishioners, devotes its whole attention to the inculcation of certain formal observances

---

[1] *Herbert Spencer*, " The Study of Sociology," c. XII.　　[2] *Ibid.*

utterly without relation to the matter of moral conduct,—
the result being neglect of the sublime teachings of the Gospel.
In the Protestant countries, however, the clergy have shown
a much better understanding of their duties. Especially
in the countries of the Anglo-Saxon race has the pastor made
the teaching of moral principles a chief object of his calling.
To him it is due that the cardinal principles of social conduct
have so pervaded all the social classes of the English-speaking
nations that a majority of the people is characterized by love
of honesty and hatred of injustice and violence.

One thing, however, must be noted. The power of religion
over morality seems to fail precisely in the most serious cases,
or in other words, when it encounters a decided criminal
character. This is only to be expected. Without emotion
on the part of the recipient, no useful instruction is possible.
Now, how can we expect to arouse this emotion in a man
whose moral sensibility, because of a defect in his psychic
organization, is distinctly under the normal? How, then,
can we expect him to attain the pure ideality of religion?

In conclusion, it may be said, that although religious
teaching is of limited efficacy, its sphere of action is more
extensive than that of education in general. It is a moralizing
force which an enlightened government would do well to
encourage and in no event can afford to impede. It is enough
if the State remain neutral, but its hostility can work nothing
but harm. Destruction of religious teaching would mean the
taking away of a restraining influence which, be its strength
greater or less, is at all times infinitely better than the complete absence of moral sanction.

§ 4. Economic Conditions: the Socialist Thesis

Next to be dealt with is a topic of a very different description: the extent to which criminality depends upon economic
conditions and especially upon the unequal distribution of
the public wealth.

The Thesis Stated. — According to the socialists, the collectivist régime would cause the most prolific sources of crime to disappear as by magic. By establishing perfect equality in the rewards of labor, by leveling all distinction between riches and poverty, the collectivist régime would effectually suppress every form of noxious cupidity, every anti-social activity. And this necessarily proceeds on the theory that the present condition of economic inequality, or, as the socialists term it, the capitalist régime, is the principal cause of the criminal phenomenon.

For some of them, indeed, crime is nothing else than reaction against social injustice. The unequal distribution of goods condemns a part of the population to poverty and thus, depriving it of the means of education, reduces it to ignorance. The economic iniquity protected by the laws is the true crime — the provoking cause, if not the complete justification, of all other crimes.[1] Society is therefore the original offender. By producing unfortunates who can find no place at the feast of life — whom it thrusts from the brilliantly lighted banquet-table into the squalor of the gloomy street, it makes possible the existence of the malefactor.

The fact is regrettable, but nearly all the socialistic writers come to similar conclusions. Almost always they charge

---

[1] There are socialistic groups which proclaim war against all social institutions: "Society is constituted in a fashion at once absurd and criminal . . . The acquisition of any property through the labor of others is illegitimate. The rich must be placed under the ban of the 'jus gentium,' . . . Any manner of attack upon them is justifiable, not excluding fire or sword or even false witness." ("Programme of the Black Hand" — *Laveleye,* "Le socialisme contemporain," p. 275, — Paris, F. Alcan, 1883). See also the admirable work of *A. Zorli,* "Emancipazione economica delle classi operaie" (Bologna, 1881). The pseudo-scientific socialism of today puts the exploitation of the working classes almost on the same level with murder.

The idea that communism would mean the cessation of crime is by no means new. It is met with in the classic authors, whence it passed into the writings of Fénelon, was later adopted by Owen, and finally took its place in the doctrines of Bebel and the modern revolutionary socialists. Strangely enough, Enrico Ferri, in spite of his anthropologic tendencies, does not altogether reject it. See on this subject my "Superstition socialiste," pp. 125–140 (Paris, F. Alcan, 1895).

crime to what they allege to be an artificial and vicious organization of society. The modification, or rather the radical reformation, of this organization would, they urge, result in reducing the number of crimes to a minimum and by gradual evolution, eventually work their complete disappearance.[1]

In the meantime, they cannot look upon the criminal as other than one of an oppressed class or upon crime as other than a symptom of class rebellion. For the honest majority of this class, for those who appear reconciled to their lot, many of these writers can find nothing but words of bitter contempt. "Of course," so runs a typical utterance, full of spleen and paradoxes, "even the most poverty-stricken classes of society have their martyrs, types of idiotic Christian resignation, incapable of offense, blessing the hand that smites them. These, we know, constitute the ideal of an exploiting bourgeoisie, but their example is far from being to us a source of edification. Thus the workman, who, selling his labor for a pitiful wage, causes the wages of others to fall, betrays his kind and justifies the reaction which overtakes him. When privilege dominates, every act of rebellion is a human fact to be studied with human sentiments; and even where it assumes the odious form of crime, it is a useful symptom, since it points out the necessity of radical treatment." [2] It would seem to be a rather difficult matter — we might say, in passing — for the exponents of this theory to explain why it is that the poor no less than the rich are exposed to the depredations of the criminal. A strange revolt this in which attack is directed indifferently upon friends and enemies!

The Question Considered. — This brings us to the principal question, namely: whether the so-called "economic iniquity," a condition by which all citizens are either proprietors or proletarians, is the chief cause or, at least, one of the most im-

---

[1] Owen, followed by Bebel and others, holds to the view that in a collectivistic society, criminality, properly so called, would have no existence; there would be "acts opposed to the social welfare," but only as the effect of disease Persons thus afflicted are to be placed in an asylum, etc.

[2] *F. Turati*, "Il delitto e la questione sociale " (Milan, 1883).

portant causes of criminality.[1]   The sense in which I employ
the word "crime" is already known to the reader; the meaning
of the word "proletariat" as describing the state to which,
because of its unfortunate exigencies, this theory attributes
the great majority of crimes, requires, however, some examination.   The proletarian is an individual without landed
property, who has no means of subsistence other than his man-
ual labor.   For this he receives a wage ordinarily paid by the
day, its amount being determined by the value of those articles
which, at a given time and in a given society, represent for
him the strict necessities of life.   Any capital which may result
from his savings causes the proletarian to pass into the class
of proprietors.[2]

Now, it cannot be denied that the proletarian, in a greater
degree than any other member of society, is exposed to suffer
privation.   If the wage, which is his sole means of subsistence, fail even for a single day, hunger may be the result.
This result may be followed by his stealing to procure bread,
either for himself or his family.   Such is the case of Jean Valjean in "Les Misérables."   I shall not go to the length of
saying with a French writer that Jean Valjean is not a real
figure, — that "there does not exist in France any such town
as Faverolles, where an honest workman with a reputation
for industry and known for his acts of kindness to a widow
and orphans, could not have procured some assistance in
case of urgent need." [3]   On the contrary, I believe it possible
for such a situation to exist, but I do say that a case of this
kind is extremely rare.   In the Rzhanoff tenement, one of the
largest habitations of the poor in Moscow, Count Tolstoi
found but one person actually in want of food — a sick woman

---

[1] The case of England furnishes the first answer in the negative.   Here
the economic inequalities are extreme and yet criminality is decreasing constantly and rapidly.   This fact shows that criminality depends upon causes
quite other than the distribution of the public wealth.

[2] Such is the definition given by *Block*, "Dictionnaire de la politique."

[3] *Adolphe Franck*, "Philosophie du droit pénal," p. 147 (Paris, F. Alcan,
1880).

who said that she had had nothing to eat for two days. Scarcely any one needed immediate assistance. "We find here," he says, "just as among ourselves, people more or less good, more or less bad, more or less happy, more or less miserable. Their happiness does not depend upon external circumstances; it lies wholly in themselves, and no gift of money can further it." [1] In our present state of civilization, times of crisis apart, scarcely any man who earnestly seeks work but is able to find it. If he has the misfortune not to find it, almost always some helping hand is extended from his immediate surroundings.

No doubt real indigence does exist, but its cause is generally a lack of courage and industry. It is then accompanied by a kind of apathy which "demands nothing more than the conservation of animal existence." [2] Its result is usually mendicancy and not crime, — for crime always necessitates a certain effort, and this the individual, exhausted by suffering, is wholly incapable of making. The immense majority of the working classes is by no means reduced to any such condition. It suffers, not from the pangs of hunger, but rather from its inability to procure the pleasures which it sees enjoyed by those more favored of fortune. In the great cities, especially, is the cup of Tantalus thus perpetually at its lips.

But the proletarian is not alone in experiencing the pains of privation. Needs are relative to desires; desires are relative to individual conditions. The man who works for a wage feels poor in relation to the man who employs him, the small proprietor in relation to the large proprietor, the clerk in relation to his head of department. According as we ascend the social scale, the wealth and position of each successive class dwarf those of the class next below. He who is owner of a million of capital envies his neighbor who enjoys a million of income: he is quite likely to entertain toward him the same feeling of cupidity which the tenant-farmer entertains to-

---

[1] *Tolstoï*, "Que faire?" (Paris, 1887).
[2] *Eugène Beret*, "De la misère des classes laborieuses" (Brussels, 1842).

ward the owner of the lands which he works. Now, just as
this feeling of cupidity may impel the peasant to steal wood,
it may impel the tenant-farmer to cheat his landlord, the
cashier to falsify his accounts, the rich merchant to defraud
his creditors, or the wealthy land-owner to forge a will by
which he hopes to add to his possessions. The sentiment of
cupidity exists in all men in a greater or less degree. But
what makes this sentiment capable of leading to crime is not
the peculiar economic condition surrounding the individual,
but his own psychic condition. In other words, there must be
on his part a complete absence of the instinct of probity
coupled with a disregard for his good reputation. The
latter element is not to be overlooked, because the desire to
preserve a good reputation will often enable persons without
an innate sense of probity to resist criminal temptations.

Manifestly, then, the disappearance of poverty would not
prevent the continued existence of these peculiar psychic
conditions; the social factor of crime would reappear under
other forms; the lazy thief of today would become the labor-
hating workman of tomorrow. The only situation in which
we could suppose the disappearance of crimes due to cupidity,
would be one where the offender no longer sees any profit
in committing them. But such a situation is not easily
imagined. Let the economic system be what it may, the possibility of an illicit profit is never excluded. A collective
possession of the public wealth with an equal right in all the
workers to the profits of their toil, would be no better than
any other system in this respect. Every law can be evaded,
and one must be ingenuous indeed to believe that a man so
disposed could not find means of acquiring an undue advantage at the expense of his neighbors (even though under a
different form than money) in the phalansteries of Fourier
or the agricultural and industrial establishments of Cabet.
In my opinion, the equal distribution of profits will never be
practicable. Moreover, a considerable section of the socialists,
in spite of their collectivist dreams, admit the division of

profits according to the quality of the work, substituting thus for the principle of absolute equality, that of the just compensation of labor. What then? The economic inequality would still cause honest activity to be shadowed by the activities of evil; the thirst of gain remaining, there would be the same stimulus to crime. And if, in lieu of money, the workman were to be paid in labor certificates ("bons de travail"), authorizing him to draw from the public stores goods to the extent of his services, would this mean an end of the idle and vicious? Unwilling to acquire these certificates by lawful means, the idle and vicious would use fraud and violence. The principle that each is to consume only in proportion to his production notwithstanding, the evil-inclined would find a thousand ways to live at the expense of others. The discontented, the dregs of society, would always be present. Lying, fraud, and oppression on the one hand, feebleness and sloth on the other, would not cease to exist. The calm and equable temperament would not cease to encounter the temperament which is excitable and neuropathic. We can look for no such change in human nature.

The proletariat is a social condition quite as much as the conditions which overlie it. The complete absence of capital by which it is characterized (without taking into account the exceptional cases of lack of the necessaries of life, that is to say, shelter, food suited to the climate, and, in cold countries, fuel) is a permanent economic condition which is nowise abnormal for those who are habituated to it. It constitutes a condition of stress only for those whose needs and desires are not met by their daily wage. But if in lieu of the word "wage" we use the word "income," quite the same stress may exist, and for an analogous reason, in the capitalistic classes. There is nothing to show that the disproportion between desires and the means of satisfying them is any greater in any one class than in another. If people of wealth eat well and drink well, says Tolstoi, "that does not prevent them from being just as unhappy as the poor. They also are

dissatisfied with their position, regret the past, and desire what
they have not. The better position which they keep ever
in view is the same which the dwellers in the Rzhanoff tenement sigh after, namely, a situation in which they can work
less and profit more from the effort of others."[1] In crossing the
chasm which separates the proletarians from the proprietors,
it even seems that in the case of the latter the increase of
desires outruns the increase of their fortune, because of their
more frequent opportunities of knowing and appreciating the
refinements of luxury and comfort, and of seeing what lacks
for their full enjoyment of life.

If, then, the economic stress, understood in this relative
sense, is not proportionately greater in the very lowest class,
there is no reason to suppose that cupidity is more actively
felt in this class than in the others, or that the criminal impulses are not equally potent in all the social classes. It is
true that theft, the crudest form of attack upon property,
is much more prevalent among the lower classes, but this fact
is counterbalanced by the forgeries, embezzlements, and
criminal bankruptcies of the higher classes. And both sorts
of offense are but varieties of one and the same natural
crime — merely different forms, dictated by the different
social conditions, in which an extreme degree of cupidity
comes to light — merely effects produced by absence of the
same nature of moral restraint. Common speech, which
translates the public conscience much better than do the
terms of the law, has a single name for all offenders of this
description. No less than to the vagabond who steals a watch,
it applies the word "thief" to the cashier who absconds with
the funds entrusted to his care, the merchant guilty of fraudulent bankruptcy, or the public officer who allows himself to
be bribed. In a different class of society, the man who is
guilty of petty theft would have been a fraudulent promoter,
a defaulting bank-teller, or a lawyer who embezzles his
clients' money.

[1] *Tolstoi*, "Que faire" (Paris, 1887).

Thus falls of its own weight the argument upon which the socialists place their chief dependence. Confining their attention to larceny, which they find more prevalent among the poorer classes, they come to the conclusion that crimes against property would cease with the disappearance of poverty.[1] They should speak not of the proletariat but of *economic distress* — a result attributable to the excessive disproportion existing in all the social classes between desires and the means of satisfying them, rather than to the unequal distribution of natural wealth. It is the fact of this distress which explains why, so long as illicit activity will be useful, that is to say, so long as it will be found a source of gain, crime will not cease to exist among immoral men, — and to these all the social classes contribute in an almost equal degree. We are speaking, be it understood, of that fundamental and not superficial immorality, which is the source of crime.

We have said that the social classes contribute to crime in nearly equal proportions. What then are the facts in this regard? Were there statistics showing the social status of the various offenders, the truth of the statement would be capable of exact demonstration. Then the figures themselves, perhaps, would show the error of this widespread idea that poverty is one of the principal causes of crime. But unfortunately these figures are not ready to hand: to obtain them approximately we must proceed by induction. Thus, dealing for the present only with such crimes as are directly actuated by cupidity, we may compare the number of those crimes which are in general committed by members of the lower classes, with the number of those which in all probability are due to persons less unfortunately circumstanced. Taking some of the commoner forms, we find, according to the Italian statistics of 1895, that in this year there were tried 10,024 cases of extor-

---

[1] See, for example, *Turati, op. cit.*, p. 92. "The fact that nearly all the thieves are recruited in the lower classes," he asserts, "so completely establishes the relation between crimes against property and social inequalities, that even the bourgeois sociologists do not venture to dispute it."

tion and robbery and 15,705 cases of theft accompanied by
circumstances of aggravation ("vols qualifiés ou commis
avec des circonstances aggravantes"),[1] making a total of
25,729 crimes, which for the most part we may presume to have
been committed by proletarians; although in the number of
extortions are included many for which the Camorra and
Mafia are responsible, — and these organizations are directed, not by indigent persons, but by men whose means are
sufficient to enable them to live comfortably, quite apart
from the profits of their dishonest activities. As against these
figures, the same statistics show 850 cases of counterfeiting
money, current paper, government bonds, seals and stamps,
and forgery of official documents, commercial paper, and private writings, and 1,688 cases of criminal bankruptcy — an
aggregate of 2,675 crimes which, partly from their intrinsic
nature, partly from the difficulties attendant upon their
execution, cannot in general be attributed to the indigent
classes. These crimes are the effect of cupidity, precisely as
are the crude aggressions upon property to which we give the
names of theft, robbery, and extortion. For the purposes of

---

[1] [In the French and kindred systems, theft unaccompanied by certain
aggravating circumstances is simple theft ("vol simple"); where these
circumstances exist it is aggravated theft ("vol qualifié"). According to the
French law, circumstances of this kind attendant upon a theft, "relate (1) to
the means employed in its commission: violence; climbing ("escalade");
breaking and entering ("effraction"); the use of false keys; the carrying of
weapons; threats to make use of a weapon; impersonating a public officer;
(2) to the place of its commission: public highways, dwelling houses; (3) to
the time of its commission: the fact of night-time; (4) to the number of the
offenders: the fact that more than one person takes part in the offense; and
(5) to the character of the offender: thefts by domestics, workmen, innkeepers,
or carriers ("voituriers") (*Garçon*, "Code pénal annoté," I. p. 1183, note 5).
In Italy, however, the grouping of aggravating circumstances under two
categories, by the Code of 1889, results in the recognition of three classes of
theft: simple, aggravated ("aggravato"), and super-aggravated ("qualificato"). "It may be said that simple theft ("furto semplice") is that unaccompanied by aggravating circumstances of either category; aggravated
theft ("furto aggravato"), that accompanied by circumstances which, in relation to simple theft, render the punishment more severe; super-aggravated
theft ("furto qualificato"), that accompanied by circumstances which, in
relation to aggravated theft, cause the punishment to be still further increased."
"Digesto Italiano," XI—2, p. 1031). — TRANSL.]

comparison, therefore, we have two homogeneous quantities. On the one hand, we have 25,729 crimes of proletarians, on the other, 2,675 crimes of proprietors. The former thus constitute about 91% of the whole number.

The next step is to ascertain the proportion of proletarians in the total population of Italy. According to published reports of the census of 1901, the number of persons registered as proprietors exceeded four millions. We must, however, remember that the larger part of these is made up of peasants whose sole property consists of a tumble-down dwelling and an acre or two of land. Registered as proprietors are many hundreds of thousands of persons who pay annually in direct taxes less than five francs. If we take the families whose heads are in a position which implies some degree of comfort — government officials and civil servants, persons holding salaried places outside of the public service, teachers, clergymen, lawyers, physicians, artists, musicians, as well as capitalists, "rentiers," and pensioned employees — and add the number of individuals therein comprised, we obtain a total of about 2,536,200 persons.[1] Even if we add further about a million rich farmers and merchants, factory owners and managers, stock-brokers, and the like (most of whom, indeed, have already been taken into account in our former total), we shall still fall short of four millions. But retaining the last-mentioned figure for the purposes of the argument, we have this result: that in Italy the people of assured economic position, who are not obliged to depend upon a daily wage, comprise less than one-eighth of the total population, which in 1901 was 32,475,253, — the actual proportions being 88% of proletarians to 12% of proprietors. It follows, therefore, that as against 91 proletarian crimes, we have 88 proletarians — a difference which is hardly appreciable.

Are we not therefore warranted in concluding that even with respect to that species of crime whose reason is directly

[1] *Ministero di Agricultura e Commercio, Direzione generale della statistica,* General Census of Population of 10 February, 1901.

economic, the share of the proletariat is very much the same
as that of the other classes?   And is it not also plain that as a
factor of criminality, poverty may be said to count for no
more and no less than the economic stress of the upper
classes — a stress, moreover, which will continue to exist
until it is possible not only to assign to each an equal share of
the natural wealth, but also to prevent any one man from
earning more than another?

If such is the case as to crimes against property, what is to
be said of the wider contention of some of the socialists that to
poverty is due criminality in general, including crimes against
the person?   Here their efforts are more labored.   They begin
by declaring that "in crimes against the person, the influence
of a vicious social organization is less apparent." [1]   Nevertheless, "the subtle influence of misery, directly or indirectly,
penetrates into all crime."   Misery goes hand in hand with the
lack of education, and this gives rise to "bad examples, ill-
requited honesty, impairment of nervous strength, the unrestrained sway of the basest passions, inability to weigh and
consider, and the permanent failure to satisfy vital demands —
the various elements whose secret fermentation is productive
of crime."

But there is one thing which this argument quite overlooks.   The lack of *moral* education is not confined to the lower
classes.   In spite of the care bestowed upon the training of
children, this same lack is often to be found among the classes
whose economic position is assured.   As has been shown
above, the work of instruction is not always successful.
Hundreds of examples prove that criminal propensities are
equally prevalent in all the social classes.

In the upper classes, even murder is by no means as rare
as might be thought.   The space of a single year will often
yield many conspicuous instances.   At Bologna, a brother
and sister are accused of murdering the latter's husband,
in complicity with her lover, — for the reason that the victim

[1] *Turati, op. cit.,* p. 96.

was not the intellectual equal of his wife — a motive to which was probably joined the desire of getting possession of the husband's estate. The father of the two principals is a well-known physician of means. The accomplice is likewise a physician. Some months afterwards, at Bari, a sea captain just returned from China is charged with killing his wife, by shooting her while she slept, — solely for the purpose of getting rid of her. The case occurs at Milan of a well-known stock-farmer who invites to his house a wealthy acquaintance to look over his pictures. Upon his arrival the unsuspecting guest is seized, bound, and forced to sign certain bills of exchange. This done, he is turned over to an ex-convict to be suffocated in a vapor bath. A leading citizen of Palermo, formerly a member of the Chamber of Deputies, is held under arrest for upwards of three years, charged with murdering in a railway carriage a director of the Bank of Sicily. A clerk whose mother has mysteriously disappeared is accused of her murder and released only after the elapse of many months, merely because the fact of her death cannot be proved. A law-student of the University of Rome is committed for trial before the Court of Assizes, for having killed a fellow-student in the night-time with the object of robbery. In the Court of Assizes appears, as a prisoner, a wealthy member of an aristocratic French family, to answer the charge of murdering the illegitimate child of his wife. Desiring to put the infant out of the way, he had taken it to a remote place on the coast, where from the top of a steep cliff, he had thrown it into the sea. Some years later, another Frenchman — a manufacturer, this time, — takes his young wife to the very same place and gets rid of her in exactly the same manner, — first having insured her life in his own favor. — These few cases have been discovered by chance. How many others must there be which have never been brought to light? Discovery is especially difficult where the people involved are clever and far-sighted, and possessed of the means to buy silence and to travel to distant countries.

The morality of the lower classes is not in general very refined, but the most elementary, the least developed moral sentiments are all that are needed to keep them from crime. In these classes, just as in the higher classes, murder is an exceptional fact. Their lack of education can have in general no other effect than a rudeness of feeling ("rudesse"), that is to say, a lesser degree of sensibility to the moral sufferings of others, an honesty which is somewhat more elastic. Mark Tolstoi's poor, the peasants and workmen described by Zola. Some of them, to be sure, are criminals, but at their very first appearance, care is taken to tell us of their antecedents, to explain the causes of their exceptionally perverted natures. We meet with others, again, who are exceptionally virtuous. No doubt, the great majority of the characters in "L'Assomoir" and "La Terre" are beings for whom we can have but little sympathy, who even inspire us with feelings of disgust. Sometimes they are disloyal and uncharitable, completely taken up with their own selfish interests, and devoid of the slightest trace of idealism, but, on the other hand, they never look to crime as the means of gratifying their passions, and even if the occasion presents, they never succumb.

So long, therefore, as a majority of the population will possess in common a certain sum of the instincts and repugnances of which I have spoken in a previous chapter, these instincts and repugnances will be hereditarily transmitted in all classes alike, rich and poor, learned and ignorant, and will be strengthened by tradition, examples, and family education. We are not here concerned with that delicacy of feeling which is the moral appanage of a comparative few, any more than with the virtues or the noble and generous sentiments. We have to do solely with a negative quality, that is to say, repugnance for a determinate number of acts, the immorality of which is universally recognized in the lower as well as in the higher classes of the population.

If it be true that the moral instincts are the evolutionary resultant of countless experiences of utility undergone by

past generations, it would seem to be plain that experiences
of the inutility of murder, theft, and similar crimes, must have
been taking place quite as constantly in the lower as in the
higher classes of society. The instinct of pity, as also a certain
very crude instinct of probity, appears in the lowest walks
of life. We find there the same repugnance for bloodshed,
the same aversion to violence and treachery, which are found
in higher places. The process of evolution which above has
pursued an even course and has there given birth to delicacy
of sentiment, is arrested or hindered below; here, morality is
confined to a few aversions, a very limited number of sentiments, but these aversions and sentiments are encountered
in an equal measure, an equal proportion, both above and
below; individuals destitute of this rudimentary morality
are equally rare and abnormal at the bottom as at the top of
society. Poverty, no doubt, is an obstacle to education, and
the want of education prevents moral development, but poverty does not necessarily bring about the total absence of
sentiments like those of benevolence and justice. Proof
of this assertion has already been furnished and that, too,
in the very field where its truth has most often been challenged,
that is to say, in connection with the instinct of probity.

And now for proof that criminality in general is not due
to proletarian conditions. In the year 1895, 8% of those
convicted of felonies ("crimes") and misdemeanors ("délits")
in Italy were persons classed as land-owners, farmers, managers
of business enterprises, salaried employees, government officials, capitalists, and "rentiers," or as engaged in the liberal
professions or the fine arts — a proportion by no means
flattering to the middle classes, if we stop to consider that
the misdemeanors comprised a multitude of petty agrarian
thefts, such as the stealing of fruit, fire-wood, etc., which
could only have been committed by persons in indigent circumstances, and ought not really to figure in the criminality of
the country. And yet, regard being had to their respective
numbers in the population, the proportion of poor is little dif-

ferent from that of the rich and well to do.   The number from
the higher classes convicted in the Court of Assizes is proportionately smaller, but this, to my mind, has but one
meaning.   It tends more and more to confirm belief in the
common remark that money may serve to defeat the ends of
justice.   Too often are verdicts influenced by the eloquence
of some gifted advocate whom only the rich can afford to
employ, or — what is a much more threatening evil, — by
sordid barter and sale.[1]   Nevertheless, we learn from the
prison statistics for 1900, that in the penitentiary establishments of Italy there were then 3,102 persons (being one-tenth
of the total number of inmates) who did not come from the
proletarian classes, since they are described as "rentiers,"
merchants, bankers, innkeepers, brokers, salaried employees,
government officials, clergymen, or members of the liberal
professions.   This gives us a proportion — 10% — which
almost equals the proportion of proprietors to the total
population.[2]

Turning now to the matter of education, we encounter a
host of facts which prove that the ignorance which almost
always goes hand in hand with poverty is without effect upon
the criminal phenomenon, — that this is wholly independent
of social condition or individual culture.   For instance, if
we take the persons convicted of criminal offenses who were
inmates of the Italian penitentiary establishments in the year
1900,[3] and classify them according to trade or profession,
we find the most poverty-stricken and ignorant group to be
that of the agricultural classes, who constituted 28.9% of
the whole.   This is a proportion very much less than that which
these classes bear to the total population, since, according to
the census of 1901, they numbered 16,836,557 out of a total
population of 32,475,253.

---

[1] Unfortunately, there is such a thing as the professional juryman. There
are places where he plies his trade almost publicly, and where he sometimes is
known even to have a fixed scale of charges.

[2] "Statistica delle carceri per gli anni 1899 e 1900," (Rome, 1902).

[3] *Ibid.*, p. x.

Again, in Germany (according to statistics of 1896), the liberal professions contribute a much larger quota than does the agricultural class to the number of crimes involving fraud and breach of trust. On the whole, the class which is there most productive of criminality is that of persons engaged in commercial and industrial pursuits. In France, persons engaged in commerce and members of the liberal professions are more largely represented than the agricultural and manufacturing classes in the more serious crimes against the person. Moreover, in 1900, the agricultural class, which comprises "a little less than one-half of the actual population of France, counted only for one-fourth in the number of accused having any sort of trade or profession. . . . The criminality of the commercial class (one of the farthest removed from illiteracy) constitutes 15% of the total criminality of the country, although this class represents but one-seventh of the whole population."[1] As for the liberal professions and the public service, we find the number of crimes ascribed to their members to be nearly double that of the agricultural class.   D'Haussonville, in remarking upon the small number of persons of superior education among the accused, has, strangely enough, forgotten to take into account the proportion existing between this small number and the small number of liberally educated persons in relation to the entire population.[2]

It therefore becomes plain that there is, in general, a lesser degree of criminal activity, and, in particular, a lesser degree with respect to the more serious offenses, among the very people who form at once the poorest and most ignorant portion of the population. In fact, this agricultural class comprises in France, besides the owners of small farms, more than a million tenant-farmers ("fermiers et cultivateurs") and upward of two million agricultural laborers and farm-

---

[1] "Compte général de l'administration de la justice criminelle pendant l'année 1900," p. xxvii (Paris, 1902).

[2] "Le combat contre le vice" (Revue des Deux Mondes, 1 April, 1887).

servants ("journaliers, hommes des peines et garçons de
ferme"). It goes without saying that women and children
are not included in these figures. Everywhere, as is well
known, but more particularly in France, the poverty and
ignorance of the peasant are in marked contrast to the education and comparative comfort of the city workman. What,
then, can be answered by those who believe in the effective-
ness of literacy and economic well-being as counter-agents
of crime, when they are told that out of every 100,000 persons
accused of crime, the manufacturing classes furnish 24%
and the commercial classes 27%, as against the contingent of
8% attributable to the agricultural classes?

But there are still other facts which tend to a more direct
demonstration. On the one hand, in France the wages of
workmen underwent an increase of 45% between 1853 and
1871; the consumption of wheat, estimated in 1821 at an
average of 1 hectolitre 53 per capita rose to 2 hectolitres 11
in 1872; the consumption of meat, which was 20 kilogrammes
8 in 1829, increased to 25 kilogrammes 1 in 1862. On the other
hand, the number of pupils in the primary schools which was
57 per 1,000 in 1832, attained a proportion of 122 per 1,000
in 1877.[1]

What then of public morality? — has it kept pace with this
remarkable growth in the general prosperity and education?

Between 1826 and 1878, as has been estimated, the total
number of felonies ("crimes") and misdemeanors ("délits")
more than tripled. Since then, the increase in wages and the
progress of popular education have been unabated, yet the
tide of crime did not cease rising until 1895.[2] It began to
ebb only in 1896, and then by no means on account of the
spread of prosperity and education (in this respect there
is no appreciable difference between the period from 1891 to

[1] See "Le combat contre le vice" (Revue des Deux Mondes, 1 April, 1887).
[2] In France, from 1861 to 1865, the annual average of convictions for
felonies ("crimes") and misdemeanors ("délits") was 95,357. In the period
from 1891 to 1895, this average rose to 130,412, but in the ensuing five-year
period fell to 124,806.

1895 and that from 1896 to 1899), but as the direct result of a group of statutes which were enacted, to quote from an official report, "with the object of making exceptionally severe the punishment of incorrigible offenders, while rendering possible an early release from custody of such prisoners as exhibited tendencies to reformation."

It cannot be said that the increase in criminality up to 1895 is attributable either to the increase of wealth or to the spread of education, but, on the other hand, the figures which we have been considering make it equally plain that poverty and ignorance are not the true causes of crime.[1]

At this juncture we may look for an objection.

If criminality is not the effect of the economic condition of the proletariat, how do we account for the constant relation which, as shown by statistics, exists between the number of thefts, on the one hand, and the abundance of harvests and the price of breadstuffs, on the other? This is a well-known statistical law, which has been the subject of repeated confirmation. In Bavaria, for example, it was observed that in a population of 100,000, every increase or diminution of

---

[1] *Van Kan* in "Les causes économiques de la criminalité" (Paris, 1903), is disposed to doubt the accuracy of my figures with respect to the middle classes and the proletariat. In dealing with France, I have taken my data for the present edition from the "Compte général de la justice criminelle pendant l'année 1900," without having had to change in the least my former conclusions. As for Italy, Van Kan acknowledges that he has not been able to obtain direct access to the figures, whereas I have indicated the source of my data and believe them to be exact. In this edition I have taken advantage of the first published extracts of the census of 1901 as well as of the prison statistics for 1900.

What particularly impresses Van Kan, is Marro's estimate that the proprietors in Italy constitute 27% of the non-criminals, as opposed to 9.4% of the criminals. I cannot, however, admit the first of these figures, since it would make the proprietors more than one-fourth and almost one-third of the total population. My own result, taken from the official census, seems much more probable. The estimate made by Fornasari de Verce, again, errs in its conception of what constitutes the proletariat. Besides 56% of indigent persons, there are others amounting to 32.15% who have only the strict necessaries of life. I fail to see why these latter should not be included in the proletarian class. For proletarianism does not mean indigence: it means only the total lack of capital.

six kreutzers in the price of cereals was attended with a
corresponding increase or diminution of one in the whole
number of thefts. Similar results attended observations in
Sicily for the period from 1875 to 1895. But another phenomenon which nearly always accompanies this last, must
not be forgotten. Fluctuations in the price of grain affect
crimes against the person in just the opposite manner to
crimes against property. Thus in Bavaria, the fall in the
price of foodstuffs was marked by an increase in offenses
against the person and vice versa.[1] Similarly, in Prussia in
the year 1862, when the price of many kinds of foodstuffs was very high, the proportion of crimes against property was 44.38%, and of those against the person 15.8%;
upon a fall in prices, the former descended to 41%, and
the latter rose to 18%. And if the movement of rise or fall
in prices is not confined to a single year but continues for
any considerable period, we may generally look for the one
form of crime to follow the progress of prices, while the other
form correspondingly moves in the opposite direction. If
the impulse, the occasional cause, the object of theft were
to be absent, theft itself would no longer exist. But this would
bring no basic modification in social immorality: it would
simply cause the form of criminal activity to undergo a decided
change. Abundance of food and drink would cause the passions to be more easily excited, and since the greater number
of crimes against the person are immediately due to the effect
of passion, it is plain that crimes of this character would
become much more numerous. The workman who had dined
well and had no economic fears for the morrow, would straight-
way go forth in search of amusement, — and this would
frequently be amusement of that questionable sort which
leads to brawls and bloodshed.

Thus, while France's improvement in social well-being, as
shown by the increase of wages, and the greater consump-

[1] *Mayr*, "La statistica et la vita sociale," pp. 556, 557 (2d Italian ed.,
Turin, 1886). As to Sicily, see a study by *A. Niceforo* (Rome, 1897).

tion of wheat, wine, and alcoholic liquors,[1] resulted, from 1836 to 1869, in the diminution by one-fifth, of crimes against property; on the other hand, crimes more especially directed against the person, showed, during the same period, an increase of more than one-third.[2] These figures conclusively prove that the oscillations in the always unstable economic equilibrium are not the real cause of criminality, but merely determine the form under which it manifests itself. They may be compared, in their effect upon the social organism, not to the microbe, which, accidentally introduced into a healthy body, infects and destroys it, but rather to the cold wind or the damp dwelling which hastens the outbreak of phthisis, or to the violent exertion or emotion which brings about the premature rupture of an artery. Had those causes never been brought to bear, the subject would sooner or later have succumbed to phthisis or arterio-sclerosis. In the same way, the circumstances which make life easier or harder, do but determine at a given moment, under a certain form and in a special manner, the manifestation of this immorality which, sooner or later, would have come to light in the form of crime.

In relation to criminality, the variations in the social environment and the economic fluctuations which are often their result, produce a phenomenon similar to that of the ocean tides. The movement of the tides neither increases nor diminishes the volume of water; it is nothing more than the water alternately advancing and receding. Thus the variations in question, — and especially those variations which recur at fixed intervals, such as the seasons of the year, — cannot be said either to increase or diminish the total volume of criminality.

It has long been recognized that the maximum, in summer, and the minimum, in winter, of crimes against the person

---

[1] The consumption of wine doubled from 1829 to 1869; that of alcohol increased more than three-fold from 1829 to 1872.

[2] *Ferri*, Studi sulla criminalità in Francia dal 1826 al 1878, pp. 39, 40 (Rome, 1882).

coincide respectively with the minimum and maximum of crimes against property (Quételet). Urged by the needs of the moment, the criminal activity prefers to fasten itself upon a single object, to the disregard of everything else. It is this which explains the constant relation between the increase of one species of crime and the decrease of another. Although immorality is often limited to the absence of but one of the elementary moral instincts, yet we not uncommonly find improbity combined with inhumanity in the same individual. The best proof of this is the fact, shown by the statistics of recidivism, that the most varied forms of crime may alternate in the case of the same individual — a fact, too, which completely refutes those juridical theories which would have the penal law direct its attention to none other than special recidivism.

This transformation of crime from one species to another, because of the vicissitudes of seasons and the abundance or scarcity of crops, with the attendant fluctuations in prices, may appear strange, but it is a phenomenon which we are obliged to take into account. We are equally compelled to recognize the similar effect produced by *annual* variations in temperature and the persistent rise and fall of prices during a series of years. Thus, in France, the crimes of murder, rape, and wounding ("blessures") showed a progressive increase during a period of five consecutive years, — from 1848 to 1852, — which, as evidenced by the extremely low prices of meat, wheat, and wine, was a time of general prosperity.[1]

All the facts, therefore, concur to render untenable the position of the socialists. The easier life and increased comfort of the lower classes have not effected a diminution in the total sum of criminality. On the contrary, the increase of wages and the extension of education in the second half of the 1800s, have been accompanied by a marked increase in some of the more serious forms of crime. "Thus it is curious to see," says a French writer, "how cupidity grows with riches, and

[1] See *Ferri*, "Socialismo e criminalità," p. 77.

how, likewise, keeping pace with the progress of urban life and the increasing freedom in sexual relations, the sexual passions increase in force, as is attested by the immense number of indecent offenses. There could scarcely be a better illustration of the truth that desire feeds upon its own satisfaction." [1]

From what has been said up to this point, the two following conclusions may be drawn:

(1) The present economic order, that is to say, the distribution of wealth, as it exists today, is not a cause of criminality in general.

(2) The fluctuations which are wont to occur in the economic order may bring about the increase of one form of criminality, but this increase is compensated by the diminution of another form. These fluctuations are, therefore, possible causes of *specific criminality*.

There remain to be considered such *abnormal* economic disturbances as are attendant upon commercial crises, famine, floods, wars, and revolutions. Events of this description, inasmuch as they totally alter the usual conditions of life, wear the appearance of true occasional causes of criminality. To them would seem to be due manifestations of the criminal phenomenon, which otherwise, under normal conditions, would perhaps not have occurred, because of the absence in the social environment of impulsions sufficiently strong to determine immoral individuals to commit the anti-social act. At first glance this view appears to be confirmed by past experience. An immediate increase in the number of robberies, homicides, and crimes of fraud has nearly always followed upon the heels of sudden disturbances of this description. And yet a closer study of the question would probably result in altering our opinion. Under such circumstances, it is true, statistics do show an increase in the more serious crimes. But after all, perhaps even here nothing more is really signified

---

[1] *G. Tarde,* "La statistique criminelle du dernier demi-siècle" (Revue philosophique, January, 1883).

than a change in form. To my notion, neither flood nor famine necessarily increases the number of criminals; what it does is merely to turn the vagabond or sneak-thief into a foot-pad, just as a war or revolution, perhaps, will do no more than transform the common thief into a brigand. The question then would seem to be purely one of specific criminality — increase on the one hand, diminution on the other; although the gravity of the crimes subject to increase causes the compensatory decrease to be felt but little. This, moreover, is a mere opinion, which I have no means of supporting with actual figures.

No doubt a political, social, or economic crisis may be the occasional cause of crime, since it makes harder the struggle for existence under all its aspects. Nevertheless, there is every reason to believe that the want of moral instincts (an indispensable condition of crime) will always encounter at some time or other, in the various contingencies of life, some impulsion which will bring about the manifestation of the criminal phenomenon.

§ 5. The Same: Theory of Direct Proportion between Crime and Material Prosperity

The conclusions which we have just arrived at are wholly at variance with the socialist thesis: as it has seemed to us, the economic condition of the proletariat — that is to say, the lack of capital or savings — is entirely without influence upon criminality as a whole; its influence is exerted only upon certain special forms which constitute the specific criminality of the lower classes, just as the other forms constitute the specific criminality of the classes possessing a better economic position. Extreme indigence ordinarily results in mendicancy, sometimes in vagabondage; the only crimes for which it is clearly accountable are such trivial offenses as the stealing of fire-wood, articles of food, and other objects of insignificant value.

The Theory Stated. — We doubt if it has occurred to the reader that an almost opposite thesis could seriously be urged, namely, that the increase of well-being, of work, of business, in short, the whole advance of material prosperity, brings with it a proportional increase in the number of crimes. And yet this theory of the *proportion between evil activity* (crime) *and honest activity* (commerce, industry, and affairs) is one which is not without its adherents. It rests upon the principle that when the latter increases, there necessarily is a fillip to the former, so that the increase in crime would be merely apparent, if it were exactly in proportion to the progress of honest activity. With this as his starting point, Poletti, in no spirit of hostility to civilization, comes to the conclusion that to the last is due the increase in criminality which has appeared almost everywhere in Europe, — in France, since 1826; in Italy, since 1865.[1] This result, however singular, is nevertheless logical. If we admit his premise that an increase in the number of crimes proportionate exactly to the increase in material progress, is without importance, signifying in reality that crime is stationary, then it follows that an increase in crime proportionally less than the increase in prosperity, really means that crime has diminished. We might therefore find in a given period double the number of crimes of the preceding period, and at the same time be obliged to recognize an actual diminution in criminality.

This idea is not entirely new. Under a slightly different form it has for many years been a subject of debate. "Civilization, which is merely the progress of liberty," wrote Lucas in 1828, "widens the abuse of liberty, precisely because it extends its use. To obtain an exact notion of the morality of civilization, we must, instead of contrasting liberty and civilization, place in one side of the balance the use, and in the other, the abuse of liberty. Let us establish the rule that the morality of civilization is to be judged by comparing the use with the abuse." This principle once posited, he sees

[1] See following chapter.

little ground for alarm in the larger number of certain classes
of offenses appearing in France, as compared with Spain:
"We are not called upon," he says, "to give especial credit
to a poverty-stricken and ignorant people because of the
small number of harmful acts occurring in their midst. This
fact is due to the lack of occasion for inflicting harm; to nothing else than an animal-like ignorance. The greater number of
such acts occurring among civilized peoples is merely the
result of a larger development of human liberty."

Taking issue with such a view, Romagnosi vigorously
denied that a civilization thus capable of augmenting crime,
could be a real civilization: "Does civilization consist solely
in more commodious dwellings, more elegant apparel, a larger
number of taverns, the development of industries, and the
like? By no means. What constitutes the true civilization
is moral, economic, and political perfectionation. . . . It is
said that crime increases with progress. One might as well
say that sin increases with progress in piety; that diseases
multiply with the regular development of a sound body;
that as men become more industrious and grow in mutual
respect and friendliness, so increases the number of the idle,
vicious, and criminal." [1] This answer, however, does not meet
the question. No one would venture to assert that civilization
in this high sense of the word is productive of increased
criminality. But such is not the scope of the theory under
discussion. It refers only to economic and industrial progress,
— with which individual morality has no necessary connection. In its support statistics are adduced showing the increase
of crime as compared with the expansion of commerce, the
multiplication of industries, and the increase in the public
wealth. And with these figures as a basis, the attempt is
made to establish a constant relation between the two series
of progressions.

The Theory Considered. — Noting that Poletti's statistical

[1] *Romagnosi,* "Observations statistiques sur le compte rendu général de
l'administration de la justice criminelle en France pendant l'année 1827."

matter is now old, — his work having been published in 1882, — we may look at the arguments which he advances.

French statistics show that from 1826 to 1878 there was an increase of crime at the rate of 100 to 254. This is merely a numerical increase and not a proportional increase. To obtain the latter, it is necessary to compare this increased sum of the criminal energies with the other energies which, under the impulsion of the same factors, have contributed in an ever-increasing degree to the conservation of society and the growth of its operative power. Criminal activity is merely the residuum of the social actions obtained by a process of elimination, in which all the just actions, viz., the activities of production and conservation, of morality and law are set aside. Although it is impossible even approximately to determine the sum total of the last, we can nevertheless ascertain their more certain and important effects.

Thus the author compares the increase of criminal activity in France with the increase in the activities of production and conservation, during the period from 1826 to 1878. He finds: (1) that during this period imports increased at the rate of 100 to 700, and exports almost in the same measure; (2) that the treasury balance (indicating the national financial power) showed an increase from 109 to 300, proportionately; (3) that the real and personal property transmitted by inheritance, which in 1826 was valued at 1,346 millions, had, by 1869, attained a value of 3,646 millions; (4) that transfers of real property "inter vivos" had doubled in value; (5) that in 1876 the charitable institutions were able to make disbursements for relief in an amount four times as great as in 1833, while between these years the capital of the mutual benefit societies had increased five-fold; (6) that the annual average of the wheat crop rose from 60 million hectolitres in 1825–1829 to 104 million in 1874–1878; (7) that from 1853 to 1871 wages increased almost one-half (45%); (8) that the consumption of wheat, estimated at 1 hectolitre 53 per capita in 1821, attained the figure of 2 hectolitres 11 in 1872,

while the consumption of alcoholic liquors almost doubled
between 1831 and 1876; (9) that although, from 1841 to
1878, the *quantitative* criminality increased at the rate of
100 to 200, still, if we are to judge by the public force deemed
necessary to maintain order (the incremental rate of which
was only from 100 to 135), social security remained about the
same at the end of this last-mentioned period as at its beginning.

From the foregoing data the author concludes that in the
period from 1826 to 1878 the social activities of France underwent a prodigious development; that in fact they may be
said to have increased three-fold. The increase in the proceeds
of taxation as from 100 to 300 constitutes the surest synthetic
expression of this general increase. The destructive or criminal energies increased not at the same rate, but in a proportion somewhat less — as from 100 to 254. It results, then,
that during the period in question there was not an increase
but a positive diminution of criminality.

Turning to Italy, he finds that there convictions for crime
between 1863 and 1879 showed an increase of 70%. On the
other hand, the rate of increase in the commercial movement
of Italy between 1862 and 1879 was from 100 to 149 in the case
of imports, and 100 to 183 in the case of exports; the funds
raised by taxation, which amounted to 617 millions in 1866,
reached the sum of 1,228 millions in 1879, while, during the same
period, the balances of the communal treasuries doubled in
amount, and those of the provincial treasuries increased four-
fold; from 1863 to 1875 the funds of the charitable institutions
increased by 38 millions; the capital of the savings banks
which amounted to 188 millions in 1863, rose to about one
billion in 1881, having become quadrupled during the last
two years of this period. Notwithstanding, therefore, the
laborious transformation of the country which had been taking place during the years under investigation, — a transformation in which there were occurring many exceptional
circumstances favorable to the development of criminality, —

the conclusion is, that the increase of the latter was not proportionate to that of the social activities.

Poletti professes to see in these examples the confirmation of his law that criminal activity in relation to honest activity develops in a proportion which continues stable so long as the causes which produce the two sorts of activity remain constant. The time of this constancy of causes the author calls the "criminal period." During such a period, he continues, the fluctuations in the quantum of criminality are inconsiderable, not exceeding one-tenth, more or less, of the average number of offenses committed in the same lapse of time, while from one period to another, as the effect of increase in honest activity, the proportionate quantum of criminality tends to a slow and progressive diminution.[1] According to the author such a result necessarily follows, because the development of the intellectual faculties and the economic activities, as well as the general social perfectionation enhance the power of resistance to crime. This, moreover, is proved by the increasing number of ill-nourished unfortunates in Northern Italy, who fall victims to pellagra, or prefer to emigrate or commit suicide, rather than risk resort to crime as a means of bettering their condition.

The theory in question is highly ingenious, and its appearance of truth is such as to make it especially appeal to those who are on the outlook for arguments to justify their own temperamental optimism. "Summed up," says Tarde, "it consists in appraising criminality as one would judge the safety of a means of locomotion. To determine whether criminality in France has grown or lessened during the past fifty years, it would have us proceed exactly as we would to determine whether the modern railway passenger travels with a greater or less degree of safety than did his grandfather of, say 1830, who made his journeys by stage-coach. Just as in the latter case we solve the problem not by comparing the

[1] *Poletti*, "Il sentimento nella scienza del diritto penale," c. VIII (Udine, 1882).

number of travelers killed or injured under the two kinds
of travel, respectively, but by ascertaining the number respectively killed or injured out of the whole number carried, so
in the present case, this theory obliges us to proceed by saying,
for example, that in 1830, for so many transactions likely to
afford occasion for criminal breach of trust, there was one crime
of this character prosecuted annually, while at the present day
there is one such crime to a different number of such transactions. Why not add, that in consequence of the greater facili-
ties for social intercourse and the more dangerous allurements
of urban life, the enormous increase of adultery witnessed
of late years is in no way surprising, and is really proof of
an actual improvement in feminine virtue?" [1]

A close examination of Poletti's argument shows that its
whole rationale is based upon a decidedly arbitrary idea,
namely, that to a given number of honest acts must correspond a proportionate number of crimes, and that this proportion is constant, except in times of crisis and social transformation. In his own words, "As long as a society lives under
equal and invariable conditions, the relative number of criminal acts will remain the same. . . . In its relation to the
social forces, criminality will in all cases adjust itself proportionately to the sum of their activities."

But where are we to go for this proportion? To France,
where the economic development is much greater, and the
amount of crime much less, than in either Italy or Spain?
To England, where criminality is constantly on the decrease,
notwithstanding the extraordinary increase in population, as
well as in commerce and industry? Or to some other country
of Europe, — but which?

Does this proportion vary with different nations and according to their difference in social condition? If so, then all comparison fails between nation and nation, and we are left wholly
without means of verifying the truth of the law which Poletti
thinks to have discovered.

[1] *G. Tarde,* "La criminalité comparée," p. 73 (Paris, F. Alcan, 1886).

The theory is untenable in another respect. It is impossible to compare the social value of a criminal offense with that of a moral economic fact. "It is wholly illogical," says Ferri, "to analyze and compare the respective growths of two such dissimilar activities with the aid of percentage and statistics alone. How can we be sure that a 600% increase of commerce represents proportionately three times as much as a 200% increase in crime? I am unable to accept any such theory. To my mind, an increase of 10% in the number of crimes is something of much more vital import from the social standpoint than an increase of 30% in the exports of cotton and cattle." [1]

"Both in its facts and the inferences which it seeks to draw therefrom," says Tarde, "the preceding calculation could hardly be more erroneous. In its facts, because it is not true that to a six-fold increase in crimes involving breach of trust, to a seven-fold increase of indecent offenses, there has corresponded a parallel multiplication of occasions calculated to give rise to such crimes. In its inferences, because, as it seems to me, with respect to criminal offenses as a whole, they involve a confusion of ideas. To continue my comparison, nothing is gained by demonstrating that railways are the least dangerous mode of travel, or that gas is the least harmful means of illumination. The fact remains that a Frenchman of 1826 ran less risk of meeting death by accident of travel, less risk of being burned to death, than does his descendant of the present day. Half a century ago there were fifteen accidental deaths for every 100,000 inhabitants; today there are thirty-six. This is due to the inventions of the latter-day civilization. Nevertheless, the average span of life on the whole has not been shortened. Indeed, I am aware that it is generally believed to be on the way to prolongation, but this is a notion which serious study of statistics has shown to be unfounded. All that we know is, that a man has now fewer

---

[1] *Ferri*, "Socialismo, psicologia e statistica nel diritto criminale" (Archivio di psichiatria, scienze penali, etc., Vol. IV, No. 2).

chances than formerly of dying in his bed, but quite as many of dying in other ways. For the evils which follow in their train, the inventions of civilization have also brought us remedies. So too, have they brought us remedies for the needs and covetous desires which they have created or aroused — incentives to crime as well as to industry. But however it may be compensated, an evil is an evil, in itself nowise lessened by its accompanying good. If the one can be wholly detached from the other, this is clear; if they are forever indissoluble (a supposition, it may be hoped, for which there is no ground), then it is still clearer. To me, it is of little concern that the safety of travel has increased or that the morality of affairs has improved, when the morality of men, be they travelers or merchants or what not, has deteriorated (or appears to have deteriorated) to the extent of one-half or two-thirds. In proportion to a given sum of affairs, it may be that the number of crimes has not increased, — I may even concede that it has diminished, — but does a French citizen today run less risk, yes or no, of being cheated or robbed than he did fifty years ago? That and not a mere abstraction or metaphor is the thing of vital concern. Can it be aught but an evil, a distinct and positive evil, that any class or division of citizens, however active or occupied, should now furnish a contingent to the criminal ranks thrice and six times its former size, — as witness the case of persons engaged in industrial pursuits and that of married women? And, granted that the development of commerce has increased in the ratio of more than two to one during the past forty years, can it be aught but an evil that in this space of time, the number of commercial failures has doubled? That this evil was far from being inevitable, in spite of the purely arbitrary principle which is Poletti's starting point, is clearly shown by the fact that a lesser evil, that of commercial litigation, has diminished since 1861, notwithstanding the continued growth of business. Civil litigation of other kinds, strangely enough, preserves regularly the same level in the face of the growing complexity of interests, the multiplication of contracts and agreements, and the increasing tendency to division of landed property. Yet, 'a priori,' what would seem more plausible than to regard the increase of civil or commercial litigation as a constant and necessary sign of prosperity, of civil and commercial activity? What is true of internal affairs is true of external. To civilization is it due that occasions of war were never so numerous or important as from 1830 to 1848 — the most peaceful period of the 1800s." [1]

Crime is undeniably an activity: it represents a sum of energies which appear side by side with the other energies of society. But because the sharper and the forger live among upright merchants, why should they increase in number, according as the rewards of honest trade are more easily acquired? Ought we not to expect the very opposite result? Does it not seem that the broader fields open to honest activity and the greater success which attends it, should constitute motives sufficient to attract thither a greater number of persons, many of whom no doubt would otherwise have found their source of income in unlawful expedients? When, therefore, we are confronted by the fact that notwithstanding a country's economic progress, criminality is increasing, although at a slower rate than the march of this progress, does it not seem fair to conclude that without the expansion of honest activity, the number of criminal offenses would have undergone a still greater increase? And such a result, of course, would be diametrically opposed to Poletti's conclusion.

It is impossible to believe that progress in civilization contributes to the increase of crime. On the contrary, we cannot escape recognition of the fact that, to the extent of diminishing the habitual development of crime, its effect is quite the opposite. The clear stream of honesty by its gathered strength and speed carries with it the waters which otherwise would have been drawn into the foul torrent of criminal activity.

[1] *Tarde, op. cit.,* p. 74 *et seq.*

At any rate, it cannot be denied that from 1826 to 1895 criminality in France (as in Italy and elsewhere) showed not only an *absolute* increase, but an increase *relatively* to the increase in population. In thirty years alone, from 1866 to 1896, the average annual number of felonies ("crimes") and misdemeanors ("délits") rose from 245 to 345 for each 100,000 inhabitants. This is the only proportion important to consider — the proportion of crimes to the number of inhabitants. The greater or less activity and wealth of the population count for nothing in determining the question of increase or diminution in criminality. If in place of ten crimes we find fifty, manifestly there is an absolute increase of crime. And if its increase surpasses that of the population, then it is equally plain that we have a proportional increase of crime. The relation in which its fluctuations or its tendencies to increase or diminish stand to the various social activities can be important only as denoting the influence which these activities respectively exercise upon the special forms of criminality. It can never afford ground for contending that the total number of crimes has diminished, when in fact it has increased.

Nor is it true that the increase of any species of activity is always attended by an increase in its abuse or in the faults incident to its exercise. Tarde expresses himself thus on the subject. "'It might be supposed' says Block, in his 'Statistique de la France comparée avec les divers pays de l'Europe,' 'that the increase in the number of letters carried by the Post-office (following the reduction of the postal rates of 1848), would have brought about an increase in the number going to the Dead-letter Office. Such however was not the case.' Then follows a table from which it appears that during the period from 1847 to 1867, the number of dead-letters diminished not only proportionally, but even absolutely, to the extent of about one-fifth, notwithstanding the fact that in 1867 there were 342 million letters posted, as against 125 million in 1847, — both the increase on the one hand and the diminution on the other having been gradual. . . . And it is

not to be supposed that the postal officials had become more
honest or intelligent, or the public more careful. With an
equal degree of honesty, intelligence, and care, the faults de-
creased, while the activity continued to increase. A further
example even more in point is also afforded by the Post-office.
In 1867 the number of registered letters was two and one-half
times as large as in 1860, yet the number annually missing
(that is to say, probably stolen) during these seven years underwent a progressive decrease from 41 to 11; nor is there any
reason to believe that the honesty of the Post-office employees
had in any way changed. If we were to adopt Poletti's point
of view, we ought, 'a priori,' to look for exactly the opposite
result. But in reality the matter is easily explained. If I
may be permitted a rather commonplace simile, I would compare a society always more or less disposed to transgress its
own laws to a horse, somewhat weak in its forelegs, and hence
ready to fall. To prevent the animal from falling the best
plan is to make him strike a faster gait. The faster he goes the
less he stumbles. This is a rule with which all drivers are
familiar. The engine-driver likewise knows the value of a
full head of steam on a bad track. The faster you spin a top,
the longer it remains in a vertical plane. These are a few
examples from among a thousand, of a mobile equilibrium
whose stability depends on the degree of speed. In the same
manner, if you stimulate a nation's production, its civilization,
its regular activity, then, always supposing that its propensity
to evil remains unchanged, you diminish the volume of its
crime. If, then, we suppose the number of crimes, in spite of
the progress of civilization, — and this unfortunately is our
own case, — to show, if not a relative increase, at least an
absolute increase, we are thus warranted in concluding that
there must have been a still greater increase in the force of
the criminal propensities."

Summary of Conclusions. — To sum up, it may be said that
the increase of a people's productive activity in nowise tends
to an increase in its criminality. Statistics show us that one

beneficent effect of civilization is to specialize criminality, to limit it to certain special forms, the practice of which becomes the peculiar industry or profession of the refractory classes. It follows that in a nation of a high degree of advancement, criminality tends to contract its boundaries and to become concentrated in a single class, as is shown by statistics of recidivism. But this movement of concentration is exceedingly slow; it will be accomplished not in the present generation, but only after the lapse of many centuries. In any event, it behoves us to take care how we bring any such charge against civilization as to assert that its progress is promotive of crime.

But we must not demand of it the impossible. Civilization does not create the criminal; it is without the power to destroy him. He existed before civilization, — for was not Cain his ancestor? He profits by civilization only to change the external form of his crime. Since the invention of railways, the criminal can no longer stop the stage-coach on the open road. But he adapts himself to the changed conditions: he becomes a passenger himself, travels in a first-class carriage, to all appearances a gentleman, and awaits a favorable opportunity to chloroform his sleeping fellow-traveler or throw him out of the carriage window. If criminality has increased in a large measure and in a proportion exceeding that of the population, the fault is not to be attributed to civilization any more than to the unequal distribution of wealth. For the causes we shall have to seek elsewhere.

CHAPTER III

INFLUENCE OF THE LAWS

§ 1. Legislation Affecting the Causes of Crime

FROM our last topic of discussion it is an easy transition to the question of the influence exercisable upon criminality by the law-making power of the State. But the problem itself is a complex one and requires us at the outset to distinguish between two classes of laws, namely, (1) those whose *direct* object is the prevention or repression of crime, and (2) those which, although aiming directly at another end, may nevertheless affect criminality in an *indirect* way. It will be convenient to speak first of the latter.

Modification of the Environment — Quételet and Lacassagne. — Is it not possible for the State to change or abolish certain social facts, certain institutions, certain modifiable conditions of the life of the people as a whole or of a given class of society — environmental elements recognized as the most frequent occasional causes of a great many offenses—and by this means effect a diminution in criminality? For if the moral imperfection of the criminal is always the necessary condition of crime, external circumstances are very often the causes which determine its manifestation. Some of these external causes are due to the physical environment, and this it is not in the power of man to modify. Every one understands the helplessness of the legislator in the face of climatologic and meteorologic conditions. But let the fact be social and not physical, and the cry is at once raised that the law-maker can suppress it if he will.

"Change the established order," exclaims Quételet, "and with it will quickly change the constantly recurring facts of which we complain. . . . Here the law-maker can fulfill a noble mission. By modifying the ambient in which we live, he can ameliorate the condition of his fellows. Let me breathe a purer air, modify the ambient in which I am forced to live, and you will give me a new life. However strong my moral constitution, it may nevertheless be impossible for me to resist the deleterious influences with which you surround me. . . . Your institutions tolerate, nay, even encourage, a multitude of snares and pit-falls, and if in a moment of weakness I suffer myself to be entrapped, then it is that you smite me. Should not your effort rather be to make less dangerous this precipice along whose edges I am forced to grope my way, or at least, to dispel the darkness from my perilous path?" [1]

Lacassagne makes a similar appeal: "To the immobilizing fatalism, which is the inevitable consequence of the anthropologic theory, rises in opposition the social initiative. If the environment, which is everything, is sufficiently defective to favor the development of vicious and criminal natures, then it is to this environment and the conditions of its operation that reforms must be directed." [2]

All this no doubt is very admirable. It is based, however, upon an utterly false notion of State omnipotence. It completely ignores the fact that society, like any natural organism, undergoes a development which is slow and gradual, a development in which the law-maker is a minimum factor. But what of the practical side of the question? Has this, at least, been approached? For if crime is a symptom and its cause is recognizable, it is the business of a good system of social therapeutics to deal with this cause, provided that it is capable of yielding to treatment. In this lies the whole question: What are the means?

[1] *Quételet*, "Physique sociale," Book IV.
[2] Actes du 1er Congrès d'Anthropologie criminelle, p. 167.

Romagnosi's Theory of Prevention of Crime. — Romagnosi, one of the greatest of Italian thinkers, referring the most common and constant causes of crime to defects in (1) *subsistence* and (2) *education*, — appertaining, respectively, to the economic and moral orders, — and (3) *vigilance* and (4) *justice*, — appertaining both to the political order, — was the first accurately to define the limits of governmental action in seeking remedies for such defects.[1] In his view, the action of the State in this regard must seldom be anything but negative. Destroying privilege and monopoly, it should allow the untrammeled expansion of commerce and the unhampered development of industry; it should put no obstacles in the way of individual enterprise, nor subject free labor to any species of tutelage. All this, he believes, can be brought about by prudent social and economic legislation and a wise administration of justice.

The only positive action which Romagnosi demands of the State, is the adoption and enforcement of iron laws against idleness, together with the active and unremitting surveillance of the dangerous classes of society. Idleness for him is a true social crime. To make it inexcusable, however, work must be given to all who seek it. "It is therefore necessary that the State provide work and wages, or else indicate sure and practical means of obtaining them."[2] With an optimism which is contradicted by experience, he believes that the number of seekers for this State-provided work would be inconsiderable, and would constantly grow less.[3] The expense, according to him, would be a small matter, but, he hastens to add, whatever its amount, the State is called upon to bear it, just as it must bear the expense of a standing army. "As the army defends us from external and remote enemies, so the establishments, of which we speak,[4] will defend us from internal enemies — enemies who dwell in our midst, attack

---

[1] *Romagnosi*, "Genesi del diritto penale," § 1021 *et seq.* to § 1155.
[2] *Ibid.*, § 1098.   [3] *Ibid.*, § 1102.
[4] *I. e.* public industrial establishments.

us from ambush and keep us in a state of continual alarm."

The last word yet remains to be said on this contention. Vigorously assailed by Malthus, who maintained that it contradicted the most obvious laws of supply and demand, and subjected to attack by many subsequent writers, it presents a question still unsolved in theory, possibly, as Fouillée suggests,[1] because of the opposite exaggerations characterizing the views of the socialists, political economists, and Darwinists.

"Manifestly," says this last author, "the State cannot undertake in a vague and general way to give work to all who apply, to furnish physicians with patients, lawyers with clients, and poets with a public: it cannot engage in business as wholesale ironmonger, milliner, cabinet-maker, or interior decorator. In a word, it cannot substitute itself for the individual, or artificially create employment for those who lack it. Nor can it artificially continue the production of a given species of commodity when the inactivity of the market announces an excessive supply.[2] On the other hand, the State should never grant assistance to able-bodied persons except under certain specified conditions, — in particular, to prevent increase in the number of indigent, that of abstention from marriage."

Proposals of Ferri. — These are serious questions, and their discussion would lead us too far afield. Apart from the question of State-provided work, Romagnosi's views can be easily accepted. But latterly Ferri has made an attempt to specify further instances in which the State should seek the prevention of crime by suppressing or making less frequent certain social facts which are ordinarily its occasional causes. He proceeds on the theory that it is the duty of the State to ascertain what sources of criminality exist among the institutions,

[1] *Fouillée,* "La philanthropie scientifique" (Revue des Deux Mondes, 15 September, 1882).

[2] *Fouillée,* "La propriété sociale et la démocratie," p. 134 (Paris, Hachette, 1884).

customs, and prejudices of the people, and having found them, to effect by special laws, their disappearance, or at least a diminution of the evil to which they give rise. "Throughout all its legislative, economic, political, civil, administrative, and penal institutions, from the highest to the lowest, it should always be the object of the State to impart to the social organism such an adjustment that human activity may be thereby continually guided in a channel directly opposite to that of crime. This it may accomplish by giving individual energies the freest possible hand and at the same time diminishing temptations and occasions of crime." [1]

To these means of indirect prevention, Ferri gives the name of "substitutes for punishment." It would be just as appropriate, remarks Tarde, "to call them 'substitutes for crime.'" Neither, perhaps, is right. It is difficult to see an equivalent of crime in a governmental action which, among its other effects, is calculated to prevent the manifestation of crime. And still less does that action strike us as an equivalent of punishment, for punishment is not called into existence until crime has been committed. But without stopping to debate this question of words, let us examine the practical programme which Ferri submits.

His plan involves nothing less than the complete making over of a whole system of social and economic legislation. He recommends establishing free exchange of commodities, whereby, he thinks, unusual advances in the price of breadstuffs would be obviated and many criminal acts, in consequence, prevented; the abolition of government monopolies, a step which in his view would result not only in the disappearance of offenses against the revenue laws, but also of many other species of crimes; and the removal of certain taxes whose existence is a source of continual agitation. Since the abuse of strong drink is a fertile cause of poverty, disease, and crime among the working classes,

---

[1] *E. Ferri*, "Nuovi orizzonti del diritto e della procedura penale," p. 376 (Bologna, 1884).

he demands, with Despine and Lombroso, the imposition of duties upon the manufacture and sale of alcohol. He proposes also the doing away altogether with paper money, and the use in its stead of gold and silver coin, with the object of making counterfeiting more difficult; the construction of inexpensive but sanitary dwellings for the working classes; institutions to provide care and assistance for the infirm poor; workmen's savings banks which by encouraging accumulation would tend to lessen crimes against property; wider and better lighted city streets, the effect of which would be to discourage nocturnal crimes of violence. Infanticides and abortions, he thinks, would be diminished by a popularization of Malthusian doctrines. He advocates better laws on the subject of descent of property, the acknowledgment of illegitimate children, and the ascertainment of paternity, as well as legislation providing for divorce and damages for breach of promise of marriage, all of which would tend, in his opinion, to counteract unlawful cohabitation, infanticide, adultery, bigamy, uxoricide, and offenses against chastity. With the object of rendering criminal bankruptcies less frequent, he would also reform such provisions of the commercial laws as relate to the personal liability of officers of corporations, the procedure in cases of commercial failures, the rehabilitation of bankrupts,[1] etc. Further proposals are the supervision of the manufacture of deadly weapons, so as to limit their use; the institution of juries of honor to prevent resort to the duel; the prohibition of pilgrimages; marriage of the clergy, suppression of convents, the abolition of many holidays ("fêtes"), the institution of public gymnastics, public baths, theatres, foundling asylums, the prohibition of obscene publications and accounts of notorious trials, the exclusion of young people from the spectator's benches in the criminal courts, and other like measures calculated to influence public moral-

---

[1] [In France and Italy, bankruptcy ("faillite"; "fallimento"), apart from any question of crime (see *ante*, p. 41, note 1), involves the suspension of various political and civil rights. — TRANSL.]

ity in general and to counteract certain classes of crime in particular.

Conclusions. — It is far from my idea to belittle the great utility of a wisely conceived legislation in the prevention of crime. But we must steer clear of the notion that the law-maker can work any such Utopian transformation as to effect the disappearance of temptations and the occasions of crime. Moreover, Ferri himself acknowledges that a large proportion of crime is due to causes quite other than those which we have just been considering, causes which lie out of reach of his proposed measures. Again, if it is the duty of the law-maker to concern himself with the effect of legislation upon crime, he must nevertheless not overlook other interests of equal importance. He is not to sacrifice all else in the single end of removing what are temptations solely for persons of criminal tendencies.

Following this general sketch of Ferri's plan, it becomes necessary for us to distinguish such of his proposals as have a bearing upon education or social economy, and tend merely to the reform of existing laws, from such as aim directly at stamping out the cause of certain specific crimes. The former are a natural and constant effect of civilization, and from them can be hoped the gradual moralization of the people and, resultingly, the diminution of vice and crime. As for the second class of proposals, their sphere of action is but limited, since they are concerned with a few criminal specialties. In this regard, Ferri proposes to remove certain existing restrictions such as taxes, monopolies, etc., and set up new restrictions applying to holiday celebrations, the retailing of liquor, and the like.

Now, if we abolish a restriction, it is evident that crimes directly due to its violation will cease. If we repeal all tariff legislation, there will be no such thing as smuggling. But, on the other hand, every new restriction will have its transgressors, and consequently result in the creation of offenses which before had no existence. And besides, none of these

restrictions which are thus to be removed or adopted at the
legislative will, in anywise concern the kind of crime which is
the sole object of our present study, namely, that natural
crime whose definition before appears. Smuggling, contraventions of special regulations, the purely political crime, the
fact which does not wound the altruistic sentiments — none
of these has anything to do with true criminality. Neither the
adoption of new prohibitions nor the removal of the old can
have any influence, direct or indirect, upon natural crime.
The tavern, for example, does not produce homicide. It is, to
be sure, a meeting place which attracts drinkers and gamblers.
Among these, quarrels may arise, leading to the exchange of
blows and sometimes culminating in the taking of life. But
almost the same thing may be said of what for the higher
classes is the equivalent of the tavern — the café or club.
Even here, dislikes and hatreds may be engendered, resulting
in insults and duels. Certain other usages and institutions,
which are indispensable conditions of specialized offenses,
are permanent social facts. If money did not exist, there
would be no counterfeiters. If there were no marriage, the
crime of bigamy would be non-existent. The same is true of
all the other economic, political, religious, and family institutions essential to social life.

It is therefore wholly useless to carry the question into this
field. Moreover, the proposal is only to remove the most
frequent causes of crime arising from certain ordinarily dangerous customs or usages which it is possible to limit or forbid
in the general interest. In respect of certain liberal institutions, Ferri agrees with other writers that the "first thing is
to see whether it is not a lesser evil to endure these institutions
with their attendant ills, than to lose all the good which they
undeniably bring. Especially must it be remembered that
as law is inseparable from society, so crime, the violation of
law, is always inseparable from the law itself. The abuse of
human liberty will always exist: all that can be done is to
reduce it to the narrowest possible limits."

The same argument might bear application to certain proposals of the author himself, relating to the economic, political, and domestic orders. Free trade, he believes, would prevent many criminal acts, as would the abolition of monopolies. True enough, but who, from this consideration alone, would counsel the State to remove its import duties or relinquish any useful monopoly? So too, the fact that enlisted men are not allowed to marry is no doubt a frequent cause of immorality: it is responsible for a great deal of unlawful cohabitation and the unhappy plight of many deserted women. Yet what government would forego the undoubted advantage of possessing an army which in its lower ranks is composed of men unhampered by matrimonial ties?

On the other hand, suppose that we had numerous such changes in law or custom. Could we be sure that the decrease in one specialized form of criminality would not be compensated by the increase of another? If you take away from the lower classes their holiday celebrations, will you not add to their isolation and thereby lessen their sociability? If their daily labors are not interrupted by an hour of careless pleasure, will their fatigues be as easily borne? Will they not become sullen, morose, perhaps even grow to hate their fellow-men, — a change in their character attended with new danger of crime? By authorizing divorce, can you legislate jealousy out of existence? Consider the rancor of the husband, turned away from his own door and shut out from the society of his own family. Finally, in view of the unconquerable resistance of inveterate usage, what assurance is there that such measures will accomplish what is expected of them?

As a means of diminishing alcoholism, Lombroso and others have advocated the imposition of very heavy duties upon the manufacture and sale of spirituous liquors. But this question cannot be decided in the affirmative without affecting economic interests which the State is bound to protect. Moreover, such measures are not always successful. Illustration of this is afforded by the French laws of 1871 and 1872. Although by these enactments the duties on alcohol were suddenly raised to twice the former rate, this did not prevent a continued increase in its consumption.

As Despine has already suggested, a means of directly preventing the evil produced by alcoholism, would be absolute prohibition of the sale of intoxicants. But it is vain to hope for any such reform in Europe.[1] It would be more feasible to employ a less radical measure, such as the fixing of a maximum number of liquor licenses for each commune, to be attained by gradual restriction. Holland many years ago adopted this course. Although, within the space of a few years, the duties had been raised from 22 florins to 57 florins per hectolitre, the continual increase in the consumption of whisky became a matter of serious national concern. From 224,885 hectolitres in 1854, it had attained the figure of 328,000 hectolitres in 1881, an increase from 7.08 to 9.81 litres per capita. In the campaign against this vice, "which not only was responsible for the moral and physical ruin of hundreds of citizens, but was also an evil which threatened family life and the peace and safety of the public," the Government took the initiative. For, "in view of the fact that to the State was entrusted the task of providing for education by means of its schools, of furthering prosperity by encouraging commerce, and of seeing to the public safety by the aid of its prisons, it would be strange indeed were it to be denied the right to make war upon one of the deadliest enemies of the same education, prosperity, and public safety."[2] In accordance with these views, a bill was introduced, passed by the Chambers, and published on June 28, 1882. By its provisions a maximum number of licenses was fixed for each commune. These were to be granted upon payment of a duty or license fee.

[1] I say in Europe, because many of the States of the American Union, beginning with the State of Maine, have taken the resolute step of prohibiting absolutely the sale of any kind of alcoholic liquor. See *Despine*, "De la folie," etc., p. 104.

[2] Report of the Minister (Moddermann). See *Drucker*,"Das niederlandische Gesetz von 28 Juin, 1882 " (Zeitschrift für die gesammte Strafrechtswissenschaft, Vol. III, p. 573).

The terms of the law were such that within twenty years from
its passage the plan would be in full operation. Penalties were
added for drunkenness and for encouraging drunkenness.
Six months of this law sufficed to show excellent results.
From 45,000 in 1879, the number of taverns fell to 32,983,
and the receipt of duties on whisky became less by 100,000
florins, while the consumption of beer and sugar exhibited an
increase. Holland has shown us what a firm and prudent
government can do to lessen the ravages of a vice whose
prevalence was such that a member of the States-general
could contend for the necessity "of allowing the workman
to take in peace his two glasses of 'schnapps' per day." [1]

Why not follow this example where the vice is more recent
and therefore more easily extirpated? In Italy there has been
a rapid increase in the number of places for the retailing of
liquor. Milan, for example, had 848 more in 1877 than in
1872.[2] Neither in the Roman provinces nor in those of the
South, does the consumption of strong drink attain large
proportions, but here the drinking of wine, while less harmful from the standpoint of public health, nevertheless, because of the excitable nature of the people, produces even
worse effects from the standpoint of public safety. It is responsible, beyond question, for many crimes of bloodshed.
Direct proof of this is furnished by the fact that in the province
of Naples the removal in 1876 of all restrictions upon the retailing of liquor and the consequent increase in the number
of wineshops were attended by an increase in the number of
strikings and woundings ("coups et blessures volontaires").
From 1,577 in 1877, their number rose to 2,191 in 1878, to
3,349 in 1879, and to 3,980 in 1888. Since the last-mentioned
year the number has continued to be very high. It would
therefore be a wise measure to impose a heavy license tax and
limit the number of licenses to a maximum for each locality,

---

[1] *Drucker*, article cited (at p. 580).
[2] During the same period, 1872 to 1877, the number of bottles of spirits
and liqueurs imported into Italy increased from 17,876 to 27,883. Archivio
di psichiatria, scienze penali, etc., Vol. IV. No. 2, p. 273 (Turin, 1883).

making interim provision for the gradual reduction of the existing number of retailers of liquor in a manner similar to that of the Dutch law.

But returning to the theory under discussion, it is to be noted that many of the other measures advocated by Ferri lie outside the State's sphere of action. Such are his recommendations that workmen's societies should expel members addicted to drunkenness, that healthful amusements be provided for the people at a low price, that the custom of paying wages but once a week and on Saturday night be discontinued, and that cheap and sanitary dwellings be constructed for the working classes, as well as his proposals for temperance societies, coöperative mutual benefit associations, workmen's savings banks, charitable committees, the admission of women to the practice of medicine, and the popularization of the doctrines of Malthus. With respect to all these measures, it is clear that if it is possible for the government to exercise any influence at all, it can be only of a very limited kind. Matters of this character are not the proper subject of legislative reforms. They all depend upon the natural progress of civilization, upon the development of thrift and economy — in fine, upon individual initiative. To say that by these means criminality would decrease is exactly the same thing as declaring that as a society acquires an increased appreciation of the value of labor, thrift, and good order, it produces fewer crimes — something which no one will deny. Even if the State were to set its hand to some of these reforms (that of Malthusian checks apart, since action of the State would be here out of the question), it is a matter of grave doubt whether its efforts would be crowned with success. Such interference, however, would be opposed by sound political considerations.

What, then, is here the true function of legislation and administration? In the prevention of crime, legislative measures of general application cannot go beyond the maintenance of a good police system, the wise administration of justice, and the indirect development of a public moral education which will tend to counteract certain vicious habitudes ordinarily the cause of crime. Upon these habitudes it cannot act directly except in some special cases, as in the regulation of liquor-selling, gambling, and the carrying of arms. Aside from such instances, the State should be careful how it interferes with the individual rights of the citizen. For notwithstanding the laudable object which moves it to act, its interference is bound to develop abuses, to degenerate into unendurable violation of personal liberty, and to be productive of new disobediences on the part of the citizen.

Schools directed by persons of intelligence and morality, lecture halls for the education of the public, agricultural establishments for dependent children, prohibition of obscene publications and immoral plays, exclusion of young persons from notorious criminal trials, restriction of the retailing of liquor, suppression of vagabondage, police surveillance of persons suspected of crime, good civil laws, and a speedy and inexpensive procedure — these are the only indirect means of counteracting criminality that fall within the scope of governmental action.

§ 2. Penal Laws

Having thus considered the practical value of indirect means of prevention, it is time to turn our attention to the question of direct means, or, in other words, to the problem of punishment. According to some of the writers on sociology, punishments are almost destitute of preventive effect, while for others they represent instrumentalities of the highest efficacy. Either side of the question may be supported by examples from history: on the one hand, of cruel and barbarous punishments which have signally failed to prevent the frequent recurrence of certain crimes; on the other, of severe forms of repression which have almost entirely stamped out the offenses at which they were aimed.

Criteria of Utility of Punishment. — In my opinion, the question is quite capable of solution if we remember that there are *different classes of criminals*. With this fact before us, it becomes plain that the *extreme criminals* — men wholly destitute of moral sense and capable alike of murder or theft — are not greatly impressed by the menace of imprisonment, whether for years or for life. They are too improvident, too brutalized, of too little sensibility, to appreciate the disgrace of the prison, or to feel the suffering, moral rather than physical, which loss of liberty entails. Yet they set store by their lives. For this reason, the death penalty alone has for them any power of intimidation. But its infliction must be swift and certain. When too seldom applied, it begins to lose its effect upon them.[1]

With respect to *impulsive criminals*, whether such from temperament, from neurosis, or as the effect of alcoholic excitation, it has been too hastily concluded that they are unaffected by the menace of punishments. Even the insane, as physicians assure us, may feel the effect of threats. Although in the impulsive criminals reflection is absent, yet there may be produced a counter-movement quite as independent of reflection as the criminal impulse, and due to the vague idea of an evil which impends, if they give way to their passions. But it is by no means the so-called punishments of modern legislation which can thus appeal to their imaginations. To produce the requisite impression, the threatened harm must be serious and immediate. If every one were convinced that to strike another with the hand meant the instant loss of that hand, many supposedly irresistible impulses would cease to be irresistible: perhaps the very word which describes this act would disappear from our active vocabulary.

It is no answer to say that the barbarous punishments of

[1] In the Italian Chamber of Deputies, at its sitting of 10 March, 1865, Conforti related the history of a case in which certain persons who had plotted a murder and robbery were frightened from their purpose by the fact of two capital executions occurring on the day fixed for the crime.

the Middle Ages were not more efficacious than the punishments of the present day. For one thing, we are without the statistics which would enable us to institute a comparison. Moreover, there was then a greater uncertainty of punishment. Numerous ways of escaping it existed, such as immunities, the right of asylum, and the protection of the great nobles. Then, too, the irregular working of the police system and the defective administration of justice in that day must be taken into account.

The case of *professional malefactors* requires to be envisaged from a different point of view. By offenders of this description, the chances of evading punishment are calculated with a considerable degree of accuracy. They boldly face the danger, because in this trade, as in any other, some risk must be run, — and there are much more hazardous trades which do not lack craftsmen. Yet here, as elsewhere, the smaller the risk and the more certain the reward, the greater the supply of recruits. But of this more in the sequel. In dealing with such offenders, therefore, legislation cannot accomplish much in the way of *prevention*. What it must principally aim at in this case is *elimination*. No laws, whatever their plan of operation, can be expected to cause the complete discontinuance of the work or the total discouragement of the workers. To diminish the number of offenders by suppressing those who are captured and convicted — such must be here the object of any really effective penal measures.

The value of punishment in relation to *endemic criminality* — due principally to social prejudices, to class customs, old and new, and to popular tradition — must next be considered. Here, particularly, from the standpoint of prevention excellent results may be accomplished by severity of punishment. A recent illustration is afforded by the rapid decrease of murder in Corsica. In 1854 two laws were passed specially applicable to the island, one forbidding the carrying of arms, the other directed against persons harboring or concealing bandits. Fifteen years of these exceptional measures

proved fully their wisdom. The disarmament of the whole
population had struck, as it was supposed, a decisive blow at
traditions which had been a constant source of bloodshed.
But unfortunately this legislation was repealed in 1868, with
the result that crime took on a new lease of life. From time
to time the magistrates in their public addresses have em-
phasized the fact "that the present situation suffers by comparison with that which existed during the fifteen years when
Corsica underwent the salutary discipline of being excluded
from the benefits of the general law."[1] In the province of
Naples, as the result of a special law which threatened
offenders with thirteen years' penal servitude at hard labor,
the practice of disfiguring young women with razor slashes
— the customary revenge of disappointed admirers — had
almost ceased in 1844. It recommenced after the adoption of
the Code of 1859, which provided for a much milder punishment, and its presence became especially marked after the
establishment of the Courts of Assizes. So numerous did
offenses of this description become that the Government was
obliged to take them out of the jurisdiction of the Courts of
Assizes and make them a matter for the Correctional Tribunals,
where trial by jury does not prevail, — for the double purpose
of saving time on their trial and ensuring more certainty of
conviction. But other difficulties have arisen. In the first
place, according to the Italian procedure nearly all persons
accused of misdemeanors ("délits") are entitled to provisional liberty,[2] and consequently to remain at large not only
during the judicial investigation ("instruction"), but until the
termination of proceedings for review in the Court of Cassation,
— and the convicted prisoner seldom fails to invoke the action
of the last-mentioned court.[3] This feature manifestly robs a

[1] *Bournet,* "La criminalité en Corse" (Lyons, 1887).

[2] [See *post,* p. 345, note 2. — TRANSL.]

[3] [CRIMINAL COURTS OF FRANCE AND ITALY. — The French and Italian
criminal courts are similar in organization, but differ considerably in respect
of the jurisdictional subject-matter of the several branches.

(a) *France.* — The general scheme of the French criminal courts consists

criminal prosecution of much of its terror.   Again, the sentences imposed are for terms of imprisonment much too short,

in a tripartite division answering to the tripartite division of offenses and punishments (see *ante*, p. 59, note 1).   "There are in France twenty-six Courts of Appeal.   There are an indeterminate number of Courts of First Instance.   There is in every commune one "juge de paix" at least.   Others are divided between two or more.   These are the French courts from which are taken the Criminal Courts as follows: The *Cour d'Assises* is taken from each Cour d'Appel.   It consists of three judges, one of whom is president. . . . The Cours d'Assises try by a jury, and the proper subject of their jurisdiction are "crimes" as distinguished from "délits"; but they also have a special jurisdiction in some particular cases, and if a case tried before them turns out to be a "délit," or even a police offense, they may deal with it. — The *Tribunal Correctional* is the Tribunal of First Instance sitting as a criminal court.   It consists of three judges taken from the Court of First Instance.   They try without a jury and have jurisdiction over "délits," that is to say, over offenses which can be punished with more than five days' imprisonment and more than 15 francs' fine, but not with death, "travaux forcés," or "réclusion."   The highest punishment which they inflict is five years' imprisonment, or, in cases of a second conviction, ten years.'   They may also in many cases try persons under sixteen for "crimes" punishable with "travaux forcés" for not exceeding twenty years or "réclusion."   Lastly the *juges de paix* are judges in regard to police offenses punishable with a fine not exceeding 15 francs, or imprisonment not exceeding five days. — If the "juge de paix" sentences any one to imprisonment or to a fine of more than 5 francs, an appeal lies to the Tribunal of Correctional Police. . . .   An appeal lies from the Correctional Court to the *Court of Appeal* in the case of all final judgments, and of such interlocutory judgments as have a direct bearing upon the final judgment. . . .   There is no appeal, properly so called, from the decisions of a Cour d'Assises. — All the courts, the Cours d'Assises as well as the rest, are subject to an appeal, as we should say, on matter of law only, to the *Court of Cassation*.   This court sits at Paris, and is composed of three chambers, in each of which there are sixteen judges. . . .   To use the language of English law, the Court of Cassation must either confirm the judgment appealed against or order a new trial."   (*Stephen*, History of the Criminal Law of England, I, pp. 517–520).

For all matters triable by the "Cour d'assise," after the prisoner has been held for trial by the judge of instruction, there must be a "mise en accusation" (analogous to our indictment).   "This is the business of the *Chambre d'Accusation*, a body which answers roughly to our grand jury, though they differ widely, both in their constitution and in their functions."   It is composed of judges from the "Cour d'Appel" and in fact forms a division of that court. (*Ibid.*, pp. 535, 536.)

(b) *Italy.* — In Italy the lowest criminal court is that of the *pretor* ("pretore").   His jurisdiction is much more extensive, however, than that of the French "juge de paix," since it includes, in general, offenses punishable with less than three months' imprisonment.   Above the pretor are the Penal Tribunals ("Tribunali penali"), the Courts of Appeal ("Corti d' appello"), the Courts of Assizes ("Corti d' assise") and the Court of Cassation ("Corte di cassazione").   The *Penal Tribunals* (constituting the criminal side of the "Tribunali civili e penali") have, in first instance, a jurisdiction embracing

and even these short sentences the pardoning power is too
ready to commute. The result wears the appearance of a
semi-impunity, and in the meantime the practice thus in-
effectively sought to be repressed has become so much the
fashion that there are villages in the neighborhood of the city
of Naples where a young woman of any personal attractions
at all has little chance to escape this manner of disfigurement,
unless she is willing to marry the first razor-wielder who asks
her.

Similar considerations apply to the reckless use of the
revolver. The exchange of shots in the streets and taverns
of Naples became a matter of such frequent occurrence that
here, too, it was found necessary to take the offense out of the
sphere of the jury. By treating it as a mere attempt to wound
("tentativo di ferimento"), or as the discharging of fire-
arms in a quarrel ("sparo d' arme da fuoco in rissa") and not
as an attempt to commit homicide ("omicidio mancato"),
the Government has conducted its prosecution before the

most offenses punishable with imprisonment of more than three months,
where the minimum which may be inflicted is less than five years and the
maximum not more than ten years.   In second instance, they hear appeals, which in certain cases lie from the pretors. Each *Court of Appeal* has
a division — the Section of Accusation ("Sezione d' Accusa") — answering
to the French "Chambre d'Accusation," and performing the same function,
namely, that of determining whether persons held for offenses coming within
the jurisdiction of the Court of Assizes should be put on trial.   Another
division of the Court of Appeal hears appeals from the Penal Tribunals.
The Italian *Courts of Assizes*, like the French, are composed of judges from the
Court of Appeal, and are the only courts in which trial by jury obtains. Their
chief item of jurisdiction consists of offenses involving a punishment of five
years or more in the minimum or (whatever the minimum) more than ten
years in the maximum. — Since 1889 there has been but one *Court of Cassation* for criminal matters.   This sits at Rome and has jurisdiction throughout the kingdom.   As in France, it reviews on questions of law only.   (Code
of Criminal Procedure, §§ 9–11; "Digesto Italiano," VII— 3, pp. 467, 475;
Mortara, "Istituzioni di Ordinamento giudiziario," p. 217 *et seq.*).
   In distribution, the jurisdiction of the Italian courts was materially affected
as a consequence of the Code of 1889 and the substitution of the bipartite for
the tripartite classification of offenses.   Prior thereto, it corresponded very
nearly with that of the French courts (upon which indeed the judicial organization was modeled), inasmuch as the Penal Tribunals (then known as Correctional Tribunals) heard most cases of "delitti" and "crimini" in general
were dealt with by the Courts of Assizes. — TRANSL.]

Correctional Tribunals. But the very fact of thus lessening
the gravity of the offense has led to its further encouragement,
with the result that in most instances it is innocent passers-by
who are its victims. And in the majority of cases the offenders
are let off with a sentence of a few months in prison. In
France the same deplorable consequences have followed acquittals of "vitrioleuses." In Scotland, on the other hand,
the practice of vitriol-throwing was completely stopped when
the British Parliament enacted, for that country, a statute
making the offense a capital one.[1]

In these and similar cases, the existence of the evil must
be principally attributed to the lightness of the punishment.
For here we are not dealing with habitual offenders who take
the chances of punishment as a risk incident to their trade.
Offenders of the present description are men who, although
lacking in the altruistic sentiments, become criminals only in
a given situation — a situation governed by a barbarous
usage which they do not find repugnant and which consequently they hasten to follow. But although urged to this
course by their instincts, they could quite as well relinquish
their purpose, if its accomplishment presented too many disadvantages. And a very serious disadvantage indeed would
be a punishment certain and severe — a punishment which
would be a life-long burden, which would overturn all their
plans for the future, and end with reducing them to an inferior
condition of life.

It is by no means a few months of correctional imprisonment
which is capable of effecting this result, especially if there be
taken into consideration the chances of a second judgment
on appeal, followed by a favorable decree of the Court of
Cassation, the criminal in the meantime being provisionally
released and left free to leave the country if he chooses.

It is easily understood that in such cases the severity of

---

[1] *Aubry*, "La contagion du meurtre " (Paris, F. Alcan, 1888). [The statute
referred to is 6 Geo. IV, c. 126, § 2 (reënacted in 10 Geo. IV, c. 38), relating
to the throwing of "sulphuric acid or other corrosive substance, calculated
by external application to burn or injure the human frame." — TRANSL.]

penal laws is not without its influence. Another thing which is important in this connection: What makes criminality endemic or imitative in a city, a district, or a nation is the fact that public blame does not bear sufficiently hard upon the offense involved. It is therefore for the law to show that facts of this description are not to be tolerated: upon it devolves the task of correcting the improper tendencies of public opinion. Far from allowing itself to be caught in any backward current, it must aid the moral evolution of the people: it must stamp endemic crimes not as trivial faults, but as reprehensible acts, abstention from which is vigorously to be insisted upon. And this end can only be attained by severity of punishment.

Plainly, then, it is not to be hastily concluded that severity of punishment is without any general or indirect effect. The question is solely one of distinguishing one class of offenders upon which its power can be generally exercised, from another which is able to feel this power in but a slight degree. The absence of morality, or even the presence of the criminal instincts, being much more prevalent than is commonly supposed, it is necessary to adopt such measures as will make crime disadvantageous and honest conduct the better policy. For that reason, it is possible for the mitigation of punishment to be a true source of crime.

Effect of Mitigation of Punishment in General. — When it is considered that in the first half of the 1800s criminality, in its more serious forms, had been reduced to no very alarming proportions, and that in the second half of the same century it underwent an immense increase in the very countries where punishments had been made less severe and of shorter duration, one cannot help reflecting that the first of these periods had been preceded by centuries in which capital punishment had been dispensed on a vast scale. And it is precisely the second of these periods which has witnessed the transformation of the penal system and that progressive mitigation of punishment which continues today, and is acclaimed

by the juridical school as a true mark of civil progress. Here
are the facts:

In France, from 1828 to 1884, the annual number of murders
("assassinats") increased from 197 to 234; of infanticides,
from 102 to 194; of indecent assaults upon children, from
136 to 791; of misdemeanors ("délits") specified in the
Penal Code and not the subject of special laws, from about
41,000 to about 163,000; of strikings and woundings ("coups
et blessures"), from 8,000 to 18,000; of thefts ("vols"),
from 9,000 to 33,000; of cases of obtaining money by
false pretenses ("escroqueries"), from 1,171 to 6,371; of
offenses against decency, from 497 to 3,397; and of cases of
vagabondage, from 3,000 to approximately 16,000. During
this time the population, which was 31,000,000 in 1826, increased only by 7,000,000, since it amounted to but 38,000,000
in 1884. It is thus apparent that the increase in criminality has far surpassed that of population.

Now, it is exactly in this period of more than half a century
that a multitude of punishments had undergone mitigation,
that juries had become more and more lenient, that the new
teachings of the correctionalist school had impressed upon
the judges the necessity of taking into consideration all the
circumstances which might tend to diminish the moral responsibility of the accused and then to strike, but to strike
in a mild and almost paternal fashion. Thus, by degrees,
punishments have come to wear the appearance of the dis-
ciplinary measures applied to unruly school boys. Indeed,
the former are much the less severe of the two, since under the
prison regulations no inmate can be deprived of light or compelled to undergo the temporary deprivation of food.

In the same country there has become apparent, since
1886, a gradual diminution of the more serious forms of crime.
The average number of murders per annum in the period from
1896 to 1900 fell to 183, that of cases of incendiarism, 196
in 1881, to 164, that of aggravated theft ("vols qualifiés") —
835 in 1881, to 636, and so on. In 1886 the number of crim-

inal cases tried before juries was 3,252. This number dropped
to 2,950 in 1889 and to 2,283 in 1900. As we have suggested
above, it is clear that the greater severity of punishment
has not been without its effect in this movement of decrease.

Nor can it be denied that the death penalty has a reflex
influence upon all the lesser criminality. The mere fact that
this punishment exists and is inflicted from time to time is a
check upon all men of criminal propensities, inasmuch as
they are not acquainted with the exact limits of its possible
application. All that they know is that the State has the power
to take the lives of certain criminals. They cannot be sure
that they do not fall in this class. Thus they become more
seriously impressed with the power of the law.[1] It may
even be said that the death penalty has most terror for those
whom it does not directly menace, that is to say, the lesser
criminals, the least improvident, the least brutalized, the least
incapable of subduing their passions.

A member of the Italian Chamber of Deputies, by profession a lawyer, in a speech before the Chamber declared
that on many occasions persons charged with inflicting wounds
had admitted to him that they would have killed the object
of their attack, had it not been for the fear of the gallows.[2]
I may cite a corroborative fact of which I myself was almost
an eye-witness. In the year 1884, in Santa Maria di Capua,
a small town in the South of Italy, three death sentences had
been pronounced by the Court of Assizes, at brief intervals.
Some days after the last conviction an inhabitant of the town,
seeing an enemy of his house pass in front of his windows,
became seized with an access of rage, grasped a rifle, and took
aim at the man. But suddenly he was seen to lay down his
weapon without discharging it, and was heard to cry: "You
may thank the Court of Santa Maria for reviving the death
penalty." Now, if this man had fired and had killed his foe,
he would have been punishable, according to the Italian law,

[1] See *Turiello*, "Governo e governati," c. III (Bologna, Zanichelli, 1884).
[2] *Chiaves*, at session of 8 March, 1865.

only by penal servitude, for his crime would have been culpable homicide ("meurtre") and not murder ("assassinat").[1]
In his excitement, however, he could not stop to make this
distinction; what vividly presented itself to his mind was the
recollection of the recent death sentences. And by this very
circumstance a human life was saved. Is it likely that he
would have had the same fear of the law, if it had been the
case,[2] and he had known it to be the case, that even for the
most extreme crimes the State could not punish except by the
prison or penitentiary?

Moreover, Italy as well as France has had experience in the
mitigation of punishments. In the old kingdom of Naples,
where the criminal laws were much more drastic than those of
modern Italy, where there was no trial by jury and no recognition of extenuating circumstances except such as were distinctly specified by law, and where the death penalty was
inflicted with considerable frequency, the proportion of criminality was much less than it is in the same territory today:
since the changes introduced by a so-called progress, the
increase of crime has been immense.[3]

The admission of extenuating circumstances — true of 80%
of the cases in which the accused have been found guilty
of taking human life — has resulted in homicidal criminals
and even murderers being let off with temporary and often
correctional punishments. — Is it possible that such a relaxa-
tion of criminal justice has nothing to do with the rapid
increase of crimes of bloodshed in Southern Italy? For my
part, I cannot believe so, especially in view of the fact that
this is by no means an isolated phenomenon. Throughout the
whole of Italy there has been a general increase of criminality

[1] ["Assassinat" = premeditated homicide; "meurtre" = intentional but
unpremeditated homicide. For the French law, see Stephen, "History
of the Criminal Law of England," III, pp. 93, 94. — TRANSL.]

[2] [The death penalty was not abolished in Italy until January 1, 1890, when
the present Penal Code went into force. See post, p. 201. — TRANSL.]

[3] Many of the more serious forms of crimes have more than doubled in
number, without any proportionate increase of the population. This last was
about 6 millions in 1833 and had attained little more than 7 millions by 1880.

since 1863, that is to say, since the mitigation of punishment began to make itself evident.

To this fact the following figures of judgments of conviction in the Courts of Assizes bear witness: For parricide, 12 in 1863, 22 in 1869, 34 in 1870, and 39 in 1880; for killing of the wife by the husband and vice versa, 15 in 1869, 38 in 1870, and 92 in 1880; for infanticide, 44 in 1863, 52 in 1869, 51 in 1870, and 82 in 1880; and for murder, 285 in 1863, 419 in 1869, 450 in 1870, and 705 in 1880. From 1860 to 1870, the number of crimes punishable by death showed an increase of 22%; the number of those punishable by penal servitude for life an increase of 64%.

From 1881 on, a tendency to diminution began to be noticeable. But it was not long before the legislature took the unwise step of abolishing capital punishment. Effective in 1890, this measure was attended by an immediate arrest of the movement of decrease. The number of homicides annually brought to the attention of the prosecuting authorities is still in the neighborhood of 4,000, and up to 1899 there was a continuing increase in the more serious forms of criminality.

In the period from 1891 to 1895, the average annual total of convictions for felonies ("crimes") and misdemeanors ("délits") was 254,591. During the subsequent three years, this increased to the alarming figure of 303,258. In 1885 we had not quite 800 convictions for every 100,000 inhabitants: today we have 966.

Nor is the phenomenon confined to France and Italy. It is observable in all countries where punishments have been the subject of mitigation. The increase has been very appreciable and far in excess, proportionally, to the increase in population.[1] In the German Empire, taken as a whole, during the period from 1882 to 1899, the common felonies ("crimes") and misdemeanors ("délits") underwent an increase of 42%.

[1] Chile, of which this is true, shows an enormous number of homicides. See *Newmann*, "Notas sueltas sobre la pena de muerte" (Santiago de Chile, 1896).

Similarly in the Austrian Empire, the annual total of felonies ("crimes"), which was 18,154 in 1861–65 and 27,304 in 1871–75, rose to 31,000 in 1896–98. That of misdemeanors ("délits") rose from 202,903 in 1871–75 to 306,007 in 1896–99. During the same period, the number of convictions for inflicting serious wounds ascended from 3,907 to 4,870, for simple theft ("vol simple") from 83,172 to 111,178, for criminal bankruptcy and offenses involving fraud and breach of trust, from 12,018 to 20,955.

It may be said that almost everywhere, throughout Continental Europe, there has been a general increase of criminality. In the most civilized of the European countries, it is true, certain barbarous forms of crime, such as arson and highway robbery, have shown a sensible diminution, but this has been more than offset by the increase of woundings ("blessures"), larceny, forgery, and crimes of fraud. In England alone, there has been apparent for many years an almost general movement of decrease of criminality, especially in its more serious forms. Homicide has there become very rare. In 1878 the average number of prison inmates was 20,833; in 1893 it had fallen to 12,178. Convictions for larceny and forgery diminish every year, as do those for crimes against the person. And England, be it noted, is the one country where the modern penal theories have exercised the least influence, where the murderer almost invariably meets the death penalty, and where other punishments are exceptionally severe. In France the similar movement of decrease, which became evident after 1896 and was still in progress in the year 1901, attests the efficacy of the more energetic repressive measures introduced in that country of recent years.

No doubt, it would be wrong to attribute the almost general increase of crime in Europe of the 1800s solely to the lighter impression produced by modern punishments. It is unquestionably the effect of a number of social and legislative causes. But punishments have manifestly become less efficacious. Not only is it true that their preventive power has diminished, but the notion that the typical punishment should be a temporary one, that, even in the case of criminal as distinguished from correctional convictions, a proper sentence is one which prescribes a short term of imprisonment, three or five years, for example — almost never more than twelve or fifteen — has resulted in all but nullifying their power of elimination. It is this sort of thing which enables the most hardened offender to become a recidivist, which makes possible the spectacle, not uncommon in Italy, of a man on trial for his second or third homicide. It is responsible, too, for the existence in all civilized countries of professional thieves and sharpers — offenders who will not cease their aggressions until compelled by some material obstacle and whom, consequently, it is farcical to release upon the expiration of their so-called punishments.

Crime as a Trade. — Tarde concludes his review of latter-day criminality with these significant words: "In taking on the aspect of a trade, crime becomes specialized. . . . The unfortunate part of it is that the profession of malefactor has become a profitable and prospering one, as is evidenced by the number of offenses and of persons arrested, even if we exclude recidivism and recidivists. . . . Upon what, in general, does it depend whether any species of trade is in a flourishing condition? First, that its revenues tend to increase; next, that its cost tends to decrease; finally, and most important of all, that there is a growing aptitude and a more frequent necessity for its exercise. Now, all these circumstances combine to favor that particular industry which consists in despoiling others. Its profits have augmented and its risks diminished to such an extent that in any civilized country the profession of pickpocket, vagabond, forger, fraudulent bankrupt, etc., — if not that of murderer, — is one of the least dangerous and most productive that a work-hating individual can adopt." [1]

[1] *G. Tarde*, "La statistique criminelle du dernier demi-siècle" (Revue philosophique, January, 1883).

The case is not otherwise in Italy. The emoluments are
most attractive. In a single year the pecuniary damage sustained by the public amounted to the sum of 14 million francs,
— which, moreover, does not include pecuniary loss arising
from criminal bankruptcies. This sum has therefore passed
into the hands of thieves, sharpers, and murderers, and but a
very small part of it has been recovered. As appears from
the records of the Courts of Assizes, in 1,372 cases of crimes
against property, in which judgment of conviction was
rendered, the juries' findings show damages aggregating the
sum of 2,458,000 francs.[1] Assuming that the total number of
criminals convicted is one-third more than of the crimes for
which conviction is had, this would give us 1,826 criminals and
consequently an average of 1,346 francs for each criminal.
But if it be considered that about 60% of those guilty of theft
either are never discovered, or else are acquitted for lack of
evidence, we cannot go far wrong in multiplying by two the
sum thus arrived at. The result, then, seems to be that from
a material point of view the trade of criminal presents many
advantages over most honest callings. It is attended by almost no danger, a minimum of work, and financial returns
which are all the more significant if we remember how difficult it is for an honest workman at any one time to command
a sum in excess of his weekly wage.

Evasion of Punishment. — The chances of impunity are so
numerous that the thought of prosecution and punishment,
unless aided by some other motive, will seldom deter from
crime. In Italy, as has already been intimated, the number of
criminals who escape punishment because of the failure of
the police to discover them, from lack of evidence to warrant
their trial, or from being wrongfully acquitted, may be computed at about 60% of the total number of crimes.[2] The

---

[1] Statistica penale del Regno d' Italia, 1889.

[2] Of the whole number of prosecutions, 30% terminate by an order of dismissal for lack of evidence ("ordonnance de non-lieu") entered by the judge
of instruction. In the case of felonies ("crimes"), we must add a further
proportion of 7.37%, in which such orders are entered by the Chambers of

offender (and, especially, the thief, the sharper, and the forger, since it is this sort of criminal who most often avoids detection) has therefore more than five chances in ten of going unpunished.   And this is true even where the offense has been discovered and reported to the police — something which in cases of theft, swindling, and criminal breach of trust does not happen once out of ten times.[1]   The risk of the crime being discovered is remote, that of conviction equally remote, and that of serving out of the sentence still more remote.   Following a judgment of conviction in the Court of Assizes, there is always the chance of reversal by the Court of Cassation, and of subsequent acquittal on a new trial.   There is the further hope that executive clemency will reduce or modify the sentence.   Again, for prisoners convicted by the Correctional Tribunals, there is an appeal, which stays the sentence and allows the provisional liberty, where that has been granted, to continue without interruption.   And if the Court of Appeal decides against him, the defendant may always carry the case to the Court of Cassation, and thus keep out of prison for sometimes a year or two after the original judgment.   Finally, when the worst comes to the worst, the offender, living in a large city where he is not widely known and being wholly free from police surveillance, can always find it possible to change his name by the aid of a forged birth certificate, which may be had for the price of the stamped paper,[2] and under the

Accusation and of 33% in which a verdict of acquittal is found by the jury. Then, too, it has been computed that out of 5% of reversals by the Court of Cassation, there is a proportion of 39% in which the defendant is acquitted by the remanding judgment ("d'acquittements dans le jugement de renvoi"). As for offenses cognizable by the Correctional Tribunals we have, first, 30% ended by orders of dismissal for insufficiency of evidence ("ordonnances de non-lieu"), next, 30% in which the defendant is acquitted after trial before these courts, and again, 10% in which he is acquitted in the Court of Appeal; finally, of the cases in which judgment is reversed by the Court of Cassation, 10% show an acquittal of the defendant on a new trial.

[1] *Minzloff* ("Caractères des classes délinquantes," — Messager juridique of Moscow, No. 10, 1881) estimates at 82% the total number of offenders who go unpunished.

[2] See on this subject, *Bertillon*, "Question des récidivistes" (Revue politique et littéraire, 28 April, 1883, — Paris).

protection of his assumed character of honest man he is safe
from molestation as long as he likes.

Futility of Prison Sentences. — It must therefore be admitted
that to get into prison requires much goodwill.[1]   But it is
also true that there are many individuals to whom this goodwill does not lack.   On the other hand, recidivists and persons
who at the time of their arrest are under police surveillance,
are not admitted to provisional liberty.   This is why the correctional prisons are always filled.

But for delinquents of this description, of what avail is a
sentence of three or six months' imprisonment?

Two Sicilian songs quoted by Lombroso, throw an interesting light on the intimidatory effect of prison sentences.   One
runs thus:

"Who speaks ill of the Vicaria,[2] deserves to have his face
cut to ribbons.   What a fool is he who says that the prison is a
place of punishment." [3]

And the other:

"Only here will you find friends and brothers, money,
good things to eat, and merry ease.   Outside, enemies ever
surround you; work you must or perish of starvation." [4]

Suppose that, as a punishment for some adventure of gal-
lantry, a man of the upper classes is forbidden to leave the
precincts of his club for a period of some weeks.   Here he

---

[1] Turiello cites the cases of the priest De Mattia who, having been admitted
to provisional liberty when his offense was regarded as a matter for the correctional courts, took to flight as soon as it was made a subject of criminal
jurisdiction.   As the author observes: "This circumstance proves that our
existing laws are ineffectual to lay hold of the rich or influential offender, save
perhaps in some clear and exceptionally flagrant cases" ("Governo e governati," c. III, p. 338, note).

[2] A prison in Palermo.

[3] "Cu dici male di la Vicaria
   Ci farrissi la faccia feddi-feddi;
   Cu dici cà la carcere castia
   Comu v'ingannati, puvireddi!"

[4] "Qua sol trovi i fratelli e qua gli amici,
   Danari, ben mangiare e allegra pace;
   Fuori sei sempre in mezzo ai tuoi nemici;
   Se non puoi lavorar muori di fame!"

foregathers with his most intimate friends. With them he can dine, play cards and billiards, and in general while away the time in most agreeable fashion. Nor do these friends think any the less of him for his fault. Far from it, they look upon him rather with feelings of envy. We can imagine what jest is made in that sympathetic circle of the foolish law which has thus thought to punish. And can any one believe that the fear of incurring again this same sort of punishment would in anywise deter the offender from resuming his ordinary habits of life and repeating the punishable act?

Now, the case is precisely the same with the habitual inmates of the prisons. They are furnished free food and lodging; they find themselves in the midst of companions and friends; they form new acquaintances which may be of use in the future. Nothing is heard resembling blame or criticism. On the contrary, the entrant who has committed a masterpiece of crime at once becomes an object of admiration — an admiration which contents his vanity quite as much as the prison bill of fare satisfies his stomach.

The same thing is true of the penitentiaries. After the fatigues and troubles of a long career of crime, the veteran offender makes no secret of his satisfaction in having finally achieved admission to so commodious a shelter.

Much has been made by sentimental romancers of the grinding toil exacted of offenders condemned to penal servitude ("galériens"). But I venture to say that none of these writers ever saw the inside of a penitentiary. The actual fact is, in Italy at least, that the majority of such convicts are engaged in nothing more terrible than knitting! Compare with this, in point of severity, the lot of the workman who sweats in foundry or rolling mill, or that of the peasant toiling under the burning rays of a midsummer sun, and say, if you can, that the expression "hard labor" [1] of the penal sentence is not the bitterest sort of irony.[2]

---

[1] ["Travaux forcés" in the original. — TRANSL.]

[2] "It is unquestionably true that, in its material aspects, the life in the

But grant that the criminal does suffer from deprivation of liberty, or at least from cellular confinement,[1] — grant, even, that the prison appears to him a real evil. What is the result? If an evil, it is one which he will endure with patience, with a sort of philosophic resignation. Regret for his own maladroitness in allowing himself to be caught will be accompanied by the resolve not to fall into the same error on a second venture. But will this transform him into an honest man? What craftsman will abandon his trade because of some incidental disadvantages, disadvantages with which he has long been familiar? Are there not plenty of honest vocations — even vocations for entrance to whose ranks men eagerly strive, — which are attended by the almost inevitable ruin of the workers' health or by continual hazard of life and limb? The soldier, the policeman, the fireman, are all at times called upon to face death in the discharge of their public duties. How, then, can we expect that the fear of a brief term of imprisonment will dissuade the professional criminal from continuing to exercise his lucrative calling?

On the one hand, there is the risk of encountering the evil — a risk which we know is very remote; on the other, the evil itself, felt but little, and hence but little feared. Judge, then, if the menace of imprisonment can mean anything for the man who is under no other restraint, whose reputation for honesty

penitentiary is for most of the convicts better than that which they were accustomed to before their arrest" (*Beltrani-Scala,* "La riforma penitenziaria," p. 294).

[1] Until 1895, the only cellular prisons in Italy were those in the cities of Milan, Turin, Cagliari, and Perugia. All the other Italian prisons were constructed on the old plan of common rooms. In many of them no means were provided for separating prisoners awaiting trial from those who have been convicted. Often many of the latter would be held a number of years before being taken to the penitentiary, with the result that not uncommonly their term would expire long before their sentence had been served out.

In France, in the year 1887, there were but fourteen departmental prisons built on the cellular system or adapted to its use, and seven in process of construction. The former contained in all 600 cells. On December 31, 1884, the total number of persons in detention was 25,231, of which number 10,087 were not provided with any species of work (*D'Haussonville,* Revue des Deux Mondes, 1 January, 1888, p. 135). The situation had undergone little change in 1892, there being then only some twenty such prisons.

— a thing of vital necessity in every social class — is already
gone, who has been publicly pronounced guilty of an infamous
crime. Terror of the word "thief" has the capability of restraining rapacious tendencies. But once a man has this brand
affixed to him, and is punished as a felon, generally all is over.
The prison may not, as some contend, create recidivism, but
at all events it does not hinder its creation. It follows that
the mitigation of punishments in respect of their duration is a
mistake. In the case of professional offenders, abridging the
term of imprisonment means increasing the number of offenses.
This has been experienced in Italy as a result of the various
proclamations of amnesty, which reduced by six months the
terms of all prisoners sentenced for a longer period, and wholly
remitted the punishment where sentence was for six months
or less. In each instance, a very perceptible increase of criminality throughout the whole of Italy was shown by the statistics of the following year.

Recidivism. — It is manifest that the universal increase of
recidivism is due to the spirit of lenity which at the present
day is everywhere prevalent. Since criminality is in large
part concentrated in a single class, its increase or diminution
necessarily depends upon whether or not the individuals of
this class find it possible to commit acts of crime. Moreover,
it is doubtful if the menace of even the severest punishments
of the penitentiary system can have any restraining effect
upon hardened criminals. In Sweden, for instance, it is the
custom for the sovereign to grant a pardon to life-convicts
after ten years of good conduct on their part, provided that
some respectable citizen is willing to take them into his employment. A life-convict of exemplary conduct for whom a
respectable citizen is ready to act as sponsor! Could one well
imagine a situation with better assurances of reformation?
Nor does this state the whole case. Pardon is here subject
to the condition that if the liberated prisoner offends anew,
he will be sentenced to *hard labor* ("travaux forcés") for life.
On the one hand, then, we have the presumption of reforma-

tion; on the other, the menace of a drastic punishment. Yet, in spite of "this sword of Damocles always hanging over their heads, the percentage of recidivism among this class of pardoned convicts is very high. In 1868 it attained the remarkable figure of 75%. In other words, out of every four prisoners thus pardoned, three, because of fresh offenses, were sent back to the penitentiary and compelled to serve out their life sentences under more rigorous conditions." [1]

This example suggests another consideration. Taking the total number of prisoners who, as shown by Italian prison statistics, were discharged from the penitentiaries in the year 1880, either because of the expiration of their term of imprisonment or because of being pardoned, we find that of 2,181, the conduct was good; of 583, fair; and of 172, bad. As to the duration of this good conduct in such cases, we are not informed. Moreover, the prisoner with us is not required to find a sponsor, as he is in Sweden. On the other hand, good conduct in prison consists of nothing more than quietness and obedience, and these qualities the object of securing a reduction of punishment would make it worth while to feign. But if any one be credulous enough to believe in the reformation of the 2,181 (three-fourths of whom would have been recidivists in Sweden), what can we expect of the 583 whose conduct was fair and of the 172 whose conduct was downright bad? It needs no prophet to predict their recidivation. Is it then to be wondered at, that in 1900 the recidivists in the Italian penitentiaries constituted 55% of the total number of inmates, — "proving," to quote the official report, "that the number of recidivations, which has long been the subject of serious concern, still continues to grow larger from year to year." [2]

In France, before 1885, the situation was the same. "From the fact," says Cazot, "that seven-tenths of the accused

[1] *D'Olivecrona*, "Des causes de la récidive et des moyens d'en restreindre les effets," pp. 46, 47 (Stockholm, 1873).

[2] "Statistica delle carceri," p. lxxx (Rome, 1902). From 35,958 in 1890, the number of recidivists in prison rose to 45,579 in 1895.

with criminal records have never received sentences of more than a year of imprisonment, the number of recidivists twice convicted in the course of one year increased from 6,851 in 1878 to 7,556 in 1879, the number of those convicted at least three times from 2,045 to 2,237 during the same period." Crime, when stimulated, increases. Now imprisonment, especially that of brief duration, is a stimulus to crime.[1] Short punishments invite the criminal, monstrous as it may seem, to mock the law, to snap his fingers at justice. For the hardened apprentices of crime, what is a few weeks' imprisonment? A happy accident which assures them lodging, food, and clothing — a breathing space in their life of adventure. Nay, better, in summer they arrange to be arrested in the North, in winter, in the South, "quite as people of fashion who spend August at Trouville and December at Nice." The vagabonds of Paris prefer to be taken into custody on Wednesdays and Saturdays because the dépôt bill of fare includes meat on Thursdays and Sundays. "Well may the workman shake his clenched fist at the jail walls and mutter: 'In there, are criminals who want for nothing, while I and my family try to live honestly, and find it hard to get enough to eat.'"[2]

The extremely large proportion of recidivists found by Ducpétiaux in the penitentiaries of Belgium — 70% in the period from 1851 to 1860 — proves, according to this author, "that it is the same individuals who continually commit the same crimes, and that criminality tends more and more to contract its limits and to become concentrated within a definite circle."[3] Indeed, the increase of recidivism in a ratio exceeding that of crime in general indicates that professional offenders as a class are multiplying and prospering, while, among the rest of the population, the diminution of crime is keeping pace with the advance of civilization. This hypothesis is borne out

[1] "Half of the discharged convicts commit new felonies ('crimes') or misdemeanors ('délits') almost immediately after leaving prison" (Rapport du Garde des Sceaux, — Journal officiel, 13 March, 1883).

[2] *Reinach*, "Les récidivistes," p. 126 (Paris, 1882).

[3] *Beltrani-Scalia, op. cit.*, p. 194.

by the fact that it is precisely in the most civilized countries that we find the largest amount of recidivism, — simply because in those countries criminality is in a greater degree confined to a single class of persons. Sweden, England, Belgium, and France have more recidivists than either Austria or Italy; Northern Italy has more than the Southern provinces. As one effect of a progressing civilization, the criminal offender becomes every day more differentiated from his honest neighbors, exhibits a sharper contrast to the population in the midst of which he lives and upon which he continually makes war — a war disastrous to the public whichever way victory lies, for the assailant, if uncaptured, lives on his booty, — if taken, he lives as a parasite.

This continual concentration of an army of common enemies should render much less difficult the struggle against crime. The disease does not affect all the members of the organism; the corrupt humors of the body do not enter the blood, but go to the formation of a superficial tumor. The situation is one which should readily yield to treatment.

France, in its legislation providing for the penal exile during life [1] of certain classes of recidivists, has recognized the remedy and resolutely applied it.[2] The other nations continue to put faith in the efficacy of their improved penitentiary systems, always repeating the same experiences and never meeting with anything but failure.

[1] ["Relégation perpétuelle" (or simply "relégation "). This punishment consists in internment for life in a penal colony beyond seas ("relégation collective"), or, by exception, in any French colonial possession ("relégation individuelle"). As distinguished from "relégation," exile to a penitentiary colony attending penal servitude ("travaux forcés) is called "transportation." — TRANSL.]

[2] From 1886 to 1900, 15,837 habitual criminals were thus banished for life. A few years of this legislation have sufficed to produce a marked decrease of criminality. As already seen, the more serious crimes have constantly diminished in number since the closing years of the 1800s. The system of anthropometric identification named after Bertillon has materially aided in the detection of recidivists. This system has been introduced in Buenos Aires, where it is in regular operation, thanks to the intelligent efforts of Señor J. Vucetich, the Director of Statistics. See his book, "Instrucciones generales para el sistema de filiacion " (La Plata, 1895).

"It is easy enough," says Tarde, "to throw overboard the thing that annoys you, but where are you going to draw the line?" True, there may be danger in this method as in every other, unless it is safeguarded with definite conditions and restrictions. And it is precisely the ascertainment of these restrictions and conditions with which we shall next proceed to deal in studying the theory of elimination.

PART III

REPRESSION

CHAPTER I

THE LAW OF ADAPTATION

"This preservation of favorable individual differences and variations, and the destruction of those which are injurious, I have called Natural Selection, or the Survival of the Fittest."

(*Darwin*, "Origin of Species," c. IV.)

§ 1. Elimination and Reparation: Theory and Applications

THE sense in which we use the word "crime" was defined at the outset of our discussion. It has already been made clear to the reader that crime in this sense — natural crime — stops short of embracing all the immoral and injurious acts which ought to be restrained by every civil society. Thus it excludes attacks, of a purely political character, upon the form of government and, in addition, all such legal disobediences as in nowise violate the altruistic sentiments.[2] Offenses of this description are to be repressed by the State quite as sternly as crime proper, but in so doing the State must be careful not to confuse the two. For the stamping out of these non-criminal offenses, it will employ punishments of greater or less severity as necessity dictates, keeping principally in view their intimidatory effect — their influence as an example and warning to would-be wrong-doers.

The Natural Law of Elimination. — Then, too, there are other immoral acts injurious to certain special aggregations, acts which violate the rules of conduct necessary to the exist-

---

[1] [§§ 3 and 4 = § III of original; § 5 = § IV. — TRANSL.]
[2] See *ante*, Part I, c. I.

ence of private associations with a definite object, be it religious, political, or artistic, or connected with the exercise of a particular trade or profession or the carrying on of some other branch of human activity. In such cases the intervention of the State is seldom found necessary: a reaction against the attack spontaneously occurs in the aggregation itself, and this reaction suffices to cancel the effect of the disturbance. Every organism reacts against a violation of the laws which govern its natural operation. The same thing is true of every aggregation.

This analogy will be of value to us in determining the manner in which, following natural laws, the State, as the representative of society, ought to react against crime. According to the concept which I have previously explained, natural crime is an offense sustained by the moral sense of mankind, taking this moral sense as we find it as soon as it has ceased to be the slave of the animal instincts or the ferocious and indomitable passions of the predatory life, or in other words, when it has reached the first stages of civilization. Besides this intimate, deep-seated, universal sense, we find a large number of sentiments properly appertaining to particular classes or aggregations of individuals and corresponding to the rules of a higher and more relative morality, or again, merely to rules of ceremony, etiquette, and good-breeding. Suppose that one invited to the home of a cultured family should exhibit defects of breeding incompatible with the habits of life of his hosts? What will the latter naturally do? They will take good care not to invite him a second time, and if, notwithstanding, he repeats his visit, they will decline to receive him. So, with somewhat more publicity, the member of a club will be expelled if he is found guilty of conduct unbecoming a gentleman. Likewise, the public official will be removed from office if he is found unworthy of the trust reposed in him. In general, it may be stated that if, by the violation of rules of conduct regarded as *essential*, a member has incurred the reprobation of the class, order, or association to which he belongs, the reaction always assumes an identical form, namely, expulsion. Mark, however, that I am not referring to *any* breach of the rules of an association. I speak only of a breach which offends the relative morality of the aggregation — the sentiments which are, or must be assumed to be, common to all the members of the association. The reaction consists in the *exclusion* of the member who is shown to be deficient or lacking in adaptation to the conditions of the environment.

A single fact, it may be added, often suffices to reveal this defect or lack of adaptation. Indeed, the particular circumstances in which a man finds himself may be said to constitute the touchstone of his character. Outside of these circumstances there may be no occasion for his defects of breeding or morality to become noticeable. The fact that in a single instance an individual has failed to govern himself according to the requirements of some fundamental principle of morality or good behavior is enough to warrant the inference that he subordinates either the one or the other to his own profit or pleasure. Now, there is a possibility that if he were placed under the same circumstances a second time, he would submit to the rule. But this possibility will avail him nothing. The presumption of his good breeding and honesty existed so long as there was no reason to doubt their presence, but it exists no longer, and he has now lost the confidence which this presumption inspired.

Elimination the Logical Form of Reaction against Crime. — If, then, we turn from the act which is an offense to a few people, to the act which shocks the moral sense of society at large, we shall find that the reaction can logically take place only in an analogous manner, that is to say, by *exclusion from the social circle.* Just as the family of refinement has expelled the ill-bred guest as soon as by word or gesture he has disclosed his social deficiencies, just as the private association has driven from its ranks the member who has failed to conduct himself as a gentleman, so society as a whole must cast out from its midst the criminal man whose single act has sufficed to make plain his lack of adaptation. In this way, the social power will effect an artificial selection similar to that which nature effects by the death of individuals inassimilable to the particular conditions of the environment in which they are born or to which they have been removed. Herein the State will be simply following the example of Nature.

Means of Elimination. — The first difficulty arises when we come to consider the means of realizing this exclusion from society. While it is comparatively easy to expel an individual from a definite circle of people, it is quite another thing totally to deprive a man of the social life. In the ancient world, each country was exclusively concerned with its own existence. In the case of capital crimes it shut out the offender from its own society: it gave him the alternative of death or exile.[1] Apart from the fact that this second form would be impracticable, because of the mutual objection of the nations, it seems today to be an insufficient form of reaction. For the sentiments of pity and probity, which first included only the family in their scope, and next included successively the tribe and the people, today extend to the whole of mankind. Crime is no longer looked at as an injury to the national sentiments: it is now regarded as a violation of human sentiments. To be adequate, then, the reaction must not only shut out the offender from his fatherland but also from the possibility of any social life.

Death, the ordinary means of intimidation or vengeance, has also been used in the case of convicted criminals and rebels, as the simplest and surest method of elimination. As an equivalent, recourse has been had to *transportation* ("déportation") which is a form of exile and the only one possible in the present state of civilization. But, like exile in general, transportation does not operate a complete deprivation

---

[1] At Rome as at Athens, the two punishments had the same end: "Capitalia sunt ea quibus pœna mors aut exilium est, hoc est aquæ et ignis interdictio, per has enim pœnas eximitur caput de civitate" (Dig. Lib. XLVIII, Tit. 1, De pub. jud. § 2; *Thonissen*, "Droit pénal des Athéniens").

of the social life. It could attain this end only if the offender
were to be removed to a place not only uninhabited, but
wholly cut off from communication with any human society.
Such places, however, are not to be found. We can hardly
imagine that there is an island in Oceanica past which a ship
does not sometimes sail.

Another equivalent is *imprisonment for life* ("réclusion
perpétuelle"). This, however, always leaves open the possibility of escape or pardon. The only absolute and complete
means of elimination, therefore, is *death*.

Without entering upon a discussion of the death penalty
in general, I desire at this juncture to anticipate a possible
criticism, not of my premises, but of my conclusion. "Crime,"
it might be urged, "reveals the man who lacks adaptation for
the social life. Deprive him then of society, but not of animal
life. The taking of life is an excessive reaction." To Rousseau, who believed in a natural state of man as distinguished
from the social state, this objection would have seemed well
taken. But at the present day, we cannot admit the existence
of any natural state other than a state of society, whatever
stage of evolution the particular society may have attained.
Death alone can deprive man of the social life. Set down in
the midst of the Sahara or the fields of polar ice, he will inevitably perish, unless he encounters human beings; encountering them, he will be a participant in a social life, however
crude it may be. Moreover, since social life is the object of
human existence, what is the good of preserving his animal
existence, if society shuts its doors against him? The fact of
irrevocableness, which opponents of the death penalty use
as a bugbear to frighten the unthinking, is in my judgment
the chief argument in its favor. For the reaction begins and
ends at the same instant, without leaving open any door to
false pity. Nor is it any answer to the main question to say
that inasmuch as "infinite forms of social life" [1] exist, there

---

[1] *Carnevale*, "La questione della pena di morte nella filosophia scientifica"
(Turin, 1888).

is no such thing as an absolute impossibility of adaptation to the social life, — that if the extreme criminals represent an inferior stage of moral evolution, they are capable of being assimilated to the savages, who are on the same moral level? How can we apply the term "social life" to the existence led by the cruelest, the most degenerate, the nearest the brute creation, of all mankind? If the idea is to make the savages a present of our criminals, well and good; but this would be no more than a disguised form of the death penalty.

It has already been explained why the punishment of death violates the sentiment of pity in appearance only, and it has been pointed out that if there is an identity between the fact of crime and that of execution, there is none between the sentiments which these facts respectively provoke.[1] But this statement is applicable only to a single group of criminals, to those who are entirely destitute of this very sentiment of pity, which is so organic and congenital in the normal man of the higher races, that the individual who wants it appears as a sort of psychic monstrosity and hence repels the feeling of sympathy from which pity is derived. In sundering, to use the words of Dante, "lo vincolo d' amor che fa natura," such an individual has placed himself without the pale of mankind. Henceforth nothing can re-unite him to associated men. It is therefore society's right to rid itself of his presence.

On the other hand, the moral sense of mankind will not tolerate the application of the death penalty to offenders of other categories, — to those whose nature does not appear entirely inexplicable, whose psychic anomaly is less pronounced, who, in fine, although differing from the normal man, fall short of being psychic monstrosities. Such are the offenders of the two classes which we have distinguished from that of the extreme criminals.[2] The first of these classes is characterized by an insufficient measure of the sentiment of pity. Its members, as we have explained, are persons without any great repugnance to crime, who are capable of committing

[1] See *ante*, Part I, c. i, § 8.   [2] See *ante*, Part II, c. i, § 6.

criminal acts under the influence of social, political, or religious prejudices, or who may be impelled to such acts by a
passionate temperament or alcoholic excitation. In the second
class are comprised offenders who are destitute of probity,
a sentiment of more recent origin than pity, less enrooted in
the organism, and due not only to heredity, but also, in great
part, to tradition and the examples of the family circle and
the environment in general. So that, even when the absence
of this sentiment is complete, these men appear to us as the
evil products of society rather than of nature, as unfortunates
rather than monsters. Despite the lacunæ in their moral
instincts, they do not cease to be our fellows, and, although
they are a source of harm, we cannot reconcile ourselves to
the idea of taking their lives as a means of eliminating them
from the social life.

This is a lesson which history teaches. The laws of Draco
were repealed immediately upon the termination of his archon-
tate, in deference to the public conscience, which had been
wounded by these laws more than by the offenses at which
they were aimed. So too, in later times, irrespective of its
being sanctioned by law, the death penalty has always excited
public indignation when inflicted for offenses not seriously vio-
lating the moral sense. This revolt of the popular conscience
admits of easy explanation. Man is by nature a social being.
Without having entered into any compact with society, he
forms a part of it. He is there because he has nowhere else
to go, and whatever he may do, he must stay there, except in
one instance. That instance is where he presents anomaly
such as deprives him of the capability of becoming a social
being and consequently renders his adaptation impossible.
This is why, in human society, the absence of the qualities
essential to the aggregate existence changes the necessity of
social life into the opposite necessity, namely, that of severing
every bond of union with the inassimilable individual. And
it is precisely into this idea of necessity that the idea of law
resolves itself. The individual has a right to the social life

because he has absolute need of it. But his personal necessity in this regard must be subordinated to the necessities of society. Metaphorically speaking, the individual represents but a cell of the social body.[1] Consequently, when he is a source of harm to the body, he can have no right longer to remain a part of it.

But let the reader not misunderstand. Such a necessity does not exist in every case of offense to the moral sentiments of the aggregation. It exists only where their violation is the symptom of a permanent psychologic anomaly which renders the subject forever incapable of the social life. Now, this sort of incapacity cannot be predicated of other than criminals of our first class — those offenders, who, as pointed out in a former place, are prone to commit murder solely from egoistic motives — the influence of prejudices or the faults of the environment in nowise contributing. In none of the other classes does this absolute incapacity exist. To apply the death penalty to members of the latter classes would cause the public conscience to revolt. Hence it is to be employed only against criminals of the first class.

For the others, adaptation is always possible, but the difficulty is to find the environment which will make it probable. We encounter individuals who are incompatible with any civilized environment. Their savage instincts are incapable of yielding obedience to the rules of pacific activity. They are fit only for the life of nomadic hordes or primitive tribes. To protect society against them, but two means exist: imprisonment for life or permanent expulsion. In many cases the first method would be an excess of cruelty. If a nation possesses colonies, lands still uninhabited, the second method would be

---

[1] In this view of the case lies the complete answer to the suggestion of *De Aramburu* that the principle contended for serves only to establish the right of might, the power of the majority ("La nueva ciencia penal" — Madrid, 1887). For this is very far from being true. We are here concerned with neither might nor numbers. It is not a case of one part being destroyed by the other parts, but of an organism ridding itself of a noxious element — an entirely different matter.

the preferable one. For in such surroundings his evil activity would stand the offender in no stead, while the necessity of preserving life would be a continual stimulus to labor, which would thus become an indispensable condition of his existence. *Transportation* ("déportation") is therefore the means of elimination necessary in the case of professional thieves, vagabonds, and habitual offenders in general. Only in these entirely new conditions of existence will their adaptation to the social life become possible — a conclusion which is borne out by numerous historical examples.[1]

With respect to offenders who lack repugnance to acts of cruelty, but who commit such acts only under the influence of their environment, as, for example, the authors of endemic crimes, it is evident that the elimination to be aimed at should not be absolute but should be limited by conditions of time and place. Here *internment in a penal colony or settlement beyond seas* ("relégation") is the appropriate form. While it takes the individual out of his deleterious environment, it does not, like the prison, degrade him or destroy his activity.

In the case of youthful offenders whom there is still a possibility of reclaiming to honest activity, the elimination should always be *relative*. For such persons the agricultural colonies of Northern Europe have worked wonders. French experiments in this direction have also been attended with favorable results.[2]

Finally, there are cases where elimination need not go beyond the *expulsion of the offender from his particular social situation*. Thus, he may be permanently prohibited from exercising the profession of which he has rendered himself unworthy, or deprived of the civil or political rights which he has made the subject of abuse.

We have here a number of methods of elimination not less logical than that of absolute exclusion of the criminal from all

[1] See *Reinach*, "Les récidivistes" (Paris, 1882).

[2] For a description of these colonies, see *D'Olivecrona*, "Des causes de la récidive," pp. 167–190 (Stockholm, 1873).

social relations. All depends on the greater or less possibility of adaptation to a given environment and upon the conditions which render this adaptation probable.

Enforced Reparation as a Form of Repression. — In descending the scale of criminality, we come to a class of offenders whose moral anomaly is hard to define. Although guilty of crime, of true natural crime, and hence inferior beings, they cannot be said to lack moral sense. The fact of their crime, it is true, demonstrates the insufficiency of one of the altruistic sentiments, but this fact has been chiefly due to the force of really exceptional circumstances, or to the pressure of a situation which is not likely to recur. Suppose, for example, that a criminal breach of trust is committed by a man who had hitherto followed an honest calling and been in the receipt of an adequate income. Nothing in his previous conduct, let us say, or in his conditions of life, appears in any way to be capable of impelling him to crime. Yet it will not do to say, because of this fact, that we are here dealing with a normal man. Hardly anything could be more inaccurate, in my opinion, than the adage: "Occasion makes the thief." To be true, the phrase should be: "Occasion enables the thief to steal." For a deficiency in the innate sentiment of justice or, more exactly, in the instinct of probity, is in all cases an indispensable condition of every crime against the property of others. Nevertheless, if the occasion has been an exceptional one, if there is little likelihood of its future recurrence, there is no need of employing any means of elimination. For the fact that the individual in question, in spite of his fundamental lack of honesty, has successfully resisted ordinary occasions, has yielded but once and then to an occasion which in all probability he will never again encounter, leads us to conclude that he is not a continual danger to society. Especially will this be the case, if his offense is made a distinct source of detriment to him, if besides losing what he had hoped to gain by breaking the law, he sees himself obliged to suffer the loss of money out of his own pocket.

This result will be attained by compelling the offender to make good the material and moral damage caused by his crime. He may be made to pay its amount in money, or else to work for the benefit of the injured person until restitution is effected. Such a measure could be adopted in the case of ordinary larceny ("vol non qualifié"), certain species of criminal fraud, criminal bankruptcy, wilful injuries to property ("dégât volontaire a la propriété," "dévastation"), setting fire to crops and to growing timber, strikings and woundings ("coups et blessures") in the course of a quarrel, defamation ("diffamation"), the use of insulting language ("injures"), minor offenses against chastity, and the like, when the same conditions surround the commission of the crime as in the case before put, that is to say, when neither the past or present conduct of the offender nor his conditions of life are such as foreshadow a relapse into crime. If the injury is reparable and the offender is willing to make reparation, elimination would be both needless and cruel.

We have thus what appears to be a new form of repression: *enforced reparation.* It is a means which will prove sufficient in many cases, provided that the reparation is full and complete and that the assessment of damages is made to include not only the material injury but also the mental suffering occasioned to the injured person. The injury, however, is not confined to the latter. Society as a whole suffers both moral and material injury — moral injury from the fact of the crime, material injury because of the expense of the police and the courts, which the public is called upon to defray. The reparation then must not stop with the indemnification of the injured person: it is necessary that a fine be paid to the State. Under such conditions, reparation in frequent instances could be very advantageously substituted for elimination. But for the enforcement of this measure some means much more effective than the present procedure will have to be devised. There must be a sure method of preventing the offender, if solvent, from evading payment, or, if in a state of insolvency, real or feigned, of forcing him to devote his labor to the benefit of the injured person.

Spencer's Theory of Restitution and Liberation. — The present theory amounts, in effect, to a narrowing of that outlined by Herbert Spencer. The distinguished philosopher proposed to make the time it would take the offender to repair the damage occasioned by his crime determine the length of his punishment. Upon making restitution, he would be discharged from confinement, provided that some person of good character and means would give bail for his good behavior. In this way, according to Spencer, we would have "a self-acting regulator of the period of detention." Persons convicted of "heinous crimes" would never be able to find liberators, and hence would remain in prison for life. For second offenders, the finding of the requisite bail would be a matter of considerable difficulty. On the other hand, individuals guilty of but trivial transgression, whose previous reputation had been good, could easily procure the proper surety, and thus, after having repaired the damage, obtain their immediate release from custody.[1]

The fault of this theory, in my judgment, is that it overlooks the general principles of the very philosophy of which Spencer is the exponent. If the latter had thought of applying to criminality the laws of adaptation and selection, he would have immediately realized the necessity of classifying criminals according to their psychologic characteristics, of distinguishing them so as to ascertain, on the one hand, the cases in which adaptation is possible and, on the other, those in which no hope of adaptation being left, it is merely a question of ridding society of an injurious element. Had he proceeded thus, he would have perceived, in many cases, the need of an *absolute elimination* from all social environment, in others, that of a *relative elimination.* Since this need is one which criminology is quite capable of determining, any such demonstration of it

[1] *Herbert Spencer,* "Essays Scientific, Political, and Speculative," "Prison-Ethics," in Vol. III.

as would be afforded by the failure of a person of good
character to come forward in behalf of the offender would
be wholly superfluous.   It is Spencer's belief that persons
guilty of "heinous crimes" will be wholly unable to find
liberators.   But he does not give us any criterion by which
we may distinguish heinous crimes.   Then, too, there is always
a lenient minority: there are places where no convict, whatever his crime, would be long without the required sponsor.
Moreover, friendship, as every one knows, is ever ready to
condone even the gravest fault.   And where friendship falters,
money will always prevail.   The bail, it is true, is to be furnished by persons of good character.   But where does good
character begin and where does it end?   I have no doubt that
in the business world every man who makes a fair living and
is without a criminal record, would be regarded as a person of
good character.   It is further true that, in certain cases, the
liberation in question may be withheld: "No bail could com-
pensate for murder; and therefore against this, and other
extreme crimes, society would rightly refuse any such guarantee, even if offered, which it would be very unlikely to be." [1]
But what are the extreme crimes to which the author has reference?   This expression seems to presuppose a distinction which
he does not make, or which, at least, is not his point of departure.   Does it intend such crimes as the rape of a female
child, the wilful infliction of cruel physical injuries ("sévices"),
mayhem ("mutilations"), woundings occurring without warning and as the result of premeditation, or robbery with a
deadly weapon?   But should it not also include all other
offenses which equally reveal the deep-seated, incurable
immorality of the agent?   We believe that it should.   In a
word, it is of the highest importance to single out a class of
criminals whose adaptation to the social life, if not impossible,
is, at least, of so little probability, that society cannot unques-
tioningly suffer them to remain a part of itself, but has the
right and even the duty to effect their elimination with all
possible speed.   [1] *Op. cit.*

§ 2. The Same : In Relation to the Different Conceptions of Punishment

The notions involved in the preceding view of social reaction against crime are present in the basic consciousness of all civilized peoples.   Although the apparent end of punishment is social vengeance, that is to say, the desire of making the offender suffer a harm approximately equal to that of which he has been the cause, it is easy to see that what society actually desires is, first, to exclude the criminal from its midst, and, secondly, to compel him as far as possible to repair the evil which his offense has occasioned.

Vengeance. — All punishment undoubtedly originated in individual sentiments of vengeance.   The law of the talion is there to prove it.   But today these sentiments, while still persisting, have acquired a much milder character.   This result in no inconsiderable degree is due beyond question to the moral teachings of the Gospel.   What has chiefly effected the minimization of these sentiments, however, is the fact that for generations men have been accustomed to see the offender punished by the social power.   This is why these sentiments reappear in all their pristine ferocity, in lands where the laws are of insufficient severity or else are laxly enforced. Especially do they come to light in the lower social strata, in the classes which in respect of the moral sentiments remain unaffected by the slow working of the centuries and are laggards in the march of moral progress.

Expiation. — Among some ancient peoples the idea of equivalence to the injury was ennobled by associating with it that of expiation.   The same thing characterizes certain modern theories.   The belief is that the harm caused by the offense cannot be repaired, even in the soul of the offender himself, except by means of suffering on his part.   Suffering alone can purify the wicked: it is the necessary consequence of sin.   Suffering contributes to the repentance of those who experience remorse, and gives rise to this sentiment in those

who are without it. Such is the conception of punishment
found among the ancient Semites and the Hindus, a conception which prevailed in the ecclesiastical law and throughout
the Middle Ages, and which had its highest scientific expression in the philosophy of Plato and Kant.

At the present day, however, this doctrine can find no
place. The hypothesis upon which it rests is contradicted by
experience. It is generally recognized that in criminals the
faculty of repentance and remorse is almost non-existent, and
that, in any event, it cannot be originated by the infliction
of physical suffering. The only individual who can commit
crime, is the man who has not kept abreast of other men,
either because his moral sense has always been lacking,
or else because it has failed him at a particular juncture.
No other hypothesis is possible. It is evident that if the
common morality had exerted any influence over this man,
he could not have become an offender. In every such case,
then, we have to do with a permanent or transitory anomaly.
The idea of moral expiation by means of punishment, that is
to say, through suffering to be undergone by the offender, proceeds on the assumption that the latter thinks and feels as the
generality of men, and in spite of this fact, has voluntarily
committed the crime to gratify his passions. But note the
obvious antinomy. If passion has overcome duty, it is because duty was not strong enough to overcome passion:
in any struggle, it is always the weaker which succumbs.
It is manifest, then, that the morality of the offender is lacking
in energy or, at least, is inferior to that which commonly
prevails. This is why he feels and thinks differently from the
normal man. The absence or weakness of a sentiment we can
try to remedy by education, or when that appears impossible,
by impeding the acts which this absence or weakness
occasions. But it is inconceivable that the social suffering
can be morally compensated or neutralized by any suffering
which the offender himself is made to undergo. One evil,
in other words, cannot be repaired by another.

The expression is still sometimes heard in the common speech, that blood is washed out by blood. But this is an idea which embodies the sentiment of revenge: it is something quite other than the mystic concept of moral expiation. The latter is derived from the fact of remorse which is produced in an unperverted conscience, a conscience, that is to say, still accessible to the moral sentiments; these after having remained latent for a time, come to light anew and give rise to repentance. Thereby is occasioned a state of sorrow, a true state of suffering, which sometimes lasts while life endures and saddens every waking moment. But the idea that such feelings can be aroused by physical suffering is a strange one. It recalls the belief of the Hindus that water could wash away the stains of the soul, or the doctrine prevailing in the Church of the Middle Ages that heresy was purged by fire.

No doubt, the punishment suffered by the offender sometimes brings about repentance, because he knows that his crime is the cause of his suffering. But between this sort of repentance and remorse for having caused harm to others, there is an immeasurable gulf. Only upon the latter sentiment can moral expiation be founded. And this sentiment is one which needs no physical suffering to produce it. It may indeed exist contemporaneously with physical suffering but purely as an accident.

Elimination a Demand of Public Sentiment. — However slight be the stress laid upon the idea of expiation, it becomes plain how difficult it is completely to dissociate it from the idea of vengeance for crime, the basis of which, manifestly, is the desire to inflict suffering upon him who has been the cause of suffering. Nor can it be denied that even among the most civilized people punishment seems to be the expression of social vengeance, that is to say, the returning of evil for evil. The criminal offender, undeniably, is the object of universal hatred and indignation. And necessarily so, because the organic conditions that explain the anomaly

to which the crime is due, are a subject for the study of
scientific specialists and cannot well be a matter of popular
knowledge. Moreover, even if hatred disappears from the
minds of those who know the causes, another sentiment not
very dissimilar will take its place, namely, repugnance —
a feeling of aversion for a maleficent being who is unlike
other men. But whether hatred or repugnance, the result
is the same: there is the same desire to be delivered from
possible contact or relationship with such an individual.
If his disappearance can be effected, that is sufficient. A
civilized people will no longer tolerate unnecessary cruelty
in punishing. Tortures such as were inflicted upon Damiens [1]
would not be countenanced today: even in the 1700s the circumstances of his execution aroused the indignation of the
people of Paris. If the death penalty still exists, it is because
it is the only complete, absolute, and irrevocable means of
elimination that we have at command. Were it possible to
find another of equal efficacy, which would spare the offender's
life, we may be sure that it would be speedily adopted. The
moral sense, basically injured, cannot consent that the man
who, in an egoistic end, either has destroyed or has shown himself capable of destroying his fellow-man, shall longer participate in the social life. When the news of some atrocious crime
reaches us, the first thing we inquire is whether the perpetrator has been arrested. Nor do we omit this question, even if
the circumstances convince us that there is no danger of his
taking to flight. Public opinion, the true public opinion and
not that of legal theorists, demands that the thief, the murderer, the forger, when there is reasonable probability of his
guilt, shall be immediately separated from society, and this

---

[1] [Robert François Damiens, who, in 1757, attempted the assassination
of Louis XV of France. "He was condemned as a regicide, and sentenced
to be torn in pieces by horses in the Place de Grève. Before being put to death
he was barbarously tortured with red-hot pincers, and molten wax, lead,
and boiling oil were poured into his wounds. After his death his house was
razed to the ground, his brothers and sisters were ordered to change their names,
and his father, wife, and daughter were banished from France." (7 Encyc.
Brit., 11th ed., p. 788). — TRANSL.]

without waiting for the fact of his guilt to be legally determined. To see him free and master of his fate, pending the
result of the proceeding against him, is a thing repugnant to
the moral sense. And precisely for this reason, imprisonment
pending trial ("prison préventive") is an institution which
still exists and will always continue to exist, despite the contrary views of certain doctrinaires whose habit it is to consider
all the social problems in the same superficial and one-sided
fashion.

Since, then, segregation and elimination are in point of fact
realized by punishment, society demands that punishment
be applied, and since punishment necessarily is painful,
suffering is necessarily involved. So far is this true, that the
law in nowise changes the punishment, even where the offender
has committed the crime for the sole purpose of incurring the
punishment. Men are known to kill so as to be put out of
existence themselves, or to steal for the sake of gaining
entrance to the shelter and idle life of the prison. Although,
in such cases, death on the gallows or a term of imprisonment
does not represent an evil for the offender, it is nevertheless
applied, and society is quite as well satisfied, as if the punishment had been dreaded and detested by the offender. Suffering, therefore, is not the end of the reaction demanded by
public sentiment, but in the nature of things is always associated with the real end, namely, elimination of the inassimilable individual.

Public sentiment thus coincides with the rational method
of social reaction and, perhaps unconsciously, has no other
tendency than that of bringing about the same effect. It is
important, however, to notice that this tendency is not the
direct result of any process of reasoning by which is demonstrated the social utility of elimination, in so far as this makes
impossible future, and otherwise probable, offenses on the
part of the same criminal. All that we can say is that this idea
of prevention, as well as that of making the punishment an
exemplary one, arouses the sentiment in question and rein-

forces its expression. That the desire of society to extirpate
an inassimilable individual in no way depends upon any
direct consideration of utility, the following examples will
show:

Suppose that a man who has received, or believes that he
has received, an injury, who has been wronged, or thinks that
he has been wronged, is impelled by implacable hatred to kill
his real or supposed enemy. It is quite probable that he will
never again shed blood in the course of his life, for no other
person could be hated by him as much as he had hated his
victim.

Again, suppose the case of a man who, because of his strait-
ened circumstances, is unable to maintain the same standard
of living as others in his social circle. By poison or other
means, he hastens the death of a millionaire uncle of whom he
is the sole heir, and obtains his estate. This object attained,
he will in all probability never have occasion to hurt a hair on
another man's head.

The same thing is true of an infanticide committed by a
betrayed girl who hopes thus to save her reputation, or of a
parricide committed through some peculiar motive which
will never reappear. Since for offenses of this description the
common sentiment exacts punishments of great severity —
of much greater severity than it invokes in the case of thieves,
incendiaries, and forgers, who are a permanent source of danger
to all citizens alike, — fear for the future is evidently not its
mainspring.

The public conscience therefore demands reaction against
crime, even where it is not concerned with the thought of the
future. It seeks the punishment of the criminal not only
"ne peccetur," but also "quia peccatum."

*Justification of the Principle "Punitur quia peccatum":
its Reconcilement with the Principle "Punitur ne peccetur."* —
The question now presents itself whether this sentiment whose
existence, we have seen, is incontrovertible, is a reasonable
sentiment, and hence capable of being reconciled with the

theory for which we contend, or whether, on the other hand, it must be regarded as one of those errors of the human mind which are to be corrected and not to be followed. It might be urged that, according to our theory, the reason why elimination is the rational mode of reaction against crime, is that the latter is the symptom of a want of adaptation, and that want of adaptation is something which plainly has reference to the future, because if the individual thought to be inassimilable later shows his fitness for the social life, elimination would be no longer in anywise justifiable. This is no doubt true. But it is one thing to say that an individual has become fit for society, and quite another to say that he *probably* will not commit a second crime in all respects the same as that of which he already has been guilty.

As occupying the foremost place in the criminal ranks, we have described a class of men who are complete moral degenerates, whose natures are exclusively egoistic, and yet who are at the same time capable of energy and activity when it comes to satisfying their passions. Now, the instant it becomes clear that we have to do with a character of this type, we are compelled to say that the individual is unfit for the social life. And this is true even though there be little probability of his repeating the *same* manner of crime. The fact remains that we have discovered a man in whom the moral sense offers no resistance to his perverted instincts and criminal impulses.

It is then that society may say to this individual: "Under present conditions my existence is founded upon the sentiments of pity and justice. You are destitute of these sentiments. You cannot therefore belong to me. You who have murdered your father, may say that I have nothing more to fear from you, because you had but one father to murder. But your words are vain. Your crime has made it manifest that you totally lack the sentiment of pity, that in you there is nothing which can restrain your savage impulses. Whosoever looks upon you will fear for his reputation, his property, his happiness, his life. Your anomaly is too great for you to participate in that sentiment of sympathy which is a common bond among honest men. You cannot participate in this sentiment, precisely because you are incapable of experiencing it. In you, men no longer see their fellow-man; between them and you every tie is sundered. For you there remains naught but suppression."

This utterance would be characterized by the strictest logic. The mode of reaction which society thus would follow finds its exact analogy in that which every other aggregation with a definite object is accustomed to use. As has already been seen, in every lesser association the violation of principles of conduct regarded as fundamental means the expulsion of the offender. From this very fact, if society did not react in an analogous manner, prohibition of crime would be proportionally less effective than the prohibition of other immoral actions. For in that case, while the infringement of the lesser association's rules results in the loss of participation in the advantages of the association, crime, on the other hand, a violation of the essential laws of society at large, would not bring about the loss of participation in the social life. The lesser association knows well how to rid itself of a member whom it has disqualified. And its judgment of disqualification is based upon his deficiency in respect of the kind of character which it requires of all who belong to it.

The greater association which, by antonomasia, we call "society," acts in nowise differently in eliminating such of its members as are proved to be destitute of the commonest, most elementary, and most necessary of the human sentiments. Hence the parricide who cannot repeat the same offense, the infanticide mother who has no more infants to smother, the man who lying in wait slays his one mortal enemy — each and all are beings incompatible with society. They are destitute of one of the fundamental sentiments of public morality, namely, the sentiment of pity; and it has been proved that in the absence of this moral resistance their criminal impulses are without other restraint.

To recapitulate: Reaction in the form of elimination is the socially necessary effect of the commission of crime ("quia peccatum"). And if it be true that the social organism, like every other physical organism, is governed by invariable laws upon which its existence depends, then, in addition to being a necessary effect, this reaction is a natural effect. It is a principle of biology that the individual succumbs as soon as he becomes unable to withstand the action of his environment. The difference between the biologic and moral orders is, that in the former, selection takes place spontaneously by the death of the unfit individual, whereas in the latter, since the individual is physically fit for life and since he cannot live outside of the social environment (to which, however, he cannot be adapted), selection must take place artificially, that is to say, by the act of the social power in effecting that which in the biologic order nature herself accomplishes.[1]

In the second place, elimination tends to the conservation of the social organism, by ridding it of members who are without the requisite fitness ("ne peccetur"). Between the two formulæ which exponents of the two antagonistic schools have been accustomed to place in opposition, there exists, then, no real contradiction. On the one side, for example, is Kant: "If civil society were on the verge of dissolution, it would be its duty to put to death the last murderer found in its prisons, so that every offender might bear the punishment of his crime." On the other, Romagnosi: "If but one crime had been committed and it were morally certain that no others would follow, society would have no right to punish."[2] Fantastic as is the first idea, the second cannot be any more

---

[1] Nature scarcely troubles herself about immorality. She distributes impartially the vital force throughout the whole universe, without stopping to inquire whether or not it will serve the interests of morality. In bestowing strength and genius, she makes no distinction between the natural child and the child born in lawful wedlock. Normal conditions of development and a propitious soil are all that she requires. . . . (*Prins*, "Criminalité et répression," p. 72, — Brussels, 1886).

[2] See *Liszt*, "Der Zweckgedanke im Strafrecht" (Zeitschrift für die gesammte Strafrechtswissenschaft, 1882).

readily accepted, since, according to our theory of natural crime, it involves a contradiction in terms.

Every natural crime signifies a total or partial lack of adaptation to the social life. It brings to light the moral anomaly (curable or incurable). In other words, it indicates that the individual in question has the *capacity for crime* — a capacity which in other men is either not recognizable or cannot be definitely ascertained, or else is presumably non-existent. In the case of a true natural crime, therefore, there is no room for "the probability that its author is not capable of committing other offenses." This probability can exist only where the offender is a normal being. But in such case there would be no crime, because crime is incompatible with the existence, or at least the energy, of the moral sense. Absence or weakness of the moral sense always carries with it the possibility of new crimes. Once recognized, this capacity is not to be tolerated. It severs the tie between the individual and society, for the only common bond which unites asso-ciated men is the presumption that all possess this minimum measure of certain sentiments, the violation of which is crime.

Notwithstanding the fact of crime, it is not always neces-sary to eliminate the offender. As we have indicated, repres-sion sometimes may properly take the form of enforced repara-tion. This should be the case when the psychic anomaly is not strongly accentuated and when the offense is of such a minor character that society can afford to experiment, before adjudging that the offender is unfit for the social life and that, therefore, the community must be freed from his presence. In the last chapter of this work we shall endeavor to determine with some degree of accuracy the cases in which elimination and enforced reparation are respectively appropriate.

§ 3. Intimidation

It has been objected that the measures thus proposed com-pletely ignore the element of intimidation, that they are solely concerned with preventing a repetition of the criminal fact on the part of the individual who has already offended and not on the part of others; that, in short, they pay no attention whatever to the effect of example. "As if," says Tarde, "the vicious disposition of the individual were alone to be feared, and contagion and dangerous customs were matters with which legislation had no occasion to deal." [1]

In order to determine the validity of this criticism it will be necessary for us, in the first place, to summarize certain general notions as to the preventive effect of punishment, and, in the second place, to inquire whether this preventive effect would be in anywise lessened by the adoption of elimination and reparation in lieu of the punishments of the present system.

The Moral Motive. — At the outset, it must be noted that penal repression gives rise to certain motives of conduct, by the very fact that it excites and upholds the sentiment of duty. There can be no question that the common moral sense, in the course of many generations, sometimes undergoes a gradual modification, as the result of the law recognizing the criminal character of a given act or divesting a given act of its previously recognized criminal character. "If discovery of prohibited acts were not to be followed by punishment, the number of such acts would no doubt increase. But this increase would not be immediately perceptible. It would come about only in a slow and indirect fashion, as the result of a series of motives other than the fact of impunity, because if it were to be seen that acts formerly forbidden are now permitted, the sentiments of honor and justice, as they relate to such acts, would be gradually destroyed in men's minds." [2]

All the sentiments may be traced back to primitive ratiocinations which have since become transformed into instincts, or indeed, to experiences of utility undergone by our ancestors.

---

[1] *Tarde*, Positivisme et pénalité (Archives de l'anthropologie criminelle, Vol. II, p. 55, — 1887).

[2] *Von Holtzendorff*, "Das Verbrechen des Mordes und die Todesstrafe," c. VII.

And among these experiences must certainly have been that of the pain-bringing reaction provoked by immorality and crime, a reaction which, at first individual, becomes social as soon as the State has taken form. The ratiocination to which experiences of this sort were bound to give rise, culminated in the instinctive feeling of the evil in crime, and this feeling has been transmitted by psychologic inheritance. The element of coerciveness "originates from experience of those several forms of restraint that have . . . established themselves in the course of civilization. . . . This sense of coerciveness becomes indirectly connected with the feelings distinguished as moral. For since the political, religious and social restraining motives, are mainly formed of represented future results; and since the moral restraining motive is mainly formed of represented future results; it happens that the representations, having much in common, and being often aroused at the same time, the fear joined with the three sets of them becomes, by association, joined with the fourth. Thinking of the extrinsic effects of a forbidden act, excites a dread which continues present while the intrinsic effects of the act are thought of; and being thus linked with these intrinsic effects causes a vague sense of moral compulsion." [1]

Even where the moral sense is organic and highly refined, as it is in individuals of advanced psychic development, it is always accompanied and reinforced, so to speak, by the idea of obligation or duty resting upon the menace of a harm. No doubt, for many persons, the consciousness of the evil involved would destroy any pleasure which the criminal act might afford and is therefore sufficient to cause abstention from crime. But even these persons involuntarily think of the extra legal social reaction attendant upon the offense, namely, of the certainty of being distrusted and shunned by their honest neighbors; and this thought is continually strengthening their resolution to abstain from the acts in question. Such relative sanctions were perhaps the same which gave rise

[1] *Herbert Spencer*, "The Data of Ethics," c. vII.

to the moral sense in our ancestors, whence it has come to us by inheritance. But although this moral sense is now innate in us, these sanctions are still present to arouse it and bring it to light. Without their stimulus, the moral sense would tend to weaken and even, in the course of time, might altogether disappear.

And it may likewise be said that with instinctive repugnance to crime there is always associated the idea of the hurtful effects of arrest, prosecution, and punishment. The representation of these effects, therefore, even in the case of persons who are not degenerate, is still a force which contributes to the conservation of the moral sense. It is the moral sense which has created the law, but this in its turn sustains, reinforces, and creates the moral sense. The motivation of punishment is not without its appreciable part in the slow, unnoticed, secular evolution in which ratiocination has become transformed into organic instinct. The repugnance inspired by words suggesting the punishment of felons, has much to do with the aversion which we feel for the felon, and undoubtedly increases our aversion to his crime. Thus it is in France and Italy, with the word "galley" ("galère," "galera").[1] The idea of the chain and the yellow cap makes the criminal more odious.

The legislator, assuredly, has no power to stamp as infamous any act which public opinion views as praiseworthy or even as indifferent.[2] But although debarred from opposing public morality, he may encourage its development, strengthen it,

---

[1] [For a period of about two centuries, France and the Italian States followed the practice of manning their State galleys, as far as possible, with convict rowers. Labor in the galleys was in fact the prevailing form of penal servitude. This method of punishment went out of use in France in 1748 and in the Italian States somewhat later. The terms connected with it still persist, however, in the common speech, "galère" in French, and "galera" in Italian being colloquially equivalent to "travaux forcés" and "lavori forzati" ("forced labor" = penal servitude). — TRANSL.]

[2] "It is for public opinion alone to say what actions are infamous. And this public opinion, while subject to the rectification of science and experience, is never to be violated or debased by the laws" (*Filangieri*, "Scienza della legislazione," Book III, c. xxxi).

stay its enfeeblement, and prevent its disappearance. In short, the representation of evil to which the fact of punishment gives rise, reinforces the moral motive of conduct in the minds of honest men: it furnishes a new resisting force, a new sustaining power, for the moral sense. More than this, it presents, in many cases, the aspect of a real reward for persons of integrity, and for the following reasons:

Honesty is never exempt from temptation. For the poor man bent under the burden of toil, there is time and again the attraction of some illicit gain, which would soften the rigors of his existence. The man who feels that he has been the victim of an outrage, experiences the temptation of seeking vengeance, the pleasure of the gods. But the moral sense overcomes the vicious impulse, not, however, without a struggle or without some regret. Now, it is clear that, having found that he himself possesses this strength of resistance, a man experiences a feeling akin to satisfaction, when he sees another who lacks this strength, suffer the pain and disgrace of trial and punishment. And this feeling affords him distinct recompense for the exertion which he has undergone in conquering his own evil instincts. Such a sentiment, no doubt, is egoistic, but its social utility is indisputable. Proof of its existence appears in the almost universal satisfaction with which the news of some well-merited sentence of conviction is always received.

Since, in the majority of men, the moral sense has now become organic, the abolition of punishment would not prevent the honest man from remaining honest. But his efforts to subdue temptation would be more painful, his satisfaction after victory much less, than under the existing state of things. The idea of the utility of good conduct would grow faint and in the course of generations the moral sense would become gradually weakened. Enthusiasm for good would disappear, for what would be the advantage of unexceptionable conduct, if bad conduct were not to render the man any less happy?

It is thus that the harm befalling the offender, as the classic world uniformly believed, "ceteros meliores reddit."

Does then the adoption of our plan mean the loss of this beneficent effect of repression? Clearly not. For the production of this effect it is enough that the punishment be such as to reduce the offender to a state of social inferiority. Is not this very thing accomplished by elimination? Does it not necessarily produce suffering? And in enforced reparation, as proposed in the case of the less serious crimes, have we not a measure which represents a real punishment? Public morality, therefore, would suffer no impairment by the substitution of our system of repression for that prevailing today.

The Motive of Fear. — We come now to a still more direct motive of conduct, namely, the fear of punishment, operating upon those who are predisposed to crime. "Oderunt peccare mali formidine pœnæ," is another maxim bequeathed to us by antiquity, but one which is not quite as exact as the preceding. Experimental science has shown us how far a preventive effect may be expected from the menace of punishment. The limits thus set have already been indicated.[1] In brief, our conclusion was that for the extreme criminals or murderers, the death penalty, inflicted with considerable frequency, is the only punishment with any power of terrifying; that professional offenders boldly face all the risks incident to their trade, and in their case, imprisonment for life has at most the effect of discouraging a small number; that impulsive or neuropathic criminals do not think of the consequences of their crimes, unless, indeed, these consequences are serious and immediate; and finally, that in the case of endemic criminality alone, severe (although not cruel) punishments are an efficacious preventive measure.

Some writers, however, viewing the matter quite prescinded from the evidence furnished by direct observation of the criminal, have essayed to establish a criterion of intimidation expressed in the following terms:

[1] *Ante*, Part II, c. III, § 2.

"For the harm threatened by the law to become a determining motive of conduct, it is necessary that it more than counterbalance the pleasure which is hoped from the crime " (Feuerbach and Romagnosi).

This is what is known as the theory of psychologic coaction. Its formula presupposes three conditions, namely:

(1) That criminals are foresighted, calculating individuals, capable of weighing exactly the pleasure to be derived from the crime (something which is as yet unknown to them) against the harm which punishment will bring (this also being often an unknown quantity to the offender).

(2) That the offender looks upon the punishment as a certain harm — as the inevitable consequence of the crime.

(3) That the prevision of the remote, even though certain, harm is sufficient to dissuade the offender from procuring an immediate pleasure and gratifying a violent and instantaneous desire.

After all that has been said, it would be merely repetition to point out that each and all of these three propositions are contradicted by experience. No doubt, fear is one of the most potent determining motives, but its effect cannot be calculated even approximately, save when we are called upon to deal with endemic criminals, or with the lesser offenders whose moral nature closely approaches that of normal man.

Intimidation properly an Effect, not a Criterion of Punishment. — Any attempt to construct a penal system based upon intimidation would involve us in the most banal empiricism, for a scientific criterion is absolutely lacking. How would we set about determining whether five years' imprisonment is sufficient to prevent a domestic theft ("vol domestique")? [1] — how are we to know whether the sentence should not be for ten years or whether even a five years' sentence is not excessive? And moreover, why not retain corporal and

---

[1] ["Vol domestique" = theft by a servant in the household of his master, or by a workman in the premises of his employer — a form of aggravated theft ("vol qualifié"); see *ante*, p. 151, note 1. — TRANSL.]

degrading ("infamantes") punishments, the lash, the "carcan," [1] or even mutilation or the branding iron? Up to the beginning of the 1800s the tendency was to an undue severity of punishment; since then, the tendency has been just the opposite. Both have been harmful. In the 1700s, for example, domestic theft, in the kingdom of Naples, was a capital offense. But because of this the employer seldom or never brought charges against the offending servant, but was content with dismissing him from his service.[2] The very cruelty of the punishment thus brought about the impunity of the offender. On the other hand, undue severity of punishment may become the cause of serious crimes, as in France in the 1700s, when hanging was the punishment for robbery. "The robber," says Filangieri, "almost always adds murder to his crime, simply because, without exposing him to a severer punishment, it puts out of the way a witness whose testimony would be the means of sending him to the gallows."

And yet, if intimidation alone is looked at in determining the question of punishment, experience of the inefficacy of mild measures makes it an easy step to draconism. For if the death penalty does not terrorize all offenders, it cannot be denied, at least, that it has a wider terrorizing effect than any other species of punishment.

In the 1500s England was overrun with numbers of vagabonds. As Karl Marx has it, these were, in large part, the descendants of peasants who toward the close of the preceding century had been wrongfully dispossessed of their holdings, as a result of feudal abuses or of laws in the interest of the mercantile classes.[3] In 1530, in the reign of Henry

---

[1] [The "carcan" served a purpose analogous to that of the pillory. It consisted of an iron collar which was clasped around the prisoner's neck. A chain attached to the collar secured the offender to a post. This form of punishment was abolished in France by the law of 28 April, 1832. What seems to have been the same instrument was at one time in common use in Scotland under the name of "the jougs." — For an account of the jougs, see *William Andrews*, "Old-Time Punishments," p. 108 (Hull, 1890). — TRANSL.]

[2] *Filangieri, op. cit.*, Book III.   [3] *Karl Marx*, "Das Kapital," c. XXVII.

VIII, a statute was passed providing that for a first offense
every able-bodied vagabond should be whipped at the cart-
tail and compelled to return to labor in the place where he
belonged. An amending act adopted five years later punished
a second offense with the loss of "the upper part of the gristle
of the right ear," and a third by hanging. These acts were
followed by the Statute of Vagabonds, enacted in 1547, in
the reign of Edward VI. This provided that every able-
bodied vagabond or beggar should be adjudged the slave,
for a period of two years, of any one willing to buy him.
Fourteen days' absence from the master's service was cause
for adjudging the offender a slave for life. A second attempt
to escape was made punishable by the gallows. By an act
passed in 1572 (temp. Elizabeth), vagabonds were to be
"grievously whipped and burnt through the gristle of the right
ear," unless taken to service, by some trustworthy person,
for one year. In case of a fresh offense on the part of one
aged eighteen years or upwards, the penalty was hanging,
unless he could secure like employment for a term of two
years. For a third offense, there was no means of escaping
the death penalty.[1] According to Marx, who cites Holinshed
as his authority, the number of hanged, during the reign of
Henry VIII alone, is estimated at seventy-two thousand.[2]

What does the theory of psychologic coaction say to measures such as these? No doubt, idleness and vagrancy should
be regarded as true social crimes in that they are a prolific
source of all other crimes. No doubt, also, the habit of idleness is one most difficult to overcome. From the standpoint
of strict logic, therefore, the sanguinary English laws of the
1500s would be entirely justified. And yet our most intimate
sentiments protest against taking the life of men who have been
guilty of nothing more than idleness or mendicancy. Had
these poor wretches gibbeted by Henry VIII and Elizabeth

[1] [The author's account of these statutes has been slightly modified to
accord with *Stephen*, "History of the Criminal Law of England," III, pp.
269–272, and *Pike*, "History of Crime in England," II, pp. 69–73. — TRANSL.]

[2] *Karl Marx, op. cit.*, c. XXVIII.

been given a chance, they would have proved susceptible of adaptation. This is shown by the case of their successors who, under a more humane régime, were sent to the plantations of North America, as well as by that of the transported offenders who were the first Australian colonists. Intimidation has never worked aught but destruction, while adaptation has laid the foundation for rich and flourishing commonwealths.

Respect for the moral sentiments, on the one hand, justifies violent reaction against crime, but, on the other, it forbids excess of this reaction. And excess is immediately present when there is applied to the offender a punishment adopted without regard to the danger to be apprehended from him, and which is neither a bar to his vicious impulses nor a remedy for his lack of sociability. It is always present when the punishment is measured solely by considerations of the danger to be apprehended from others who, it is feared, may be led to imitate the criminal, and when, consequently, the criminal and his punishment are used as instruments to terrorize these others.

The conception of punishment as a *natural reaction* clearly defines its true intimidatory scope. Intimidation should be no more than a *useful effect* of which society avails itself, an effect which is attendant upon application of the total or partial exclusion required by the offender's defect of adaptation. If intimidation is regarded as the chief end of punishment, society can put to death an offender who is still susceptible of adaptation, or can inflict upon him useless tortures, and thus violate his right not to undergo a harm greater than that which is the natural consequence of his wrongful act. Or again, the punishment will fail to attain its end, as occurred when, to terrorize the offender, he was flogged or put in the pillory, and then left free to resume his ordinary habits of life, or, indeed, as happens today, when habitual criminals are sentenced to a few months or years of imprisonment.

In short, attempting to act upon the conscience of the dis-

honest individual, "formidine pœnæ" simply means subjecting him to sufferings more or less severe but almost always
useless, without procuring his exclusion from the social life,
or that form of the social life, for which he is unfit. But it is
something wholly incompatible with the positivist notion of
crime, with which the reader has already been made familiar,
that the malefactor, once his chastisement has been undergone,
may freely return to the social life. If crime is, as we believe,
an act which reveals the lack or insufficiency of adaptation,
this is a consideration upon which should turn the logical
reaction of society. Punishments are not, therefore, to be
chosen because of their power of intimidation. Intimidation
will none the less be present as a necessary incident of the
menace of elimination and its inherent harm.

In the absolute form of elimination, namely, death, or those
measures which in certain cases may take the place of death,
that is to say, transportation and penitentiary imprisonment
for life ("déportation et réclusion perpétuelle"), this intimidatory effect is obvious. But it will also be produced by the
partial and conditional forms of elimination, provided that in
a given case they are exactly the means required for remedy-
ing the particular defect in social aptitude. If this means be
accurately determined, it will not fail to produce the intimidatory effect desired.

For the sake of illustration, suppose that in some small
village a long standing family bitterness causes one inhabitant
repeatedly to insult or threaten his neighbor in public, or
suppose that in a like village a rejected suitor continually
waylays and annoys the young woman to whose hand he has
aspired, thus rendering his presence not only intolerable,
but a danger to the public peace. According to the happy
expression of Filangieri, such an offense may be termed a
"local" one. For it is evident that the defect of adaptation
is one which is relative to the circumstances of the social
environment where the offender has conceived, in the first
instance, his hatred, or in the second, his incurable love.

It may then be presumed that if we remove the individual
from this locality where the motives for his anti-social conduct
exist, the disappearance of these motives will render possible
his adaptation in another place. Such, then, is society's
rational mode of reaction in cases of this description. And
we believe that there can be no question of its intimidatory
effect, for if the fear of local exile will not overcome the
motives which impel to homicide or other serious offenses,
it is at least sufficient to deter from insulting language ("injures") and other offenses of minor importance.

It is not to be supposed that with this principle once
established, there would no longer be any need for the rigor
and severity of penitentiary discipline. This discipline is
required for the maintenance of order, always a difficult
task in a population of convicts. And in great part, its rigor
and severity are due to the object sought to be attained,
namely, the complete segregation of the convict.

In our opinion, then, the conclusion is warranted that when
the method of elimination is really that which the circumstances require, that is to say, when it meets the true end of
repression, intimidation by the nature of things will always
result as a reflex effect, without any necessity on our part of
making it a subject of especial concern.

Here it may be objected that, according to our previously
expressed view, there are many cases in which elimination
would be a useless proceeding — cases in which every sort of
corporal punishment even that of a brief term of imprisonment should be done away with.[1] True, and we may add
that a detention or imprisonment of a few days or weeks is a
punishment no whit less absurd than the fustigation of by-
gone days. But we have advocated, in such cases, a measure
which has an intimidatory effect of its own. In fact, our plan
of compulsory reparation for the moral and material damage
caused by the offense will be a form of repression much more
serious than the punishments for which it is substituted.

[1] See *ante*, § 1 of the present chapter.

Particularly will this be so if, as we propose, it will be enforced
by means of so energetic a character (necessarily more energetic than those of the present procedure) that it will be possible for no offender to evade his obligation. If we thus require
the offender fully to indemnify the injured party, either by
the immediate payment of a sum of money or by his compulsory labor until the sum is earned, as an indispensable
condition of being set at liberty, is it not plain that this sort
of coercion will have a much more sensible effect in the prevention of crime than any fixed term of imprisonment,
imposing on the criminal no other obligation than that of
eating the bread of idleness at the public expense?

§ 4. Selection

There remains to be examined one effect of elimination
which is substantially peculiar to this measure, being encountered only accidentally in other forms of punishment, —
namely, selection.

Selective Effect of Absolute Elimination. — From the brief
summary which we have heretofore given, it is manifest that
crime cannot escape the inflexible laws of psychologic heredity.[1]
It follows, therefore, that the elimination of the elements
least fit for the social life is calculated to bring about the moral
betterment of the race, by reason of the diminishing number
of individuals born with criminal propensities.

The efforts of the individualist school of the 1700s to support
the thesis that there is no psychologic continuity between
parent and child, that neither the good nor the bad qualities
of the father are transmitted to the son, have all been in vain.
The fact is that if the individual does not precisely inherit
the virtues and the vices of his parents and grandparents,
he assuredly does inherit their virtuous or perverted instincts,
their sentiments, their passions, and their character. Everything goes to show that psychologic heredity is but an aspect

[1] See *ante,* Part II, c. i.

of physiologic heredity.[1] Especially is this so in the case of criminals. Psychologic and physiologic inheritance are here indisputable. As has been seen, the criminal instincts are frequently found in association with a structural difference, with a peculiar anthropologic conformation which, in the case of the extreme criminals, stamps its possessors as monstrosities, sometimes atypic and often regressive.

Antiquity relentlessly punished the son for the faults of the father. In our more civilized age, the aim should be only to prevent the procreation of individuals who in all likelihood would turn out to be vicious and depraved. Not to punish the children of criminals but to prevent their birth, to effect the permanent isolation of offenders — I now refer to the abnormal authors of true crimes — and thus effect an artificial selection which will bring about a moral improvement of the race, — such is the duty which today rests upon society. Lombroso did not hesitate to ascribe the greater humanity of our times, as compared with that of past centuries, to the work of capital punishment in purifying the human race.[2] The scaffold which annually put to death malefactors by the thousand is responsible for the fact that crime is not more prevalent today. Who can say what would have been the result if this selection had not come to pass, if these offenders had been left free to multiply their kind, and if we had now among us the innumerable descendants of all the thieves and murderers of centuries gone by?

Today the race of civilized man is more benign, less swayed by passion, better able to resist brutal instincts, than it has ever been in the past. Progress in this respect has been in great part owed to selection. Why, then, should this progress be interrupted? Why should we not continue this secular work of purification? Every pause in the forward movement is a step backward. Let us then see to it lest we incur the righteous blame of future generations for not

[1] *Ribot*, "L'hérédité psychologique " (Paris, F. Alcan, 1882).
[2] *Lombroso*, L'incremento del delitto in Italia, p. 30 (Turin, 1879).

stamping under foot the seed from which otherwise will
have sprung a noxious crop to devastate their fields.

But, it may be asked, is there not even now a natural
selection continually taking place in every civilized environment, a selection which is effected without any interference on
the part of the social power? "The criminal who is such by
reason of the vices of his physical constitution represents in
most cases a product of degeneration or, at least, the beginning
of a dangerous deviation from the normal type. In both cases
nature, looking to the perpetuation of the species, either elim-
inates the defective individual at once, or else causes his posterity soon to die out."[1] This, however, is true only of a few
varieties of criminals — of those who present a marked bio-
pathologic character, such as epileptics, lunatics, and neuro-
paths. By far the greater proportion of offenders, notwithstanding their plainly revealed characteristics of degeneration
and moral inferiority, are in no way deficient as regards their
fitness for the physical life. Such are the individuals whose
physical abnormalities are limited to the regressive characteristics which approximate them to the inferior races of
mankind, or those, again, who exhibit atypic but not pathologic characteristics. These persons may be in perfect health,
in better health, perhaps, than civilized man, in whom the
moral development has often taken place at the expense of the
physical. From a purely physical standpoint the savage is
the superior of civilized man, excelling him in muscular
strength and keenness of the senses.[2] Non-diseased criminals
are therefore capable of reproducing "ad infinitum," like
normal men. In fact, their prolificacy is ordinarily greater

[1] *Venturi*, "La peine de mort" (Actes du Congrès d'Anthropologie
criminelle, p. 312, — Rome, 1887).

[2] "Intellectual development is conducive to neuropathic conditions,
and, resultingly, to the degeneration and extinction of the race" (*Jacoby*,
"Études sur la sélection," Preface to 2d ed., — Paris, F. Alcan, 1904). *Al-
brecht* has maintained that, so far as comparative anatomy is concerned,
man, as a race, is morphologically inferior to the simian, and civilized man
to the savage. See Actes du Congrès d'Anthropologie criminelle, pp. 105, 111
(Rome, 1887).

than that of normal men, as is proved by the genealogical data which we have concerning certain criminal families.

Moreover, "society, in taking the life of the offender, aids and accelerates nature's work of subordinating all things to the social interest. The necessities of the social life and the influence of the social environment have altered, for the members of society, the natural conditions of the struggle for life; the forces of nature have been replaced by those of the social conventions. It would be dangerous, indeed, for society to shrink from ridding itself, at least as far as possible, from the elements which constitute a source of infection." [1]

Selective Effect of Relative Elimination. — But, as we know, the death penalty is not the only method of elimination capable of furthering natural selection. The enforced emigration of vagabonds from Great Britain to her colonies has not been without its influence in the purification of her population, among which today the percentage of crime, at least in its most serious forms, is very much lower than in the countries of Central and Southern Europe. As we already have had occasion to notice, the number of murders and homicides in the United Kingdom has been undergoing, especially in the second half of the 1800s, such a steady decrease, that one would be justified in predicting the total disappearance of these crimes from British soil at an early day. Nevertheless, the British government still retains the death penalty, and wisely so. If the hangings under Henry VIII and Elizabeth went far in accomplishing a selection, the transportations of the 1700s and the first half of the 1800s humanely continued the work. The problem consists in this: to distinguish the typical criminals, men insusceptible of any new adaptation, from such offenders as present the possibility of a new adaptation. In the case of the former, selection will be effected by their absolute elimination. In the case of the latter, relative elimination will accomplish a relative selection, namely, a

[1] *Venturi*, in the paper above cited.

selection in relation to the environment from which they have been separated.

§ 5. The Correctionalist Theory

We have seen that the reaction of society against crime ought to assume one of three forms, according to the degree of danger arising from the psychic anomaly of the criminal, or, to put it in another way, according as his perversity is more or less ingrained in his organism and likely to manifest itself anew. These three forms are (1) *complete elimination*, by which the individual is deprived of all intercourse with society, (2) *partial elimination*, consisting in his separation from the particular environment for which he is unfit, and (3) *enforced reparation* of the injury caused by his offense.

The Theory in General. — But there would be no room for such proposals, if it were to be shown that, by an appropriate method of education, evil instincts could be overcome and the criminal transformed into an honest man. There are certain psychologists who believe in the possibility of modifying character by education, using the word in its true sense. Save for some rare cases of exceptionally refractory natures, they maintain that all men, even those who seem to be most imbruted, most destitute of good sentiments, are susceptible of normal reform; and that consequently every possible effort should be made to save them. This view has given rise to the correctionalist school, which, in combating the system of physical and degrading punishments ("peines afflictives et infamantes") [1] and treating the reformation of the offender as the true end of punishment, has had much influence upon legislation and legal thought. If the postulate of the criminal's corrigibility can be accepted, this theory ought to command adherence, even from the standpoint of social defense. For what better guaranty against the repetition of the crime could be desired than the removal of the criminal's perver-

---

[1] [See *ante*, p. 59, note 1. — TRANSL.]

sity? What need, then, to destroy the criminal himself or to surround him with physical trammels?

But, at the outset, we encounter this difficulty: Ought the moral reform to exclude the physical suffering and the shame which accompany punishment? If so, is the penal sanction to consist, not in the menace of an evil, but in the promise of a good? The effect of such a proceeding, it is evident, would be completely to overturn the motives of conduct, since the worst sort of conduct would be rewarded by especial care on the part of the State; untouched by any agency of physical suffering, the criminal would receive as the sole consequence of his crime, the privilege of gratuitous instruction. Moreover, the situation presents a practical impossibility. Without physical constraint, how is the offender to be made amenable to discipline? But just as soon as the element of constraint appears, we have the prison, the penitentiary. The mere deprivation of liberty, however benign the administration of the place of confinement, is undeniably punishment. In effect, therefore, what the correctionalist school proposes simply comes to this, that the sole office of imprisonment should be that of rendering possible the moral reformation of the prisoner.

Having reached this point, the first thing, it seems to me, which the correctionalists should consider, is whether criminals in general, or, at least, any classes of criminals, are susceptible of reformation; and the next, by what means this reformation is to be accomplished. Instead of thus examining the question, they have established the correctional prison with its compulsory labor, and all has been said. The only case in which the problem has been given intelligent study is in that of children and adolescents. And if such studies have yielded some good results, it is merely for the reason that in this case alone is there any possibility of attaining the desired end.

Limited Efficacy of Education; Impossibility of Distinguishing its Effect from that of Heredity. — In fact, it seems clear that education is an influence which acts only upon infancy and early youth, an influence which, like heredity and tradition, contributes to the formation of character. Once fixed, the character, like the physiognomy, undergoes no further change during life. And even in the period of early childhood, it is doubtful whether education can create a wanting moral instinct. Still the word "education" ought not to be taken in the pedagogic sense. It signifies rather an aggregate of external influences, a whole series of scenes which the child sees continually passing before it, and which impress upon him moral habitudes in teaching him the lesson which he thus learns by experience and almost unconsciously, namely, what conduct is to be followed under different circumstances. Family examples have a far greater influence upon him than any pedagogic instruction. But in giving to the word "education" this wide meaning, it is impossible to be sure of its effect, or, at least, in anywise to measure this effect.[1]

Almost all children during the first years of their life seem destitute of moral sense. Their cruelty to animals is well known, as is also their propensity to seize what belongs to others. They are thoroughly egoistic, and in seeking to satisfy their desires, they are not in the slightest degree concerned with what they make others suffer. In most cases all this changes with the approach of adolescence. But can it be said that this psychologic transformation is the effect of education? Are we not rather to see in it a simple phenomenon of organic evolution, similar to the embryogenic evolution by which the fœtus passes through the different stages of animal life, beginning with the most rudimentary and ending with that of man? It has been said that the evolution of the individual is an epitome of that of the species.[2] Thus in the psychic organism the instincts which primarily appeared must have

---

[1] "In order that education may exert its full influence, it is necessary that the subject be free from any defect of conformation, any pathologic state, any hereditary condition which, from having lasted throughout a long series of generations, has resulted in the absolute callousness of certain nerve-centres" (Paper by *Sciamanna*, in the Actes du 1er Congrès d' Anthropologie criminelle, p. 201, — Rome, 1887).

[2] See *Haeckel*, "Anthropogénie," p. 48 (Paris, 1877).

been those of the animal, next must have come the ultra-
egoistic sentiments, then in succession the ego-altruistic sentiments as acquired first by the race, secondly by the family,
and lastly by the parents of the child. The juxtapositions of
instincts and sentiments thus arising would be due not to
education or to the influence of the immediate environment,
but solely to heredity. "The conscience," says Espinas,
"grows in the same manner as the organism and parallel to
it. It contains aptitudes, predetermined forms of thought
and action, which are direct emanations of anterior consciences, momentarily overshadowed, it is true, in the obscurity of organic transmission, but coming again to light
with unequivocal characteristics of resemblance, very soon to
be confirmed, and in an increasing degree, by example and
education. So far as conscience is concerned, a generation is
really a phenomenon of reproduction by fission." [1]

This hypothesis is not an improbable one. To prove it with
exactness is, however, out of the question. It could not be
done without distinguishing the respective parts played by
heredity and education in the moral development of the child.
And how is this distinction to be arrived at? These two influences ordinarily act in the same direction, because they are
almost always derived from the same persons, namely, the
parents. Domestic education is merely the continuation of
heredity. That which has not been organically transmitted
will be transmitted, and in an equally unconscious manner,
by the force of examples. It is therefore impossible to determine how far the influence of one would have extended without the aid of the other.

So, on the one hand, we cannot dispute Darwin when he
declares that if an equal number of Irish and Scots were to
colonize a country, the former in the course of time would be
ten times as numerous as the latter, but that the Scots, on
account of their hereditary qualities, would hold the reins of
government and industry. But neither have we any right,

[1] *A. Espinas*, "Les sociétés animales," Conclusion, § 2.

on the other hand, to suppose that Fouillée is mistaken in saying: "Substitute the Irish children for the Scottish without the knowledge of their parents; bring up the Irish children like the Scottish, and perhaps, strange as it may seem, you will have the same result." [1] But this second experiment has never been tried, and in all likelihood never will be. No doubt, there are thousands of children brought up by persons other than their parents, but in such cases the parents are generally unknown. Finally, there always remain to be reckoned with the still obscure and undeterminable phenomena of atavism. Everything thus tends to render the problem insoluble.

It frequently occurs that the paternal instincts are stifled or attenuated by maternal examples. Sometimes, again, the converse is true. Still, this proves nothing as to the efficacy of education, for it may just as well be said that the effect is due simply to the ultimate superiority of one of the two heredities.

What may be said, however, is that when the hereditary influence is not too strong, education has a very probable effect upon infancy and early youth, — education, that is to say, especially in the sense of examples set the child by the family and the persons by whom he is immediately surrounded. But it is an influence which grows weaker and weaker as the child advances in years. While it may attenuate, it can never entirely eradicate the perverse instincts. Whatever its action, these would always remain latent in the psychic organism. This explains why, in the case of certain children, it has never been possible to correct the perversity, perhaps atavistic, manifested in their early years, notwithstanding the exemplary conduct of their parents and the persons with whom they have been brought in contact, and in spite of the greatest pains taken in their upbringing.[2] On

---

[1] *Fouillée*, "La philanthropie scientifique au point de vue du Darwinisme" (Revue des Deux Mondes, 15 September, 1882).

[2] *Bernard Perez*, who is not in general open to the charge of pessimism, lends the weight of his authority to the view that there are children whose

the opposite, it seems certain that the deleterious influence of a bad education may completely obliterate the transmitted moral sense and set in its place the most evil instincts. From which it results that a good character artificially created would always be subject to lapses, while a bad character similarly created would be unalterable. This is easily accounted for by the theory of evolution. The evil germs or anti-social instincts which correspond to the primitive age of mankind, are the ones most deeply rooted in the organism, precisely because they are the oldest in the history of the race. They are consequently stronger than the instincts which have been superposed upon them by evolution. This is why the savage instincts are never entirely stifled, but, on the contrary, as soon as the environment and the circumstances of life become favorable to their expansion, burst forth with violence. As Carlyle has said, "Civilization is only a crust beneath which the savage nature of man burns with an infernal fire."

natures are wholly insusceptible of education. "Goodwill and even virtue on the part of the parents do not always guarantee the success of their children's education. The children of couples who are sound in mind and body, of no disparity in point of age, and living under good hygienic conditions, are not always moral. In such cases we must reckon with the grievous recurrences of heredity. As for people who lead irregular lives, who are addicted to excesses, intemperance, and vicious habits, whether congenitally so or not, they are infallibly laying the foundations of a race in which vice, insanity, and crime will be the rule. It is undoubtedly true that violent and dangerous tendencies are exhibited by a considerable number of young children, but in many cases they are so pronounced, although sometimes intermittent, that we are forced to see in their possessors the unfortunate victims of the fatal laws of heredity and degeneration " ("L'éducation morale dès le berceau," pp. 109, 110, — Paris, Felix Alcan, 1888).

For *Magnan* there is no natural predisposition to crime in the *normal* individual. He admits, however, the fact of degeneracy due to nervous or vesanic heredity or to the alcoholism of the ascendants (Paper read before the second Congress of Criminal Anthropology).

Taverni, in his paper read at the same Congress, admits the existence of a natural irremediable deficiency, rendering the subject insusceptible of education, whatever be the pedagogic method employed, which insusceptibility constitutes the natural predisposition to crime.

See, upon the same question the interesting remarks of *Molet* and *Herbette* in the proceedings of this Congress. Mme. *Pigeon's* protest that there are no children who are insusceptible of education seems to be inspired by womanly tenderness of heart rather than based upon experience.

If the influence of education upon the moral sense is thus open to question even when exerted upon infancy, what can we expect it to accomplish in later years?

Fixity of the Character Type. — Sergi represents the moral character as formed of superposed layers which may cover and entirely conceal the congenital character. The social environment, the effect of examples, and even direct teaching may operate to produce a new stratum not only during childhood but also in later life.[1] In my opinion, this theory is admissible only upon the assumption that the more recent strata never produce alteration of the type of character already formed. The psychic organism, unquestionably, has its period of formation and development just as the physical organism. Like the physiognomy, the character takes form at a very early age. It may become more flexible or more rigid, its angles may become subdued or accentuated, in ordinary life it may be dissimulated; but how can it lose its type? Now the man who is destitute of the elementary moral sentiments has a special type of character. It is organically defective from heredity, atavism, or a pathologic condition. Is it reasonable to suppose that this congenital defect can be repaired by external influences? The artificial production of the racial moral sense of which, by exception, the individual is devoid, would be in effect a creation "ex nihilo."

Such a result is difficult to conceive under any circumstances. When the subject is past the years of childhood it appears absolutely impossible. We are not to be understood as denying the power of education. No one can doubt the prodigies which it accomplishes, when its task is that of perfecting character, of refining the already existing sentiments, in a word, of weaving the threads into the completed fabric. But what we cannot concede to it is the power of making something out of nothing.

Views of Despine. — In this regard, it seems to me that Despine has fallen into a singular contradiction. We are

[1] *G. Sergi,* "La stratificazione del carattere e la delinquenza" (Milan, 1888).

indebted to this author for a multitude of observations confirming the existence of criminal anomaly. Moreover, he has formulated a theory closely approaching our own, as to the absence of the moral sense, not only in murderers, but also in the extreme, violent criminals.[1] So too, he has declared that "education, even in the best sense of the word, cannot create faculties; it can only cultivate those already existing, at least in germ"; that "the intellectual faculties, alone, have no power to produce the instinctive cognitions, these being derived from the moral faculties"; that "it is easy to recognize in the moral faculties the origin of the motives of action which ought to present themselves to the mind of man under the varying circumstances of life";[2] and finally, that "no amount of reasoning or intellectual exertion will suffice to establish the existence of the sentiment of duty any more than it will that of the affections, fear, hope, or the sense of the beautiful."[3]

And yet, holding these views, he proposes for criminals a palliative and curative moral treatment, the leading features of which he summarizes as follows: All communication between persons morally imperfect is to be prevented. Such persons, however, are not to be left in solitude, for their own consciences afford no means of reformation. It is to be arranged that they shall be constantly in contact with moral persons, fitted to keep them under observation and to study their instinctive nature, persons who are capable of impressing this nature and giving to their thoughts a right direction by inspiring them with ideas of order and imbuing them with the liking for work and the habit of working. It is, then, for the State to undertake this unremitting and assiduous care of the prisoners, to keep watch over their progress in the manner of a schoolmaster, and to endeavor by examples, experiments, and direct teaching, to mitigate their char-

---

[1] *Despine*, "De la folie au point de vue philosophique," etc., Part I, p. 39 (Paris, 1875).
[2] *Ibid.*, p. 40. [3] *Ibid.*, p. 46.

acters and render them affectionate, honest, charitable, and zealous.

In the first place, the idea of applying such a moral therapy to many thousands of criminals is plainly Utopian. It would require that to every inmate there be assigned, so to speak, a guardian angel. Such an employment would demand persons endowed with the noblest and rarest qualities of man, patience, vigilance, and just severity. To an intimate knowledge of human nature, they would need to unite education and devotion. Where are we to find a sufficient number of these soul-physicians? And what of the expense of such an undertaking? But, assuming, for the moment, that the practical difficulties of the system are not insurmountable, what would be its effect?

The offender, separated from his former surroundings and removed from the continual temptations to which he was there exposed, would undoubtedly no longer think of committing crime, inasmuch as both its occasion and possibility would have become non-existent. But in spite of all teaching, the criminal germ, in a latent state, would continue to reside in his being, ready to make itself manifest with the return of his former environmental conditions. Therefore, even if the reformation were not feigned, it could never be more than apparent.

Impossibility of artificially creating Moral Instincts. — The idea of reforming criminals by means of an experimental pedagogy can no longer be taken seriously. For, if it be true that the moral instincts of mankind are the result of countless experiences of utility undergone by our ancestors throughout thousands of centuries, how can we suppose it possible for these experiences to be artificially reproduced in as short a space of time as the life of a human being? How, then, are we to believe that the man whose instinct has not inherited the product of these experiences of past generations, can be artificially raised to the moral level of other men? And for that matter, how can such experiences be possibly undergone by a prisoner deprived of all contact with the outside world?

The uselessness of trying to effect a moral cure in any such direct fashion as that involved in the Utopian plan of Despine, has at length come to be recognized. The belief, however, still persists that this moral cure can be indirectly effected by means of a proper penitentiary regimen. Solitude, silence, labor, and instruction, it is maintained, will lead to repentance and good resolutions and tend to the reformation of the convict.

Respecting solitude, it is to be observed, in the eloquent words of Mittelstadt, that "what the wretched and unhappy, the outcast and the fallen are in need of, is not separation from society, but rather the love and contact of their fellow-beings." And as for labor, to quote the same author, "all that our prison humanitarians have left to them is the hopeless dilemma of coming to an understanding as to the meaning of the formula: 'Educative labor for prisoners.' Would they employ labor as a useful corrective of habits of life? If so, they must remove all coercion and substitute freedom for imprisonment. Or would they retain coercion? Then they are simply dispensing punishment as before, and reformation, as an object, vanishes." [1]

But the correctionalists answer that with labor there must be combined mental and moral education: that for this purpose we must have schools where the ordinarily rude and ignorant convict may acquire the knowledge which he lacks, of the true and the good. Experience, has shown, however, that in general the school is almost entirely destitute of influence upon individual morality. Take an adult criminal devoid of a part of the moral sense, namely, the instinct of

---

[1] *Mittelstadt,* "Gegen die Freiheitstrafen" (1880). On this subject, *Spencer* says: "It is to no purpose that you make him (the prisoner) work by external coercion; for when he is again free, and the coercion absent, he will be what he was before. The coercion must be an internal one, which he shall carry with him out of prison" ("Prison-ethics"). And *Lord Stanley,* speaking in Parliament, expressed the same idea when he exclaimed: "The reformation of man can never become a mechanical process."

pity. Try to inculcate this instinct in him by teaching, that
is to say, by repeating over and over that one of the duties of
man is to be sympathetic; that morality forbids us to harm
our fellows; and the like. What will be the result? The subject, we may well suppose, will have thus acquired, if indeed
he did not already have it, a criterion for distinguishing and
recognizing what is good conduct according to the principles
of morality. In a word, he will have acquired ideas but not
sentiments. What will be the effect of these ideas upon his conduct? If goodness in man springs not from reflection but
from instinct, and if it is precisely instinct which is lacking in
the case put, how can any reception of ideas supply his organic deficiency? He will know the good, but will do the evil,
when this accords with his pleasure.

> " Video meliora, proboque;
> Deteriora sequor."

It would be idle to reiterate to him that the social interest
is far more important than the interest of the individual;
that in the long run the latter identifies itself with the former;
that, as members of society, it is our duty to sacrifice our egoism
in order that others may do likewise toward us. It would be
equally fruitless to use the argument of religion, to speak to
him of the eternal happiness in store for the just man and the
eternal damnation which awaits the wicked. What he is told
in either case, simply comes to this: "If you do a certain act,
a certain harm will befall you. To avoid this harm, therefore,
you must refrain from the act."

Unfortunately, the offender prefers to satisfy the passion
or desire of the moment rather than sacrifice this passion or
desire to the vague hope of a future and far-off benefit. The
argument, then, is without effect upon him. Ability to see
clearly what others regard as a predominant interest will not
prevent him from offending anew. What is necessary is that
he experience the same repugnance to crime as other men,
because, in the ultimate analysis, it is the character of the
individual and his general manner of feeling which explain

every human action.[1] Instinct can never be created by ratiocination.[2] It cannot be other than congenital, or else unconsciously acquired through the effect of the physical or social
environment.

We are thus brought back to our two principal agencies:
heredity and environment. Education, in so far as it is that
of the school-room, is of little or no effect if the environment
is unchanged, that is to say, if, upon the termination of his
punishment, the criminal is allowed to return to his former
surroundings. The story is well known of the negro children
who in infancy were taken to Europe and, after having been
there brought up and educated, were sent back to civilize
their tribesmen. No sooner did they find themselves among
the latter than they forgot all that they had learned, their
grammar as well as their habits of life, and throwing away their
civilized garments, they fled into the forest, there to become
savages like their fathers, whom, moreover, they had never
known.[3] This is exactly how the correctionalist principle may
be expected to result, if the trials of it, which have already
been made, viz., in the cellular system, the system in use at
Auburn, the Irish system, etc., are any criterion.

The Elmira System. — In the Elmira Reformatory,[4] a
system of coercion has been adopted which aims at improving
the physical and mental structure of the inmates, with a view
to creating in them new habits of life and thought. The means
employed are hygienic conditions of living and diet, baths,
massage, gymnastic exercises, military drill, and instruction
both academic and in the industrial trades. Strict rules
of deportment and the sternest sort of discipline prevail.
Inmates whose future good conduct seems assured, may be

[1] See *Ribot*, "Les maladies de la volonté," (Paris, F. Alcan, 1883).
[2] *Despine*, "De la folie," etc., p. 39.
[3] "In Brazil, not long ago, a doctor of medicine of the University of Bahia
abandoned civilized life and returned to wander naked in his native forests.
Instances of the same kind have been noted in Australia and New Zealand "
(*Victor Jeanvrot*, "La question de la criminalité," Revue de la réforme judiciaire, Paris, 15 July, 1889).
[4] Elmira, N. Y., U. S. A.

released on parole after one year's detention. They are then kept under surveillance for a further period of six months. If their conduct continues to be good, they are at the end of this period granted their absolute release, whatever be the maximum term of their sentence. It is to be noted that there are no recidivists among the inmates of this institution. These are mostly youths, their average age being twenty-one years. Furthermore, they are here under a regimen which keeps them continually active, and, upon being released, places of employment are found for them. Yet in spite of these facts, about 20% of them commit a second offense within the six months following their release on parole. While the rest are lost to sight, it is asserted that they are no longer heard of as criminals. But the question of time is not mentioned, nor are there any proofs adduced in support of the statement. Moreover, what possibility is there of extending this system to habitual offenders, to hardened criminals? Then again, the administration of such an institution could only be intrusted to persons with extraordinary qualifications, such qualifications in short as are possessed by Mr. Brockway, the first director of the Elmira Reformatory. "The head of an educational institution of this sort," writes Charles Dudley Warner, an enthusiastic admirer of the school, "must be a man of high character. . . . He must be an educated man, a man of executive ability and capable of enforcing discipline. His subordinates must be like him in degree. They must be pervaded with the spirit of the system." [1] Under such conditions — which, it is needless to say, are extremely difficult of fulfillment — similar institutions may yield good results, but always upon a small scale as at Elmira, where, as has been seen, the treatment in question is confined to youthful first-offenders.

Statistics of Recidivism a Refutation of the Correctionalist Theory. — The fact is indisputable that in all countries

[1] "The Elmira System": Paper read before Am. Soc. Science Ass'n., 9 September, 1894 ([Am.] Journal of Social Science, No. 32, pp. 65, 66).

recidivism tends to increase according as punishments are made shorter and less severe. In France the proportion of misdemeanors ("délits") which were not first offenses rose from 21% in 1851 to 44% in 1882, that of felonies ("crimes") similarly representing cases of recidivism, from 33% to 52%, during the same period. "Recidivism," to quote from a report of the Minister of Justice, "continues its march of invasion. . . . In ten years the number of criminals who have undergone more than one conviction, has increased by 39%, — almost two-fifths." [1] The average annual number of recidivists reached the figure of 104,070, being almost one-half of the total number of convictions, in the period from 1891 to 1895. In the following four-year period, however, it began to show a decrease, quite evidently as the result of the new laws relating to recidivism and conditional sentences. In Germany, between 1889 and 1899, the number of recidivists increased by more than 100%, — specifically, from 88,270 to 187,136. Italy from 1876 to 1895 suffered under a steady growth of habitual offenses. In the latter year, of the 45,579 recidivists in custody, 3,000 had undergone upward of six convictions.

In all this, we have a practical demonstration of the futility of the correctionalist theory, or, at least, of its applications. The result could not be otherwise, in view of the obvious contradiction which its principles involve. While, on the one hand, it maintains that the aim of all punishment is the reformation of the offender, on the other, it establishes a fixed measure of punishment for every offense, that is to say, detention in a State institution for a certain number of months or years — a proceeding which, as Willert has said, "is much as if a physician, in prescribing hospital treatment for a patient, were to indicate the exact day on which he must be discharged, irrespective of his state of health." [2] In institu-

---

[1] "Journal officiel," 13 March, 1884.

[2] *Willert*, "Das Postulat der Abschaffung des Strafmasses mit der dagegen erhobenen Einwendung."

tions for dependent children and for adolescents who have begun to exhibit evil propensities, we find the only salvage from the wreck of this theory. In the case of adults, all that we can do is to try to make them acquire such a habit of life as they will desire permanently to continue, because more useful to them than any other species of activity, in the new social environment to which they will have been transported. Only in this way will the offender, who is not entirely degenerate, cease to be harmful to society. Such a result, however, can be realized in no other manner than by *transportation* ("déportation"), or by *internment in agricultural colonies* to be established in the more sparsely settled districts of the mother country. It is an indispensable condition, moreover, that this sort of exile shall be for life or at least for a term not fixed in advance. The use of indefinite sentences would permit release in those rare cases where the reformation of the offender through labor could be regarded as an accomplished fact.[1] Such cases do occur; but they are exceptional. In the ordinary case it would be out of the question to suppose that the offender, however long his absence, could return to the environment which for him is a miniature fatherland, without being affected by the influences which had impelled him to crime.

[1] The idea of punishment without fixed duration was advanced by me in 1880 (see my "Criterio positivo della penalità," — Naples, Vallardi), and by *Kraepelin*, the same year, in his brochure, "Die Abschaffung des Strafmasses" (Leipzig, 1880). Liszt lent it support in his lectures at the University of Marburg in 1882. More recently, a number of other authors have taken it up; and it has become the subject of legislative adoption, as for example in the Argentine Penal Code of 1903. An excellent commentary on this code exists in "La ley penal Argentina, Estudio critico," by *Rodolfo Moreno* (La Plata, 1903).

CHAPTER II

THE EXISTING THEORIES OF CRIMINAL LAW

§ 1. General Considerations

THE simplicity and self-evidence of the principles set forth in the preceding chapter, are such, I am confident, as to commend them to the intelligent reader, regardless of his acquaintance with the natural or social sciences. Indeed, it may be that a perusal of the chapter in question will move him to declare that it contains nothing new. For it not seldom happens that the mere enouncement of an idea carries persuasion of its truth. The reader is convinced that the idea has always been his, although he has never clothed it in words, or believes, at least, that had he studied the subject in hand, he could have come to no other conclusion.

And yet the doctrines of the prevailing criminal law are essentially different from everything which we have advanced. It therefore becomes important to explain wherein this differ-

---

[1] [§§ 1 and 2 = § I of original; §§ 3, 4, 5, and 6 = § II; §§ 7 and 8 = III and IV respectively; §§ 9, 10, 11 and 12 = § V; and § 13 = § VI. — TRANSL.]

ence consists, so that such of our readers as are unfamiliar
with legal science, may better appreciate the significance of
what we have been advocating. For this purpose, we shall
present a brief analysis of the generally accepted theories of
the modern criminal law, comparing as we proceed, its various rules with those which are the logical corollaries of our
principles.

It has been explained in a former place,[1] that the jurists
do not, like us, regard the criminal as an abnormal being, in
varying degrees insusceptible of adaptation. In their eyes,
he is merely a man who has disobeyed a law of the State and
deserves the punishment which constitutes the sanction of
that law. For each of the two principal schools which have
hitherto dominated the field of criminal law, punishment, it
is true, has a different signification. The idealist school looks
upon it as the moral compensation for the harm occasioned
by the crime. The juristic school properly so called (which,
especially in Italy and Germany, has become the classical
school) declares, on the other hand that it represents the
defense of the juridical order.[2] Of the idealists I have already
spoken of in connection with the theory of expiation.[3] I may
add here that it is impossible to solve the problem of punishment by the idea of absolute justice, for it will never be
discovered what is the absolutely just punishment which
corresponds to any given crime. The theory, moreover, is without any criterion of its own, and is compelled to borrow the
"punctum ubi sistat" from the penal system of a particular
nation and period. Finding in this system the death penalty

---

[1] See Part I, c. II.

[2] "In the view of the classical school, the criminal was not a sentient
being, but an abstract type conceived by pure reason and existing wholly
apart from real life. It regarded the crime not as a portion of this real life,
but as a legal formula inscribed in a code. For it, the punishment was not a
means of social defense adapted for attack, but a theoretic system devised
by savants with whom the nature of the criminal was a matter of no concern"
(*A. Prins*, "Les doctrines nouvelles de droit pénal," — Revue de l'Université
de Bruxelles, 1895–1896).

[3] See preceding chapter.

prescribed for murder, it comes to the conclusion that for mere homicide death is an unjust punishment, and that in this case a lesser punishment as, for example, life-imprisonment would be a just punishment. But suppose that the death penalty disappears from the system. This same life-imprisonment will necessarily take its place. As a result, life-imprisonment would cease, over night, to be a just punishment for mere homicide. It is thus apparent that the theory of absolute justice exists in nothing but the name.

On the other hand, what we have termed the classical school, justifies punishment by the necessity of defending the rights of the citizen. But over this social necessity it sets "justice" as a regulator or modifier. With this school, justice is thus something imported from without, superior to social necessity. The fact of seeking this regulator elsewhere than in social necessity itself, shows a lapse into metaphysics. To say that the just punishment is the necessary punishment, is exactly equivalent to saying that an unnecessary punishment is an unjust punishment. The thing important to establish, therefore, is the criterion of necessity, for by this all excess will be avoided. But such a criterion will never be arrived at by metaphysical hypothesis: the method of experiment alone will give it to us. This criterion once in our possession, there will be no need of invoking any adventitious element. Social necessity, taken in its true sense and stripped of all exaggeration, will itself be the best guaranty of the individual's rights.[1]

But it is necessary that we subject to a closer examination, this element of justice by which the classical school limits the exercise of social defense. It has given rise to two principles, the adoption of which is responsible for the strictly juridical character of present-day criminal science, viz.:

(1) Crime does not exist unless the agent is morally responsible for his act. From which it follows that the gravity of the crime varies with the degree of moral responsibility.

[1] See, on this subject, *Von Liszt*, "Der Zweckgedanke im Strafrecht," § 32.

(2) The quantum of punishment must be in direct ratio to the gravity of the crime.

"Moral responsibility"; "penal proportion": these two postulates continue to form the keystone of criminal law, notwithstanding that science has demonstrated their inherent impossibility. The stone has already been loosened, but the ideas in question are too intimately bound up with commonly obtaining philosophic prejudices for any hope of its immediate dislodgment. The task will be a difficult one, but ultimate success cannot be doubted. For the rules we are dealing with, erroneously looked upon as the safeguard of individual rights, are in reality the source of the criminal law's weakness and failure.

§ 2. Moral Responsibility

Fallacies of the Principle. — To those who, regarding punishment as a means of social defense, at the same time decline to admit the existence of crime without free will, one might put this pertinent question: When the criminal act is the result of a permanent pathologic condition or of an internal impulse, violent or even irresistible, but such as may be expected to recur in the same individual, what reason exists for abating the social defense? Are we not obliged to say that against the individual whose manifest total absence of free will makes him incapable of controlling himself or resisting his vicious impulses, society requires increased, instead of lessened, protection? In the case of criminals formally declared insane, a remedy, to be sure, is found in the asylum. But the evil of the situation is that with moral responsibility regarded as an essential element of crime there follows the logical consequence of an almost complete impunity, even when the case is not one of true insanity.

Without entering into the question of free will, we venture the assertion that the consciousness of our moral liberty does not extend so far as to warrant us in believing that we possess the power of thinking and feeling in any different way from

that in which we felt and thought on a given occasion. We
know that the Ego cannot create itself, and that the character
has already been formed by a series of anterior facts, for the
most part ignored by the consciousness at the instant of its
determination.[1] Were this not so, we would be compelled to
acknowledge that in every man there takes place at each
instant a veritable miracle, that is to say, a movement of
mind not subject to the universal laws of nature, an initial
movement in nowise the effect of preëxisting or supervening
conditions, by means of which he is perfectly competent to
decide whether he will be good or bad, just or unjust, discontented or resigned, amiable or irascible. In such case the free
will would be a force continually creating the Ego,[2] — and
this is not a fact, or at least we have no proof that it is. If,
on the contrary, we regard the expression "free will" as
denoting not that which creates the Ego, but simply the consciousness that we have, at any given moment, of the Ego that
wills and decides, the impossibility of any penal system based
upon the idea of moral responsibility immediately becomes
clear. For this element is always limited by the circumstances, intrinsic and extrinsic, which may have acted upon
the individual's will. It is always relative, always the
subject of infinite gradations, and always liable to reduce
itself to an insignificant and inappreciable minimum. Heredity, atavism, and the particular circumstances of life, such as
environment, education, profession, climate, diet, and disease,
all of which exert an unmistakable influence, would therefore
operate to limit or restrain without "entirely doing away

[1] *Tarde's* view of free will comes very close to ours. "The Ego," he says,
"is the bundle of habitudes and prejudices, abilities and acquirements, which
accord with the slowly changing character. . . . If the will at the opportune
moment has not sought to make use of the moral forces at its disposal, it is
because the Ego, of which it is the strongest expression, sympathized with the
cause of temptation, appropriated it to itself, made it its own. That being so,
the Ego, there is no doubt, has not been able to will what it has not willed.
But this very thing proves the evilness of the Ego."

[2] See on this subject a most important study by *Piperno*, "La nuova
scuola di diritto penale in Italia" (Rome, 1886).

with" — I quote from a writer of the juristic school — "this spontaneous circle of movements which it is given to man to execute in the attainment of an end." [1]

From this standpoint, the problem of punishment completely defies solution. How are we going to distinguish, in the individual criminal, that which is the effect of circumstances of the kind indicated from that which is the effect of free will? How are we to fix a responsibility which is subject to infinite circumstantial limitations?

Suppose, however, there were some means of lifting the veil from the life of the offender, of disclosing this life in all its intimate details, in all its relations with the external world, from the first faint cry of the new-born child up to the instant of the criminal act. Nevertheless, this would not help us. We would still be without the history of his ancestors: we would still be unenlightened as to how far his tendencies may have been influenced by heredity and atavism. And even suppose that this knowledge could be acquired, how, again, are we to say what part has been played by psychic anomalies for which the man is not to blame, and what by anomalies due to the brain-structure, which only an autopsy can reveal?

The principle of relative or limited responsibility cannot therefore be applied to penal theory. The diagnosis to which it leads is one of purely scientific interest, — lacking completeness and uncertain in its conclusions.

The Italian Penal Code has an article which contemplates the case of a semi-responsibility. If we are to be guided by the principle of moral responsibility, then the provisions of this article ought to be the rule: they ought to be applied to all offenders alike — to those in whose cases the circumstances limiting responsibility are least apparent as well as to those in whose cases these circumstances are conspicuously present. For no offender is without some such circumstances, and where not evident they should be searched for, or at least presumed

---

[1] *Pessina,* "Il naturalismo e le scienze giuridiche" (Naples, 1879).

to exist. To do otherwise — to take such circumstances into consideration only when they chance to come to the surface, is to work a manifest injustice. Logically, then, this article would govern in every case. And as a result, the punishments established by law would prove useless, since they could not be administered in the prescribed measure.

But by what criterion would we mitigate punishment in the individual case? The problem is not solved: it looms just as large as before. With the principle of relative responsibility admitted, how are we going to maintain that this responsibility is equal in all men, in the face of our knowledge that the circumstantial limitations of free will vary "ad infinitum"?

In short, the principle of moral responsibility simply serves to defeat the ends of penal repression.

Irresistible Force. — But this is not all. In modern legislation there has been admitted the principle of irresistible internal force, an event which the doctrinaires conceive to be significant of real progress. To our mind it is quite the opposite. In the first place, it is plain that the adoption of this principle places the criminal law in subjection to the dominant philosophy of a given period. For the determinist, as has been made clear in the preceding pages, every criminal act, like every other action, good, bad, or indifferent, is a necessary effect, a manifestation of the will under the influence of a motive which prevails over other motives, as the result of preëxisting causes. The force which directs a man's acts on the most ordinary occasions of life, is not less irresistible than that which impels him to the most extraordinary actions. If all things are determined, all things are equally inevitable ("tout est également nécessaire"). The resistible impulse is the one which has met another stronger than itself. The irresistible impulse is the one which has proved stronger than any other. The act itself is evidence of the irresistibility of its impulse. If the impulse had been resistible, the act would not have taken place.

"Moral responsibility," is a phrase void of meaning, except in so far as we admit free choice, that is to say, the arbitrary or undetermined choice of the will. With this as an element of crime, how can any sentence be intelligently pronounced?

The danger, we may be told, is not serious, for determinism is not yet, and may not be for years to come, a doctrine sufficiently popular to lead judges and juries to the systematic acquittal of offenders, merely for the sake of consistency. However this may be, it is nevertheless true that instances may occur, and in fact have occurred, of the acquittal of desperate scoundrels on the plea of the irresistible force of their criminal impulse. This formula, in the plainest way, neutralizes the action of social defense, because the worst offenders, the criminals most to be feared, are the very ones in whom the impulse to evil is most imperious.

The commentators, it is true, are not without assigning definite limits in the present regard. Many of them teach that to come within this principle, the impulse, blind as it is, must be derived from a plausible motive: that the lowest and vilest motives will never serve for its recognition. But all such attempts at qualification are merely opinions which may change over night, while the formula itself, without disguise and making its own applications, continually stares us in the face. It speaks of irresistible force, of a force which no one can resist. Who will tell us whether the cupidity of a cashier, excited by the sight of the money which another has entrusted to his care, is an impulse more resistible than the unrequited passion of a disappointed lover? Who, again, will tell us whether the passion of the latter is more resistible than that of the lover who has been forsaken for another? And how are we to measure the degree of resistance which, in different individuals, the impulse *ought* to have encountered, but which in fact it did not encounter?

These suggestions are borne out by the facts. In Italy, the principle of irresistible force no longer obtains, having been omitted from the new Penal Code. But during its existence as a rule of criminal law, it resulted in homicidal criminals of all sorts escaping conviction. Hundreds of such instances

occurred. Indeed, on one occasion it was responsible for the
acquittal of a ruffian who had been hired to disfigure the faith-
less mistress of his employer. Sometimes, too, it was successfully invoked in favor of forgers, and even thieves. In short,
with this principle in force, there is no offender for whom it
does not afford a shelter. And if, in Italy, it was not always
set up as a defense in prosecutions for extremely atrocious
crimes, this was because the defendants' counsel were persuaded that the jury would turn a deaf ear to it. For there
is a universal feeling which discountenances the showing
of indulgence to certain kinds of criminals. Irrespective of
whether it is or is not the law that the man who has committed
a criminal act through irresistible impulse shall be unpunishable, juries will invariably convict the murderer whose motive has been none other than sheer brutality, the pleasure
of shedding blood, notwithstanding that his impulse is evidently blind and pathologic. The oftener the thief has
offended, the more severe will be the punishment which he
meets at their hands. And yet, take the case of a professional
thief, born of criminal parents, taught to steal from early
childhood, barred from the society of honest men, associating
continually with other criminals — who is wholly devoid of
fear or restraint, and without possibility or desire of changing
his mode of life. Where can we find a more perfect specimen
of the man who is unable to resist the criminal impulse?
If in such a case the defense of irresistibility has so scant a
prospect of success that the prisoner's counsel does not dare
to raise the question, the inconsistency is manifest. If the
principle is to be recognized at all, how can it be conscien-
tiously rejected in this instance? The truth is, that the consideration in question is overborne by a greater, namely,
the dictate of the social interest that dangerous criminals shall
not be allowed at large. To deprive them of liberty it is necessary that the jury find them responsible — find that they are
able to resist their perverse impulses. But how can they
resist if they are without a single good instinct, if in them is

neither self-respect, nor fear of God or man? Need one be a determinist to conclude that so circumstanced, the criminal cannot be other than a criminal ?

That being so, he is not responsible; therefore, according to the theory under discussion, he cannot be punished. Society has reason to be thankful that juries do not always see the matter in this light. In fact, the instances in which the existence of irresistible impulse has been ground for acquittal do not constitute a hundredth part of the number in which, logically, it should have been admitted. While the principle prevailed in the Italian law, complaint was heard from time to time of its abuse, in spite of the fact that in the most evident cases it was scarcely ever urged. The few instances of this character in which the defense was sustained sufficed to bring down upon the heads of the jurors a storm of popular indignation. They had answered according to their conviction the question that had been put to them: they had found what they believed to be the fact. Still, in the popular judgment they had done wrong, because their verdict resulted in the acquittal of a desperate criminal. To be honest, should they have answered the question against their consciences? Men could hardly have been put in a false position.

Such is the situation brought about by the principle which makes responsibility depend upon the possibility of resisting criminal passions and impulses. And this principle is a consequence of the equally absurd doctrine that a criminal is not a criminal unless he had deliberately willed to be such.

§ 3. The Same; Insanity

The criminal science of the jurists does not concern itself with the insane. As soon as the fact of alienation is established, it hastens to disclaim jurisdiction. And here we encounter a question which logically forms a continuation of our last subject of discussion. If the element of moral responsibility is to be laid aside, in determining who and what is the criminal, does it not therefore follow that society ought to react against the crime of the lunatic, without regard to the insanity which has been its cause? We may expect the immediate answer:— "Of course, society ought to react, and it does in fact react by confining the dangerous lunatic in an insane asylum — a proceeding which is nothing else than a means of eliminating him from the social life. Society is even induced to take this step by the mere fact of insanity, regardless of whether or not the lunatic has committed a harmful act. For his pathologic condition of mind makes it probable that he will commit all sorts of harmful acts, just as the fact of idleness, a morally pathologic condition, gives rise to the probability that the subject will commit all sorts of crime. But when this course is adopted toward the insane author of an act, which if committed by a sane person would be a crime, it is a very different thing from *punishing* him."

Unquestionably, the act of an insane person may exhibit the external appearances of crime without being criminal in reality. Take the case mentioned by Maudsley, of the woman who "had dreamed that her children cried out to her that the house was on fire, and in the confusion of waking had thrown her youngest child out of the window in order to save it." [1] No one would ever think of calling her a criminal. For unless the act corresponds with the intention, crime does not exist. The same rule would govern in cases where the act is the result of an epileptic access, of impulsive insanity, or of any mania which has caused the extinction of conscience. But does the fact that the madman intended to do what he did justify us in classing his act as a crime? We know that in many instances insane persons have really the intention of damaging or setting fire to property, or even of killing. The answer must be in the negative, because, according to our theory, crime exists only as a revelation of character, the effect of an improbity or cruelty, which may be either congenital or

---

[1] *Maudsley*, "Responsibility in Mental Disease," c. VII.

acquired, but which in all cases has become instinctive. And being instinctive, it gives rise to the apprehension of new crimes from the same individual. It is therefore essential to the existence of crime, that the disease shall not have deprived the individual of the faculties of ideation. For if he is destitute of these faculties, it is no longer a modification, but a total annihilation of his character, with which we have to deal. In a word, he has ceased to have any psychic individuality — a result which occurs in the case of mania, dementia, and progressive paralysis.

In the case of certain phrenoses or neuroses which do not altogether destroy the faculties of ideation, but result in more or less serious disturbance of these faculties, the character of the individual very often becomes changed to such an extent as to be unrecognizable. The alienation, it is true, is the cause of the moral transformation, but this does not prevent the production of a persistent character, as in the case of hysteria and melancholia. If, then, insane persons of this class are subject to criminal impulses, if they reveal tendencies to homicide, theft, incendiarism, rape (impulsive lypemania and homicidal mania, kleptomania, pyromania, erotomania), or to crime generally, by reason of any form of mania which destroys or impairs the moral sense, we are obliged to conclude that they have become the possessors of a criminal character, and that further crimes on their part may be expected.[1]

The question then finds itself solved. These are, in fact, criminals, but *insane criminals*. In other words, they are criminals of a species apart. Their moral anomaly is likely to

---

[1] It may be said in this case, to use the expression of Tarde, that the offender, who is the cause of the act in question, is identical with himself. For Tarde, the basis of responsibility is the personal identity: for us, it is the moral character. In my opinion the two come to the same thing, and the result should be that when the insanity in point of fact consists in systematized criminal ideas, or in the destruction of the moral sense, it ought to be dealt with by the criminal law. See on this subject an excellent article by *Puglia* who has unreservedly declared in favor of this theory: "Il principio genetico del diritto di punire" (Scuola positiva, Naples, 15 and 30 January, 1892). See also *G. Fioretti*, "Genio e follia" (Naples, 1902).

fluctuate with the varying phases of their disease; their character is capable of improving or even of returning to its former
state; complete restoration or total disappearance of the moral
sense are both possibilities.

Such being the case, it seems plain that for insane criminals
there ought to be reserved a special treatment — a treatment
adapted to the disease which is the cause of their crime.
Nor does this result involve us in any contradiction. On the
contrary, it is merely a reaffirmance of our central principle,
namely, that repression is to be regulated by the particular
nature of the criminal, — on the one hand, by his degree of
insociability, on the other, by the possibility of his adaptation.
The most important implication of the present conclusion
(and in this we are at one with the jurists) is that the death
penalty cannot be inflicted upon the insane. Here, again,
we may seem inconsistent. But the fact is quite the opposite.
For if the man's moral sense has been impaired, his character
corrupted, by disease, the ensuing perversity cannot be viewed
in the same light as that of other criminals. If he has lost his
idoneity for the social life, its lack will wear the appearance
of an unfortunate accident, and although he may be dangerous
as any murderer, he will not be the object of the same detesta-
tion. The death penalty is not proper in the case of the insane
criminal, because a necessary condition of its application is
that sympathy for the criminal has ceased to exist. In the
case of disease, sympathy is intensified rather than destroyed,
for the subject is in need of aid and it is society's duty to aid
him. As a result, society, in reacting, has no right to destroy
the individual. If elimination is required, it can only be
effected by his confinement for life in an asylum provided
for criminals of this species.

The criticism that our theory tends to extravagant consequences is therefore wholly without foundation. Writing in
1880, Paulhan has this to say: "If we are to accept Garofalo's
principle, how, I would ask, are we to distinguish between a
criminal and an incurable lunatic? Moreover, why should

we not execute the dangerous madman whose disease is
beyond remedy?"[1] For the distinction we need go no further
than the principles themselves, which I have laid down, beginning with the concept of crime and ending with the conditions under which the death penalty is to be applied. It
is impossible to conceive of the application of the death penalty
to an individual whose character is not permanently perverted
— to a criminal, that is to say, who is not typical but fortui-
tous. Insanity does not engender a permanent moral character: the perversity in this case is transient and capable
of change. The repression of insane criminals forms part of
our system of punishment, because the word "punishment"
does not always mean for us the same thing as it does for the
jurists. But this repression ought to have different forms
appropriate to the modifications of character for which the
disease is responsible, and which fluctuate with the phases of
the disease itself. No doubt, from the determinist standpoint
the monster is no more to blame for being a monster than the
lunatic for being a lunatic. Both, however, are equally
dangerous to the community. Hence there must be repression
in both cases, but not the same kind of repression. For if the
violation of the sentiment of pity constitutes crime, the same
sentiment would be violated by killing the insane criminal —
a result which does not occur when the criminal monster is
conducted to the gallows.

But, we may be asked, is it not likely, that with the advance
of knowledge this social sentiment, which denies sympathy
to the instinctive criminal, will undergo change? When all
men come to understand that the ferocity of the murderer
is the fault of his psychic organization, will he not become an
object of compassion? Will not his anomaly be viewed in
the same light as insanity, epilepsy, and other nervous dis-
orders? To which I would answer that no such change is possible, for the sentiment in question is in complete accord with
the conclusions of reason. The two cases are utterly different.

[1] Revue philosophique, July, 1880 (Paris F. Alcan).

In the one, as progress in the science of anthropology will make clear, we have to deal with an individuality which is intrinsically maleficent, and immutably so; in the other, with an individuality which has become maleficent as the result of an accident, but in which the maleficence is not necessarily a permanent condition. In short, the distinction is between the natural instincts, innate in the individual, the instincts which go to make up his real and irreducible character, and the adventitious instincts resulting from a physical deterioration. The latter may disappear as suddenly as they have come, because they are not created by a force inherent in the organism, but, on the contrary, by a force which is warring upon and seeking to destroy the organism.

The foregoing is but one of many considerations which go to justify the death penalty as such. But with this justification I am not at present concerned. What has just been said is for the purpose of assigning to the application of this punishment the fixed limits which are demanded by the theory of natural crime.

Insane criminals, then, form a class apart. Here we differ from the jurists in but one respect. According to their doctrine the fact of alienation prevents the existence of crime: once this fact is established, the case passes from out the cognizance of the criminal law. We maintain, on the other hand, that crime may exist notwithstanding the fact of alienation. It is, however, crime of a species distinct from all other crimes — crime which is the effect, not of a moral character determined by a permanent cause, but of a moral character determined by a transient pathologic condition and susceptible, therefore, of amelioration, pejoration, or transformation. As his disease undergoes mutations, the dangerousness of the criminal may increase, may diminish, or may even entirely vanish. Hence there should be, in this case, repression of a special form, not absolute elimination, but confinement for an indefinite period in an asylum for the criminal insane. If, for example, the mania of persecution which is the initial cause of a homicide, gives way to dementia, as is frequently the case, this repression will no longer be needed, and the subject can be cared for elsewhere or returned to his family. We have thus a form of elimination suited to the case of criminal alienation, just as the other forms of repression are suited to the case of ordinary crime — a means by which society will defend itself against the insane criminal, just as by means of a different description it will defend itself against the non-insane criminal. Why, then, should it be found necessary to exclude this species of crime from the domain of the criminal law?

It should further be noted that internment of the lunatic in an asylum conforms to the requirements of what we regard as true repression, in respect of the selection to which it gives rise. One effect only seems to be lacking, namely, intimidation,— for, as has been said, "a man does not go mad at will." But for us, it will be remembered, intimidation is only a subordinate and accessary effect and not an effect which constitutes the true criterion of punishment, as is taught by the classical school. Again, the problem is not to prevent insanity, but to prevent the crime which the lunatic is capable of committing. If the lunatic is merely a monomaniac, the menace of an indefinite term of imprisonment may not be without influence upon him. For, as Maudsley has pointed out, insane persons are to a certain extent influenced by the same motives as sane persons in what they do or forbear to do, and for the most part regard the deprivation of their liberty as a grievous suffering.[1] Then, too, when even insane criminals may be convicted and sentenced to an indefinite term of detention, this is likely to put a stop to the practice of feigning insanity, which, be it observed, is by no means as uncommon as might

[1] *Maudsley*, "Responsibility in Mental Disease," c. I.
"There can be no doubt that the insane inmates of asylums are to some extent deterred from doing wrong and stimulated to exercise self-control by the fear of what they may suffer in the way of loss of indulgence or the infliction of a closer restraint if they yield to their violent propensities" (*Ibid.* c. v).

be supposed. Taylor assures us that he examined a large number of true criminals who had been acquitted on the plea of insanity, without finding one who exhibited the least symptom of alienation.[1] Instances have been known in Italy where murderers acquitted on the ground of lypemania appeared so sure of future impunity as openly to boast that they had nothing to fear from the law. Indeed, in one such case, an offender who had murdered two persons and attempted the death of a third is said to have publicly declared that he might kill whom he pleased without incurring the slightest risk.[2]

Furthermore, the jurists are under the necessity of setting arbitrary limits to the defense of insanity so as to exclude from its benefit the accused who is suffering from monomania.[3] By making criminal insanity a subject of penal repression, such a limitation will be no longer required. Without doing violence to the teachings of science, society will find adequate protection in the plan outlined above. Under this, monomaniac criminals will be treated as criminals of a species apart. Against them will be employed the requisite mode of elimination, namely, confinement for an indefinite term in an institution, half prison, half hospital. And to the judicial power will be entrusted the duty of trying and sentencing them, as well as that of seeing to their liberation, when they have wholly ceased to be dangerous.

A decidedly senseless feature of the present system is that of treating semi-insanity as an extenuating circumstance. In such case, the punishment prescribed by law is inflicted, but the length of its term is greatly cut down. It is because of this feature that there have occurred, and in fact occur every day, instances of homicidal criminals and incendiaries, monomaniacs perhaps, but nevertheless extremely dangerous offenders, escaping with a sentence of a few years' imprisonment. If we were to take the resolute stand that these indi-

---

[1] *Taylor*, "Principles and Practice of Medical Jurisprudence."

[2] See *Lombroso*, "Incremento del delitto in Italia," p. 107 (Turin, 1881).

[3] See on this subject *Adolphe Franck*, "Philosophie du droit pénal," c. v, p. 140 (Paris, F. Alcan, 1880).

viduals are really insane, the result would be their confinement for life, or what appears much more practicable, for an indefinite term.

This sort of extenuating circumstance, indeed, seems to exist for the sole benefit of the alienist experts. As one author has justly observed: "However great may be the faults of the criminal law, the harm which they work is as nothing compared to what is suffered from insanity experts. There is hardly a criminal case in which at least one expert may not be found ready to testify to the partial responsibility of the accused, that is to say, when he does not see fit to declare him completely irresponsible. Were it not that judges and juries sometimes have the courage to disregard such testimony, or else become thoroughly disgusted with the witness' answers, the acquittals continually ensuing would be a public scandal." [1]

§ 4. The Same: Drunkenness

A further difference between the doctrines for which we contend and that of the prevailing criminal law, exists with respect to the state of drunkenness. To determine how this shall be dealt with by the criminal law many different theories have been evolved, some of which, unfortunately, have been embodied in criminal legislation. The attempt has been made to determine the question of responsibility by provisions of general application. Drunkenness has been placed on substantially the same footing as alienation, in such wise that the severity of punishment is made to depend upon the degree of the offender's intoxication. The result is that he is punished more or less severely, but always less severely than if he had not been drunk.

The criminalist of the positive school, on the contrary, will not seek the establishment of any general rule. He will distinguish drunkenness, the effect of which is merely to exaggerate the character, from alcoholism, which is a true disease and capable of entirely changing the character. In the first

[1] *Frassati*, "Lo sperimentalismo nel diritto penale," p. 327 (Turin, 1892).

case, the offender will be dealt with in the same manner as if the act had been committed in his normal state, for the excitation of the alcohol is merely the occasional cause, the fact which reveals the criminal instinct. No matter how much liquor the man of mild character may consume, he will never be guilty of stabbing his companion to death in a tavern brawl. The drunkard may then be compared to a choleric man who, in a transport of rage, does what would not have been done by a man of calm temperament, — who, although capable of shouting, gesticulating, and proceeding to other extravagances of deportment, is quite incapable of committing true crime. Incapable, that is, unless the criminal instinct is conjoined with his rage, in which case he will become a murderer in his transport, just as the man of calm temperament, possessed of the same criminal instinct, will become a murderer in his apparent phlegm. What we are here confronted with, is not the question of an augmented or diminished responsibility, but that of preserving society from murderers, the phlegmatic and choleric, the insane and the drunken, alike. The necessary means, perhaps, will differ, but each and all will conduct directly to their end, without wandering astray in the useless quest for the precise degree of responsibility.

To determine whether the drunken man has committed a crime, we must ascertain whether the nature of the crime corresponds with the character of the individual; we must see whether the inhumanity or improbity of the act is so in keeping with the propensities of the offender as to make it plain that the drunkenness has had merely the effect of determining these propensities, and rendering them unmistakably manifest. Cases abound of crimes committed in a state of drunkenness, where the accused have undergone previous convictions for the same sort of offense. There are other cases where, although not previously convicted, the defendant is known to have had a bad reputation. What is to be done with such criminals? Their drunkenness must be wholly disregarded: they must be dealt with precisely as if they had not been drunk. But, again, cases may arise (especially in crimes other than homicide and theft) where there is a clearly evident incompatibility between the punishable act and the character of the offender, the existence of which incompatibility requires us to attribute the crime to the alcoholic excitation alone. This situation oftenest occurs in the case of offenses such as strikings ("coups"), insults ("injures"), incendiarism, indecent assaults, and defamation. If it be found that the punishable act has not been premeditated before the drunkenness ensued, that the offender has not sought by the use of the liquor to strengthen a purpose already formed, then the act in question must be regarded as an involuntary offense, and not as a true crime.

The case is otherwise with the impulsive criminal who has become what he is as the result of chronic alcoholism. We have here a continuing cause of crime, a cause which will persist until the causes of the vice disappear. Consequently, what is needed for offenders of this description is not leniency of punishment, but special treatment. Like insane criminals they should be confined in an asylum combining the features of both prison and hospital, from which they will be discharged only in the event of their being completely cured of the vice.

§ 5. The Same: Hypnosis

The subject of hypnotic suggestion need not long detain us. As yet, few instances are known where hypnotism has been employed to induce the commission of crime, and these, moreover, are not very well authenticated. Should, however, the art of hypnotism become a matter of more general knowledge and be taken advantage of by criminals, there would be need of a definite rule. In that event, it is plain, under any sort of theory, that the hypnotizer would be properly punishable as the real author of the crime, while the person hypnotized could only be regarded as the passive instrument, — guilty, perhaps, of an involuntary offense for having imprudently subjected himself to the hypnotic influence, but of nothing more. A very different case, however, would be presented where the agent has been hypnotized at his own instance, to guard against the possibility of his resolution weakening at the last moment. Here, according to the principles of the classical school, no guilt on his part would exist. Whatever may have been his previous design, if at the instant of the rape, homicide, or other crime, he had no longer moral liberty and consequently could not recede from the accomplishment of this design, the jurists to be consistent would have to declare him unpunishable.

The logic of our theory conducts to the opposite conclusion. In such a case, where the suggestion is merely a means of rendering the criminal intention irrevocable, of strengthening the resolution already formed, there is nothing to diminish the necessity of social defense. The situation is similar to that where the offender intentionally makes himself drunk immediately before the commission of the criminal act. Furthermore, it seems to be true that the subject obeys the suggestion only when the thing which he is ordered to do is not repugnant to his moral character; otherwise he resists, and renders the suggestion unavailing. This is a view which I advanced many years ago, and which is now generally accepted. Although many examples might be cited in its support,[1] proofs, however, are still insufficient to warrant a definite conclusion on the point — to enable us to say with certainty whether, in the act dictated by suggestion, all voluntary participation of the subject is to be excluded, or whether the suggestion merely operates to provide him with the impulse to do what he desired to do.

§ 6. The Same; Infancy

It remains to consider the application of the principle of responsibility to the *age* of the offender. The codes following the theoretic ideas upon which they are based, fix an age

[1] *Sighele,* ("La foule criminelle," French transl. — Paris, F. Alcan), relates a large number of cases of this character.

limit under which there cannot be complete responsibility, setting this, for the most part, at eighteen years. In the case of childhood, adolescence, and early youth, they admit a limited responsibility, the legal effect of which is a reduction of punishment, varying from one or two degrees to as much as one-half or three-fourths.

This rule of thumb leaves wholly out of account distinctions of sex, maturity, and disease, as if these circumstances were of no possible importance. Needless to say, it cannot be accepted by positive criminal science. As has been already pointed out, criminal psychology and anthropology furnish us with the means of recognizing in the child the born criminal, of recognizing in the youth corrupted by bad examples, whether of his family or of his associates, the incorrigible offender. "A certain proportion of offenders," say Marro and Lombroso, "have been such since their earliest years. This result may or may not be due to hereditary causes, or to put the case more clearly, if some of them are the victims of a bad education, for most of them education has accomplished no good." [1] This opinion is substantiated by a multitude of examples. The propensities to violence and bloodshed sometimes begin to manifest themselves at a very early age: they result in the child inflicting a series of violent physical harms, trifling in importance, perhaps, but entirely without provocation. Such acts the law ordinarily punishes with a few days or months of imprisonment. They are repeated, too, with a frequency which would hardly be credited by one who has never had occasion to inspect the record-sheets ("casiers judiciaires") [2] of criminals. And these sheets,

---

[1] "I germi della pazzia morale e del delitto nei fanciulli" (Archivio di psichiatria, scienze penali, etc., Vol. IV. No. 2). See further on this subject a very interesting article by *Gino Carlo Speranza*, "Criminality in Children" (Green Bag, November, 1903). See also *Perez*, "L'éducation morale dès le berceau," p. 110 (Paris, F. Alcan, 1888).

[2] ["Casier" literally signifies a filing case: a cabinet furnished with pigeonholes. From the use of such a cabinet in filing data, the term "casier judiciaire" has come to be applied to the record of an individual's convictions.

"In criminal and correctional matters . . . investigation of the suspect's

be it noted, tell but a part of the story: they speak only of such of the offender's acts as have been the subject of judicial cognizance.

In very many instances a brutal murder is simply the sudden revelation of an instinct for bloodshed on the part of the offender, which the anthropologist might have discovered long before. And yet, we are aways ready to excuse the former crimes of such an individual, solely on the ground of his youth at the time of committing them. They are not a subject of especial concern, being always attributed to the heat of the passions, while as a matter of fact they often involve the manifestation of an innate and indomitable perversity, which will only increase with the added years. It is in such cases, particularly, that anthropology could render a most important service to criminal science, completing for us the description of the *typical physiognomy*, both physical and moral, of the instinctive murderer or thief. The criminalist, convinced that in this youthful offender he has to deal with an individual born to crime, an individual who with his advance in years will be an ever-increasing menace to society, ought to demand the adoption of the adequate means of repression. He ought to insist that segregation for life, or at least for an indefinite term, take the place of the few months of imprisonment in a so-called "house of correction" (deserving rather to be termed a "house of corruption"), usually meted out to such an offender under existing laws.

antecedents is rendered possible by the system of 'casiers judiciaires,' the essential idea of which consists in keeping a local register, in the judicial record-office ('greffe') of the arrondissement wherein the individual was born, of every sentence pronounced against him, at any time or place. . . . Whenever a suspect or an accused appears before a court, nothing is easier, with knowledge of his birthplace, than to procure his judicial biography. The 'casier judiciaire' is therefore an accessory mechanism in the application of the laws relating to recidivism." Upon request, the keeper of the records furnishes a "bulletin" or extract enumerating the prior convictions. The system was suggested by Bonneville de Marsangy and put into effect by an administrative order of the French government in 1850. It was subsequently adopted in Italy and other countries. (*Garraud,* "Traité de droit pénal français," III, pp. 168–170). — TRANSL.]

The authors last cited (**Marro** and **Lombroso**) suggest the use of the Froebelian method of education, supplemented by a special hygienic regimen, as a means of overcoming the criminal tendencies of children. If, however, these tendencies are found to be tenacious and ineradicable, they have no hesitation in proposing "the confinement for life in an appropriate institution ('una casa di perpetuo recovero') of minor offenders under the age of twenty-one years."

Even in the case of the most heinous offenses, the codes punish criminal children under fourteen or sixteen years of age by a few years of imprisonment or surveillance, and lessen the punishment to correspond with their limited responsibility. How far apart criminal law and science are in this regard, is painfully obvious.[1]

From our summary examination of the subject of moral responsibility, are we not warranted in concluding that such a doctrine is in manifest contradiction to the object of social defense? And ought not the fact of this contradiction to be patent, even to those who to some degree believe in the existence of free will on the part of the criminal? As we shall see later, the legislation to which this doctrine has given rise, while professing to have as its end the protection of society, in reality protects nothing. The utter failure of the doctrine in practice is such as might be expected from its invalidity in theory.

---

[1] The former Italian penal code, which fixed at twenty-one years the age of complete responsibility, did not allow, however, a reduction of punishment in the case of minors between eighteen and twenty-one years guilty of the offenses most shocking to the sentiment of humanity, such as parricide, robbery accompanied by murder, and the like. This exception offended the jurists' notions of uniformity, and they were successful in keeping it out of the new code. As a result, instances have occurred of criminals, comparable only to ferocious beasts, turned loose to prey on society after serving some years in prison. The draft code, it must be said, fixed at eighteen years the age of complete responsibility in all species of crimes, but the consensus of opinion in both chambers being in favor of twenty-one years, the limit was so fixed in the code as finally adopted.

§ 7. Proportionality between Crime and Punishment

Our attention must now be directed to the other cardinal principle of the classical system, namely, the rule of penal proportion, or in other words, the necessity that the quantum of the punishment shall correspond with the quantum of the crime. At first glance, this rule may not appear an objectionable one, but a very slight examination serves to disclose its inherent unsoundness. Scrutiny of the two terms which it involves immediately makes clear the impossibility of establishing between them any relation useful to social defense.

The Gravity of the Crime. — The first term, viz., the gravity of the offense, is insusceptible of exact determination, for the reason that a uniform criterion is lacking. Sometimes it is the damage, sometimes the alarm, occasioned by the criminal act. Sometimes, again, it is the importance of the duty which has been violated. Different authors have different opinions in this regard. Thus the Italians give preference to the first two, while the French school, founded by Rossi, declares for the third. Certain it is, however, that no one of these elements by itself furnishes an adequate test for the solution of the question. The conclusions arrived at, it is true, are not dissimilar, because, as a practical matter, the alarm must very often depend upon the immorality of the act and, at the same time, upon the damage. Nevertheless, the graduated scale of offenses, with its distinctions of species and sub-species, is nothing more than the result of an arbitrary compromise of conflicting juristic theories.

For the advocates of the *damage* criterion, the question of criminal attempt presents serious difficulties. Confronted with this question, they are either compelled to abandon their test altogether, or else invent for their purposes a new species of damage which they call *indirect*. This consists in the danger which has been incurred as a result of the criminal act. But in adopting such a course, they signally fail to explain why the danger which is past should be called upon to measure the importance of the crime. How, moreover, are we to compare, one with another, the heterogeneous facts which constitute *direct* damage in different cases, such as the physical pain of a wound, the moral suffering engendered by a calumnious accusation, the loss of money or property attendant upon some crimes, the shame and dishonor attendant upon others? Who will tell us which of these harms is the most keenly felt, the most irreparable, the one which brings in its train the most serious consequences?   Any attempt to fix the gravity of the direct damage occasioned by the various offenses, in such wise that it shall furnish a basis for determining the relative gravity of the offenses themselves, seems to us utterly hopeless. If, then, we would use the test of damage, we are driven to an estimate of the indirect or social damage, that is to say, the alarm and the effect of the evil example.   But here we can only proceed by the sheerest empiricism, for the relative gravity of offenses would be dependent upon a thousand circumstances of time and place.   Their importance would be measured according to the public appreciation of the danger, the alarm, — and not according to their true quantum. This it is impossible to appraise without an acquaintance with the life history and the psychology of the offender. The social danger is not that to which an individual has already been exposed, but that which continues. Of itself, the past danger is without sociologic importance: it is important only as one of the elements which enable us to determine the future danger.

The importance of the duty violated, when applied as a criterion, serves merely to create a fresh problem.[1] How are we to recognize the relative importance of different duties? "Ask the human conscience," — answers Rossi, — "that conscience which speaks even from the lips of childhood, whose notions of justice assuredly do not find their source in the law." [2] But how far will the responses of this conscience be certain and uniform? Rossi himself is obliged to admit that

---

[1] See *Carrara*, "Programma del diritto penale," § 184.
[2] *Rossi*, "Traité de droit pénal," Book III, c. IV.

the "fact of conscience" cannot be studied in the individual
case, — that his method can do no more than fix the principal
categories.   But here again doubt takes the ascendant.
"There may exist a constant moral criterion to determine that
certain acts are evil, but there is certainly no universal and constant moral criterion by which we may judge that one of these
acts is more evil than another." [1]   "For," adds a German
author, "it never can be said, under any circumstances, that
from the moral point of view any given offense surpasses
another in gravity." [2]   The different species of duties are too
differently appreciated, not only by individuals but by the
social classes as a whole.   It must be noted, also, that the terms
of the comparison are not homogeneous.   The public conscience, unquestionably, will have no hesitancy in declaring
that theft, rape, swindling and malfeasance in office, for
example, are crimes, but it can only stand mute when asked
as to the degree of intrinsic immorality pertaining to each of
these crimes.

The truth is that no method whatever will enable us to
determine in an absolute manner the relative gravity of
offenses.   There are too many elements to be taken into
consideration.   We have to deal with the gravity of the material harm, that of the immaterial harm, that of the intrinsic
immorality of the act, that of the danger, and finally, that of
the alarm.   What right have we to single out any one of these
and ignore the others?

The Gravity of the Punishment. — In spite of these difficulties, there was formed, at least for the principal species,
a scale of crimes graduated according to their supposed gravity,
over against which was set a similar scale of punishments.
The penal problem was regarded as solved when the highest
and lowest degrees of the one were made to coincide with the
highest and lowest degrees of the other.   In this, we have

---

[1] *Carrara, op. cit.*, § 184.
[2] *Von Holtzendorff*, "Das Verbrechen des Mordes und die Todesstrafe,"
c. 19.

what the classical school terms "penal proportion." The greatest thinkers, it is true, have not yielded assent without misgiving. Rossi, for example, declares that "this method does not offer enough landmarks to ensure our keeping on the right path." But he was unable to suggest any other. With the two parallel catalogues of crimes and punishments in front of us, he says that "there would be a chance, as we descended the scale, of recognizing the relation of the several punishments or degrees of punishment with the several crimes." Subsequently, however, he admits that a valid point of departure is lacking, and that therefore the problem remains unsolved.[1]

Still, if this distinguished scholar was able at all to reconcile himself to the method in question, it was only because he did not regard the social defense by the prevention of crime as the true end of punishment. He was a believer in absolute justice, and hence in the necessity of repairing evil by evil. The inexplicable thing is that the same method is adopted by those for whom prevention is the principal object of punishment. For logically it would seem that to accomplish prevention, our first step should be to discover the degree of prevention which the menace of the various punishments is capable of exercising, rather than to set up a purely theoretic proportion which can be of no possible aid in this regard.

The theory advocated by Romagnosi and Feuerbach is somewhat more rational. Here, the punishment is proportioned to the degree of desire or criminal impulse, so that it may serve as a counter-impulse, capable of overcoming the former. But this theory, as has been already suggested, verges on intimidation — tends, that is to say, to make the guilty person an instrument wherewith society may terrorize others. According to these authors, punishment ought to increase in direct ratio to the criminal impulse, because, as they view it, the stronger the impulse, the greater the danger to society. This, if I am not mistaken, is the weak point of the

[1] *Rossi, op. cit.*, Book III, c. vi.

theory. For it may be that once the crime has been committed, the danger in question has diminished or become nonexistent. On a future occasion the impulse may not possess the same energy, for its force at the time of the criminal act may have been the effect of exceptional circumstances which will never recur. In that case we would be punishing the offender, not on account of the danger arising from himself, but because of the danger to be apprehended from others. On the other hand, if the impulse to which the crime was due, was a weak one, this does not argue an absence of violent impulse in the future. The very weakness of the reaction may encourage the force of the impulse. The desire need not be very keen nor the passions greatly excited: the absence of the moral sense alone is sufficient to cause the criminal movement ("mobile") to prevail. In the present case, then, the counterimpulsion would be inadequate, just as in the former case it would be excessive. The sole object of the punishment, therefore, would be indirect prevention. The offender would be punished not for that which he is capable of doing, but for that which others, moved by his example, are capable of doing in his place. The reasons which prevent us from adopting the theory of intimidation have already been fully explained, and need not be here repeated. We believe in inflicting a harm upon the offender only so far as this harm is made necessary by the danger deriving from the individual himself. *Special* prevention ought to be the direct object of punishment. *General* prevention will be its occasional effect — an effect which, as has already been seen, will never fail of production, when the means adopted are those exactly suited to the individual.

What we must measure, then, is not the force of the criminal desire, but rather the strength of resistance to this impulse — in other words, the moral sense of the individual. Only by thus proceeding can we attain to the knowledge of what is to be feared from him. If this is possible, the problem is all but solved. Nothing more remains than to adapt the means of

prevention to the agent's degree of constant perversity.
Search for a quantitative criterion of crime therefore becomes
utterly useless.

The difficulty of arriving at such a criterion, because of the
lack of homogeneity in the terms of comparison, has just
been pointed out. Even if it were possible to confine our
comparison to crimes of the same species, our efforts would
come to nothing. The use of the damage test would lead us
no further than the measure of the material or pecuniary
reparation owed to the injured party. As for the other criteria
referred to above, they are never of any importance save
as representing elements of the constant perversity of the
offender.

The graduated scale of punishments must then be entirely
discarded. With its disappearance, the relation sought to be
established loses one of its terms, and the question of penal
proportion ceases to exist.

The True Inquiry — the Question of Adaptation. — In its
stead, the question with which we are called upon to deal
is that of the *adaptation of the offender to the social life*, in the
various classes of crimes. Our efforts, in other words, are to
be directed, not to measuring the quantum of harm to be
inflicted on the criminal, but to determining the kind of restraint best fitted to the peculiarities of his nature.

"What!" some one may exclaim, "Would you make no
distinction in punishment between the man who has stolen
twenty francs and the man who has stolen but twenty
centimes?"

My answer is that I do not know, for the question is one
which cannot be decided abstractly. The thing important
here to determine is — which one of these two thieves has the
greater criminal aptitude, and is thus the greater danger to
society? It may well be the former, but it may quite as well
be the latter.

What we are aiming at is not to fix the quantum of suffering
occasioned by the offense, on the basis of the value of what has

been stolen, but to designate the repressive means which shall be exactly appropriate, that is to say, the obstacle capable of averting the danger. The problem then can be formulated in but one way. "By what means are we to determine the offender's degree of constant perversity and the degree of sociability which he still retains?"

To answer the question requires us, first of all, to recall the distinctions arrived at in our study of criminal anomaly. Having before us the different groups fixed by our analysis, we shall proceed to compare the particular criminal in question with one or other of these groups. We shall be careful not to exclude the "objective" circumstances of the crime — the circumstances from which the existing law determines the seriousness of the offense. On the contrary, we shall select from among them, such as are really indicative of perversity, as well as those which will enable us to assign the case in hand to its proper class. For example, the circumstances which characterize aggravated theft ("vol qualifié") will no doubt be subjected to examination, but only as constituting one of the elements which will enable us to determine whether the author of the offense ought to be classed as a thief from instinct, from idleness, from the effect of a neglected and depraved childhood, from the effect of bad company, or simply because of the evil examples of his family surroundings.

For this purpose, we ought to know the previous history of the offender, — and it will therefore become necessary to investigate as closely as possible his family and social relationships. The age of the criminal will be a most important circumstance. Inquiry must also be made as to the education which he has received, his occupations, and his general aim in life.

Stress has been laid upon the difficulties of such an investigation. The fact is, however, that very much the same sort of inquiries are made daily in the criminal courts. The difference is that their results are not sufficiently taken into consideration in passing sentence. Under the prevailing law, these circumstances affect only the measure of punishment, while for us they operate precisely to determine the repressive means required and the kind of punishment thereby entailed.

These repressive means will be naturally pointed out by the possibility of the offender's adaptation, that is to say, by the conditions of the environment in which presumably he will cease to be dangerous.   If, for example, the case is that of an offender who has committed a theft, the first thing to be determined, — and from the subjective characteristics, — is whether we must apply to him a means of elimination, or whether mere enforced reparation will not suffice.   Should elimination be found requisite, then we must see whether it ought to consist of internment in an oversea penal colony ("relégation") for life or for an indefinite term, or, in the event that the age of the offender is such as to offer the hope of his moral reformation, whether it should not take the form of his commitment to an agricultural colony or industrial establishment.

Poletti, while recognizing the validity of the criterion thus proposed, has endeavored to harmonize it with the theory of responsibility, that is to say, relative responsibility, for he can conceive of no other.   "So far as prevention is concerned," he says, "we can effect this reconcilement by adding to the sentiment of responsibility for the act, fear of the punishment which in ordinary cases is deemed sufficient to thwart the offense.   With respect to repression, we accomplish the same result, if to these two sentiments which have not been sufficient to prevent the offense, we add the carrying out of the threatened punishment in such measure as the law deems sufficient for its own defense, ("che la legge reputa sufficiente a tutelare il diritto"), and to suppress the desire of committing new crimes."   But is the law to deem sufficient that which experience has shown to be insufficient?   It seems hardly possible that such can be the author's idea, for a fiction of this sort could serve no useful end.   If, then, the punishment established by law must be really sufficient for the prevention of new crimes on the part of the same individual, does it not logically follow that the proposed criterion is the only one which furnishes a practical solution?

If, as Poletti would have us, we are to adopt the view that the phenomenon of crime is the result of a lack of adaptation to the legal relations of associated men, the remedy for which is to be sought in punishment,[1] why should we stop short of the consequences which such a point of departure necessarily involves? Why, when it comes to a criterion of punishment, should we not follow whither these consequences lead? Why, for example, discarding the death penalty, should we reduce all punishments to a single type — that of imprisonment for a term definitely fixed in advance? We are told that the human personality has rights which must be respected. Such an answer quite overlooks the fact that every punishment necessarily violates some of these rights. All such rights are circumscribed by arbitrary limits representing a compromise between individualism and the social necessities. But the word "individualism" has no meaning for criminal science. Society cannot defend itself without encroaching upon the rights of those individuals, who by committing crime have trampled under foot the rights of others. What then do we gain by trammeling social reaction? We are not directly concerned with finding a means whereby more or less suffering shall be inflicted: all we ask is the recognition of a minimum relation between the end and the means of attaining it. The whole matter reduces itself to the question of the true social necessity. To fix this, and fix it accurately — such is the problem upon which all our efforts must be brought to bear. Any attempt to discover a criterion elsewhere is to engender errors — errors which, finding their way into legislation, are attended with disastrous results.

In my judgment, therefore, the old criterion of proportionality must give way to that of *idoneity*. This criterion was

[1] *Poletti,* "Il sentimento nella scienza del diritto penale," pp. 126, 127 (Udine, 1882).

suggested by me under a slightly different form in one of my earlier works.[1] To designate the active and constant perversity of the agent and the quantum of harm to be apprehended from him, — or in other words his capacity for crime, — I invented the term "temibilità," a word which has no equivalent either in French or English.   Such a test is merely the logical complement of the theory that punishment is the weapon of social defense.   If there is any element of strangeness in the present situation, it consists, not, certainly, in the enouncement of the criterion in question, but rather in the fact that the advocates of the social defense theory have never thought to make use of it.   For when it comes to establishing rules to govern the infliction of punishment, they have recourse, some to the objective gravity of the offense measured by the damage or the alarm, others again, to the force which impelled the criminal act, subject in both cases to the limitations imposed by the theory of moral responsibility.   None of them regards it as worth while to examine in the various cases the intrinsic value of punishments with reference to the end sought to be attained.

It is not easy, however, to overcome the prejudices which attach to certain words. The "merit" or "demerit" of human actions, the "justice" of rewards and punishments — these, it is charged, we would empty of every significance. But let it not be thought that we hold any such view. They are words which will always express something real — words which will endure as long as man is man. But what else is the merit or demerit of human actions but the indication of their dependence upon the character and the will of the individual, whatever may have been the process of character formation and the derivation of the instincts and tendencies which go to make up the character, whatever may have been the causality of the motives which determine the will. There are certain moral qualities whose display is invariably regarded as meritorious by public opinion, despite the fact that they visibly depend

[1] "Di un criterio positivo della penalità" (Naples, 1880).

upon the temperament, and hence are impossible of attribu-
tion to the free choice of the individual. Such are courage,
fortitude, coolness, self-possession. Is the soldier to be denied
our plaudits for his deed of valor, because we know that
courage is hereditary in his family? Are we to withhold our
blame from the cowardly deserter, because we know that he
is unable to resist the impulse of fear? It has been often said
that some men by dint of constant efforts form their own characters. True, but whence came the strength of will which
brought this to pass? Its origin can only be found in the natural qualities of the psychic organism. But so far as philosophy is concerned, what does it matter whether the motive
is plainly evident or remains hidden in obscurity, if we are
convinced that a motive does in fact exist?

The same may be said of what we are accustomed to call
the "natural gifts." Physical merits, such as strength, beauty,
grace, talent, command admiration, while their opposites
awaken repugnance and disgust. Now, the expression of
admiration necessarily results in an increase, the expression
of disgust or repugnance in a decrease, of happiness on the
part of the persons who are its object, although these persons
were not free to have or not to have the qualities or defects
in question. The praise of virtuous and the blame of vicious
acts really present the same case. If these acts are peculiarly
our own, that is to say, if they are a derivation from our character, from our individuality, — this is sufficient for the surrounding world to grant us that increase or diminution of
happiness with which it is accustomed to requite acts which
are manifestly devoid of moral merit.

If the determining force is none other than the Ego, why
should we refuse to recognize the praiseworthiness or blame-
worthiness of a determined act? [1] Is the Ego the determining

---

[1] "It remains then to be inquired if the moral sentiment cannot quite as
well be applied in deciding whether to praise or blame a determined act.
For my part, I believe that it can . . ." (*Fr. Paulhan* in review of my brochure: "Di un criterio positivo della penalità" — Revue philosophique, July,
1880).

force, or is it not? — this is the only inquiry made by public opinion — the only thing which it seeks to know in order to bestow admiration or censure, reward or punishment. With the residue of the problem, namely, the reason why the Ego is what it is, it concerns itself but little. For us, it is true, the wicked, the imbruted, the vicious, the criminal, are no more able to transform themselves into persons of honesty and virtue, than is the crawling reptile to fly through the air. But the world itself no more than the criminal is master of its conduct: it is not free to give or withhold its sympathy or repugnance, its praise or its blame, its reward or its punishment. Necessity on the one side confronts necessity on the other. "Merit" and "demerit" have always relation to acts dependent upon the moral qualities. The words themselves require no change. All that is needed is a correct understanding of their meaning.

But, it is insisted, to inflict suffering upon one who is merely the victim of his own depraved organism is to do injury to justice. Be it so: if the suffering inflicted is necessary for the preservation of society, let abstract justice take such offense as it may. The entire world affords a continual spectacle of similar injustices. Men suffer because of mental and physical defects, because of the lack of energy and intelligence, because of an unfortunate situation in life, which they are without power to change. The child who is deficient in memory or attention will never receive good marks at school. However great a source of mortification he may find it, he will always remain at the foot of his class. For the clerk of small intelligence there is no hope of preferment; sooner or later he may expect his dismissal. Must we call these injustices? Is the law itself unjust, when it condemns the children to poverty because of the debts of the father? Is elegance unjust when it shrinks from squalor? Do we speak of injustice when an audience hisses from the stage a tenor who cannot sing? — when the populace hoots an incompetent general?

Life is never free from afflicting situations. What the rich

may enjoy to the poor is denied. On the one hand is the re-
cluse, on the other the Don Juan. The smiles of some women
are eagerly courted; their sisters have never attracted a passing glance from the meanest of men. We see men full of health
and vigor, and others who bear the burden of incurable ail-
ments. The strong man dominates: the weak man obeys.
Why must this be so? Why should not all men be equally
strong, handsome, rich, attractive, and happy? Why, at
least, is there not vouchsafed to all the possibility of enjoying
our few years of earthly existence? Why should nature, so
prodigal with my neighbor, deal so niggardly with me?

But no such justice is found in creation. In one climate
man freezes, in another he burns. There are planets surrounded with brilliant rings, others inundated with light and
heat, others again, which are arid and desolate. Not even two
leaves can be found exactly alike. Nature abhors equality.
How then can we hope for equality in human society?

Since the world knows no such thing as equality, there are
bound to be human beings who are happy, and others who are
not, — neither responsible for their lot. And such injustice
is inevitable. Human justice cannot do otherwise than imitate
the justice of nature, by excluding the unfit. But just as the
care which a hospital patient receives is measured by standards quite other than the degree of the possibility, existing at
the time of contracting the disease, that he might have
avoided its causes, so repression cannot be measured by the
degree of the possibility, existing at the time of the criminal
act, that the criminal might have avoided the causes of his
crime.

If this works injury to justice it is assuredly not the existing
system of criminal law which offers anything better. According impunity to irresistible impulses, it recognizes among the
causes of irresponsibility neither innate degeneracy nor that
corruption in childhood which stifles every virtuous sentiment,
uproots every good instinct, and destroys the possibility of remorse. Its hand falls upon idleness, regardless of whether it is

voluntary or involuntary. It imposes the same fine upon the man of wealth to whom the sum is a trifle as upon the poor wretch whose little hoard accumulated by long years of toil is swallowed up in the payment. It shuts up in the same jail the man for whom imprisonment is unimaginable torment, and the vagabond to whom it furnishes comfortable quarters and congenial company. It buries in the same penitentiary the man who has committed a crime solely for food and shelter and the man who finds himself in a living tomb. And this is said to be justice! Is justice of this sort not a thousand times farther away from the ideal than that which would result from our system? For, instead of requiring the judge to weigh what is to him an unknown quantity — the resistibility of the criminal impulse, we would have him estimate from experimental data the probability of future danger. Instead of advocating the infliction of a useless punishment proportioned to the hypothetical and indefinable quantity which represents the criminal's free will, we propose that he adapt to the case in hand the preventive means which it requires, keeping strictly within the limits of social necessity. Under this method, the criminal will undergo the punishment which has been merited, not by a doubtful faculty of his mind, but by all that which constitutes his personality, namely, his psychic organism, his instincts, and his character.

The aim is not to strike at misfortune, but to preserve society from new misfortunes whose advent is already foreshadowed. The human sentiment of sympathy intervenes to preserve the lives of offenders whose death is unnecessary, for whom there is yet the hope of adaptation to the social life. But in the case of the others — those men who by reason of a moral monstrosity can never be aught but enemies of society — this sentiment is silent; none will lament their death. In this case, it is to be said with Shakespeare:

"Mercy but murders, pardoning those that kill ";[1]

or with Dante:

[1] "Romeo and Juliet," Act. III, Scene I.

"Qui vive la pietà quando è ben morta." [1]

The real injury is done to justice, when to prevent the crimes of others, there is put to death an offender whose complete perversity has not been established. The punishment which is inflicted for the sake of example is very likely to be unjust, as is seen in times of war or revolution or under despotic governments, whether of the individual or the mob. But punishment cannot be other than just, when it has the single aim of disarming an enemy of society, when it is solely a means of *direct* and *special* prevention, when it is adapted to the *individuality* of the offender. It will be no doubt exemplary, but only by a natural effect which is not at all to influence its determination. Such is the true justice — the justice by which is tempered the maxim: "Salus populi suprema lex est." None is to suffer either more or less than his individuality has merited. By this rule alone can we foreclose the possibility of exaggerations, whether of individualism or utilitarianism.

§ 8. Criminal Attempt

Supplementing the doctrines of responsibility and penal proportion in the existing criminal law are certain lesser theories which it now becomes necessary to examine. The first and most important of these is the theory of criminal attempt ("tentative") — a theory which is made to adjust itself to the principles of the classical school only with considerable difficulty.

Objective Doctrines of Attempt. — In Germany and Italy there exists an objective doctrine of attempt, under which the attempt is punishable only when the intent has been in part carried out. In this view, therefore, the attempt is simply a fragment of the crime meant to be committed and, like the

---

[1] ["Here pity most doth show herself alive,
When she is dead."
"Divina Commedia," Book I, Canto XX, 26, 27 (Cary). — TRANSL.]

latter, has an objective side (Osenbrüggen; Geyer). There is also a more recent doctrine which defines attempt as "an act adapted to produce the intended result and possessing the material character of a crime" (Cohn).[1] In France and Italy it is required that the criminal intent be manifested by acts directed to its accomplishment ("actes d'exécution") which are intrinsically capable of bringing about the crime. This consequently exempts from punishment cases of attempt in which the agent has mistakenly employed means which are insufficient or inapt to produce the desired result. Moreover, the distinction is made between the absolute insufficiency and the relative insufficiency of the means. It is acknowledged that there is criminal attempt when the means would in general have proved sufficient, although they have turned out not to be so in the particular case (Carrara). The further conclusion is reached that when the agent, although selecting means which would have proved effectual, yet by reason of some circumstance of which he is in ignorance, actually employs other means which proved insufficient, the case is not one of punishable attempt. Thus if A, believing that he is aiming a loaded gun at X, pulls the trigger with intent to kill X, his act is not punishable, if it transpires that the weapon was not loaded. The same would be true if, unknown to A, the mechanism of the piece had been so out of order as to prevent its discharge.

These views are in keeping with the principle that attempt is a partial carrying out of the intent, or, as it may otherwise be expressed, a material part of the fact which would have constituted the crime. For, it is contended, the law cannot take cognizance of acts of no immanent hurtfulness. It is of little moment that the agent is immoral or even danger-ous: the thing to be looked to is whether the danger was inherent in the act. Crime cannot exist without an act

---

[1] See articles in the Zeitschrift für die gesammte Strafrechtswissenschaft for 1881 and the Gerichtssaal for 1880, where this subject is discussed with much learning and refinement.

of criminal efficacy.[1] "Punishment is directed not to the criminality of the agent displayed by his external act but to the *fact* accompanied by the criminality of the agent" (Carrara).

The True Theory of Attempt. — The true rule, in our opinion, should be exactly the opposite. In this respect the divergence between our system and that of the jurists could not be more marked. The view of criminal attempt which we regard as the correct one, closely approaches the so-called subjective theory advocated by many German writers, notably by Herz, Schwarze, Von Buri, and Von Liszt. According to the teaching of the Roman law, the intent alone is of value in determining the question of attempt: the material fact is without significance. When no damage has been occasioned, there is nothing to strike at but the will. That this will has made use of means which presented no probability of success is a matter of small importance. Moreover, it is impossible to appraise simultaneously both the will and the fact, for they come together only in the accomplishment of the act. In the attempt they are separate, and the objective quantity, that is to say, the accomplished part of the fact, can mean nothing to us as long as the design has not been carried out. The fact has no bearing upon the case except as an expression of the agent's will. Now, the very circumstance that the intended result was not produced always indicates an impossibility either specific or relative. It serves no purpose to inquire if the means which the agent believed to be sufficient, would have been so regarded by others. A man walking toward a given point, let us say, finds further progress impossible because of the fall of a bridge. From the moment he started until he reached this point, all his acts have been useless. And yet so far as he knew, so far as any one knew who had not been apprised of the accident, the acts in question were the directest means of reaching his destination. On the other hand, from the standpoint of one

---

[1] *Geyer,* "Ueber die sogenannten untauglichen Versuchshandlungen" (Zeitschrift für die gesammte Strafrechtswissenschaft, Vol. I, p. 30.

who knew of the obstruction, what he did was futile: his acts represented an insufficient means.

This accomplished part of a design is completely devoid of objective value. "Take the case of a traveller who finds himself, tortured by thirst, in the midst of a trackless desert. All at once he descries far off a low hill crowned with verdure and dotted with human habitations. If, notwithstanding his utmost efforts, his physical forces will not enable him to reach more than half-way to this place of safety, he must inevitably perish, unless some one comes to his aid. Traversing half the distance which separated him from the oasis has not quenched half his thirst." [1]

Furthermore, there is no human act which is absolutely incapable of producing a given result, none, on the other hand, which will necessarily bring about that result. "An act can never be the cause of an effect which has not come to pass. The fact that the means employed by the agent have failed to produce the intended effect, of itself demonstrates the insufficiency of the means to accomplish the design. It may be said, generally speaking, that there are no means absolutely insufficient under all circumstances, just as there are no means absolutely sufficient. . . . Every aborting of a design is the fault of the agent, who has failed to foresee the circumstances which intervened to prevent its accomplishment. What then do we gain by seeking to differentiate the circumstances which have operated to deceive the agent? Why should it be necessary to ascertain, for example, if the obstacle existed from the outset, if it intervened during the course of the action, if the agent was mistaken in estimating his own strength and abilities, if he neglected to examine, with respect to species and quantity, the means of which he made use, or if he failed to select the instrumentality most adapted or apply it in the most effectual manner?" [2]

---

[1] *Von Buri,* "Versuch und Causalität" (Gerichtssaal, Vol. XXXII, Book 5, pp. 367, 368, — Stuttgart, 1880).

[2] Decree of the Supreme Court of the German Empire (Reichsgericht)

This subjective theory of attempt is however rejected by the jurists of France and Italy and even in Germany encounters bitter opposition. But as already suggested, it is the only theory which has any points of contact with our own.

Once punishment is measured by the perversity of the criminal, the question of attempt by insufficient means completely disappears. If the attempt, quite as much as the executed crime, suffices to reveal the criminality of the agent, there can be no difference between the two. Regardless of the sufficiency or insufficiency of the means, what must be done is, first, to ascertain whether the criminal will has been displayed in an unmistakable manner, and secondly, to determine if this criminal will is dangerous. The second branch of the inquiry is necessary, because perversity which cannot be translated into action requires no repression on the part of society.

In this last respect, there is involved a qualification of the subjective theory. For here, in some cases, examination of the means employed will not be without its use. The choice of means may serve to demonstrate the intelligence or stupidity of the agent. Such would be the case where A thinks to poison X by the use of sugar or table salt, or to shoot him with a gun which he, A, knows not to be loaded or else by firing it from a wholly impossible distance. No crime would exist in these instances, not because of the insufficiency of the means, but because of the ineptitude ("incapacità"; "inaptitude") of the agent, which this insufficiency establishes. The agent's criminal desires are nothing more than velleities. In point of fact he is harmless. In such case, therefore, penal repression would be uncalled for.[1]

But a very different case is presented if A in his attempt to poison X uses sugar which, on the representation of the

24 May, 1880: (Rechtsprechung des Deutschen Reichsgerichts, Vol. I, p. 819 *et seq.*), quoted by *Geyer* in article before cited. See also *Von Liszt*, "Das fehlgeschlagene Delikt and die Cohn'sche Versuchstheorie" (Zeitschrift, etc. before cited, p. 103).

[1] The former codes of Hanover, Brunswick, Nassau, and Baden, provided that attempt with insufficient means should not be punishable, when the choice of such means was the result of superstition or imbecility.

chemist from whom he bought it, he believes to be arsenic.
So too, the case is different if the gun with which A seeks to
take the life of X, had been loaded by A himself, but unknown
to him had been unloaded by another; or again, if instead of
an impossible distance, the distance at which he fired at X
had chanced to be merely a trifle beyond the range of any
species of fire-arm. The agent's mistake does not make him
any the less a criminal, since it in nowise proves his ineptitude.
The act in itself, we may concede, is not dangerous. But this
fact does not prevent the act itself from revealing the danger.
A similar situation exists when the means are such that their
insufficiency could not have been known without special
study, as, *e. g.*, a mistake in the quality or dose of a poison.
An error of this character does not in any way demonstrate
the agent's ineptitude. The fact of a false calculation cannot
render a poisoner harmless.

With respect to youthful offenders, it is somewhat more
difficult to arrive at a rule which will fit all cases. Frequently
the child's ignorance of matters of the commonest knowledge
is not sufficient to establish his harmlessness. He may be a
born criminal and yet his maladroitness may be such that if
he were older it would be reason for declaring him harmless.
All we need to know is whether he is possessed of discernment
and resolution. If so, this is enough to convince us that when
he outgrows his ignorance, he will become an object of danger.
In spite of the differences arising from the varying facts of
particular cases, every difficulty may be overcome by the aid
of this general rule: "Whether or not ineptitude exists on the
part of the agent is to be determined not alone from the
examination of the means employed, but by the fact taken in
its entirety." For the choice of means is important only when
it shows the harmlessness of the agent. It is a quantity without absolute value. Adoption of insufficient means may be
quite compatible with an intelligent and persevering will.[1]

---

[1] On this subject see my brochure: "Il tentativo criminoso con mezzi
inidonei" (Turin, Loescher, 1882).

The Question of Punishing Attempt. — Having thus determined the cases wherein attempt is punishable, we may now proceed to consider the measure in which punishment is to be applied. The criminalists of a former day, as we know, have marked out for us the several steps of the "iter criminis." They distinguished the acts which were merely those of preparation ("actes simplement préparatoires"), the "conatus remotus," and the attempt properly so called ("tentative proprement dite"). More recently there has been added the frustrated crime ("délit manqué"). The first two are punishable as a general rule; the last two only in special cases. And yet nearly all the modern penal codes concur in punishing the attempt ("tentative") and the frustrated crime ("délit manqué") with much less severity than the executed crime. The French Code is perhaps the only one which treats every attempt to commit crime as the crime itself.[1] But this provision has been sharply criticized by legal theorists and in practice is constantly evaded by resorting to extenuating circumstances as a means of reducing the punishment. It is supposed that the punishment should vary in severity according to the degree of forwardness in the execution of the design. Accordingly, the Italian Code, strictly logical in this regard, provides a much heavier punishment for the frustrated crime ("délit manqué") than for simple attempt ("tentative").

The reason assigned for the gradation in question is that in the attempt ("tentative"), since the agent had not arrived at the end of the "iter criminis," there is a possibility that he might have desisted before doing the final act. But this is a possibility insusceptible of determination, because the agent has been halted midway by an intervening obstacle. In case of frustrated crime ("délit manqué") it is even more difficult to justify mitigation of punishment. For here there is no room for doubt as to the resoluteness of purpose, inasmuch as the agent has done everything necessary to carry his design into execution.   [1] Art. 2.

"But," explains Rossi, "it is impossible to ignore either the distinction, natural to the human mind, between reparable and irreparable injury, or the tendency to judge the importance of human actions by their outcome." [1] This, as we view it, is a consideration entitled to no weight. The different importance accorded the success or failure of a project, depends solely upon the sensation of pain in the one case or relief in the other. When a crime has been committed, we sympathetically participate in the suffering of our fellow-being who is its victim. When, on the other hand, the commission of the crime has failed, relief succeeds anxiety in the mind of the person at whom the aggression is aimed, and in this sentiment we likewise share. If we estimate the importance of the fact by the dangerousness of the agent, the question of whether the crime has been accomplished or has been thwarted by some intervening circumstance, becomes relevant in but a single instance, namely, when this circumstance is one which could easily have been foreseen by the agent. Not having foreseen it, the agent for this reason ceases to be a true criminal and an object of danger. Nothing else, in our opinion, need be looked at. The distinction between the several stages in the acts of commission, so far as it is sought to be used as a standard for measuring punishment, seems wholly without value.

Nor can I regard as well taken the criticism which another aspect of the situation draws from Tarde.[2] He is unconcerned, he premises, with the "petty logic" of the jurists and is of the opinion that, even unexecuted, the attempt or suggestion which reveals a criminal propensity, proclaims a danger to society. But he goes on to say that the peril is increased two-fold if the crime has in fact been executed, since to the nascent criminal habitude there is joined the nascent criminal example, both objects of repression. For my part, I

[1] *Rossi, op. cit.*, Book II, c. xxxiii.
[2] *Tarde*, "Positivisme et pénalité" ("Archives d'Anthropologie criminelle," Vol. II, No. 7, pp. 35–37, — Paris-Lyons, 1887).

am unable to see how a theft accompanied by a frustrated murder ("assassinat manqué") can ever serve as a discouraging example to criminals, if the agent has in fact been able to attain his end, namely, that of robbing his victim.

The victim, let us say, has survived his wounds or escaped by the merest accident. How can either of these facts operate to lessen the force of the criminal example? It may be suggested that discovery and identification of the assailant are thereby facilitated. But this circumstance will have anything but a dissuasive effect upon other evil-doers. It will merely teach them that their safety lies in striking more effectually and insuring their victims' death. Such is the invariable result in like cases. The method which has been hitherto employed will always be dropped when they learn of a better. The experience of the malefactor who has fallen into the hands of the police is not lost upon the apprentices of crime who sit on the spectators' benches in the Court of Assizes. Far from being induced to give up their trade, they resolve to profit by the mistakes of their predecessor. Tarde admits, however, that his distinction "does not furnish the true reason why it is difficult to make judges and juries see the identity, insisted upon by Garofalo and embodied in many of the penal codes, between the consummated offense and the attempt to commit that same offense, which has been frustrated by accident." The true reason, according to Tarde, is very nearly that assigned by Rossi, namely: "the unconscious feeling common to all, of the major importance which must be accorded to the accidental and casual." We are accustomed "to admit that nothing so legitimately belongs to a man as his good or ill fortune. When the man who has attempted to dynamite a railroad train is brought to trial, every one experiences the thought that it was a fortunate thing for him, as well as for his intended victims, that the fuse went out before the sparks had reached the explosive." Our author, it is true, does not appear to justify this popular feeling. "It makes no difference," he continues, "that the criminality of this offender is

the same as if he had accomplished his design; his good fortune is his indisputable property in the eyes of all. It is
vaguely felt, — by virtue of a sort of symmetry, constant
although unconscious, unjustifiable but ineradicable, — that
to deny him this species of property would logically lead to a
denial of most of the established rights of property. This is
perhaps absurd, but the irrational is strongly rooted even in
the essence of our reason."

Such indubitably is the case and will always remain the
case, so long as criminal judgments continue to be popular
judgments. It is not upon an unjustifiable, absurd, and irrational sentiment that we should found a system of repression
which looks to the social defense. "A jury," we are told,
"will always display leniency toward the author of an unsuccessful attempt to commit murder or theft." It does not
follow, however, that the law must conform itself to this irrational tendency. What is needed is the substitution of a
rational judgment for that which is dependent upon the
verdict of the jury. Let us have judges who possess the requisite fitness to determine the fact of the criminal's perversity — to say whether or not he is a continuing source of
danger; let logic and consistency characterize their decisions;
let them inflict such punishment as is adequate, not merely
for the purpose of allaying the public alarm, but for that of
really preventing the threatened harm. Then we shall see
what leniency will be shown to the offender whose attempt
to murder or steal the merest accident has thwarted.

Our conclusion, therefore, cannot be other than this, that
an attempt to commit crime must be treated as the crime itself when the same danger proceeds from the agent. It will
always be possible to ascertain whether the agent is really a
criminal or whether, in spite of his display of criminal intention, the fact of his ineptitude must be regarded as established.
In the case of frustrated crime ("délit manqué"), the inquiry,
then, will be directed solely to discovering if the manner in
which he has set about the execution of his design, does not

reveal complete impotence for harm, and this, as before explained, irrespective of the intrinsic sufficiency of the means
adopted.　In the case of attempt proper ("tentative"),
it must further be inquired whether or not it appears that in
the absence of the unforeseen circumstance, the agent would
have voluntarily desisted before doing the final act.　The
punishment, instead of being reduced for every such case,
should be applied in the measure demanded by the consummated crime, or else dispensed with entirely, according as
the judge shall find that the criminal resolution was or was
not irrevocable.　Even acts which are merely those of preparation ("actes simplement préparatoires") may sometimes
afford a basis for the like determination.　Why, then, should
not such acts be considered in the light of a true attempt?
What possible difference can it make that one or more stages
yet remain to be traversed, if we are convinced that the
agent, if unhindered, would have persisted to the end?
Then, too, it has been admitted by many of the classical
jurists that acts of preparation may become punishable as
true attempts (Ortolan, Geyer, Rossi).　Moreover, in the
Roman law an act of preparation might assume the significance of a "conatus remotus": "cum quis, exempli gratia,
gladium strinxerit."

The lex Cornelia sanctioned the infliction of capital punishment upon the following offenders: "Qui furti faciendi causa,
noctu, cum telo ambulaverit"; "Qui in alienum cœnaculum
se dirigunt, furandi animo"; "Is qui cum telo ambulaverit,
hominis necandi causa"; "Qui, cum vellet occidere, id
casu aliquo perpetrare non potuerit"; "Qui emit venenum
ut patri daret, quamvis non potuerit dare."　Now, it is plain
that in every one of these instances, the criminal is still very
far from the final act of execution.　Nevertheless, there has
been unequivocal manifestation of his resolution and aptitude.
His acts are convincing evidence that if he had not been prevented by external force he would have accomplished the intended crime.　Why, then, should we distinguish between

a direct and an indirect act of execution? Why should the extent of the punishment be influenced by the nearness or remoteness of the terminal act? This was not the method of the Roman law: "Pari sorte leges scelus quam sceleris puniunt voluntatem."

When we have to do with an act which is simply one of preparation, there are two things to be seen: first, whether the object of the agent might have been something other than the commission of the crime, or whether the fact of his criminal resolution is beyond dispute, and secondly, if there is no doubt that the act was directed to a criminal end, whether it is conclusively shown that the agent would have persisted until the crime was accomplished. In the case of true attempt, the second inquiry is the only one necessary.

But, we may be asked, how are we to attain the requisite degree of definiteness in our conclusions? Hard as it may be to formulate any general rules, the particular case will present no great difficulties. Suppose, for example, that near the door of a well-furnished dwelling which stands some distance away from any other, two professional housebreakers are caught hiding, with burglars' tools in their possession. Can there be here any reasonable doubt of the criminal intent? If common sense calls this an attempt to commit burglary, why should the law apply to it any different name? Given a professional criminal and an act necessary in the particular species of crime which forms his specialty, there can be no doubt as to the intent. This is of course an hypothesis, but in no department of science is a principle deemed worthless solely because hypothesis is its basis. We have no right to reject the principle until it is shown that the hypothesis itself is wholly unsound or at least ignores a contrary probability important enough to be taken into account.

In acts which are simply those of preparation the criminal resolution as a rule is difficult to prove. Hence, in this case as well as in every case of "conatus remotus," it becomes necessary to subject the agent to examination. If from this we

discover in him an instinctive criminal who is totally devoid
of altruistic sentiments, or who is the prey of covetous desires
or unrestrained passion, or who is actuated by such a degree
of lasciviousness as renders him totally insensible either to
punishment or public opinion, then we may be certain, as
far as it is humanly possible to be so, that he would not have
voluntarily relinquished his purpose: the danger is there quite
as much as if the crime had been accomplished. To make
any distinction in respect of repressive measures between the
two cases would be out of the question. If, on the other hand,
our examination discloses that the agent was under the sway
of a transitory influence which in all likelihood will never
repeat itself, that in spite of his inferior morality, he is not
entirely destitute of moral sense, then the possibility may be
admitted that at some intermediate stage of his criminal
enterprise, the resistance of his good instincts or the fear of
discovery and punishment would have caused him to desist
of his own accord. For this reason the danger, although
possible, is not probable, and a mere possibility gives society
no right to strike.

In treating attempt by insufficient means as always unpunishable, the existing law is irrational; in punishing the
attempt with less severity than the executed crime, it is
absurd; in never punishing acts of preparation and always
punishing attempt proper, it is unjust. These results represent a false progress — a progress detrimental to social defense. The positivist doctrine, which in this instance comes
much nearer to the Roman law than does that of the modern
jurists, reaches very different conclusions. It holds that
attempt is punishable notwithstanding the insufficiency of
the means, provided that the choice of these does not establish the fact of the agent's ineptitude; that in certain cases
acts of preparation may be regarded as a true attempt ("tentative"); that the crime which has been frustrated by accident ("manqué par hasard") ought to be punished as if the
criminal had accomplished his purpose; and that the more

remote attempt ought in certain cases to be punished as the crime itself, in others, not at all.

§ 9. Criminal Participation

The next theory to be looked at is that of criminal participation ("complicité").[1] It cannot be gainsaid that in this respect a distinct step in advance is marked by the principle that the personal circumstances ("circonstances personelles") ought not to be imputed to the accomplice, while the material circumstances ("circonstances matérielles") ought so to be imputed only in so far as the accomplice is chargeable with knowledge thereof.[2] But while this effects a difference in the

---

[1] ["The expression 'complicité,' in a strictly legal sense, indicates only the secondary participation in the offense, but used in a general sense it denotes every participation, principal or secondary" (*Garraud*, "Traité de droit pénal français," II, p. 600, note 2). The Anglo-American classification of participants into principals of the first and second degrees and accessories before and after the fact has no counterpart in Continental law. The French law divides all the participants into the two classes of principal authors and accomplices (Art. 59, Penal Code; *Chauveau* and *Hélie*, "Théorie du code pénal," I, pp. 409, 410). In the Italian Code of 1889, three classes are recognized, viz., principal authors, principal instigators, and accomplices (Art. 63; *Lacointa*, "Code pénal d'Italie," pp. lvii, lviii). — TRANSL.]

[2] [The circumstances here referred to are those which serve to aggravate the offense and bring about an increase in the degree of punishment. By "personal circumstances" also called "subjective" or "intrinsic" is meant "in general such circumstances as relate to the understanding, the will, the mental condition, the natural, legal, or contractual relations which exist between the accused and the injured person. . . ." (*Lacointa*, "Code pénal d'Italie," pp. 48, 49, note). "Material circumstances" (frequently referred to as "objective" "real" or "extrinsic") are such as arise out of the body of the crime; such, in other words, as inhere in the acts themselves, preparatory, intermediate, or final (*Ibid.*; *Garraud*, "Traité de droit pénal français," II, p. 723). The distinction between the two sets of circumstances occupies an important place in the Continental law of criminal participation, as affecting the determination of the degree of guilt of the several offenders. For example: a servant commits a theft in the household of his master. The fact of his service is a circumstance of aggravation and, because arising out of the personal relationship of master and servant, a personal circumstance. This circumstance being taken into consideration he will be deemed guilty of domestic theft ("vol domestique") and thus incur a heavier punishment than provided for simple theft ("vol simple"). But suppose that he was aided by an accomplice who was not in the service of the master. The question then arises whether the personal circumstance which serves to aggravate the servant's offense can be imputed to the accomplice, so that he, too, can be found guilty of domestic theft.

degree of punishment, we would go still further. We are unable to understand why the same *kind* of punishment should be applied to both principal and accomplice when they cannot be ranked in the same class of criminals. The man who for the purpose of avenging an atrocious injury which his family has sustained at the hands of another, hires a bravo to kill the wrong-doer, is a very different sort of criminal from the paid murderer who actually does the deed. Why should the same kind of punishment be the portion of both? Why, again, should the same sort of treatment be meted out to the professional thief as to the novice whom he has influenced to participate in the criminal act?

Another principle of the juridical school, and one which we believe to be wholly unsound, is this: where, for example, A employs X to commit a crime and X voluntarily relinquishes the undertaking, A is exempt from punishment notwithstanding X's acceptance of the employment ("mandat"). "For," says Rossi, "no process of reasoning can establish the existence of something not yet begun, and it would be unjust as well as irrational to hold a man guilty of a crime which never had any existence." [1] Nevertheless, the same author concedes that taken by itself the fact of employing another to commit a crime might in certain cases be considered as a special offense and punished accordingly.[2]

Again: a theft is committed with violence. The fact of the violence is an aggravating circumstance, and because it is inherent in the crime itself, a material or objective circumstance. Is then the accomplice who did not participate in the violence to be affected by this material circumstance of aggravation and punished for aggravated instead of simple theft? Under the principle referred to in the text, the accomplice in the first case would be guilty merely of simple theft, because the aggravating circumstance, being personal to the servant, could not be imputed to the accomplice. In the second case, the accomplice would be guilty of aggravated theft, only if he had knowingly permitted the violence.

Circumstances of excuse and extenuation admit of a like division. The inquiry in this instance is whether a given circumstance of excuse or extenuation, plainly existing in favor of one of the participants, will inure to the benefit of his co-participant. — Transl.]

[1] *Rossi, op. cit.*, Book I, c. xxxvi.

[2] The Sardinian Penal Code of 1859 treated the case in question ("mandat

In my judgment, the true solution of the problem lies in the application of the same principles with which we would govern the case of attempt by insufficient means. The agent ("mandataire") who weakens and desists, represents exactly the insufficient means. What must then be ascertained is whether the criminal had good reason to believe that his agent would prove an effectual instrument for the accomplishment of the crime. Suppose that in one of those unhappy regions where the trade of hired assassin still exists, a man has engaged a notorious member of this guild to commit a murder. The task in hand is an easy one, the risk almost nothing. If the bargain has been struck and the money paid down, must it not be granted that the employer has left nothing undone? So far as his criminality is concerned, what can it matter if the attempt has failed, or even if the agent has taken no step toward the execution of the crime? Can my innocence or guilt be made to depend upon the act or omission of another? There is nothing left for me to do in order that crime may result, and yet what I have done may be all or nothing, contingent upon what another, without my knowledge, shall decide! Such a result indicates how the views of the idealists have really brought about the materialization of criminal law. In striking contrast is the utilitarianism of the positive school which, by directing the law-maker's attention to the criminal rather than to the crime and thus according a greater importance to the element of intent, conduces to the elevation and dignity of this science.

§ 10. Plurality of Offenses

A further matter deserving notice in the present connection is the plurality of offenses by the same individual ("concours de plusieurs délits"). This is a situation to be distinguished from that of recidivism, since, unlike the latter, it does not

---

inexécuté") as an attempt to commit crime (Art. 99). The Penal Code of the German Empire, the Italian Code of 1889, and others are silent on this subject.

suppose the fact of a previous conviction. In the case of recidivism the offender has undergone trial and sentence and
thereafter has committed a new crime. According to the prevailing doctrine, the fact that the criminal has been warned
by one or more prior convictions and, notwithstanding, has
persisted in defying the law, makes his guilt greater in the case
of recidivism than in the present case. Since society has been
unable to find the requisite means of repression, it ascribes the
fault to the criminal: it is just as if a physician were to hold
his patient responsible for the harmful effect of an improperly
prescribed or badly compounded medicine. On the other hand,
where there is repetition without previous conviction, the same
school advocates lenity to the offender, arguing, not without
a certain unconscious humor, that because he has not had the
warning of a previous punishment, less guilt attaches to his
repeated infractions of the law.

Such a criterion might do to regulate the discipline of an
infant school, but applied in the field of natural criminality,
it is nothing short of farcical.

Under the same theory, which finds acceptance in a majority
of the codes, the judge, in a case of repetition without recidivism, is without power to vary the nature of the punishment.
However many the swindles or frauds perpetrated by the
criminal before him, he may impose only so many correctional
punishments, keeping in each instance within the limits
assigned by law for a single offense. Upon the criminal who
has committed three or four murders he has no power to pass
a sentence of life-imprisonment, if no one of the offenses in
question is punishable by more than a term of years. In
short, the law obliges him to treat the habitual criminal in
nowise differently from the first offender. A striking commentary this on the wisdom of the doctrine.

It seems hardly necessary to specify here the totally different conclusions to which our system would lead. It is our
belief that the man who has committed a number of unpremeditated homicides may in certain cases be still more per-

verted, still more dangerous than the author of a single premeditated homicide. We are unable to see, therefore, why the former should always be punished more leniently than the latter. In our opinion, too, there may well be ground for declaring the professional sharper an habitual offender despite the fact that he has never undergone previous conviction. Why, then, should so much importance be attached to the fact of a previous conviction, if it be shown that we have to do with an habitual or incorrigible malefactor? The only reason is the prejudice which exists in favor of the supposed reformatory effect of punishment.

§ 11. Recidivism

More astonishing still is the circumstance that certain writers of the strictly juridical school have begun to attack the distinctive punishment of recidivists, or at least to contend that the fact of recidivism ought to have no influence upon the *kind* of punishment imposed. "The fact of recidivism gives the law-maker no right to substitute a criminal punishment for a correctional punishment, or imprisonment for life in lieu of imprisonment for a term of years, still less to sanction the death penalty, for this fact can in nowise change the nature of the punishable act." [1] The order of reasoning is ever the same — always irreconcilable with our own. What we are concerned with is not to see whether recidivism changes the nature of the act, but whether it demands the transference of the agent from one class of criminals to another. Mere common sense told men this in past centuries before the juridical theorists had exaggerated the importance of the objective side of crime.[2]

---

[1] *Haus*, "Principes du code pénal," c. III, § 624.

[2] In the Middle Ages, the second recidivation was ground for extreme punishment, even though the offense itself was not a serious one: "Si tamen reiteratur tertia vice, potest pro tribus furtis, quamvis minimis, pœna mortis imponi" (*Farinacci*, Praxis et th. crim., Questio XXIII). Under Henry VIII and Elizabeth, the death penalty was inflicted upon vagabonds who recidivated. The Code Napoléon sanctioned capital punishment in the case of

But the reformers go still further. Not only are they opposed to changing the nature of the punishment, but they also insist that increase in the degree of the punishment is admissible only in the case of special recidivism, that is to say, where the second offense is identical in kind with the first. This theory has gained ascendancy in Germany, where the penal code is entirely silent on the question of recidivism, save in the case of repeated offenses against property. It has all but prevailed in the Italian Code of 1889, under which there are no measures of severity prescribed for the recidivist, except where his new offense is of the same kind as his past.[1]

To our way of thinking, on the contrary, the fact that a man who has committed theft, later commits a murder, furnishes conclusive evidence that he does not possess the sentiment of pity any more than he does that of probity, or in other words, that he is destitute of every fundamental altruistic instinct. It follows, therefore, that he is utterly lacking in sociability and that in consequence his elimination should be absolute. This is not to deny, however, that there are cases where recidivation in a different kind of crime proves little or nothing. But the existence of such cases only goes to show the impossibility of any "a priori" laying down of rules, and the necessity of recognizing many distinctions. Recidivism, special or general, is for us merely one of the elements which determine the classification of offenders, but still one of the most important and useful of these elements.

In the system which we propose, it is inconceivable that the punishment applied to the recidivist should be of the same nature as that reserved for the first offender. For the fact of the new crime is the best proof in the world that the means employed in the former case has failed to attain its end. Up to a certain point, I can readily understand the propriety of a second experiment which materially increases the quantum

recidivists who had committed a crime punishable with penal servitude ("travaux forcés") for life.

[1] See my paper on the subject of recidivism in the Actes du Congrès pénitentiaire de Paris, 1896.

of the remedy, but what would we say of a physician who, after a second failure, obstinately clings to his original method, without trying any of the other therapeutic measures recommended by medical science for the case in hand?

Finally, it is laid down by the jurists that legal recidivism exists only when the second offense occurs within a fixed period of time after the first conviction — five or ten years for example, depending upon whether the offense is a felony ("crime") or misdemeanor ("délit"). For, as has been said, the fact of good behavior for many years makes evident the efficacy of repression.[1] We have here one of these legal fictions which always have been the subject of deplorable abuse. It is supposed that the offenses which have been brought to light and whose perpetrators have undergone trial and conviction, are the only offenses which have been committed, whereas the fact is that they constitute but a slender part of the whole number. Take the case of a sharper who has already one conviction to his score and yet cannot be legally declared a recidivist, because of the elapse of five years since its date. Who can tell us how many crimes of fraud are actually to be laid to the charge of this man?

Suppose, however, we lend credence to this fiction. Suppose that the offender's behavior has in fact been good for five or ten years. If, then, after such an interval, the same individual relapses into crime of the same description, does not this fact furnish strong indication of firmly rooted criminal instincts which, it may be, are rarely manifested, and yet await but a favorable occasion to come to light? The evil tendency suddenly reappears when all might think that it has disappeared forever. Must we then render thanks to the offender for refraining from crime during these years? Must we by way of recompense for this boon, ignore the existence of the element of criminality found in his previous life, notwithstanding the powerful aid which it affords in determin-

[1] See the report of the Minister of Justice (Mancini) on the draft of the new Italian Penal Code, p. 227 (Rome, 1877).

ing his classification and ascertaining the repressive measures which his case most requires?

In our system, the fact of recidivism is altogether too important a matter to be under any circumstances left out of view. It is sometimes one of the surest signs of the instinctive and incorrigible offender. But if we are to appraise it at its just value, as will be seen in the last chapter of this book, it will not do to study it as an isolated fact: inasmuch as its significance very greatly depends upon the kind of criminality, it must be studied in its relation to the different classes of criminals.

Praise must be accorded the French government for its good sense in brushing aside juridical sophistries and setting on foot energetic measures for the suppression of recidivism. As long ago as 1854, it enacted a law whereby criminals sentenced to penal servitude ("travaux forcés") for terms of eight years and upwards were, upon the expiration of their imprisonment, forced to reside for life in the colony of New Caledonia. This, as might be expected, resulted in a marked decrease of recidivism. The average annual number of cases, which was 1,200 in 1851–55 fell to 864 in 1861–65. In 1871, out of 1,710 accused, only 80 had undergone a previous criminal conviction.[1] But the movement did not stop here. In 1885 there was passed a law which made internment for life in a colonial possession ("relégation perpétuelle") the punishment of. recidivists guilty of even the less serious offenses, whenever the number of previous convictions exceeded a fixed minimum varying with the species of crime. Similar proposals have been advanced in Germany since the acquisition of its African colonies.[2]

In other countries, because of the all-powerful influence of the juridical theorists, the current unfortunately is setting the other way. Volumes have been written to prove that morally the recidivist is no more responsible than the first offender —

[1] *Reinach*, "Les récidivistes," p. 58 (Paris, 1882).
[2] *Bruck*, "Die Gegner der Deportation" (Breslau, 1901).

something which is no doubt true. And from this premise is drawn the wholly unsound conclusion that the former ought not to be punished any more severely than the latter.[1]

Nor is this a mere matter of the harmless pastime of some closet logician who diverts himself in the deduction of corollaries from his principles. What we are faced with here is the alarming fact that those legislatures in whose membership the juridical element is preponderant, make no scruple of translating these same faulty conclusions into provisions of law, — the effect of which can be none other than to lend countenance to the enemies of society and embolden them in their merciless warfare.

§ 12. Extenuating Circumstances

In passing, a word may be proper on the subject of extenuating circumstances. The principle here involved is one which effected its entrance into the law in connection with the doctrine of moral responsibility. Its logical consequence is that the punishability of the act decreases in inverse ratio to the strength and irresistibility of the criminal impulse. Setting thus at naught the true aim of repression, it furnishes an additional proof that the doctrine of moral responsibility is wholly irreconcilable with the social defense.

Replace this consideration with that of the offender's perversity, and it will be perceived that many circumstances which are ordinarily regarded as matters of extenuation become wholly indifferent, or else require a form of repression other than that which would have been prescribed in their absence, but one in nowise regulated by the words "mildness" and "severity." These words, indeed, are bound to disappear from the criminalist's vocabulary, for the notions which they import are without relation to the object of punishment.

One of the absurdest institutions due to the recognition of

---

[1] See *Orano*, "La recidiva nei reati" (Rome, 1883), a work which *Barzilai* has keenly criticized in his brochure: "La recidiva e il metodo sperimentale" (Rome, 1883).

extenuating circumstances is the practice of making what are really felonies the subject of correctional punishment ("correctionalisation des crimes"). For example, a theft aggravated by breaking and entering ("vol qualifié par effraction")[1] may lose its character of felony ("crime"), and become a misdemeanor ("délit"), if the court chooses to regard the insignificant value of the stolen articles as an extenuating circumstance. The fact that the property has been recovered is often treated as a circumstance of this sort. So too, the age of the offender quite often serves as an excuse for applying the practice in question to very serious crimes. The distinction between felonies and misdemeanors thus loses every reason for existence. Such a distinction is justified only so long as we confine the latter class to mere legal disobediences, offenses of no particular intrinsic immorality, and harmful acts occasioned by thoughtlessness or inadvertence. But the reforms introduced by the Code Napoléon and the practice here referred to, have been tending more and more to departure from this conception of the distinction. And today it is a common thing to see violations of the most intimate human sentiments forced into the category of misdemeanors and resultingly exempted from the punishments prescribed for felonies, — which, it is to be noted, alone of the existing punishments do accomplish a measure of elimination, however incomplete and temporary this may be.

§ 13. Punishments of the Present System

The punishments which find place in the present system need not long detain us. In the preceding chapters we have shown the inefficacy of temporary imprisonment for a period fixed in advance. And this, be it observed, is precisely the type of punishment which today predominates, the type, moreover, with which the juridical school would completely supersede every other. It is of little moment whether we speak in terms of penitentiary, jail, or house of correc-

---

[1] [See *ante* p. 151, note 1. — TRANSL.]

tion,[1] the method is always in essence the same, varied only by the form of regulation. Other types, however, still survive: the death penalty, life-imprisonment, exile, internment in an oversea penal colony ("relégation"), and fines. But the last, where the offender cannot pay, is converted into a fixed term of imprisonment; internment in penal colonies is a measure used only on a small scale and by a few countries; exile or banishment is possible only in the case of political offenders; while the death penalty almost everywhere in Europe is inflicted only in extraordinary cases.

To complete our examination of the existing criminal law would require us to show the legal relations between the several crimes and their punishments. But this would lead us too far afield and besides would be without profit from the standpoint of results. For a people recognizes as law, not that which the law-maker has written, but that which it sees applied by the judges. The principle of moral responsibility in conjunction with the extenuating circumstances fixed by the law itself or left to the sole determination of the trier, has brought it about that the punishments prescribed by law are almost never applied.

For example, the Sardinian Code, like that of France, contained a provision punishing homicide without premeditation or lying in wait, with penal servitude for life. But just as soon as the Courts of Assizes adopted the practice of limiting the punishment for this crime, as a general rule, to six or seven years of penitentiary imprisonment, the law became a dead letter. Any efficacy which the punishment possessed must be attributed to this sentence of six or seven years which the public actually saw imposed, and not to the useless menace of life-imprisonment, known only to those who had studied the code. "I know of an instance," says Cosenza, "where a prisoner who had been convicted of homicide and sentenced to twenty years' penal servitude, had not the slightest doubt

---

[1] ["Maison de force, réclusion, travaux forcés, prison cellulaire ou prison correctionelle," in the original. — TRANSL.]

that this punishment was illegal, because up to that time no homicide committed in his part of the country had met with a sentence of more than a few years' imprisonment. In another case, a sentence of twenty-five years' penal servitude for homicide and attempted homicide was such an unheard of thing in the community where it took place, that it was generally believed to be the result of error or abuse of power."[1] In these temporary punishments — segregation for a few years fixed in advance — we have, therefore, all that is left of the punishments established by law. And at that, this segregation is only relative, for in the penitentiary establishments maintained at a heavy expense to the public, absolute and continual isolation is never the case. Elsewhere the cellular régime brought to that state of so-called perfection which consists with the teachings of the correctionalist school, allows the inmates a certain degree of contact: if they no longer sleep in a common room, they at least work together.

Yet, in spite of the fact that these sentences of three, five or ten years of imprisonment, are wholly without effect upon the offender himself, it cannot be denied that they are productive of some social gain. For the segregation such as it is, spares society a greater or less number of crimes. Five years' imprisonment, for example, inflicted upon a professional thief, means from one to two hundred thefts the fewer. This is always something to be considered; and the punishments of the present system, if strictly applied, would at least have this relative utility. But, unfortunately, the statute law is one thing, the judicial law ("jurisprudence"), another. The sole object which the latter seems ever to keep in view is to mitigate punishment as far as it possibly can. This circumstance is due to certain principles which have taken firm hold in the juristic mind, among others the principle that in construing the law the magistrate must lean to the side of the offender. "Where the question of human slavery was involved," to quote again from Cosenza, "the ancient juris-

[1] Inaugural address at the Tribunal of Santa Maria Capua-Vetre, 1884.

consults decided 'pro libertate,' because they felt that the
institution of slavery, while recognized by the law, was not
in accordance with humanity and justice. Looking at the decisions of our courts on questions of criminal law one might
easily suppose that we have the same notion of that important
institution which we call the punishment of criminals, as the
Roman jurisconsults thus had of slavery. For we study to
moderate, nay, even to annul as far as possible, the legal consequences which appear to bear too heavily on the offender.
On one occasion, I was present when a criminal was acquitted
because through error a negative answer was written to the
principal question propounded to the jurors, notwithstanding
that the answers to the subordinate questions clearly evidenced the mistake.[1] It counted for nothing that the jurors
desired to rectify the verdict. The court held that the negative answer returned to the principal question created a right
in favor of the accused. The decision recalled to my mind that
rule of the Roman law whereby the child of a female slave
acquired the right to liberty from the fact that the mother,

---

[1] [In France (and the practice in Italy is substantially the same) . . .
"the President is required by the Code to state to the jury in writing the
questions which they are to answer. . . . The object of the questions, to
each of which the jury must answer Yes or No, is to constitute when taken
with the answers a statement of fact which will enable the Court to discharge
their duty. The result, therefore, of a French trial by jury is not to get a
verdict of guilty or not guilty, but to get the facts stated in a form analogous
to a special verdict with us, or to a special case in civil matters" (*Stephen,* "History of the Criminal Law of England," I, pp. 553, 554).

Supposing the prosecution to be for theft by a workman from his employer,
the questions might assume the following form:

"(1) Is N. the accused guilty of having, within the past ten years, stolen
('frauduleusement soustrait') timber and tools to the prejudice of X?

"(2) At the time of such theft, was N. a workman employed by the said X?

"(3) Was such theft committed in the workshop of the said X?

"(4) Was this workshop connected with the dwelling occupied by X?

"(5) Was the theft above mentioned committed by means of breaking
and entering ('effraction')?

"(6) Was it committed in the night-time?"

From the answers the court will be enabled to say whether the defendant is
guilty of theft and if so, which if any of the aggravating circumstances referred
to in the questions enter into his offense. See *Garçon,* "Code pénal annoté,"
I, p. 1236, note 481; from which the foregoing set of questions is taken. —
TRANSL.]

during her pregnancy, had enjoyed some period of freedom, were it even as the result of a mistake. The humanitarian part which our fathers acted in this regard, we seem to imitate by permitting the malefactor to escape his just deserts. We smile at the mediæval Roman custom which extended clemency to the culprit who chanced to meet a cardinal by the way. But at the present day an accidental happening of no greater relevance — the fall perhaps of a drop of ink on a juror's ballot — may mean nothing less than a judgment of acquittal." [1]

No subtleties are too refined, no sophistries too extreme, to receive a favorable hearing in courts of justice, when the question is one of mildening a punishment thought to be over-severe. The recognition of extenuating circumstances, which should be the exception, has instead become the rule. There are courts which accord this recognition almost as a matter of course and justify it by the most trivial reasons, such, for example, as the fact that the accused has confessed, notwithstanding that it would have availed him nothing to deny the charge. In the few instances where the court does not see fit to cut down the statutory punishment by this means, it seldom imposes more than the legal minimum. Then too, the fact of recidivism is almost lost sight of. In my own experience, I have seen criminal record-sheets (" casiers judiciaires") which told an almost unbelievable story: of extenuating circumstances recognized in the case of recidivists with as many as ten previous convictions; of thieves and sharpers sentenced to two and three months of imprisonment for their fifth or sixth offense; of bloodthirsty scoundrels with whom the law had many times dealt for inflicting wounds by shooting or stabbing, escaping with a few weeks of detention for a fresh offense of this character.

In those districts where the use of the knife and revolver is habitual among the criminal element, the number of shootings and stabbings has given rise to the practice, adopted

[1] Address before cited.

for the purpose of preventing congestion in the Courts of Assizes, of making these offenses the subject of correctional jurisdiction. This is effected either by allowing extenuating circumstances, or else by treating the case, not as an attempt to commit homicide, but as a wounding of the grade of misdemeanor ("délit de blessures"). As a result there is a very large number of criminals whom the fact of plunging a knife in their victim's breast or firing a revolver at his head, has not served to class as homicidal offenders ("meurtriers"). Their fault forgotten, they are today free citizens in full possession of their legal rights. To cite one instance from a thousand, it was held, where the accused had placed the muzzle of his pistol against the mouth of his adversary, and while it was in that position pulled the trigger, that these facts did not constitute an attempt to commit homicide. Inasmuch as the weapon had missed fire, the court took the view that the evidence of homicidal intent was insufficient, and that the only offense here was the misdemeanor of putting in fear with a deadly weapon ("menaces à main armée").

When a homicide has been actually committed and the fact of intent is beyond dispute, the most trivial circumstance is made to serve as an excuse. If the crime has been preceded by an altercation, then, without any pains being taken to see how the quarrel originated or on which side lies the blame, it is at once concluded that the accused acted under provocation. Let a man who has been outrageously insulted but raise his hand against the offender or tap him with his cane, — he does so at his peril. For by this act he has given to the other power of life and death over his person. Like as not, the aggressor will go in search of a revolver and returning at the end of half an hour, when the insulted man has perhaps dismissed the incident from his mind, will leave him a corpse in the public street. The judges, or if they do not take the initiative, the jurors, will not be long in finding an absence of premeditation from the fact that at the time of the act, the feelings of the accused were still smarting from the slight physical retaliation of his victim. They will find also, and for the same reason, that he acted under provocation. Moreover, they will give him the benefit of extenuating circumstances, if, indeed, they do not see fit to apply in his favor the principle of irresistible force. If an acquittal does not follow, the punishment ordinarily imposed in such cases, at least in Italy, is but three to five years' imprisonment. This explains why the same individual can have to his score three or four homicides separated by short intervals. The murderer of this type knows so well that the fact of a slight dispute preceding the criminal act will save him from serious consequences, that he purposely arranges that this shall take place, provoking his adversary until the latter retaliates with a blow. That done, the criminal can work his will. And when arrested with the still reeking knife in his hand, he exclaims: "All right. I will get some eighteen months in prison for this, but I have done what I long wanted to do." Thus it is that we tolerate murder in the midst of our so-called civilization.

There is nothing in these pages but what is drawn from some case with which I have been connected in an official capacity. I have had no occasion to borrow from others; still less, have I given rein to my imagination. Minutes of the facts above cited are still in my possession, and if need be, proof of my assertions can be furnished to any who, unfamiliar with the courts and the bar, might be inclined to tax me with exaggeration.

But, it may be said, these abuses are not the fault of the law itself but of its application. This is perhaps true but cannot alter the case. For to what is this fault of application due, if not to the principles of the dominant theory. It is these which have given rise to a judicial law which ever leans to the side of the offender. If it becomes the duty of the judge to determine the question of guilt by the standard of moral responsibility, what right have we to demand that he shall not look for extenuating circumstances. According to this standard, such circumstances actually exist in most cases; sometimes, indeed, they are wrongly ignored.   For when we undertake to ascertain whether a man is really responsible for what he does, we always end by discovering that he is not.   It is to the fallacy which pervades the entire system that the present ineffectiveness of repression is due. The whole blame rests with the two principles of moral responsibility and penal proportion.

For these principles disarm the judge, and render him powerless to take any active share in the struggle against crime. How, for example, can he consistently say that the recidivist is guiltier than the first offender and punish him accordingly, when he knows that, because of the infamy attaching to his past, the prisoner has been unable to obtain employment, has been shunned and despised by honest men, and in consequence, to use the expression of Tarde, has found his only welcome in the criminal microcosm whence he emerged ("sa petite patrie criminelle")?   How is it possible for the judge to suppose that this man can resist his criminal propensities as easily as the man who is restrained by the fear of losing his yet untarnished reputation?   The judge is more logical than the law. When we see him imposing punishments so ridiculously ineffectual, so utterly useless from the standpoint of social protection as to wear the appearance of some ironic jest, the fault is not his, but that of the theory in which he finds his justification.

CHAPTER III

Defects of the Existing Criminal Procedure

THAT the dominant theory and the judicial law which has conformed itself thereto seem to exist for the purpose of protecting the criminal against society rather than society against the criminal, the reader has already learned from the preceding chapters. But it is not till we come to the rules governing criminal procedure that we find this purpose at its fullest expression. For here it is the statutory law itself which, by suggesting to criminals the means of escaping punishments or insuring protracted delay in their execution, has in one of its branches undertaken to render difficult the application of the provisions contained in another branch.

§ 1. The Distinction between Public and Private Criminal Actions

We may begin with the distinction between public and private criminal actions. This distinction is often based upon the objective nature of the offense, regardless of the perversity of the agent; sometimes upon the kind of punishment pre-

---

[1] [§§ 1 and 2 = § I of original; §§ 3, 4, 5 and 6 = § II; §§ 7 and 8 = § III; and § 9 = § IV. — TRANSL.]

scribed by law or imposed by the court. For example, indecent assaults ("attentats à la pudeur") for the most part do not fall within the category of public actions, or, what amounts to the same thing, they require complaint on the part of the injured person before the offender can be prosecuted. The same is true of those cases of threats, and strikings and woundings ("coups et blessures"), which are punishable as police offenses ("contraventions"), and by the Codes of some countries, of false pretenses, whatever be the punishment imposed. In Italy, there has been an increasing tendency to narrow the class of public actions. And with it all, the personality of the agent is completely forgotten. Whether he is a recidivist, whether the manner in which he has planned and consummated his crime indicates the dangerous criminal, whether he has made reparation for the damage — these are matters to which not the slightest attention is paid. A private citizen thus becomes the arbiter of the social function of repression. Upon him it devolves to say whether the violator of a social law shall be punished, whether he shall be imprisoned or allowed at large. To this citizen the State puts the question: "Do you desire that the professional sharper who has made you his victim shall be prevented from fleecing others, or is it your wish that he do to others what he has done to you?"

Such an attitude on the part of the State almost leads one to wonder if we are not in a fair way to return to the times when punishment was merely the vengeance of the victim or his family.

To us, the expression "private action" as applied to a criminal prosecution is wholly devoid of meaning, so far at least as concerns what we have termed natural crimes. In cases of strikings and woundings ("coups et blessures"), threats to kill, rape, false pretenses, and forgery, whether complaint has or has not been lodged, society, once it learns of the crime, cannot remain inactive. And when the State thus takes the initiative it will be impossible for the offender to defeat the ends of justice, as in certain regions is often now the case, by intimidating the injured person into withdrawing his complaint.

It is of small moment that viewed objectively the crime does not appear especially grave. The thing is to know what sort of offender we are dealing with, to become acquainted with his personality, to determine his type, to see if he is not to be numbered among those who because of their lack of adaptation to the social environment, must be made the subject of eliminative measures. If investigation discloses that the offender does not belong to the class of true criminals, that in spite of a slip he is not of a nature very different from that of the generality of men, then and then only, as has been said in the preceding chapter, repression, always necessary, may assume a different form, — namely, coercion to make reparation of the damage, both moral and material, resulting from his injurious act.

§ 2. Enforcement of the Judgment for Damages

On this question of reparation we differ yet more decidedly from the jurists. The latter have been content with the principle that conviction of the offender carries with it the obligation to respond in damages.[1] This posited, they have stopped, for, according to their view, the enforcement of the obligation is a matter to be regulated by the ordinary rules of civil procedure; the obligation they regard as one "ex delicto" just as if it had been one "ex contractu": it is no concern of the criminalists.

In practice, even where the defendant is not insolvent, the judgment for damages in a criminal matter is in most

---

[1] [" . . . In every French criminal proceeding, from the most trifling to the most important, any person injured by the offense may make himself 'partie civile.' In certain cases he may, by doing so, be made liable in damages to the accused. A French criminal trial may thus also be a civil proceeding for damages by the party injured by the crime, and at the same time an action by the accused for what we should call a malicious prosecution" (*Stephen*, "History of the Criminal Law of England," I, p. 524). The same is true of Italy, the claimant there being called the "parte civile." — TRANSL.]

cases little else than a mockery. For no attachment can be ordered until after the entry of a judgment concluding the case ("arrêt définitif"). This means that pending the judicial investigation ("instruction") and even after judgment of conviction, where steps have been taken to have the last reviewed, the defendant is free to effect the disappearance of all his personal property. By the law of some countries, it is true, real property may be attached following the issuance of a warrant of commitment ("mandat d'arrêt"),[1] but, on the other hand, there are only a few cases, and those only the most serious, in which it is considered necessary to secure the person of the accused pending the judicial investigation. For the most part, therefore, the demand of the injured person is neither a preferred nor a secured claim. The defendant pays only when it suits him, and this, as may well be supposed, seldom happens. Since the rules of civil procedure are applicable to the ascertainment of the damages as well as to the enforcement of the judgment, sometimes years are consumed in contests, proceedings for review, and delays of all sorts. This explains the fact vouched for by Cosenza that sums no greater than three hundred, two hundred, or even one hundred francs have been known to be offered as indemnity for a murder. An instance occurred, he writes, "where the brothers of a murdered man, tired of litigation, compromised their claim by accepting fifty francs from the murderer." As for insolvent offenders, it is useless even to speak of them, say

---

[1] [The "mandat d'arrêt" issues only when the defendant is to be held without provisional liberation or bail. Preliminary writs are the "mandat de comparution" which answers to our summons and the "mandat d'amener" which answers to our warrant. . . . "When the suspected person appears before the Juge d'Instruction either upon a 'mandat de comparution' or upon a 'mandat d'amener' he must be interrogated. . . . If his answers are satisfactory, he is discharged, if not he is remanded under a 'mandat de dépôt.' This 'mandat de dépôt' may be changed into a 'mandat d'arrêt' (which, however, can be issued only upon the requisition of the Procureur de la République) at any period of the instruction. The principal difference between them is that the 'mandat d'arrêt' is definitive, the 'mandat de dépôt' provisional" (*Stephen*, "History of the Criminal Law of England," I, pp. 531, 532).— TRANSL.]

the jurists, for "Nemo dat quod non habet." The great majority of offenders, therefore, escape the obligation in question. And with those who cannot escape it, the fulfillment hardly deserves the name.

For this condition the jurists have no remedy, because, as they view it, the obligation here involved is a civil obligation and consequently enforcible only by the ordinary means of civil procedure. Any more drastic form of coercion would be an abuse worthy of a barbarous country, wholly at variance with legal progress, etc.

To our way of thinking, there is an immeasurable difference between a debt arising from contract, where default of payment is something that can be foreseen and guarded against, and a debt arising from a criminal offense — from violation, not of a rule of conduct adopted by the agreement of two persons, but of a rule of conduct universally recognized in human society. Men are not in the habit of lending to insolvents or of lending without security. If any one should do so, he is wanting in prudence and must abide the consequences. But all alike are exposed to aggression on the part of insolvents. Why, then, should insolvency enjoy this privilege? And seeing that the origin and nature of the two debts are so dissimilar, why should the means of enforcing payment be identical?

The reader has already been made acquainted with our views on this subject.[1] We regard the severest form of compulsion as just in the case of the insolvent offender. He should be kept in detention until he shall have paid his debt, together with all expenses of his maintenance in prison. Not the slightest indulgence should be shown him. As I have said elsewhere: "Let him sell his house, his shop, his forge, — cost what it may, he must find the money."[2] The essential thing is that he make reparation for the crime. To force him to do this, it is necessary that the law be relentless. If

[1] See *ante*, Part III, c. i, § 1.
[2] Actes du premier Congrès d'Anthropologie criminelle, p. 307 (Rome, 1887).

he is insolvent, then he must be made to pay over, out of his daily earnings, every penny in excess of his actual necessities — in excess, that is to say, of what is strictly necessary, irrespective of the difference in social conditions, for the maintenance of life and health. Should the offender prove refractory, or should there be reasonable ground to believe that his insolvency is feigned, this coercion will last indefinitely. In other cases, there will be fixed a longer or shorter term, according to the importance of the damage caused by the criminal act, so that there will be no danger of the prisoner being held in life-long slavery in the effort to work out a judgment for some impossible sum.

That these propositions readily lend themselves to being put into practice will be shown in the following chapter.

The foregoing considerations have made plain to the reader the radical difference between our system and that of the jurists, with respect to this question of reparation. If the strict rules which we advocate were to be adopted, every species of punishment could be dispensed with in the case of such offenders as are not sufficiently dangerous to require elimination. The result would be the complete disappearance of the so-called correctional punishments. And this means an end of congested prisons and an end, too, of the corruption of thousands who, once having experienced the prison contamination, can never again become good citizens. Moreover, it would no longer be possible for the prisoner, after having served a few months or years of correctional imprisonment, to enjoy unmolested the fruits of his maleficent activity, confided in the meantime to the hands of friends or relatives. And the foreclosure of such a possibility will be a much more potent means of disarming the enemies of society than the ridiculous punishments which are today imposed in the hope of reforming offenders.[1]

[1] See on this subject: Actes du Congrès d'Anthropologie criminelle, *u.s.* p. 23 *et seq.*, 306, 363 *et seq.*: Actes du Congrès pénitentiaire international, p. 185 *et seq.*, pp. 200, 201 (Rome, 1885); and my two brochures: "Ciò che

§ 3. The Judicial Investigation

Another feature to be looked at is the judicial investigation preceding the trial ("instruction des procès").[1] This, according to the doctrinaires, should be conducted openly, in the presence of the accused and his counsel. Only by such a method, they maintain, can impartiality be assured. They forget, however, that in the greater number of cases, the strictest secrecy is required for the ascertainment of the truth. To exhibit to the accused and his counsel the slender thread which, scarcely visible, is yet the sole guide in the labyrinth of possible evidentiary facts, is tantamount to breaking it. And even in the least complicated cases, acquainting the accused with the testimony which has been given against him would be a practice not unattended with danger.

In spite of this very substantial consideration, the French legislature in 1897 modified the Code of Criminal Procedure[2] with respect to the examination of the accused. As a result, the law of France now gives the right to counsel from the moment of arrest, and allows counsel to be present at the first examination of the accused. In my judgment this system is a very dangerous one, since it renders it possible for counsel to become the go-between of the prisoner and complaisant wit-

---

dovrebbe essere un giudizio penale" (Turin, Loescher, 1882), and "Riparazione alle vittime del delitto" (Turin, Bocca, 1887).

[1] [The following passage contained in the 2d Italian edition of the present work (Turin, Fratelli Bocca, 1891) is here reproduced for its explanatory value: "Under our procedure the judge of instruction is entrusted with the duty of examining the witnesses indicated by the accused and collecting proofs to establish his innocence or to diminish his guilt. The sole office of this magistrate is to throw light upon the case — not at any cost to find a scapegoat. The accused has the right to make legal objection ("reclamare") against the order declaring lawful his arrest. He may have the grounds of his objection presented by counsel and passed upon by the Section of Accusation (see *ante*, p. 193, note 3). The right to defend is therefore admitted at the very first stage of the cause. . . . Since the office of the judge of instruction is neither to accuse nor defend, his impartiality takes the place of contest ("contraddizione") between the parties, to the decided economy of time and labor" (p. 395). — TRANSL.]

[2] ["Code d'instruction criminelle" is the official title. — TRANSL.]

nesses. In Italy proposals have been advanced of an even more dangerous character, into the details of which I cannot enter here.[1] It is only the rapid succession of ministerial crises that has saved the Italian judge of instruction from being reduced, according to the apt figure of a newspaper writer, to the state of a dancing puppet with the two adversaries alternately pulling the strings. In cases of the most important crimes, where as yet no conclusive evidence has been discovered against the person suspected, to conduct the judicial investigation in public is to renounce all hope of arriving at the truth. Hundreds of cases might be cited in which conclusive evidence of guilt has been obtained only by preserving the strictest secrecy in the judicial investigation. It is therefore to be hoped that the public will suffer to pass unheeded the rhetorical outbursts of certain members of the bar who contend for the complete publicity of every step in the procedure from beginning to end.

§ 4. Provisional Liberty[2]

But the most debated topic of criminal procedure is that relating to the detention of the accused pending final determination of the cause. We hear it asserted that this is often an unjust measure, and one to be resorted to only in extreme cases, when there is reason to believe that the accused will

---

[1] See my articles in the Nuova Antologia, for 1900–1902 (Rome).

[2] [The natural rendering of "liberté provisoire" in terms of English law is "release on bail," but such a rendering would be inexact as applied to the Continental systems. Thus by the French law "in cases in which the maximum punishment is two years' imprisonment the prisoner has a right to be set at liberty if he has a domicile, and has not been previously convicted of a crime or sentenced to a year's imprisonment. In cases in which the provisional liberation is not a matter of right the defendant may be held to bail " (*Stephen*, "History of the Criminal Law of England," I, 535). In Italy, on the other hand, although provisional release is in general a matter of right where the punishment involved is less than three years of ordinary imprisonment ("reclusione o detenzione"), bail can be dispensed with in but one instance, that is to say, when the accused is a poor person and investigation results favorably to his previous good moral character. (Code of Criminal Procedure, Art. 214; "Digesto Italiano," XIV, pp. 848, 882–3. — TRANSL.]

become a fugitive from justice. Enounced and repeated by legal theorists without practical experience in criminal cases, arguments of this sort have become almost commonplaces; the press has caught them up; and some fine morning we shall awake to find them translated into terms of law, — made the subject of statutes hastily drafted by persons who are either incompetent or else, because of their private professional interests, opposed to severity in the repression of crime.

In the first place, it is inaccurate to say that imprisonment pending trial ("emprisonnement préventif") has no other object than to prevent the flight of the accused. It is often necessary for the purpose of keeping the accused from effecting the disappearance of physical evidence ("traces matérielles") of his crime; to hinder him from concerting measures with his accomplices or friends for the corroboration of the story which he has told; to render more difficult the intimidation or subornation of witnesses; to influence the prisoner to confess (something which not unfrequently happens); and finally, to protect the accused himself from the vengeance of the injured person or his family. As to the probability of flight, however, it must be obvious that, apart from some exceptional cases, this is always present, whenever the punishment involved is of more or less severity or threatens the offender with serious financial loss.

No doubt it is difficult to formulate general rules which will be applicable in all cases, but, subject to the power of the judge of instruction to make exceptions in proper cases, imprisonment pending trial could be defined as necessary in the following instances:

(1) Where it is probable that the accused will be sentenced to a punishment heavy enough to make it an object to him to take to flight or go into hiding, — because the punishment in question is for him the greater of the two evils.

(2) Where the case is one of striking ("coups") or wounding ("blessures"), until the victim has fully recovered from the effect of his injuries.

(3) Where it is probable that the person injured will resort to bloodshed to take revenge upon the aggressor.

(4) Where the accused is a recidivist, habitual offender, or person without visible means of support or fixed place of abode.

(5) Where the accused is a thief or swindler who has been taken in the act.

(6) And finally, in all cases where there is danger of the accused intimidating or suborning the injured person or the witnesses, or in any way hindering or thwarting the judicial investigation.

The cases in which the warrant of commitment ("mandat d'arrêt") should issue being thus determined, the institution of provisional liberty ("liberté provisoire") would lose all reason for existence. There would no longer be any such thing, except where the judge of instruction has good reason to believe in the innocence of the accused.

As it exists at present, this institution is a source of the greatest dangers. It seems expressly devised for the encouragement of the criminal classes, and testifies to the ingenuousness of law-makers in failing to take into account the new weapons with which civilization has furnished the malefactor. It is readily understood how, in the small cities of the ancient world or even in the municipalities of the Middle Ages, the person accused of a misdemeanor or, for that matter, of a felony, might be permitted at large pending the result of his trial. The difficulties of traveling were great; those of living in a foreign country still greater. Flight was voluntary exile; and exile was regarded as a punishment of exceptional gravity — according to the Roman law, a capital punishment.[1] And yet precautions were taken: the prisoner was not released without an undertaking on the part of some reputable persons to produce him at the proper time: "Si fidejussores habere non potuerit, a ministris comitis custodiatur et ad mallum perducatur." [2] The Roman law always made an exception to

---

[1] Dig., Lib. XLVIII, Tit. 1, "De pub. jud.," § 2.
[2] Cap. Karoli II, anno 873, jan. 4 (229, Pertz, Hanover, 1835).

the privilege of release in cases of the most serious offenses.[1]
Even in England, the country of "habeas corpus," a similar
exception prevails, and in other cases the law permits the
accused to be released only when the bail furnished is sufficient
to give assurance that he will appear and abide the result of
his trial.

We, in the Latin countries, have lent a willing ear to the
rhetoric of legal theorists, and, especially, have succumbed
to the influence of sensational novels, wherein are depicted
the moral tortures suffered by the innocent hero who under a
wrongful accusation of crime has been immured in some hideous dungeon. As a result, the law has in many cases established
the *right* of the accused to release pending the conclusion of the
proceedings. Moreover, the judge is left the widest discretion to grant it, even where the crime is of the most serious
character. Indigent persons are exempted from furnishing
bail of any sort — an immunity which resembles the ancient
privileges of caste, in that it is a true privilege of the proletariat. Release has come to be accorded even after the judgment of conviction, pending the delays incident to proceedings
for appeal or review. The consequence is that a man found
guilty, and sentenced to a merely correctional punishment,
may walk out of jail, and be under no necessity of returning
until the higher court has decided against him. It may even
be said that the facility of release increases in direct proportion
to the certainty of guilt. For the same individual who has been
arrested on mere suspicion and detained on evidence which is
far from conclusive ("simples indices") finds himself set at
liberty just as soon as a solemn judgment has declared his
guilt.

Is not this sort of thing utterly opposed to reason and common sense? Whatever grounds may be urged in justification
of such a system, there is no gainsaying the fact that it is not
natural; that it is unsound; that it cannot be comprehended
by the popular intelligence, least of all by that of a Southern

[1] Dig., Lib. XLVIII, Tit. 3, "De custodia reorum," §§ 1, 3.

nation. How is it to be supposed that a people with the meridional characteristics of little foresight, of little sensibility to that which is not present and immediate, can be impressed by the menace of an imprisonment which is not to take effect until after the elapse of an indefinite period — one year or two years, or even more in the event of a new trial being ordered by a higher court? Remote menaces of this description may not be without influence upon people of a cold and calculating turn of mind. Up to a certain point they are understandable in the North, but in the South, to apply Spencer's expression, "there must be penalties which are severe, prompt and specific enough to be vividly conceived." [1]

In Naples, when, by the new laws of 1865, provisional liberty was introduced even in serious cases of woundings ("blessures") the notion became prevalent with the lower classes that these offenses were no longer subject to punishment, or at most were punishable with the forfeiture of the bail-security, the amount of which seldom exceeded fifty francs. As a result, it was a common thing to overhear the remark among people of these classes that for fifty francs one could purchase the pleasure of bestowing a knife-thrust. This shows that the punishment which would be imposed by the court and executed after a long delay, was not a matter of concern; what struck the meridional imagination was the payment of the fifty francs, because this was exacted immediately.[2]

As for the impression which this institution produces on the general public, it may be said without exaggeration to be always deplorable. Effort to explain such a system is quite in vain. The fact remains that a culprit who was in the power of the law is in its power no longer, and that it is the law itself which has turned him loose. Imagine what must be thought of this proceeding by the neighbors, the friends, and the relatives of the injured person, — who perhaps is yet groaning from the pain of his wounds, who has been maimed

---

[1] *Herbert Spencer*, "Prison-Ethics."
[2] *Turiello*, "Governo e governati," I, c. III (Bologna, 1882).

for life or who, again, has been reduced to poverty by the wiles of some clever swindler, — when they see the offender after a few months' detention, and in spite of the fact that the judge of instruction has decided to hold him over for trial, released from custody and granted his full and absolute liberty until the cause shall have dragged its weary length through the Court of Appeal and the Court of Cassation. This means that the criminal is free to resume his former tenor of life, side by side with his victim — in the same house, if it suits his pleasure. One case may be cited, out of a multitude of such examples, where a peasant, to rid himself of competition for the leasehold of a farm, fired a loaded gun at his neighbor. His attempt to kill was unsuccessful, but at the end of eighteen months the man had not yet recovered from his wounds. In the meantime, the would-be murderer who had been charged only with the offense of wounding was suffered to remain unmolested at home. The house in which he lived and the dwelling of the injured man opened on a common court, their doors being exactly opposite. As a consequence, the victim from his bed of pain was forced to endure the repeated sight of his assailant enjoying his pipe and glass in the open air of the enclosure. Such is the progress of judicial institutions!

But much greater evils may and in fact do result. The criminal often takes revenge upon witnesses who have testified against him, or renews an attempt which before had proved unsuccessful. Here again, hundreds of tragic instances might be related, from which I shall select a few. Thus, a man who had been repulsed by a young woman whose affections he sought, fired at her with a revolver, the shot fortunately missing. He was arrested but admitted to provisional liberty. During the delay which ensued before his case came on for trial, he murdered the girl's brother. In another case, a Cammorist forbade a waiter to pay attention to a young woman upon whom one of the law-breaker's friends had designs. The first disobedience on the part of the waiter was punished with a razor slash on one side of the face. The young man complained to the police but continued his court. Some months later he received a like slash on his other cheek. He was thus disfigured for life by two fearful scars. The offender was arrested and sentenced to four years of imprisonment by the Correctional Tribunal. There was first an appeal, and later, proceedings for review of the judgment rendered on appeal. Four years thus passed. Meanwhile, the Cammorist daily promenaded in front of the café where the waiter was employed, taking occasion as he passed to blow cigar smoke in his victim's face. The poor fellow had repeatedly refused offers to settle, but finally, the long delay causing him to despair of the outcome, he agreed to accept the sum which was offered. A judgment ordering a new trial ("jugement de renvoi") was procured, the complaint was withdrawn, new witnesses testified to an imaginary provocation, and the miscreant was sentenced to a few months' imprisonment, and even from this he was rescued by an opportune proclamation of amnesty!

Sometimes the patience of the aggrieved person becomes exhausted and the consequent outburst of anger is the cause of a new crime. Witness the tragedy which not a great many years ago took place at Paris, in the very precincts of the Palais de Justice, when Madame Clovis Hugues shot and killed her defamer, whom she had prosecuted before the courts for many months and saw still at liberty, notwithstanding that he had been sentenced to prison.

Again, it is impossible to estimate the pernicious effect of this institution, with respect to imitative and endemic criminality. In a village of Southern Italy, a man arrested for disfiguring with a razor a young peasant woman who had refused his attentions was granted provisional release; as usual, an appeal and proceedings for review left him at large for upwards of two years. Meanwhile, other disappointed admirers followed his example, and cases of this sort multiplied to such a degree, that as I have before had occasion to point out, the best looking young women were terrified into

marrying the most desperate blackguards of the neighborhood.[1]
Are we not justified in laying the whole blame on this institution of provisional liberty? For if the scoundrel who set the
example had not been thus released, if he had been kept
in custody before and after his trial until he had served his
five or six years of imprisonment, it is not at all likely that he
would have found imitators. This is in substance the remark
of one of these same imitators when refused the provisional
release which had been accorded to all his predecessors. He
frankly acknowledged that had he expected to encounter a
treatment so different from that of the others, he would not
have committed this crime.

There is, moreover, one consideration which should foreclose all debate on the practice under discussion. Provisional
liberty leaves the accused free either to submit to the punishment which has been imposed upon him, or to avoid it. For
in our day a man may travel unhindered from one end of the
world to the other: passports, even, are nearly everywhere
unnecessary. And for that matter, why is it at all necessary
for the criminal to exile himself or indeed to go any distance?
All that is necessary is to take refuge in the whirlpool of some
great city. If he already lives there, he need only change his
abode and the police will note in their "procès verbal" that
he is not to be found. They do not put themselves about,
except in the case of sensational crimes which keep the tele-
graph lines of the whole country in a constant hum. Nor,
on the whole, are they to be blamed, for the service which
society now for the second time demands of them, has been
already performed. They discovered the criminal; and
in face of one knows not how many difficulties, they arrested
him. Then, in the name of lofty principles, in the sacred name
of personal liberty, the thief or murderer is released on his
own parole, just as in a former day a gentleman was set free
on his word of honor. And now, two years after the event,
the police are again required to find in some hidden corner of

[1] *Ante,* p. 195.

one of our modern Babylons, an obscure scoundrel whose memory has long since been forgotten, in order that he be made to undergo the three or six months' imprisonment to which he has been sentenced. Could anything be more ridiculous? [1]

When, however, the punishment involved is of as short a duration as this, the offender will not trouble himself much to hide from the police. What matters to him these few weeks of enforced inactivity? In winter the peasant criminal really welcomes such a punishment, for it means a money saving to him at a season when his labor is unproductive. But a man in good health who has been sentenced to two or three years in prison, is not apt to be solicitous about knocking on the prison door, especially if he has some money in his pocket. What is then to be said of the case where the perpetrator of some swindle of enormous proportions or of some theft amounting to hundreds of thousands of francs, having been sentenced, pursuant to the verdict of the jury, to a punishment merely correctional (a situation of frequent occurrence in Italy), is released pending proceedings on appeal or review? Is it at all likely that he will appear and obey the law? Every one knows that with two or three hundred thousand francs in his possession, such a man can laugh at all pursuit, assume whatever name he pleases, and, free from molestation, live surrounded by the respect of his neighbors.

In short, we find that the practice of granting provisional release is the most vicious of all the institutions of our criminal law, directly counteracting as it does the activities of repression. It directly encourages the criminal element; it discourages the injured person and the witnesses; it demoralizes the police. The absurdity reaches its height when the offender is released after a judgment in first instance has been arrived at, but the reign of unreason becomes inexplicable when, after his appeal has been dismissed, he is still permitted to remain

---

[1] In this paragraph I have had especially in view the law of Italy, according to which provisional release is in most cases of misdemeanors ("délits") a right of the accused.

at large pending proceedings in review, begun for the sole purpose of gaining time. Finally, there is no room for any such institution in the system proposed in this book. The cases in which imprisonment pending prosecution ("détention préventif") is a necessary measure have already been seen. Provisional release, therefore, is not to be considered except where the magistrate charged with the judicial investigation deems the evidence insufficient. But when there is reason to believe that the offender will be adjudged deserving of elimination, no manner of bail can serve. For the thing here necessary is that society rid itself of the noxious element, and in effecting this it cannot await the criminal's good pleasure or count upon his spirit of obedience and resignation.

With respect to the rare case of unjust detention, where the innocence of the accused has been completely established, I have no hesitation in urging, as many others have done, that the State make proper compensation to this victim of deceitful appearances. The right to such indemnity once recognized, there would no longer be any occasion for the outcries usually evoked by an error of this sort. In the first place, the situation is not one of an intolerable or irreparable injury, but of a disagreeable accident, the mere acknowledgment of which is in itself reparation for a really honest man. Again, the accused himself in most cases is to blame for the mistake, because of his imprudence, his lightmindedness, his eccentric conduct, or the bad company with which he has associated: it is very seldom that the fault lies solely with the police. It is therefore just that the part which the accused has himself contributed to the creation of suspicion against him should be taken into consideration in fixing the amount of the indemnity. What we are unable to understand is why, because of a few isolated cases, a trifling number of easily remedied judicial errors, any such measure should be proposed as that of doing away altogether with imprisonment pending prosecution — a step which can only mean the impairment of repression and impunity for a multitude of criminals.

§ 5. Criminal Trials; the Jury

Something must now be said as to the mode of adjudication in criminal matters. The strictly juridical character given to the repressive function has resulted in the criminal trial bearing an artificial and misleading resemblance to the trial of a civil cause. In the latter, there is a plaintiff and defendant; in the former the Public Ministry [1] takes the place of the plaintiff: it plays the part of creditor, exacting payment, under the form of punishment, of the debt owed by the accused. The court in case of conviction finds that the claim is a valid one, and declares what the accused must pay to square his account with society.

Shortsighted progressives maintain that there is nothing more admirable than this system of accusation. They would even reconstitute it on a purely accusatory basis and turn the trial into a genuine combat in which the eloquence of opposing counsel is made to do service for the weapons employed in the most barbarous centuries of the Middle Ages. As one author has observed: "The peculiar nature of the system of accusation consists in this, that it always proceeds on the theory of an antagonism between two parties and consequently has in view the verification of and conformity to, not an absolute, but only a relative certainty. The question is not whether the man is innocent or guilty but whether one side or the other has won. The gage of battle has become the bail-bond, the challenger the accuser, the challenged the accused, the peers the jurors — to the clash of arms has succeeded the clash of words, — but the primitive character of combat always remains the same." All the features of this system "bear witness that the matter is not so much a public function as a private question. . . . The system of investigation introduced by the ecclesiastical tribunals during the Middle Ages and adopted in

---

[1] ["Ministère Public": the collective designation of the officers of prosecution. For France, see *Stephen*, "History of the Criminal Law of England," I, pp. 524, 525. — TRANSL.]

France by Louis XII, undeniably marked a step in advance, inasmuch as it recognized the real essential of procedure to be the critical and impartial search for the truth, and that this should be the object of every rational and lawful judicial proceeding." [1]

That this system, especially in political matters, became the subject of abuses admits of no question. The one thing needful was the addition of guaranties for the accused and restrictions upon the magistral authority. But instead, there took place, in the establishment of the grotesque institution of the jury and the according of an exaggerated importance to the oral character of the trial proceedings, what was little short of a return to the obsolete system of accusation.

However conclusive the evidence against the accused, however unimpeachable its character, its whole effect may vanish before some sudden impression which the art of a skillful advocate is capable of producing on the minds of the jurors. Every one admits, and foremost of all the legal profession, that the result of a trial in a Court of Assizes depends on sheer chance. And yet, although public opinion at least in Italy is decidedly hostile to this "prud'hommesque"[2] institution of the jury, not a voice has been raised in the legislature to demand its abolition.

This is due to the supposition that it is inseparably connected with the political liberties of a country — a notion which is perhaps true in the case of England, where the jury

---

[1] *P. Ellero*, "Delle origini storiche del diritto di punire," p. 18 (Bologna, Zanichelli). See also *Henry Sumner Maine*, "Ancient Law," c. x. *Cruppi,* "La cour d'assises," p. 150 (Paris, 1898), is to the same effect: "It is still the ancient ordeal, the judicial duel. The question is still one of skill, of war, of victory. Who will prove the more eloquent? Yesterday these warriors were armed with the halberd, today their weapon is speech; but this difference between the two systems counts for little when we reflect on the remoteness of both from a logical and rational search for the truth."

[2] *Tarde* has so called it in praising the Italian positivists who "overwhelm it with ridicule": "Positivisme et pénalité" (Archives de l'Anthropologie criminelle, 1887). See also "Philosophie pénale" by the same author, c. VII (Lyons, 1890) [American edition, "Penal Philosophy," Criminal Science Series (Boston: Little, Brown & Co., 1912)].

is indigenous and traditional, but without common sense in the case of other countries which possess a magistracy expressly created for the administration of justice. Then too, in the case of England, the character of the people, their small sympathy for criminals, their sternness and unyielding severity toward every infraction of law, render the institution still workable. Moreover, the English jury, unlike that in Continental countries, is called into service only where the accused pleads "not guilty," or refuses to plead, in which case the plea of "not guilty" is entered for him. Again, its verdict must be unanimous. A single intelligent juror is thus enabled to render an ignorant majority powerless except to declare that an agreement cannot be reached. In the event of such disagreement there must be a new trial of the cause. And finally, its members are not allowed to separate or hold communication with outsiders until their duty has been performed. The practice, common enough in the Latin countries, of seeking to influence corruptly the juror who returns to his home or goes to dine in a café between the sessions of a cause which may perhaps be protracted for ten days or more, has therefore no chance to exist.

The injustices committed by the jury, for the most part, are due in reality to its ignorance, whether because of its inability to grasp the meaning of many legal terms and to appreciate the true significance and connection of the often numerous questions which are propounded to it,[1] or because of the lack of necessary aptitude for or experience in the critical labor of examining the evidence and weighing the arguments for and against, in a case where the fact of guilt does not appear at the first glance. Sometimes the jurors bring in a verdict of acquittal, as a protest against the government. This often occurs in Italy in the case of embezzlement of public moneys — the thief being turned loose for no other

---

[1] Here again is a difference between the English and the Continental jury. The former is only required to determine the general question of guilt, and returns a simple verdict of "Guilty" or "Not Guilty."

reason than that of spiting the Minister of Finance. In
the Courts of Assizes held in small cities, the jurors are gathered from different districts; they are lodged at the same hotel,
and exposed to all sorts of influences. "When some orator of
note, some advocate who figures in political life and enjoys
popularity as a member of the Chamber of Deputies, under-
takes the defense of a prisoner," says Turiello, "even the
most honest and intelligent members of the jury are unable
to resist a contagion of admiration for his skill. Without
properly understanding, or having had time to consider,
they experience a sort of diffidence, they succumb to a feeling of respect for what, in this atmosphere, wears the appearance of talent. They lose sight of the issues in the spectacle,
and just as a theater audience applauds the actor by clap-
ping its hands, so they applaud the orator by their verdict;
to examine the facts and find accordingly would appear dis-
courteous. In short, whether it is due to his nervous sensibility or artistic impressionability, I am unable to see how
the Italian, when called upon to act as judge, can help being
emotionally affected, unless he has undergone a special
training to prepare him for this function." [1]

It must further be added that the advocates very often
employ all sorts of means to confuse the minds of the jurors,
to create a doubt where the proof is clear. Sometimes, indeed,
they go so far as to state to the jury facts which are purely
imaginary. With us it is not forbidden, as it is in England, to
play upon the emotions of the jury and arouse their sympathy
for the lot of the accused and his family. An advocate may
thus win his case by picturing the unhappy plight of the prisoner's wife and children in the event of his conviction: that
the prisoner never had either or else has long since deserted
them, is a matter of little consequence. Another advocate
will tell you in accents of the utmost sincerity that the mother
of the accused has been rendered insane by grief and is upon
the point of death, while as a matter of fact she enjoys the

---

[1] *Turiello*, Governo e governati, c. III (Bologna, 1882).

best of health and has long since disowned her precious son. The orator speaks with tears in his voice; he wrings his hands in token of despair; the president smiles; but the jury in its simplicity suffers itself to be imposed upon; it sees tragedy in what is downright farce.[1]

Nor is this all. Besides the immense number of unjust verdicts of acquittal due either to inability to sift and weigh the evidence or else to the emotion of the moment, there are yet other instances where the result must be attributed to bad faith, timidity, or actual corruption. In Naples, for example, dread of the Càmorra operates so strongly that it is almost impossible to get a jury to bring in a verdict of guilty against a member of this organization. Speaking of the unfortunate experiment with this institution tried by Spain in 1873–75, Manuel Silvela tells us that there were provinces where a conviction could never be obtained against any person with influential relations, "even though the crime involved was of the most serious character." [2] Sicilian juries frequently obey the behests of the Mafia. In Romagna, hatred of the Government often results in the acquittal of criminals who have murdered members of the Carbineer force.[3] And finally, the frequent acquittals everywhere occurring of persons of means — forgers, counterfeiters, or criminal bankrupts — have a sinister effect upon public morality, since so evidently due to the all-powerfulness of money.

The permanent judge, it is true, is not always beyond the reach of corruption: he may also be accessible to fear or other influences. But he has a name to preserve, an honorable position to retain; from prudence, from necessity, he acquires courage and firmness, for the slightest breath of suspicion

---

[1] "The taste for development of the oratorical art is the natural product of the judicial machinery as constituted at the present day. As a mill produces flour this mechanism produces rhetoric. To modify the product would require the re-modeling of the machinery as a whole." *Cruppi*, "La cour d'assises," p. 168 (Paris, 1898).

[2] *Manuel Silvela*, "Le jury criminal en Espagne," pp. 41, 42 (Montpellier, 1884).

[3] ["Carabinieri" : Italian military police. — TRANSL.]

may suffice to accomplish his ruin. Hence, scandals from this cause will never be common, nor of so startling a nature as those which the jury every day compels us to witness.

In some provinces there are jurors who have a fixed scale of charges, with one price for acquittal and another for the admission of extenuating circumstances. An instance is reported where a Sicilian juror complained to a member of the Chamber of Deputies that a certain trial had yielded no pecuniary benefit to the members of the jury.[1] Cases have often occurred where the jury has convicted poor accomplices and acquitted the real authors of the crime who were people possessed of means. In the South of Italy, where rich men sometimes commit crimes of bloodshed from motives of revenge, the feeling is general, in every instance, that a conviction will never be reached, and very seldom is it mistaken. "At Potenza on December 16, 1879, an adulterous woman and her paramour were on trial for the murder of her husband. Although both had confessed, a dinner had been prepared at one of the hotels in expectation of their acquittal. Nor was the expectation disappointed, for in point of fact, after the conclusion of the trial, the accused, the jurors, and the audience which in the court room had applauded the verdict of acquittal, all gathered at the appointed place to celebrate the event."[2]

We are assured that in France the jurors generally do their duty. Perhaps the truth is that they have only a little more regard for appearances. Certain noted criminal trials which we recall to mind are not calculated to give us a very high idea of the French jury. Among others there is the case of the Marquis de N. who was accused of carrying off to a distant place the illegitimate child of his wife, and throwing it from the top of a cliff to the rocks below, where its dead body was

---

[1] "Relazione della Giunta parlementare per l'inchiesta sulle condizioni della Sicilia" (Rome, 1876).

[2] *Turiello, op. cit.,* p. 338.

found. Nor have we forgotten the wholesale verdict of acquittal following the occurrence at Aiguesmortes — the case in which, under the pretext that they had conspired to lower wages, some fifteen Italians were set upon and deliberately clubbed to death by their French fellow-workmen. Moreover, in France as in Italy extenuating circumstances are always found in the case of passionate crimes, and when the accused is a woman her acquittal is a foregone conclusion.

Complaint is made of the jury everywhere. In British India a large number of crimes go unpunished, and, as Brighton tells us, the most shameful manner of corruption is there practised. The Chief Justice of the High Court at Allahabad has declared that the only way to reform this institution is to abolish it.[1]

But if I were to undertake the collection of examples, volumes would be required to contain the thousands which might be adduced. No doubt just and equitable verdicts are sometimes returned, but this, which should be the rule, has become the exception. The result is that even where the evidence is absolutely conclusive, there is reason to fear that the offender will escape. In such a case we await the verdict with no less anxiety than in one where there may be room for doubt: we are always apprehensive of some blunder, some extravagant miscarriage of justice. This fact goes to show that we are without the least confidence in the integrity or intelligence of the jury. And is it not clear that such lack of confidence betokens a probability that the criminal will go unpunished — a probability which cannot fail to be an encouragement to malefactors? Certain it is, that when the Government is really interested in securing obedience to any law, it loses no time in divesting the Court of Assizes of jurisdiction over the particular violation involved. Have we not here an obvious recognition of the weakness and uncertainty of repression when exercised by means of the jury?

When the jury has not been influenced by illicit means and

[1] The Times, London, 4 November, 1903.

has been kept under close supervision throughout the trial, the ability and discernment of the judge, his clearness in putting the questions, and his patience in explaining them in the smallest details, will often bring about a reasonable verdict. But under such circumstances a criminal trial becomes a labor of Hercules. One might well exclaim with an Italian publicist: "What manner of judges are these, whom we are continually required, at great cost of time and by means of a complicated mechanism of forms, to watch, to guard, to instruct, to warn, lest they mistake what they are to decide, fall a prey to corrupting influences, or make of themselves a laughing stock!"[1]

To the argument often made that jury service is an excellent school for the citizen, a sufficient answer is that contained in Silvela's notable discussion of the criminal jury in Spain: "If it be said that the jury is a school of instruction, is this not an acknowledgment that its pupils do not gain proficiency without making mistakes? What sort of respect can we have for an institution which turns the temple of justice into a training school? Is it a part of the jurors' education that they should sometimes convict unjustly? The unfortunate accused would have difficulty in reconciling himself with this view. Or are they to learn by degrees and begin by acquitting the offender whether innocent or guilty? Here society could scarcely be expected to acquiesce."

Again, it is said that the jury represents the people, and that, good or bad, the people will thus obtain the kind of justice it deserves. It must be admitted that this idea is thoroughly substantiated by the facts. For the jury, in reality, is the faithful interpreter of all the prejudices, political, social, religious, or anti-religious, which hold sway over a people at a given period. Where the popular novels in local favor recommend the husband to kill the wife who has transgressed her marriage vows, juries never fail to recognize the excellence

---

[1] *Pavia*, "Studii sulla criminalità italiana nel 1881" (Archivio di psichiatria, scienze penali, etc., Vol. IV. No. 1, — Turin, Bocca).

of this advice by acquitting the slayer. So, in those parts of the country where a woman cannot dispose of her affections without the consent of all the men of her family, her father, brothers, and uncles, and according to the prevailing prejudice, deserves death if she disobeys, there the jury as the representative of the people invariably acquits the murderer amid the applause of the spectators. The truth of these statements is indisputable.

The one question which goes to the heart of the matter is this: Is it possible for such an institution to contribute to popular education? Is it calculated to milden the ferocious sentiments which prevail among certain peoples of a retarded civilization? What if the British had established the jury system among the cannibal Maoris and had tried the offense of cannibalism by a jury composed of natives? The principle involved is exactly the same, when we submit cases of murder to a jury chosen from among a people who excuse murders arising from passion or provocation.

That a people is not capable of administering justice is no reason for depriving it of justice. Whether deserving or not, it should have justice imposed upon it, for otherwise it will never attain a higher plane of civilization. What is needed to overcome its barbarous customs is not a jury, but judges who do not represent this people, who have neither its passions nor prejudices, who, in a word, do not resemble it at all.

Finally, there is the contention that the jury constitutes for the citizen a guaranty against abuses of authority. This argument is one which at the most deserves consideration only so far as political matters are concerned: applied to the case of ordinary crimes it is simply ludicrous. It would require a powerful effort of imagination to suppose a Minister of Justice furiously bent upon the prosecution of honest citizens, — corrupting magistrates to protect the real authors of theft, incendiarism, and murder, and to convict in their stead respectable persons entirely innocent of any such crimes. No government has ever availed itself of such weapons, even

against its worst enemies. Sometimes under despotic governments, imaginary conspiracies invented by a too zealous
police have been the subject of prosecution, but the practice
of throwing citizens in jail on false accusations of infamous
crimes, is something which has never yet been witnessed.
What modern State would be likely to resort to means so
disgraceful and at the same time so open to immediate ex-
posure? But assume for the moment that the case is possible.
Is it to be supposed that the twelve obscure citizens composing
the jury would be any less open than permanent judges to
corruption on the part of the government? The history of the
jury in its relation to political questions justifies the opposite
belief. In England in the 1500s and 1600s, and in France
during the Revolution and the Restoration, the jury almost
always proved the faithful servitor of the most powerful:
it bent the knee to every species of tyranny, that of the throne
as well as that of the populace.[1]

§ 6. Criminal Trials; the Judges

In urging the doing away with the criminal jury, we are
very far from advocating that for triers recourse should be had
to jurists whose scientific equipment consists in the main of
maxims from the Digest. However valuable such a knowledge
may be in dealing with civil cases, it is of little or no use when
the matter in hand is the judging and classifying of criminals.
Of all the officers of the government, the judges of the present
day are perhaps the least fitted for this work. Accustomed by
the nature of their studies to regard human things from an
abstract standpoint, they are chiefly concerned with formulæ.
The civil law is completely indifferent to everything relating
to the moral and physical nature: the validity of a debt is
wholly uninfluenced by the goodness or wickedness of the
creditor. This strictly juridical character is in no way to be
predicated of criminal science, the object of which is to combat

[1] See on this subject De Novellis, "Il giuri" (Naples, 1885).

a social disease, that is to say, crime. The two branches have but few points of contact: as we view them, they constitute two entirely distinct sciences. Why, then, should we employ the same officials in two departments of the public service which are essentially foreign to each other? The member of a civil tribunal who is called upon to preside at a criminal trial retains all his habits of mind. His attention is directed not to the individual but to the legal definition of the fact. He is concerned only with the interest of the law: the social interest escapes him. The operation which he performs in imposing punishment is almost mechanical. He proceeds by the use of arithmetic. He counts up the circumstances, adds them or subtracts some from the others, and to the result applies the scale which he finds ready to hand. The too general scale of the codes has been worked out in detail by what is known as the judicial law ("jurisprudence") of the court, — resort to which is a most convenient means of avoiding the trouble of examining and appraising new facts as they arise. And finally, the judge easily forgets that in the infliction of punishment the prime consideration is that it ought to be of some use; that utility is to be attained by means varying with the individual; and that, therefore, it is precisely the examination of the individual, by which the kind and measure of punishment ought to be determined.

The renovation of criminal science for which we contend, and which consists principally in the classification of criminals from a psychologic standpoint, naturally entails a distinction still more fundamental between the qualifications requisite for the two offices of civil and criminal judge. Criminal judges ought especially to be equipped with a knowledge of statistics and penitentiary systems, as well as of criminal anthropology and psychology. They ought therefore to constitute a corps apart from that of the civil judges. For the analogy between the functions of the two is merely specious and superficial, and an externality of this sort is clearly not the test for determining the true character of a function.

§ 7. Prescription of Criminal Actions

Another favor which the law extends to offenders is the prescription of criminal actions. We can understand the reason for prescription in civil cases. When for a given period of time a plaintiff has neglected to assert his rights, a tacit relinquishment of such rights must be presumed, in order to prevent the subsequent disturbance of new rights which another enjoys in good faith. But when we have to do with a crime, is it any reason for not molesting the criminal, that he has been successful for a given period of time in keeping out of the hands of the police? — And yet, this is exactly the theory upon which proceed all the codes, in sanctioning the prescription of prosecution after the lapse of five, ten, or twenty years, according as the offense is a misdemeanor ("délit") or a felony ("crime") of greater or less seriousness. Notice, then, how the law extends its protection to the enemy of society. After some notable exploit, a clever swindler changes his name and removes to a new field of operations. Finally caught, if five years have elapsed since his first offenses, he can be prosecuted only for the later ones. And if for lack of evidence he cannot be convicted of these, then perforce he must be restored to his nefarious calling!

This is not to say, however, that prescription in the case of crime should be altogether abolished. It should be retained, but only in certain cases where the conduct of the agent has furnished proof that he is not an anti-social being, and where a supervening change in the conditions which determined the crime, renders improbable the occasion of its future manifestation. Suppose, for example, that idleness and poverty are the determining cause of a crime against property, but that the offender, successful in eluding the police, is discovered only at the end of five or ten years in the course of which, like Jean Valjean in "Les Misérables," he has undergone a moral transformation and become an honest workman whose probity is recognized throughout the neighborhood. Such a

case might occur once in a thousand times, but if by chance
it presented, would not all agree that punishment is no longer
necessary, that its imposition would be a useless cruelty and
that all that should be required is the reparation of the
damage? The same thing substantially would be true in the
case of certain aggressions upon the person such as strikings
and woundings ("coups et blessures"), offenses against
chastity, etc., where the agent's subsequent good behavior
and the mature age which he has reached combine to guaranty
society against the repetition of his one criminal act. And
it would be true, again, in the case of all offenses committed
by men who are not habitual malefactors, where, in other
words, the offender falls into the intermediate zone which we
have mentioned as existing between the class of true criminals
and that of honest men.

It is a principle recognized by the criminal law of certain
countries that the fact of recidivism interrupts prescription of
the punishment. The thing for us to do is to lay hold of this
principle, or rather of its spirit, and utilize it in the case of prescription of the action, where, that is to say, no sentence of
punishment has been rendered, substituting for the *negative*
element, viz., the absence of a fresh offense, a *positive* element,
viz., proof that the offender has undergone a moral transformation. Such a rule would naturally prevent any prescription in the case of instinctive criminals of the murderous
type, whose active perversity is not susceptible of amend-
ment. And then we would no longer be compelled to endure
the repellent spectacle of malefactors living in the very theater
of their sanguinary deeds, secure from disturbance by the
sole fact that some ten years have gone by since the act was
committed.

§ 8. Prescription of Punishments

Similar considerations will serve for the solution of the problem presented by prescription of the punishment — an institu-

tion provided for by some of the codes and unrecognized by others. Here, quite as strongly as in the preceding case, the positivist theory is opposed to any absolute rule. It would have the individual case decided by the requirements of social defense. It would apply the principle that when time has worked the moral transformation of the offender and made him a useful and socially adaptable being, then the object of punishment fails. The criminal whose subsequent conduct has confirmed the diagnosis of his incorrigibility, it would therefore exclude from all benefit of prescription.[1]

§ 9. Executive Clemency

A further means made use of by the State for the protection of criminals is the exercise of the pardoning power. The granting of a *pardon* is an act of generosity understandable in the case of offenses which are such because forbidden by the government, as, *e.g.*, political crimes and violations of financial and administrative regulations; no one would question the government's right to overlook what is an injury only to itself. But we are unable to conceive by what right the government can pardon an injury occasioned to society as a whole through an act forbidden by the natural laws of the social organism which this very government exists for the purpose of protecting. It is a mystery how this power of pardoning has managed to survive all the other irrational pre-

---

[1] In a notable monograph ("La dottrina morale nel diritto penale" — (Turin, 1902), *Carnevale* declines to admit that a greater or less lapse of time is capable of annulling the fact of a crime, or that in such a case the absolute impunity of dangerous criminals is reconcilable with the moral sentiments of a civilized nation. We contribute entirely too much to the offender's chances of impunity. A self-respecting State which is cognizant of its duties ought to direct all its efforts toward minimizing these chances instead of conducing to their augmentation by institutions such as that of prescription in criminal matters. It is not, however, this author's view that the lapse of a very long period of time between the commission of the crime and the arrest of the criminal should be entirely without effect. Only he believes that, so far at least as the more serious crimes are concerned, the effect should not extend beyond a reduction of the term of punishment or the substitution of a different punishment appropriate to the new conditions of fact which have come into existence.

rogatives which have given way before the progress of institutions.

Amnesty, that is to say, the wholesale pardoning of an entire class of persons guilty of ordinary crimes, is something which for strangeness cannot be exceeded. The State in effect says to the offender: "The thing which you did was yesterday a crime; it will be a crime tomorrow, but for today only, we shall not regard it as such." For amnesty cancels the crime itself. However humorous this formula may appear, it nevertheless serves to obliterate from the record-sheet ("casier judiciaire") of the criminal every trace of his misdeed, so that the recidivist ceases to be a recidivist by the fact of the government so deciding. At the present day, fortunately, this right of granting amnesty is seldom abused in the most enlightened countries. It is to be hoped, however, that the time is not far distant when the institution itself will have disappeared.

The case is otherwise as to the right to grant individual *pardons* affecting only the matter of punishment. This right is one which we find established under all forms of government, in republics as well as in monarchies. In the former, however, it takes on the appearance of a review of the proceedings by the Chief Executive, in the most serious cases, for the purpose of preventing the execution of the death penalty where there is reason to suppose that the verdict of the jury was wrong or unduly severe. Thus limited, the pardoning power ought to be preserved, for after all it is nothing more than an additional cog in the judicial machinery, useful, perhaps, in extreme cases.

But, inexplicable as it may seem, there are many countries where this conception of the pardoning power does not prevail — where it retains all its early significance as an act of clemency, of generosity, of remission. It is an act deemed in nowise inconsistent with the object of punishment, and this simply because of the unwillingness to understand that the latter is not an act of vengeance, but merely one of the means which must be employed in the struggle against crime.

In simple justice, the government ought to assume responsibility for fresh offenses committed by criminals whom it has pardoned. It ought at least to make reparation for the damage which in the absence of its ill-advised act of clemency would in all likelihood not have been occasioned; but supposing that it was so inclined, how could it make reparation for a new taking of human life? For, to say nothing of the depredations committed by offenders whom the negligence of government officers has suffered to escape from prison, — and in some countries this is a very frequent occurrence, — the case is not rare of pardoned murderers killing some unfortunate turnkey, some gendarme placed in charge of their transportation, some prisoner less guilty than themselves. A singular sort of generosity this which enables the man-slayer to continue his killing!

And yet we find some governments consistently refusing to authorize the execution of capital sentences. Belgium, since 1863, is a case in point. Such a course of action did not appeal to King Oscar of Sweden, when in 1875 he was asked to commute the sentences of two men who had been sentenced to death for robbery and murder. He said that in such a case the exercise of the pardoning power would mean nothing else than the abolition of the death penalty established by law. "Now," he added, "regardless of my personal views as to the justice and expediency of the death penalty in general, it is my firm conviction that I have no right, by exercising the pardoning power in cases of this character, to override a law which has been adopted by the common consent of King and Parliament." [1]

This distinguished utterance leaves nothing unsaid. Assailed by great thinkers such as Rousseau, Beccaria, and Filangieri, the pardoning power is plainly incompatible with the theory for which we stand. For us, the criminal judgment is the designation of the type of the offender under

[1] *Beltrani-Scalia*, "La riforma penitenziaria in Italia," p. 241 (Rome, 1880).

examination, the punishment the means of social defense which the case requires. Nothing could be more just than that there should be provision for a review of the case by a higher court of justice or by the Chief Executive himself, when public opinion is convinced of the convicted man's innocence. Such a review may even be granted, as useful and equitable, where the punishment seems excessively severe. But that the Chief Executive should have the right to set at naught society's means of defense against its natural enemies — how can this in anywise be admitted? The pardoning of a dangerous criminal is a violation of the citizens' right to be forever rid of his presence. Under present conditions the fact that an individual has been found inadaptable, counts for nothing. The first thing we know, the government steps in with a pardon and makes him a present of his lacking social capacity. Are not such acts of generosity something worse than State-organized charity, the only effect of which, as Spencer has abundantly demonstrated, is to encourage the vagabond while impoverishing the honest workman?

CHAPTER IV

THE RATIONAL SYSTEM OF PUNISHMENT

IN the three preceding chapters we have pointed out the corollaries to which the principles contended for give rise with respect to guilt in general, criminal attempt, criminal participation, recidivism, procedure, and prescription. All that now remains is to show the practical application of the idoneity test as a substitute for the criteria of moral responsibility and penal proportion — to indicate, in other words, the means of repression suited to the different classes of criminals.

To that end, the reader is asked to bear in mind the classification outlined in our chapter on "Criminal Anomaly" [2] as well as the considerations advanced in discussing the "Law of Adaptation." [3]

§ 1. The Punishment of Murderers

Following, then, the order of this classification, we meet first with the extreme, typical criminals — men who are desti-

---

[1] [§ 2 (a) = § II of original; § 2 (b) = § III; § 2 (c) = § IV; § 2 (d) = § VI; § 3 (a) = § VII; § 3 (b) = § VIII; § 4 = § V; and § 5 = § IX. — TRANSL.]

[2] *Ante*, Part II, c. i.   [3] *Ante*, Part III, c. i.

tute of moral sense and hence of the sentiment of pity even in its lowest terms.   In certain cases this fundamental characteristic appears at the first glance from the very nature of the crime, which of itself suffices to denote such congenital psychic anomaly in the agent as to render him incapable of assimilation in a human aggregation.   The cases in question are those of murders which could only have been the result of innate and instinctive cruelty — a trait always abnormal in any social class or environment.   For criminals of this sort, we have employed a designation sanctioned by usage, namely, that of *murderers.*

Sometimes it is the motive of the crime, sometimes the manner of its execution, which constitutes the principal sign of moral monstrosity in these offenders.

First Category: Motive as Index. — Thus every murder which is committed for a purely egoistic end — such as that of procuring money, power, or favor, sexual gratification, the concealment of a previous fault or any other gain, advantage or pleasure — furnishes proof, no matter how depraved the criminal's environment, of his exceptional perversity or utter lack of the altruistic sentiments.   With murders of this last description are to be grouped those cases of taking human life, where the motive is the gratification of some monstrous desire.   Murder accompanying rape is an instance of the kind, as is also murder committed solely to enjoy the sight of blood and mangled flesh.   Then come cases where the victim has done nothing to deserve the hatred or arouse the anger of the murderer, or where on account of ties of blood or benefits received, what the murderer regarded as provocation would not have been provocation for a normal man.   Such, in general, is the crime of parricide, for even a distinct wrong, sustained at a father's hand, does not impel the normal man to revenge himself by an act of bloodshed.   Such, too, is the murder of a benefactor or a person to whom the slayer owes respect and obedience.   And of this type, lastly, is the case where some inoffensive stranger is killed, from no other motive than the murderer's desire to exhibit his physical prowess or his skill in the handling of weapons. These various manifestations of brutality — still prevalent among savages but of rare occurrence among civilized peoples — are all related by a common feature, namely, the absence of any conduct on the part of the victim capable of producing a reaction on the part of a normal man, or in other words, the absence of what for the normal man would be an injury or sensible injustice.

Second Category: Mode of Execution as Index. — A second category of murderers is characterized by the manner in which the crime is committed. Where the murder is attended by torture, where the criminal intentionally prolongs the suffering which he is inflicting, we may always be sure of his innate cruelty, — for no normal man could withstand the sound of the victim's groans, or the sight of his agonized writhing. The fact of torture is in itself sufficient proof of the complete absence of the sentiment of pity, even where the intention to take life does not clearly appear. For this reason the French Code is right when it applies the term "murder" ("assassinat") to any species of crime which in its execution has involved the deliberate infliction of physical cruelty ("sévices sur le corps de la victime").[1]

Premeditation not a Certain Criterion of Anomaly. — It may not be out of place to remind the reader that we have made no use of the criterion of premeditation, which has become dominant in the theory of the juridical school, as the means of distinguishing the most serious offenses against human life. The character of *murderer* does not depend on the length of reflection. The speed with which the act follows the resolution has nothing to do with the corrigibility or incorrigibility of the agent. Immediateness of action is not incompatible with the completest absence of the moral sense. On the other hand, there are cases where the slayer is not a typical criminal, although he has had time for reflection. This may occur

---

[1] This provision was followed in the Sardinian Code, but, needless to say, is condemned by contemporary Italian jurists.

when he has experienced some grievous injury, some outrageous wrong which has poisoned his own life and that of his family, or where he is convinced that vengeance is for him a sacred duty. Premeditation, moreover, does not signify the non-existence of passion, for the degree of swiftness with which this is manifested, is something that depends upon the individual temperament.[1]

Sometimes the murder, although unpremeditated, is nevertheless the sure sign of an instinctive cruelty, as when there has been no provocation on the part of the victim. "The extreme, violent criminals," says Despine, "are quite as destitute of moral sentiments as those who commit crime in cold blood." [2] Suppose that a man who already sustains a reputation for violence is spending the evening in a tavern. In a moment of ill-humor he picks a quarrel with the first person at hand, perhaps a table-companion, — insults him, strikes him and when goaded into retaliation the victim flings a glass at the head of his tormentor, the latter draws his pistol and shoots him down. In such a case, we may very well have a criminal presenting the psychologic characteristics of the *murderer*, notwithstanding that the deed is instantaneous and unpremeditated.

One thing, however, is undeniable, namely, that the circumstance of unmerited and absolutely intolerable provocation shows the murderer's manner of feeling to approximate that of the generality of men, and, in most cases, prevents us from attributing to him an excessively abnormal character. Circumstances of this sort may be met with in premeditated crimes as well as in those committed on an instantaneous impulse. The fact of premeditation is therefore not always a sign of the psychologic anomaly which distinguishes the extreme criminals. In many instances a homicide may be the work of an individual belonging to the murderer class,

[1] *Von Holtzendorff,* "Psychologie des Mordes" (Berlin, 1875). See also, "Das Verbrechen des Mordes und die Todesstrafe," by the same author.

[2] *Despine,* "De la folie au point de vue philosophique et plus spécialement physiologique," p. 39.

despite the absence of premeditation, while there are other cases in which the opposite would be true.

Our conclusion, then, is that the cruelty with which the murder has been committed and the absence of grave provocation on the part of the victim, are the two criteria which ought to be substituted for that of premeditation. By their means, we shall be enabled to distinguish from other homicidal criminals, those whom we have called murderers, that is to say, the extreme, instinctive, or typical criminals who may be regarded as beings morally degenerate in the last degree, and permanently incapable of sociability.

Elimination by Death the Measure Necessary. — The impossibility of adaptation in the case of these offenders once recognized, absolute elimination is plainly required. It is inconceivable that the social power should even in a single instance suffer to exist the probability, however slender, of a monstrous act of this sort being repeated by the same offender. The death penalty alone will serve in the case of these extreme criminals. The only exception to its application will be in established cases of intellectual insanity, for reasons which have heretofore been given.[1] In such cases it will be necessary to confine the agent in an asylum for the criminal insane, from which he will not be discharged until there is complete certainty of his cure.

So far as the death penalty itself is concerned, there is no need for undertaking its justification here. The matter has already been sufficiently discussed in other portions of this book.

It is contended, however, that as a means of elimination, an adequate substitute for the death penalty is furnished by imprisonment for life, in that the latter prevents the criminal from reëntering society and renders his reproduction impossible. We must challenge the accuracy of this statement. In the first place, the number of escapes annually occurring proves that the elimination which life-imprisonment effects

[1] See *ante*, Part III, c. ii, § 3.

is not absolute.[1] Then, again, there is always a considerable number of contingencies such as prison mutinies, pardons, amnesties, etc., by the happening of which the criminal is thrown back upon society. And finally, it is not a matter of rare occurrence for life prisoners to murder their keepers or the gendarmes in charge of their transportation from one penitentiary to another.[2]

The penitentiary, therefore, is not an absolute and irrevocable means of elimination. But even if it were, this fact would not be sufficient cause for giving it preference over the death penalty. We can see no good reason for keeping alive men who must be forever barred from society, — for conserving an existence which is purely animal. Nor are we able to understand why the citizens of a state should be taxed for the purpose of affording food and shelter to permanent enemies of society.[3]

Were the preceding considerations to be left entirely out of view, there is another yet more decisive. Assume that the two means of elimination — death and life-imprisonment — are equally absolute. Since we have to choose between them, why should we not decide in favor of the one which possesses the inestimable advantage of intimidation? We have, it is true, rejected intimidation as a criterion of punishment, in the

---

[1] In Italy there is an annual average of 15 escapes from the penitentiaries and of about 110 from other prisons.

[2] In one instance, a man who had been twice condemned to death and each time pardoned, committed a third homicide. A further case is that of a pardoned convict who killed a carbineer in the railroad station at Alessandria. In a third instance, the offender killed the director of the Favignana penitentiary (*Beltrani-Scalia,* "La riforma penitenziaria in Italia," p. 250, Rome, 1879). A prisoner who, serving a sentence in the same penitentiary, had attempted to kill one of the keepers was sentenced to life-imprisonment. When sentence was pronounced, he defiantly asserted in the presence of the court that it was his intention to carry out his purpose of taking the life of his keeper in whatever penitentiary he should be confined (Address of the Procurator General at Parma, — 1880).

[3] In the penitentiaries of Italy, on December 31, 1900, there were 3,041 prisoners serving life sentences and 1,198 serving sentences of more than 24 years (Prison Statistics, 1902). The expense which honest citizens are called upon to pay for the maintenance of this army of murderers may be roughly estimated at two millions of francs per annum.

sense that we believe it unjust to inflict upon a man a graver evil than his individuality demands, in the sole end of example or terrorization. We have said that for each offender there must be employed the repressive means suited to his individual nature, according to the degree in which he lacks idoneity for the social life, — to the greater or less probability that he will become assimilable: otherwise extreme injustice and cruelties might be committed with a view to the prevention of crime. In the case in question, however, the offender is incapable of assimilation; he deserves to be eliminated; and such elimination we find to be absolutely effected by means of the death penalty, without excess or injustice. It is now proposed to substitute for this means another of supposedly equal value. But, plainly, before giving up the first, we must see whether the other offers the same indirect advantages, — advantages which are not determinative but which nevertheless ought to be given due weight. Such an advantage is intimidation. In the death penalty this is a natural effect; by punishments restrictive of liberty it is produced in a measure incomparably less.

On this point no doubt is possible. Although the gallows does not intimidate *all* malefactors, it strikes terror into a considerable number who are unaffected by the menace of imprisonment, whatever its duration. If the death penalty were capable of disarming all murderers, there would be no need for its application. But there can be no question that it disarms many. Moreover, when the State puts murderers to death, it can do no more. If, however, it fails to do all it can, it is responsible for the human lives which otherwise would not have been taken. When it is sought to do everything possible to prevent a given act, it is necessary to menace him who would commit the act, with the greatest possible harm. Loss of liberty is not the greatest possible harm, for life yet remains. When the State abolishes the punishment of death, it authorizes murder: it says to the criminal: "The risk that you run in killing a human being is a change of abode, the necessity of spending your days in my house instead of your own." In reality there is no abolition of the death penalty. In relinquishing its own right to inflict this punishment, the State thereby recognizes in others the right to take life. We are here confronted with a vicious circle. Is it not better that death be inflicted by the State than by individuals? That is the sole question.

Furthermore, it must be noted that the influence of the death penalty is not restricted to the class of criminals which it directly menaces: it has a powerful effect even upon the lesser criminals, for the man who is tending to a career of crime has no exact knowledge of how far he can go, or what punishment his acts may involve. His consciousness, then, of the fact "that there exists a power capable of taking the life of certain malefactors" (he does not know precisely which), may become a motive sufficiently strong to paralyze his criminal inclinations.[1]

History and statistics establish the truth of these assertions. In Belgium, as a Procurator General of that country has said, the belief that the death penalty was a thing of the past, induced among the masses by reason of the Government's attitude toward capital sentences for some years prior to 1850, was attended by an increase in the number of the more serious crimes dating from that year. And following the year 1863 which saw a return to the practice of systematic pardoning, the graver crimes multiplied "in an alarming manner, as belief in the abolition of the death penalty became more and more fixed in the popular mind." [2] In point of fact, from 1865 to 1880, prosecutions for murder increased from 34 to 120.

As is well known, the formidable outbreak of brigandage which in the year 1861 occurred in the South of Italy was put down only by the summary shooting of convicted offenders. England, which has constantly employed hanging as a punish-

---

[1] *Turiello, op. cit.,* c. III.
[2] As cited by *Beltrani-Scalia,* "La riforma penitenziaria in Italia."

ment for murder, is the only country of Europe showing a sensible diminution of crime.[1] In Prussia, where for many years scarcely any executions have taken place, the criminal statistics exhibit a continual growth in the number of homicides during the period beginning with 1854 and ending with 1880: from 242 in the former year, it rose by an uninterrupted progression to 518 in the latter. In Switzerland, as a result of the abolition of the death penalty in 1874, it has been ascertained that there ensued an increase in this crime estimated at 75% for five years alone [2] — a circumstance which decided many of the Cantons to reëstablish the punishment in question.

As for France, so long as capital sentences continued to be carried regularly into execution, the more serious forms of crime were on the decrease. But in 1878, President Grévy, apparently desirous of experimenting "in anima vili," permitted but 7 executions, in 1880, but 2, while in 1881 he cut the number down to 1. As soon as this leniency was noticed by the criminal world, murders became more frequent. As against 31 capital sentences in 1877, there were 35 in 1880. Convictions for parricide, which had been 8 in 1878, increased to 14 in 1882. During this last-mentioned period the number of murders underwent an increase of 36. Since then, the censure of public opinion has caused the pardoning power to be exercised more sparingly. Of the criminals sentenced to death between 1886 and 1900 almost half were executed, with the result of reducing the number of murders from 224 to 175.

A correspondent writes me from Chile that with the practice there prevailing of systematically commuting the death penalty into that of 15 or 20 years of "presidio" there has kept pace an increase of murders and culpable homicides, these crimes from 1898 to 1902 showing an annual average of 950, that is to say, 35 per 100,000 inhabitants. This extraordinary frequency of offenses against human life, adds my informant, renders colonization almost impossible. The peas-

[1] See *ante*, p. 202.
[2] *Freuler*, "Für die Todesstrafe," p. 57 (Schaffhausen, 1879).

sants are kept in a continual state of fright and their chief concern is to get away from the country districts.   Yet in spite of these conditions the newspapers and politicians still make it a point to preach " assassinophily."[1]

In Italy, where, except in the army, no executions have taken place since 1876, the more serious forms of crime have attained almost incredible proportions.   Whereas in England the annual average of homicides is only 300, Italy, with an almost equal population, has an annual average of 3,814, of which nearly one-third are true cases of murder.   Since 1892 there has been little change in the figures, the number in 1899 being 3,586.   Perhaps the reason is that the criminal saturation has reached its maximum.   Whether capital punishment exists or not, in no country are all the citizens likely to amuse themselves by cutting each other's throats.   The only thing is that with the death penalty absent, those who are inclined to this form of diversion have no longer any reason for hesitation.

One or two examples in point may not be without value. In the city of Naples an officer of the fire department was murdered in cold blood by a subordinate toward whom he had shown many acts of kindness.   The murderer's confession showed that he was thoroughly convinced that the death penalty was not a thing to be reckoned with, since he declared that the motive of his crime was the desire to obtain food and shelter for the rest of his days, without the necessity of working or begging.   In 1884 occurred the case of the soldier, Misdea, who one night in the Pizzofalcone barracks at Naples, opened fire with a rifle upon his sleeping comrades, and continuing his murderous work for a quarter of an hour killed ten of them.   Condemned to death by a military tribunal,

---

[1] My correspondent subjoins a curious detail.   In Valparaiso, on the very day when the translation of my brochure attacking the abolition of the death penalty there appeared, an agitation was in progress to obtain the pardon of three convicted murderers, and not a single newspaper had the courage to announce the pamphlet's publication for fear of hurting the cause of these offenders.

he refused to take his sentence seriously, because he was fully of the belief that executions were not possible in Italy. Some days after this massacre, certain other soldiers murdered their sergeants. All the offenders were shot. Since then, there has not been a single instance of the kind in the Italian army.

If the fear of losing their lives is capable of influencing the conduct of men who from the nature of their calling are frequently required to face death, how can it be supposed that the same fear is without efficacy in the case of the population generally?

Any efforts to realize the plan of Beccaria and make the conditions of life-imprisonment so rigorous as to instill terror, would be utterly useless.[1] In the first place, the infliction of the cruelties necessarily involved would be distasteful. Then again, anything we might do to impart to the penitentiary a terrifying aspect would have no effect beyond the sinister impression produced upon those who visited such establishments out of curiosity, for the prisoner's despair does not echo beyond the walls of his dungeon.

§ 2. The Punishment of Violent Criminals

(a) HOMICIDAL OFFENDERS

We turn now to the second class of criminals. With these, crime is chiefly due to the superficial stratum of the character, in which find lodgment false notions of honor or of the duty of vengeance or other prejudices often traditional in a family or in an entire social class. Criminals of this sort do not kill from motives of purely egoistic satisfaction. Their crimes are the effect of an ego-altruism — of "amour propre," of what they conceive to be wounded honor, — or even of a true but misdirected altruism, as when they are actuated by political or religious prejudices.

---

[1] "Whoever has visited a penitentiary may flatter himself that he has seen a picture of contented crime ('un tableau du crime heureaux')" (*Lauvergne*, "Les forçats," cited by *Aubry*, "La contagion du meurtre" — Paris, F. Alcan, 1888).

As has already been indicated, the criminal's anomaly is always in inverse ratio to the gravity of his provocation: the more serious the provocation, the less remote in his manner of feeling from that of normal men. The crime may thus assume the appearance of a reaction, legitimate in principle, but excessive (and it is just this excess, be it noted, which establishes the fact of abnormality); the sentiments of the criminal, although exaggerated, may not be inexplicable. But for this, the provocation must be appreciable, it must be of such a nature as to constitute in itself an offense to the moral sentiments. Everything which relates exclusively to the manner of feeling of the criminal individual must be left out of consideration, for it is precisely his psychic anomaly which makes him feel external impressions in an exaggerated fashion, causing the fact, which for others is almost indifferent, to become for him a serious injury, a wrong which cries for vengeance. It is therefore necessary that the provocation be such as would be regarded as real by the generality of men or, at least, of those belonging to the same social class or part of the country. Then and then only does the criminal approximate more or less the normal man, according to the gravity of the injury or wrong which he has suffered.

A case in point would be that of a crime which represents an immediate and unpremeditated reaction against an extreme offense to the sentiment of self-respect. The universal prevalence of this sentiment renders the crime less shocking. This is why we are always ready to excuse the act of a man who makes use of a weapon at the very instant of experiencing some intolerable insult.

The thing to be feared is that, in practice, these circumstances of excuse will be the subject of abuse. In the Latin countries, especially, it is very difficult to get juries to convict for crimes of passion. The abolition of trial by jury should be the first step in the reform of criminal science.[1]

---

[1] In Italy, the criminal jury is retained chiefly out of consideration for the fifty or so lawyers included in the membership of the Chamber of Deputies

Again, there is the case where the motive is that of revenge for the murder of a relative. Committed in obedience to local prejudices or those of a social class, the crime may be termed "endemic." It does not, however, essentially differ from the murder which is rendered excusable by the fact of provocation. We regard an injury as real when it is such according to the ideas current in the sphere in which we move: it is of little moment whether this sphere is the whole world or merely that microcosm wherein we dwell and which alone we know. Of such character is, beyond question, the blood-vengeance prescribed by the primitive customs which still survive in some regions of the South, such as Corsica, Sicily, and Calabria.

Nevertheless, the fact of premeditation, whatever be the motive of the murder, always denotes a cruel nature. Not possessing such a nature, Hamlet passed long days of indecision, without being able to bring himself to an act against which his instincts rebelled. But the influence of the environment, the superstitious notion of a duty which calls for avenging the death of a father or the honor of a daughter, to a great extent limit the share in the production of the crime which must be ascribed to the individual character, that is to say, the moral anomaly of the slayer. It is the non-egoistic external motive which has predominated and been the determinant. Unless there are present other facts which would lead us to an opposite belief, we cannot be sure of the permanent insociability of the offender.

In none of the cases spoken of in this section can the criminal be classed as a murderer. But there is reason to suppose that there exists in him a moral anomaly, in that his sentiment of pity falls below the measure demanded by the social life. Hence some means of elimination is required. It is necessary above all, that the individual be exiled from an environment where the prevailing prejudices almost justify his crime.

whose specialty is that of trying cases in the Court of Assizes. Public opinion is decidedly adverse to this institution.

But this elimination ought to be neither absolute nor permanent nor determined in advance, — first, because it is impossible to affirm that the degree of perversity is so high as to afford ground for fearing further crimes on the part of the same offender, and secondly, because of our inability to distinguish the part in the production of the crime which is chargeable to the moral anomaly of the individual from that which is chargeable to the influences of the environment.

It would seem that the repressive treatment here appropriate should take the form of internment ("relégation") in some place — an island or colony, for example — where the criminal could be permitted freedom of movement and yet be kept under such supervision as would prevent his escape. The duration of the punishment should not be fixed in advance, but should be made to depend upon a number of circumstances, among which age and sex are the most important. For if we are dealing with a very youthful offender it may be supposed that the coming on of maturity will moderate the excessive sensibility responsible for his exaggerated tendency to resent offense, and take away from him the energy of which he has made such ill use. In the case of women, marriage and the birth of children may operate as a sufficient guaranty. With adult offenders, the approach of old age may have the like effect. Each of these conditions marks a change of life in which the dominating passions decline in strength or else disappear entirely to be replaced by others. Finally, when the interned offender during a series of years will have displayed a uniform mildness of character in an unmistakable way, this fact ought to accelerate his return to society. For these reasons, it will be necessary to establish a period of observation. This will vary with the case, care however being taken not to make it too short. At its conclusion, the magistrate having before him a detailed report of all the facts tending to throw light upon the character of the offender, will decide whether the punishment should be terminated or continued.

(b) Offenders Guilty of Acts of Serious Physical or Moral Cruelty

Offenders guilty of other crimes of the same nature — other violations, that is to say, of the sentiment of pity — should be subjected to a penal treatment very different from that which is involved in the physical ("afflictive") and correctional punishments of the present system. This category comprises individuals who commit such offenses as the infliction of wounds with intent to maim or disfigure or to bring about a physical disability either permanent or temporary, mutilations, forcible abduction, rape, the infliction of physical cruelties upon defenseless persons, false accusation ("calomnie"), and kidnapping attended by protracted detention of the victim ("séquestration prolongée d'une personne"). It sometimes happens that the criminal instinct of such an offender is persistent. Whether this is the case can be ascertained by an examination for the stigmata of degeneracy, mentioned in a previous chapter, in conjunction with an investigation of the facts relating to his habits and character, which a long period of observation will permit to be studied in all their details. It may transpire that the offender is afflicted with hysteria. This is especially likely when his offense is that of false accusation or cruelties practised upon children. So, when the crime in question is that of wounding or rape, it may appear that the criminal is an epileptic or a victim of alcoholic brutalization. In such cases it will become necessary to confine the offender in an asylum for the criminal insane.

Again, it may be that the author of an act of cruelty, without presenting any indications of phrenosis or neurosis, continues to display a brutal perversity, although he has not yet had occasion to commit murder. Here the only means capable of reconciling the necessities of social defense with the sentiment of humanity which in our day does not sanction the infliction of the death penalty upon the man who has not

taken life, is that of transportation.   And since in instances
of this kind the criminal's nature is really that of a savage,
the transportation should consist in the offender being taken
to some remote region where civilization has not yet pene-
trated and there left to shift for himself, removed from all
possibility of doing harm to civilized men.   This sort of transportation — the marooning of the offender — is in such cases
the only rational form of punishment, as it is the simplest and
least expensive to the public.   So far as concerns the question
of place, the islands of the Oceanic archipelago and the deserts
of Africa will render possible this mode of repression for centuries to come.

On the other hand, when a crime of the character under
discussion appears as an isolated instance in the life of its
author and does not prove an absolute insociability on his
part, internment ("relégation") in a penal colony beyond
seas will be the remedy most adapted to the case.   The punishment will not be terminated until after an adequate period
of observation, unless in the meantime the offender has made
full payment to the victim or his family of the amount of
compensation fixed by the magistrate and has obtained from
the latter permission to return.

(c) Youthful Offenders

A period of observation must also be had in the case of
youthful offenders guilty of wanton cruelties or of rape, when
there is a possibility that mental and moral development will
modify their instincts.   The existence of this possibility should
depend on no hard and fast rule fixing legal minority, but
should be left to the determination of the judge in the individual instance.

As we already have had occasion to point out, the instinct
for bloodshed sometimes begins to reveal itself at a very early
age in a series of acts characterized by violence and brutality.
Although the agent's lack of strength prevents them from being

of serious consequence, the situation is one which calls for
attentive consideration on the part of the judge instead of, as
under the present system, the hasty imposition of a so-called
correctional punishment involving a few days or months of
detention. These minor offenses are repeated with a frequency
at times almost incredible until at length they culminate
in some monstrous crime. Then only do we stop to consider
the offender's antecedents. The fact is that he has been all
along an instinctive murderer and this the anthropologist
would have told us long ago, had we submitted the subject
to his examination. On the one hand, the kind and frequency
of the acts, together with the offender's psychology and anthropologic characteristics, on the other, what may be called
the queen of proofs — an hereditary history of vice, madness,
or crime — would have enabled the observer to detect in the
violent, passionate, and cruel child, that type of criminal which
we have termed the murderer, and to suggest measures which,
if adopted, would have resulted in the saving of one or more
lives.

For youthful offenders of the present description there
should be a primary period of observation in an asylum for
the criminal insane. This will probably disclose the existence
of some psychopathic form. If not, and there is still hope that
the arrival of puberty will work a transformation of the instincts, then the requisite measure is a secondary period of
observation in an agricultural colony, lasting indefinitely,
that is to say, until there is good reason to believe that the
danger has disappeared. In the case of recidivism and when
it becomes certain that the offender is characterized by absence
of the moral sense and a persistent instinct of cruelty which
sooner or later will manifest itself in murder, transportation
of the kind mentioned in the last section, namely, marooning
seems to be the only means whereby the State can prevent the
taking of innocent lives, and at the same time spare the life
of the offender who has not yet committed a murder.

(d) OFFENDERS DEFICIENT ONLY IN MORAL TRAINING OR RESTRAINT

Next we have a class of offenders who occupy a place at the very edge of natural criminality, or if it be preferred, midway between criminals and normal men. The offenses which they commit are the least serious violations of the sentiment of pity and can scarcely be attributed to a true cruelty, appearing rather to be the effect of what may be termed rudeness ("rudesse") or lack of moral training or restraining influences. Such is the case of assault ("coups") occurring in the course of a fight where, the prisoner having refrained from striking his adversary after he was down, it is evident that there was no intent to kill; of causing death or physical injuries where the result is directly due to the negligence or carelessness of the offender, — to that disregard for the lives of others which always marks a low state of development of the altruistic sentiments; and of insults ("injures") and threats without serious import. In this category we may also include the case of seduction ("détournement d'une jeune fille sans violence").

It is in such cases that we could with advantage substitute for the punishment of imprisonment that of compulsory reparation, rigidly enforced, of the material and moral damage occasioned by the offender. This would take the form of requiring him to pay two fines, one for the benefit of the State as compensation for the social disturbance as well as to defray the costs of the prosecution, the other for the benefit of the injured person. The amount of each should be made to depend upon the prisoner's ability to pay, taking into consideration his private means if any, and if none, the possibility of his meeting the sum from the proceeds of his labor. With respect to solvent offenders measures of extreme severity will be necessary. The injured person should be awarded a lien ("hypothèque," "judicial mortgage") upon the defendant's real property, and as to the residue of the latter's assets, the claim should be made a preferred and secured debt ("créance privilégiée"). And in order to defeat any attempt on the part of the defendant fraudulently to convey his property, these ought to date not from the time of final judgment ("sentence définitive") but from that of the order committing the prisoner for trial ("ordonnance d'envoi en jugement"). Lastly, in case the injured person declines to avail himself of these advantages, the amount due to him ought to be paid into a Compensation Fund ("caisse des amendes") created for the purpose of making advance payments to needy persons who have suffered injury through criminal offenses.

As for insolvents, the thing to do would be to make them pay over for the benefit of the State on the one hand and on the other, for that of the injured person or (in case of the latter's refusal to accept) the Compensation Fund above mentioned, all their earnings over and above what is required for the strictest necessities of life, namely, shelter and such food as is just sufficient to satisfy the demands of hunger. In the case of factory employees and the like, it should be made the duty of the employer to withhold this overplus in making payment of their wages. Finally, all offenders who refuse obedience to these measures, together with those who are in no position to comply, — vagabonds, wilful idlers, and persons without a fixed habitation, — should be enrolled in a corps of State workmen. Their wages in this service will nominally be not less than the wages paid free workmen. The State, however, will actually pay to them only such part thereof as is strictly necessary to enable them to live: the residue will from time to time be paid into the Compensation Fund, which will make the proper payments to the injured person.

The adoption of such measures would have a three-fold effect. In the first place the resentment of the offended person would be more speedily allayed. Again, the public would be freed from the useless burden of maintaining the constantly renewed host of criminals who people the correctional prisons. And finally, the criminals themselves will be kept from becoming still more demoralized and debased by the associations of the prison and brutalized by the enforced idleness of its regimen.[1]

§ 3. The Punishment of Criminals Deficient in Probity.

We now proceed to consider the penal treatment applicable to the third main class of criminals — those who lack the sentiment of probity, either in whole or in part.[2]

(a) INSTINCTIVE AND HABITUAL OFFENDERS

It has already been seen that as the counterpart of the morbid form called kleptomania, there may exist in persons not of unsound mind a propensity to theft resulting from heredity or atavism, and that such propensities are often revealed by external anthropologic signs, in particular by a distinctive physiognomy. The presence of these characteristics in an individual who is not in a condition of extreme destitution or wretchedness, coupled with the fact of a number of recidivations on his part, makes it certain that he is a born and incorrigible thief. The same thing is true of swindlers, who, likewise, are often found to exhibit distinctive characteristics.

As I have said in a former place,[3] elimination in its absolute form ought to be applied only in the case of murderers, because, when the act of the offender has occasioned no grave and irreparable injury to the sentiment of pity, that sentiment itself stands in the way of taking his life. For the defense of society against such enemies, some less absolute means of

---

[1] These proposals have been worked out in my "Riparazione alle vittime dei delitti" (Turin, 1887); and in my papers read before the International Penitentiary Congress of Rome in 1885, the Congress of "L'Union Internationale de Droit Pénal," at Brussels in 1889, the International Penitentiary Congress, at Saint Petersburg in 1890, and also the Italian Juridical Congress, at Florence, in 1891. See in particular the proceedings of the last-mentioned Congress, p. 185 *et seq.* See also, in the Actes du premier Congrès d'Anthropologie criminelle (Rome, 1887), the notable paper presented by Fioretti; and, further, Appendix A of the present volume.

[2] See *ante*, Part II, c. I, pp. 125-130.

[3] *Ante*, Part III, c. I.

elimination is quite sufficient. First of all, we may set apart
kleptomaniacs and pyromaniacs as well as epileptic thieves
and incendiaries: these should be committed to an asylum
for the criminal insane and there placed under proper treatment. The sane criminals with which we have to deal in the
present connection are therefore thieves, incendiaries, swindlers, and forgers, who are suffering from no mental disorder
but are possessed of a criminal instinct (or according to Benedikt, a moral neurasthenia), together with habitual offenders
of this species, whether their lack of probity is congenital or,
commencing by external accident (bad training, bad examples,
and bad company), has subsequently become instinctive and
incorrigible. For these the proper measure would be that of
transportation to some distant and sparsely peopled territory,
some colony in the first stages of settlement, where assiduous
toil is absolutely necessary to the preservation of existence.
The rigid application of the maxim "Qui non laborat nec
manducet," together with the offender's knowledge that all
the rest of his days must be passed in this exile would perhaps
induce him to make some efforts; the probability is that he
would try to render his existence less precarious and burdensome. But if the neurasthenia is unconquerable and the
criminal finds the means of exercising his maleficent activity
in the place of his internment, then a further elimination will
become necessary. In that event resort should be had to the
punishment of marooning mentioned in § 2 (b) of the present
chapter.

It is contended, however, that transportation has seen its
day. In view, we are told, of the rapidity with which Oceanica
is being colonized, and of the constant invasion by civilization
of all the other waste places of the earth, there will soon be
no more available territory.

Yet France possesses New Caledonia, the colonization of
which has scarcely commenced, and sends thither its habitual
offenders in spite of the opposition of the Australian government — an opposition no doubt actuated by the fear of future

commercial competition much more than by that of Australia becoming an asylum for escaped convicts. Russia has, in Siberia, an immense area of very thinly populated territory which it uses for the exile of criminals. The government of British India continues to transport convicts to the Andaman Islands. In the prison congress held at Calcutta in 1877, the subject of debate was not the abolition of transportation, but merely its restriction to the case of habitual offenders — a measure with which our plan is in entire harmony.

Some day, perhaps, space will be lacking. So, for that matter, will the world's coal supply some day be exhausted: it has even been calculated just how many centuries it will take to bring this about. But, because of a vague probability, are we to refrain from making use of the world as we find it today? After the islands of Polynesia and Malaysia, recourse could be had to the Sahara and finally, to the innumerable coral islands, for the most part entirely uninhabited, with which the Pacific Ocean is strewn. . . . We may rest assured that for many centuries to come, there will be no default of waste lands to receive the noxious elements of the civilized nations.

There is, of course, an economic problem to be solved, that of the expense of transportation and supervision, as well as the cost of defending a population situated at such a distance from the mother country.[1] But it must be considered that the original outlay, however great, which such a plan may involve, will mean a saving in the long run. By relieving the home penal establishments of the care of all habitual criminals, — whose offenses, be it noted, constitute almost one-half of the total number of crimes, — this measure will effect a reduction, constantly growing more appreciable, in the amount of the prison appropriations. For the interned offender will be under the necessity of earning his own living by agricultural labor,

[1] On the question of transportation see the very interesting work of *Leveillé*, "La Guyane et la question pénitentiaire coloniale" (Paris, 1886). See also *Bruck*, "Die Gegner der Deportation" (Breslau, 1901); *Fani*, "La deportazione" (Perugia, 1896).

opportunity for which will not lack, whereas in the case of a
prison it is always a matter of exceeding difficulty to find
useful employment for the inmates.[1]

(b) Non-Habitual Offenders

The sub-class with which we have just been dealing, it
will be observed, is composed of offenders whose improbity
either is congenital or else has become instinctive through
habit and who, at the same time, by reason of the gravity or
number of their crimes are a constant menace to society. We
have now to do with a second sub-class consisting of individuals whose depravity is still incomplete, and who have not
yet become habitual offenders or extremely dangerous to
society.

This is a particularly numerous group. The typical case
is that of the individual with no very deep-rooted sentiment
of probity who offends because of an evil example which he
has followed from a spirit of imitation. A first fault often
leads to another. For a good reputation is a necessity of
existence even in the humblest social conditions. The domestic or workman detected in a theft will have difficulty in finding
employment. A new career, that of malefactor, then opens
to him, and since he is no longer held back by the most powerful of the restraining influences which had hitherto been
operative, — the fear of being proclaimed dishonest, — he
will lose no time in making this career his own. The only
remedy possible in the case of such offenders is to effect a
change in their territorial environment, in their habits, in the
nature of their work, — in short, to make them begin a new
life. If the punishment inflicted by the State is to improve
the situation instead of rendering matters worse, as it does

---

[1] In Italy, for example, three-sevenths of the inmates of the penitentiaries
are in a state of complete idleness, while the work of the rest counts for little
in point of productiveness (*Beltrani-Scalia*, "La riforma penitenziaria in
Italia," p. 307). In France, on 31 December, 1884, out of 25,231 prison inmates, 10,087 were unemployed (*D'Haussonville*, "Le combat contre le
vice, " — Revue des Deux Mondes, 1 January, 1888).

today, it must not lose sight of the causes which have determined the crime.   It therefore becomes necessary for us to distinguish the different cases of this character according to these causes.

Youthful Offenders Influenced by Bad Examples. — Take first the case of adolescents who have been influenced to steal by bad examples encountered in their environment or, for that matter, in their own families.   The necessity of immediately removing the offender from his deleterious surroundings is here evident, for therein lies the only hope of preventing him from becoming an habitual thief.   This necessity has long since been recognized and by nearly every writer who has treated the subject.   The only difficulty has been in settling upon the means, — in determining whether it shall consist of houses of correction, industrial asylums, or agricultural colonies.   But, according to D'Olivecrona, there is no doubt that the agricultural colony is much to be preferred.[1]

France, since 1850, has had agricultural colonies for young criminals acquitted because of inability to understand the nature of their acts ("défaut de discernment") and minors sentenced to more than six months and less than two years of imprisonment.   Of these colonies some were established by the Government; others again were founded by individuals but are now under State control.   The latter showed only 6.42% of recidivists, while the percentage in the Government colonies was somewhat higher — 11.29%.   The term of detention varies from 3 to 6 years.   Agricultural labor furnishes the principal means of employment, but other industries such as blacksmithing and carpentry, find a place.   "Never has public money been more usefully expended," says the writer last cited, "since by this means the State in 93 out of every 100 cases re-adapts to society a class of individuals who for the most part would otherwise have become inmates of the penitentiaries for the rest of their lives at the public expense." [2]   When

[1] *D'Olivecrona,* "Des causes de la récidive," etc. p. 171 (Stockholm, 1873).
[2] *Ibid.,* p. 163.

the term of detention expires, the director of the colony finds employment for his charge with some farmer, or else sees that he enters the army or navy. A complete removal of the individual from his former environment is thus brought about. Similar colonies exist in England, Belgium, Holland, Germany, Switzerland, and the United States.

Such institutions, it need scarcely be said, can be established with safety in a civilized country. The class of offenders here in question is such that their supervision would be an easy matter, and even if some escapes should occur, the danger to the neighboring residents would not be very serious. The case offers no difficulties at all to be compared with those attending the establishment of agricultural colonies composed of adults sentenced to penal servitude, as has been attempted in Italy — an undertaking which, in my judgment, is a very grave mistake.

Adult Novices. — Turning now to individuals who have emerged from adolescence, we find a large group of novice thieves who have been compelled to crime as a result of neglect, idleness, the lack of a trade, or a tendency to vagabondage. Whatever be the nature of the theft, unless it plainly appears that we have to do with an irreducible congenital instinct, the case is always one for experiment. This will take the form of assigning the offender to a corps of workmen employed by the State, where his wages, nominally equal to the ordinary standard, would be retained for the payment of a fine to the State and compensation to the injured party. In this service he would be entitled to food only when he has properly performed his daily stint, and would thus be confronted with the alternative of working or starving. Nor should the satisfaction of the amount due be followed by his absolute release. Instead, he ought to be required to deposit a small sum as security for his good behavior and to find employment in some manufactory or other industrial establishment. In case of a fresh crime, the sum deposited would be immediately forfeited; otherwise, it would be restored to him, but

not until after the lapse of a certain number of years of good
conduct on his part.   Where the State has colonial territory
in which it is desirous of encouraging settlement, the offender
might be exempted from giving security upon condition
that he immediately emigrate to one of these colonies.   In
the case of recidivism, internment for life in an oversea
penal colony ("relégation perpétuelle") is the means which
must be directly resorted to.   Since proof is here present of a
persistent individual cause, namely, aversion to work, any
other measure would be of no avail.

The same treatment is applicable to the case of novice
swindlers and forgers.

Cases of Aberration or Cupidity. — It happens with considerable frequency that the offender is neither an idler nor a
vagabond.   He follows a trade, a profession, he has an adequate income, perhaps even moderate wealth.   Yet, by some
strange aberration, he commits a theft; from pure cupidity,
he misappropriates money which has been entrusted to his
care: all at once he turns swindler, forger, or criminal bankrupt.   The circumstance furnishes proof of his improbity,
but there exists no constant motive to impel him to further
offenses.   It may well be, therefore, that he will not repeat his
fault, if by the complete disappointing of his cupidity, he is
made to realize that in his own interest, honesty is the better
policy.   To serve this purpose no course of action could be
better adapted than that of compelling him, by the means
indicated in § 2 (*d*) of the present chapter, to pay a fine to the
State and compensation to the injured party.   Such a measure
would result in still other advantages to society.   Suppose that
a dishonest cashier or fraudulent bankrupt knows for a certainty that once discovered, he will not be permitted to enjoy
the smallest fraction of his ill-gotten gains, but will be compelled to restore them to the last penny, or else work throughout an indefinite period for the benefit of those whom he has
robbed.   Is it not likely that the upshot will be the speedy
reappearance of the stolen funds, supposed to have been

squandered but in fact confided to friendly hands? And is not the plan here proposed much more useful from every standpoint than the sentencing of the offender to a fixed term of imprisonment — a proceeding which is of profit to no one, and only adds the cost of the prisoner's maintenance to the damage occasioned by his crime?

If the sum has really been squandered, then it is for the offender to devote his constant labor toward making it good. In case he refuses to seek work on his own account, he will be made to enter one of the companies of State workmen, already mentioned, where work will be his only means of escaping starvation. If, after the lapse of a number of years, he has been unable to earn the whole of the misappropriated sum, his age and good intentions could be taken into consideration. The period of this coercion might even be fixed at 10 or 15 years, subject, however, to indefinite extension, whenever there appears any tendency to shirk.

When the offender has fully compensated the injured person and paid the fine due to the State, he will be released. In this case as well as in the case just mentioned where he may be released at the end of a term of years on account of his inability to meet the whole of the sum required, he will undergo no further punishment except that of being deprived of his political rights and prohibited from holding any public office or, if the offense be criminal bankruptcy, from engaging in any commercial pursuit.

Should, however, the offender commit a new crime of the same description, then he ought to be subjected to the form of treatment which is above proposed for idlers and vagabonds. A second recidivation on his part, as on theirs, would be properly followed by internment for life in an oversea penal colony ("relégation perpétuelle"). For the fact of recidivism is sufficient evidence that the case is not one of an individual with whom crime is an isolated instance, but of an individual whose improbity of character is accompanied by a constant motive for dishonest conduct.

§ 4. The Punishment of Lascivious Criminals

It now becomes necessary to speak of those offenders against chastity who cannot be ranged among the violent criminals. Apart from the latter and requiring a different order of treatment is the class of lascivious criminals ("satyres et cyniques").[1] The members of this class are for the most part degenerates, but not always psychopaths. When a true form of psychopathy does not clearly appear, the appropriate regimen for such an offender is internment in an oversea penal colony (relégation") for an indefinite period. Release should be made dependent upon the changes brought about by new habits of life and supervening circumstances of age and family, as explained in § 2 (a) of the present chapter. But if the offender is a psychopath, — it matters not whether the case is one of sadism, senile lubricity, or any other form, — the necessary measure will be that of confining him in an asylum set apart for the purpose, like those designed for epileptics and persons suffering from chronic alcoholism.[2]

§ 5. Cases for Retention of Existing Punishments

It will be noticed that temporary imprisonment for a term fixed in advance, the typical punishment of the modern criminal law, has no place in the system just outlined. The reasons which have led us to oppose this form of punishment have been sufficiently explained in the course of our discussion, and need not be repeated. We have tried to direct all punishment to the end which today it leaves out of view, namely, that of social utility, and this we have sought to do by a strictly logical following of the principle of rational reaction against crime. Sometimes, as has been seen, the measure necessary is elimination — realized, absolutely by the death penalty, relatively by confinement in an asylum for the crim-

---

[1] See *ante,* Part II, c. i, § 6.

[2] See *Viveiros de Castro,* "Attentados ao pubor" (Rio de Janeiro, 1895).

inal insane, by marooning ("déportation avec abandon"),
by internment in an oversea penal colony for life or for an
indefinite period, the duration of which will depend upon a
number of circumstances. In other cases, as has been further
shown, there is required nothing more than reparation, the
payment of compensation to the injured person together with
a fine to the State, to effectuate which, if need be, the offender
can be subjected to enforced labor in some species of public
works, — his wages being withheld by the State, — for a
period which may be indefinitely prolonged.

Exceptional Cases, e. g., Counterfeiters. — For a few crimes,
physical restriction of the criminal's freedom of movement
must still be resorted to, as the only means of preventing the
repetition of his act. Such, for example, would be the offense
of counterfeiting, either of paper money or of coin. Exile
to a penal colony ("relégation") would not be calculated
to stamp out this criminal industry. Nor would enforced
reparation be likely to prove any more effective. Criminals
of this species are for the most part in association, and have
at their command ample funds to pay the offender's indemnity and enable him to make a fresh start. For these reasons,
it is necessary that counterfeiters be imprisoned and kept
isolated until the expiry of a period sufficient to justify the
belief that their confederates have disappeared. But cases of
this description, where a physical obstacle to the criminal's
movements is absolutely exacted by the social defense, represent but a small fraction of the whole number, and penitentiary imprisonment ("réclusion") should be here employed by
way of exception.

Cases not involving Natural Criminality. — Lastly, imprisonment or detention for a term fixed in advance would be reserved for all those offenses which we have excluded from our
categories of criminality [1] — cases involving a *special* immorality not incompatible with the altruistic sentiments which
at the present day form the basis of morality. The immo-

---

[1] See *ante,* Part I, c. i, § 6.

rality of these acts consists chiefly in a defiance of authority or a disobedience to the law.   If this political element predominates, then it becomes necessary that instead of being determined by the criterion of adaptation to the social life, the punishment should assume the form of a chastisement capable of enforcing respect for the law.   It is a question not of true criminals but of persons who set themselves against the law ("révoltés").   Falling without the scope of our study, these likewise fall without the scope of our conclusions.   We thus stop at a point where the policy of the State takes the place of the natural laws of the social organism.

PART IV

OUTLINE OF PRINCIPLES

SUGGESTED AS A BASIS FOR AN INTERNATIONAL
PENAL CODE

OUTLINE OF PRINCIPLES

SUGGESTED AS A BASIS FOR AN INTERNATIONAL
PENAL CODE

DIVISION I: GENERAL PRINCIPLES

§ 1. Purpose of the Code. — It is the purpose of the Code to provide a system, which in coöperation with the other social forces, will serve to bring about the disappearance, or at least the progressive diminution, of the criminal phenomenon.

§ 2. Its Scope. — The Code is to deal solely with *natural crime, i. e.,* such acts as offend the sentiment of humanity or violate the rules of conduct exacted by the common or average probity of present-day civilized peoples.

§ 3. Its Internationality. — (*a*) Thus limited, the Code is to be made international and will contain provision for the mutual delivering up of fugitives from justice between the several States included in the International Union thus to be formed. The fact that the offender is not a national of the demanding State will not be a bar to his extradition.

(*b*) The police of the adopting States as well as the judges of instruction and all other judicial officers will be in direct communication without the necessity of diplomatic intervention.

(*c*) In order that the punishment, hereafter mentioned, of internment in an oversea penal colony ("relégation") may be at the command of each of the several States, it will be the duty of States possessing such colonies to receive and take charge of offenders sentenced to this form of punishment in States not themselves provided with the means of carrying it into effect, always subject to the payment of proper charges.

§ 4. Excluded Punishable Acts. — Such punishable acts as do not come within the purview of the Code will be the subject of a Code of Disobediences ("Révoltes") and a Code of Police Offenses ("Contraventions") to be formulated by each State according to its individual necessities.

§ 5. Punishment: its Character and Purpose. — (a) Punishment ought to represent a means calculated to effect the cessation of the criminal's harmfulness to society. It should therefore interpose to the criminal's activity a barrier of sufficient strength to nullify that activity. This may be (1) material, consisting of the application of external force, or (2) of such a nature as to convince the criminal that from his own standpoint honest and peaceful activity will be more profitable than the activity of crime.

(b) Punishment, moreover, ought not of necessity to occasion physical suffering to the offender. In all cases, however, it should reduce him to a condition of inferiority which he will feel as something undesirable.

(c) The rule which permits the granting of extenuating circumstances at the discretion of the trier will have no place in the criminal law, nor will the institutions of pardon and amnesty.

(d) The punishment of imprisonment for a term fixed in advance will be abolished. Cellular imprisonment may be retained for temporary use in case of need.

(e) The convicted offender will be required to pay the expense of his maintenance, and by his enforced labor, if he is without pecuniary means.

§ 6. Classes of Criminals. — Every criminal (i. e., every author of a natural crime) belongs to some one of the following classes:

(1) Murderers.
(2) Violent Criminals.
(3) Criminals Deficient in Probity.
(4) Lascivious Criminals ("Satyres et cyniques").

§ 7. Murderers and Violent Criminals. — (*a*) Criminals of the first or second class may be guilty of: Murder, culpable homicide, arson, dynamiting, mayhem ("mutilations"), the wanton infliction of other physical cruelties ("sévices"), and such maltreatment of the old, of children, and of other dependent persons as is injurious to their health or (in the case of children) arrestive of their development.

(*b*) Before a person committing a crime of this description can be classed as a murderer, there must in general appear on his part: (1) an intent to kill or to inflict physical torture, and (2) an acting to an egoistic end, without any provocation on the part of the victim which can be regarded as intolerable or unjust.

(*c*) In certain cases, however, the cruelty of the act is in itself sufficient evidence that the agent belongs to the class of murderers.

(*d*) In the absence of the elements specified in sub-sections *b* and *c* of the present section, attacks upon life or physical integrity, interferences with the liberty of the person (including abduction ("enlèvement")), as also cases of insults and threats, are to be attributed to the second class, *i. e.*, Violent Criminals.

§ 8. Criminals Deficient in Probity. — (*a*) The class heretofore designated as Criminals Deficient in Probity comprises thieves and falsifiers ("faussaires").[1]

(*b*) Under the denomination of thieves are included receivers of stolen goods, persons obtaining money by false pretenses, criminal bankrupts, and persons guilty of counterfeiting manufactured products. Thieves properly so called, receivers of stolen goods, and persons obtaining money by false pretenses are either (1) novices, or (2) habitual offenders.

(*c*) Falsifiers are those who directly or indirectly injure the civil rights, property, or reputation of others by means of

---

[1] ["Faussaire" ordinarily is translatable as "forger" or "counterfeiter," but (as appears in sub-section *c*) is employed here to denote the authors of a wide range of "crimina falsi." Either of these renditions would consequently be too narrow. — TRANSL.]

the forgery of official documents or private writings, the substitution of children and the suppression of civil status,[1] or by means of false declarations as occurs in the crimes of perjury and false accusation ("calomnie").

§ 9. **Lascivious Criminals.** — To the class of Lascivious Criminals ("Satyres et cyniques") are to be attributed offenses against chastity dictated by an inordinate degree of lasciviousness (as in certain cases of indecent liberties with minors), and also acts proceeding from the form of perversion known as sadism.

§ 10. **Cases for Special Treatment.** — (a) Notwithstanding that moral apathy, the absence or weakness of moral sense, the influence of passion, may annul moral responsibility, they do not prevent the existence of crime. Cases of this character may however call for differential treatment.

(b) Differential treatment would likewise be proper for the following classes: (1) Women. (2) Persons advanced in years. (3) Children and adolescents. (4) Hypnotized persons. (5) Drunkards. (6) Criminal monomaniacs.

§ 11. **Criterion of Punishment.** — All idea of proportioning the punishment to the objective gravity of the offense or to the moral responsibility of the offender must be discarded. The punishment must be adapted to the criminal aptitude of the wrong-doer.

§ 12. **Aim of Punishment.** — The aim should be not to punish the criminal fact but to strike the criminality of the agent as revealed by the fact.

§ 13. **Criminal Attempt.** — (a) It follows that an attempt to commit crime, when it reveals the criminal aptitude of the agent, must be considered as the crime itself. The employment of insufficient means is not always proof of ineptitude, especially in the case of juvenile offenders.

(b) Acts simply of preparation may be regarded as constituting a true attempt, when (1) the criminal resolution is beyond question, and (2) there is no reason to doubt that the

---

[1] [For "suppression of civil status" see *ante*, p. 41, note 3. — TRANSL.]

offender would have persisted in carrying out the resolution had he not been prevented by an unforeseen circumstance. In general the intent is unmistakable if the agent is an habitual offender and the act of preparation is a necessary one in the particular class of crimes which he makes his specialty.

(c) Acts simply of preparation and attempts which have not proceeded beyond a remote stage will not be subject to punishment unless the elements above specified concur to remove all doubt as to the true direction of the act and the criminal aptitude of the agent.

§ 14. Criminal Participation. — (a) The personal circumstances are not to be attributed to the accomplice. The material circumstances are to be so attributed only in so far as the accomplice is chargeable with knowledge thereof.[1] Different forms of penal treatment may be applied to the principal agent and the accomplice if they belong to different classes or sub-classes of criminals and differ in their criminal aptitude.

(b) One who has employed another to commit a crime will, in the event of its failure, be deemed guilty of an attempt, even where the person employed has voluntarily desisted before coming to the final act, provided that the mandator had no reason to suppose that the mandatory would not have carried out his undertaking.

§ 15. Plurality of Offenses. — A plurality of offenses is sufficient ground for classing the criminal as an habitual offender, although he has never undergone previous conviction.

§ 16. Recidivism. — (a) Recidivism involving crime of a different species from the prior offense or offenses may be regarded as more serious than special recidivism.

(b) The offender is not to be considered as any the less a recidivist, because of the lapse of a certain number of years since his last conviction.

(c) The fact of recidivism, either general or special, fre-

---

[1] [For "personal and material circumstances" see *ante*, p. 321, note 2. — TRANSL.]

quently denotes the incorrigible offender hereafter mentioned (§§ 20, 21).

(*d*) This fact is not however a mark of incorrigibility in the case of adolescents, persons just emerged from adolescence, and persons of extreme ignorance, when there is ground for attributing the offender's criminal habits to the surroundings in which he was born and reared and to the total absence of education.

Division II: System of Punishment

§ 17. **Requisite Effect of Punishment.** — All punishment should be such as to produce at least one of these two effects: (1) elimination of the offender who has been found incapable of adaptation to the social coexistence, and (2) reparation by the offender of the harm which he has occasioned.

§ 18. **Absolute Elimination.** — For murderers, the elimination will be absolute. The only punishment capable of realizing absolute elimination is that of death.

§ 19. **Relative Elimination.** — For criminals of the other classes elimination will be realized by one of the following methods:

(1) Marooning ("transportation avec abandon").

(2) Internment ("relégation") in an oversea penal colony for life.

(3) Internment in an oversea penal colony for an indeterminate period.

(4) Confinement for an indeterminate period in an asylum (insane persons and victims of chronic alcoholism).

(5) Compulsory service in a company of workers to be employed in some species of public works. For such service there is to be a wage (nominally equal to the ordinary standard) which however will be retained by the officials in charge to defray the cost of the offender's maintenance and to indemnify the injured person.

§ 20. **Marooning.** — (*a*) The punishment of marooning

("transportation avec abandon") will be applicable only to such violent criminals, instinctively disposed to bloodshed, and such habitual thieves as have been found incapable of assimilation in a civilized environment.

(b) Such incapacity, however, will not be declared until after the offender, during subjection for a certain period to one of the forms of internment before indicated, has given proof of an irreducible and dangerous criminal character.

(c) The punishment will be carried out in some remote region entirely cut off from communication with the civilized world.

§ 21. **Internment for Life.** — (a) The punishment of internment for life ("relégation perpétuelle") in an oversea penal colony will be applicable to habitual or professional thieves. But in the case of children and youths reared in a criminal environment, this punishment will not be imposed until after unsuccessful resort has been had to internment for an indeterminate period.

§ 22. **Internment for an Indeterminate Period.** — (a) Internment for an indeterminate period (in addition to its employment for the youthful offenders just mentioned) will be applicable to thieves who are recidivists but not professionals, to falsifiers,[1] to dangerous individuals belonging to the class of violent criminals, and to lascivious criminals ("satyres et cyniques").

(b) In all cases of indeterminate punishment, there will be established a period of observation varying from five to ten years, according to the agent's degree of perversity. Upon the lapse of this period it will be in order to examine the facts capable of throwing light upon the question of the offender's adaptation to the social life. Marriage and the birth of children (especially for female offenders), the attainment of maturity or old age, are all to be taken into consideration as tending radically to modify the character. The desire to make compensation to the victim or his family, manifested

---

[1] [See *ante*, p. 407, note 1. — TRANSL.]

not by words but by acts of unmistakable import will be regarded as the only real sign of such reformation on the part of the offender as is capable of bringing about the termination of his punishment.

(c) Thieves, receivers of stolen goods, and persons obtaining money by false pretenses, will be interned, preferably in a newly established colony where the population is widely scattered. They will be released only after they have acquired the habit of work and learned some useful trade. In case such an offender resorts to criminal activity in the place of his internment, he will be subjected to internment for life.

§ 23. **Compulsory Labor.** — (a) Non-recidivist offenders whose crimes appear to be chiefly due to idleness, apathy, or vagabondage, will be made to undergo compulsory service in one of the companies of workers before mentioned (§ 19, (5)). In this service the prisoner will not be supplied with food except upon the performance of his daily stint. There will be various sorts of work suited to the age, sex, health, and education of the individual. Release will come only when the offender has fulfilled his obligation to indemnify the injured person and has, in addition, paid a fine to the State. If the sum required to effect complete indemnity is beyond his means and cannot be entirely met by the proceeds of his labor, the indemnity will be partial and in a measure to be regulated by the circumstances of the case.

(b) Upon his release, the officials in charge will lend the offender assistance in finding free labor either in the home country or in the colonies. They will, however, require him to deposit a sum of money, which will be subject to forfeiture in the event of a fresh offense on his part.

§ 24. **Enforced Reparation.** — (a) Except as before provided, violent criminals and non-recidivist thieves who are neither dangerous nor without means of support, will not be punished otherwise than by being compelled to make compensation to the injured person and to the State. This will take the form of two fines, the respective amounts of which will be fixed by the judge, in taking into consideration the offender's pecuniary means, if he has such, or if not, the possibility of his meeting the sum by the proceeds of his labor.

(*b*) If, however, the convicted person does not fulfil this two-fold obligation within a stated period, he will be made to undergo compulsory service in one of the companies of workers described in § 23, and to conform to the rules governing the offenders therein enrolled.

(*c*) The offender who, in consequence of making compensation to the injured person and the State, as before indicated, has been exempted from punishment or released, may, nevertheless, be deprived of his political rights as well as his right to exercise a given trade or profession.

§ 25. **Measure of Reparation.** — (*a*) The amount of the fine due to the State will be proportioned to the social and economic condition of the offender.

(*b*) In fixing the amount of compensation due to the injured person when the question is not one of pecuniary damage, but of moral suffering ("douleur morale"), there will be taken into account the social and economic condition both of the offender and the person injured.

§ 26. **Compensation Fund.** — The State will establish a Compensation Fund for the purpose of indemnifying: (1) persons injured by criminal acts who have been unable to obtain compensation from the wrong-doer, and (2) persons who, after suffering imprisonment pending prosecution, have been acquitted as the result of a trial on the merits.

§ 27. **Substitute for Prescription.** — (*a*) There will be no prescription either of the action or of the judgment. But when the offender's conduct and manner of life, for an adequate period from the date of his offense, have been such as to show that he has undergone a true moral transformation and thereby become a sociable and useful being, the judicial authority, either before or after a judgment of conviction, may order that further proceedings shall cease.

(*b*) Such action however will not release the offender from his obligation to indemnify the person injured.

§ 28. Hypnotized Persons and Drunkards. — A person who commits a crime in a state of hypnotic suggestion or drunkenness will be subjected to the treatment indicated in § 19, (4). If, however, other circumstances exist which prove his criminal character and the fact of his prior decision, the case is one for the ordinary punishments.

DIVISION III: PROCEDURE

§ 29. The Judicial Investigation. — The magistrate who is to conduct the judicial investigation ("instruction") will be independent of every governmental agency other than the Public Ministry;[1] and, except as hereafter provided, will act only upon the request of the latter. The investigation will be secret unless, in the opinion of the judge of instruction, publicity will be an aid in arriving at the truth. In that event he may permit the parties and witnesses for and against to testify in each other's presence, but without the attendance of counsel.

§ 30. Complaint by Person Injured. — When the Public Ministry does not see fit to prosecute, the person injured may address the judge of instruction directly.

§ 31. Commitment for Trial. — Except where taken in the criminal act, the accused will be committed for trial only by interlocutory judgment ("ordonnance") of the judge of instruction.

§ 32. Initiation of the Criminal Action. — Crimes of the character dealt with by the Code will always be the subject of official initiative ("action publique"). Complaint by the injured person is never to be treated as an essential step in the procedure.

§ 33. Imprisonment Pending Prosecution. — (*a*) Imprisonment pending the result of the proceedings is a necessary measure and will be ordered by the judge of instruction:

[1] [See *ante*, p. 355, note 1. — TRANSL.]

(1) When the punishment likely to be imposed is sufficiently heavy to make it an object to the person under arrest to take to flight or go into hiding;

(2) When it is probable that he will effect the disappearance of physical ("matérielles") evidences of the crime;

(3) When there is reason to believe that he will attempt to suborn witnesses or otherwise hinder or thwart the prosecution; or

(4) In any case where he stands in danger of violence at the hands of the injured person or his relatives.

(b) Provisional liberty will not be granted except when, in the opinion of the judge, each and all of the foregoing circumstances are absent.

§ 34. The Court. — (a) The criminal jury will be abolished.

(b) The function of criminal judge will be exercised by magistrates forming a class wholly distinct from the judges of the civil courts. To this office appointments will only be made from among persons possessing a thorough knowledge of the moral statistics of the country as well as of criminal psychology and penitentiary systems.

§ 35. Trial and Sentence. — (a) The Public Ministry will not act as accuser.[1] Its duty will be that of advising with the judicial officers as to the results of the investigation and trial.

(b) The prisoner may call for expert testimony ("expertise") or for the examination of new witnesses ("assignation de nouveaux témoins"), on his behalf. Except in case of a confession, the truth of which there is no reason to doubt, he will be allowed the services of counsel.

(c) Once the facts have been established, the public trial will conclude.

(d) The tribunal will then appraise the moral nature of the offender so as to assign him to his proper criminal class. It may suspend judgment for the purpose of investigating his

---

[1] [I. e., the procedure is not to be adversative. The trial will represent not a contest between two sides but an inquiry conducted by the court. See *ante*, p. 355 *et seq.* — TRANSL.]

antecedents, his family circumstances, and his condition of life. It may subject him to examination by a physician, or assign to one of its members the duty of studying his mental and moral nature and defining his criminal aptitude or degree of perversity. Lastly, it will determine whether the means to be applied is one of elimination or merely that of enforced reparation.

(*e*) In case of indeterminate punishment, the question of its termination as well as that of the new punishment to be imposed as provided in §§ 20, 21, and 22, will be passed upon by the same court which pronounced the original sentence.

§ 36. **Review by Higher Court.** — (*a*) Proceedings for review will lie:

(1) When the judgment has not received the unanimous concurrence of the members of the trial court.

(2) When proof is adduced that the adjudication of guilt or innocence has been brought about by perjury or other punishable facts; or

(3) When there has come to light new evidence capable of changing the result.

(*b*) Irregularities of procedure assigned as error in the court of review ("cour de cassation") will be ground for reversal ("nullité de la procédure") only when it appears that the informality complained of has materially influenced the decision of the lower court.

APPENDICES

APPENDIX A

ENFORCED REPARATION AS A SUBSTITUTE FOR IMPRISONMENT

FOR the purpose of exhibiting the more detailed working out of the plan of enforced reparation advocated in the text,[1] it may be useful to reproduce here the paper which I read on that subject at the International Penitentiary Congress of Brussels, 1900.

The question was thus stated: "On the basis of the views expressed by the Congress of Paris, what would be the most practicable means of insuring payment by the offender of the indemnity due to the victim of his crime?"

PAPER READ BY M. RAFFAELE GAROFALO

SUBSTITUTE PROCURATOR–GENERAL AT THE COURT OF CASSATION, ROME

I

My efforts to direct the attention of the legal world to the present question — in my judgment, one of the first importance for criminal legislation, — belong now to a good many years. As early as 1885, I laid before the Penitentiary Congress of Rome [2] certain proposals embodying my ideas with reference to the proper means of enforcing payment of indemnity by offenders. And a number of Congresses of

---

[1] *Ante,* pp. 226–228, 389–391, 396–398.

[2] See Actes du Congrès pénitentiaire international de Rome, 1885, pp. 185, 191.

"L'Union Internationale de Droit Pénal,"[1] the Penitentiary Congress of St. Petersburg, 1890, as well as the Juridical Congress of Florence, 1891, bear witness to my continued insistence in this regard.

These efforts, perhaps, have not been unavailing. In his paper read before the Congress of Christiania, 1891, M. Prins recognized the practical importance of my programme.[2] He added that "the idea need not be feared on the ground of novelty: on the contrary, it represents return to a principle of the ancient law"; that there was no occasion "for gainsaying the propriety of reaction against the narrow theory which attributes a magical virtue to the prison"; and that "while the obstacles to the idea's practical application are by no means to be overlooked, it is necessary to examine as to how far it would be possible to introduce it in the prevailing system of repression."

Finally, I had the pleasure of seeing the question made the order of the day at the Congress of Paris, 1895. It was formulated in the following terms:

"Does the criminal law of the present day furnish the victim of a crime with sufficient means to obtain the indemnity due him from the offender?"

That the answer had to be in the negative was a foregone conclusion. The Section charged with the examination of the question adopted the following resolution:

" (1) The criminal law ought to take into account, to a greater extent than it does today, the necessity of insuring due reparation to the injured person.

" (2) If the complaint of the injured person is held to be well-founded, judgment for costs should never go against the civil party.[3]

"The civil party who merely joins his action to that already

[1] See my papers read before the Congress of Brussels, 1889, and the Congress of Paris, 1893.

[2] Paper of M. *Adolphe Prins*, upon the second question, in the Bulletin de l'Union internationale de droit pénal, July, 1891, pp. 128, 131, 135.

[3] [See *ante*, p. 340, note 1. — Transl.]

commenced by the Public Ministry, ought, in the event of defeat, to be adjudged liable only for such costs as have been occasioned by his intervention.

"(3) Where the case requires, it will be proper to extend to the injured person the benefit of official legal aid ("assistance judiciaire") before the court having jurisdiction of the crime.

"(4) In the case of prosecution, either criminal or correctional, the Public Ministry will be required to submit to the court having jurisdiction (and without the payment of costs) the injured person's claim for damages, subject always to the right of the Public Ministry to make proper recommendation touching the allowance or rejection of the claim.

"(5) The indemnity allowed the injured person will be secured by a general lien ("privilège général") upon the real and personal property of the offender, to be enforced concurrently with that of the government in respect of the costs of prosecution.

"(6) The Congress declares that the proposals which have been laid before it with reference to subjecting to the payment of the injured person's claim a portion of the earnings of the convict in the course of his imprisonment, as well as with reference to the establishment of a special compensation fund, out of which pecuniary aid could be afforded to the victim of criminal acts, call for the most serious consideration; but, believing that, as the case stands, it is not sufficiently advised to take immediate action in the premises, it decides to reserve the above indicated questions for more thorough examination by the next International Congress."

Although I was unable to take any part in the session at which they were adopted, these resolutions as a whole were strikingly in accord with the proposals which I had previously advanced, and especially with the conclusions of my paper read at the Juridical Congress of Florence, 1891. This fact goes to show that the insufficiency of the protection accorded the injured person is everywhere recognized in an equal degree, despite the differences in the criminal laws of the various European countries. The gentleman who read the committee report, M. Flandin, and the members who participated in the discussion, notably Dr. Lydia Poët, MM. Zucker, Prins, Armengol y Cornet, Eisenmann, Slossberg and more especially M. Leveillé, all expressed views similar to those set forth on this subject in my "Criminologie"; and my proposals as to the means of insuring effectual reparation were recommended to the Congress — among these, the plan of creating a special public fund into which would be paid the moneys arising from fines imposed by the courts, for the purpose of distribution among the victims of crimes and misdemeanors who had been unable to exact indemnity from the offender.

II

I have premised so much by way of excuse for returning in this paper to a subject upon which I have been harping for nearly twenty years. As M. Dorado-Montero remarks in an introduction to one of my works, it may be said that this question of reparation has "continually engrossed my attention," and that "single-handed at the outset, later supported by many other writers" of my school, I never "lost an opportunity of urging the question, — succeeding finally in securing the important and significant support of the "Union Internationale de Droit Pénal." [1] This is why, at the risk of repetition, I have been unable to resist the desire of uttering myself anew, now that for the second time the question has been made the order of the day in the International Penitentiary Congress.

But, first of all, it is necessary to anticipate the possible objection that the present paper is here out of place. The question in hand, it may be said, is a purely legal one. What interest then does it possess for a penitentiary congress? To be sure, the section in which we are is that of "Penal

[1] *P. Dorado-Montero:* Introduction to "Indemnización á las victimas del delito," by *R. Garofalo,* pp. 14, 15 (Madrid).

Legislation," — but are we not restricted, thus, to dealing with legislation which has in view the effects of punishment? In short, what connection is there between a method of insuring compensation to the person injured, and a science which especially concerns itself with the treatment of prisoners, looking to their moral improvement as well as the safety of the public? Although perhaps not easy to be seen at the first glance, a relation does exist between the two, their points of contact being even more numerous than one might suspect.

For one thing, compulsory indemnification would be a means of prevention much more potent than the menace of brief terms of imprisonment. If offenders were persuaded that, once discovered, they could in nowise evade the obligation to repair the damage of which they have been the cause, the ensuing discouragement to the criminal world (and especially professional thieves and sharpers) would be far greater than that produced by the fear of a temporary curtailment of their liberty.

It is not the risks, but the unproductiveness, of a trade which cause men to forsake it. Now, under present conditions, the trade of thief or sharper yields very considerable returns, in fact, much larger returns than many honest trades. The risk is only that of a few months or years in prison. As against this, moreover, the wrong-doer may almost certainly count on being able to retain the proceeds of his criminal activity, because of the lack of any effective means to exact from him restitution and the payment of damages. His term expired, he withdraws the stolen moneys from their hiding place or receives them from the safe hands to which during his imprisonment they had been entrusted. What is true of forgers and fraudulent bankrupts is equally true of professional sharpers: the only difference is one of degree. They never make restitution; they never pay. In spite of repeated convictions, they sometimes grow rich; often, they have very considerable sums at their disposal — facts of which the judges cannot help being aware when they see such persons represented at the bar of the court by advocates who are not in the habit of giving their services for nothing. It cannot therefore be doubtful, that the trade would have fewer followers if the offender's sense of security as to his hidden plunder were displaced by the certainty that, as an inseparable incident of conviction, he would be forced to make restitution or indemnity.

But there is a second consideration of even greater importance. What loads down the budget and renders difficult the improvement of the prison system and the individualization of punishment, is the excessive number of inmates contained in the prisons. This number is chiefly made up of a floating population serving short sentences of from eight or ten days to two or three months. In France the annual average of persons sentenced to terms not exceeding one year is more than 120,000. Of these about 50,000 represent cases where the individual has to serve only from one to five days. Italy shows an annual average of about 100,000 convictions where the term does not exceed three months. In 1896 the total number of persons sentenced to three months or less in jail ("arrêts") and to six months or less of other forms of imprisonment ("détention et réclusion"), was 174,902. To lodge and feed this army of offenders, — most of whom pass but a few days in the prisons, — entails an enormous expense. As I have said elsewhere, "beyond the evils which the citizen must endure from crime itself, he is called upon to support the increased burden of taxation necessitated by the maintenance of these thousands of convicted offenders, — and this without the slightest social gain to counterbalance." For it is evident that imprisonment for such short terms is wholly devoid of intimidatory effect. As for its reformatory effect, it is not worth wasting words on. The most optimistic correctionalists must concede that before there can be any hope of the prisoner's moral reformation, the time of detention ought to be sufficiently long to permit of his being taught a trade and made to acquire the habit of working. I deem it

unnecessary to insist upon this point, namely, that there is
no possibility of any marked improvement in the penitentiary
régime or, more especially, of successful effort in the individualization of punishments (*i. e.*, in the acting upon different
criminal natures by specialized means) until the average
number of prison inmates can be cut down to proportions
immeasurably smaller than it exhibits today.

My ideas as to the solution of this problem, you perhaps
already know. Approaching the question from the standpoint
of the real necessities of society and the interest of the person
injured by the crime, I would confine the use of the prison
within comparatively narrow limits. Imprisonment I would
admit only for terms of considerable length, and then only in
the case of dangerous criminals, recidivists, offenders of ill-
repute, and vagabonds incapable of labor. In lieu of brief
terms of imprisonment, I would substitute coercive measures
of extreme severity for the purpose of exacting indemnity
from the criminal. In the case of minor offenses, the payment
of such indemnity would afford greater satisfaction to the person injured, wipe out all traces of the wrongful act and render
useless all measures of repression.

I shall not here repeat the exposition of this system. That
would take me too far afield and be at least an apparent departure from the terms of the present question. Yet I cannot
refrain from testifying to my satisfaction in noting how much
ground has been gained by these ideas, the same which on
their first enouncement some twenty-five years ago were
regarded as legal heresies. Today they meet with a very
different reception. For example, the admirable work of
M. Prins, "Science pénale et droit positif" (pp. 391–396),
contains a chapter wherein the author, while pointing out the
difficulties which the practical application of these ideas must
encounter, takes a resolute stand in their favor. "The end
to be attained," he had previously said, in his paper read
before the Congress of Christiania, "is simply that of introducing the economic element into the system of repression,

whenever possible. . . . A distinct result would be in our possession if the convict by his own diligent labor (being allowed his freedom for the purpose), or through the labor of his relatives, or even by the charitable aid of private persons or public officials who might interest themselves in him and his family, could afford due satisfaction to the private interests affected by his wrongful act, and thus sometimes escape the whole or a part of a punishment involving the deprivation of liberty. . . . Such a reform can only be a matter of gradual accomplishment. It requires prudence and sagacity, and demands the attentive, thoughtful, and conscientious cooperation of the judiciary." [1]

III

Enough has been said, I think, to justify discussion of the present question in a penitentiary congress. Reverting to its exact terms, what we are required to ascertain is the most practicable means of insuring indemnity to the person injured by a crime.

The measures necessary are to be distinguished into three kinds: (1) preventive measures, having place before trial with a view to defeating any attempt on the part of the criminal, after conviction, fraudulently to convey his property, or make it otherwise unavailable on execution; (2) measures having place at the time of the trial; and (3) measures to be put into effect while the offender is undergoing his punishment.

Before trial, the judge of instruction, or, where the offender is taken in the act, the Public Ministry, should have authority, as a precautionary measure, to attach ("à faire saisir") the personal property of the offender and to create a lien ("hypothèque," "judicial mortgage") upon his real property, for the purpose of securing, not only the costs of prosecution,

---

[1] M. Prins, moreover, is not alone in this. Mr. Tallack, the Secretary of the Howard Association of London, has expressed the same views in a letter to the Times appearing in the month of June, 1899.

but also the amount of compensation to be adjudged to the injured person. These measures should be resorted to, however, only when in the opinion of the magistrate the evidence against the suspected person is sufficiently strong to bring about his conviction. This is why, although the attachment should be levied forthwith where the offender is taken in the act, it would be necessary in other cases to defer these steps until after the accused had been interrogated or had evaded the service of a preliminary warrant of arrest ("mandat d'amener"). In order that such measures may be effective, a further requirement would be the adoption of legislation, declaring void any alienation without consideration, or any payment of a debt before maturity, on the part of the offender, subsequent to the date of the crime. There should also be established a presumption of fraud in respect of any alienation or payment made by the offender after the date of the interlocutory judgment remanding him for trial, thereby placing upon his grantees or creditors the burden of establishing the validity of their claims. Presumptions similar to this, and indeed of much more stringent character, already exist in commercial law with reference to the case of bankruptcy. There would seem to be no good reason why a like rule should not prevail in criminal procedure. For the class here to be protected are not mere mercantile creditors, but the unfortunate victims of sharpers, forgers, and all the other species ofi criminals.

At the trial, the Public Ministry should have authority to appear on behalf of the injured person (in case the latter is without counsel) and see to the proper presentation of his claim. The judge in pronouncing his decree will confirm the previous attachment and fix the amount of damages due to the claimant, or allow him a provisional sum pending their complete ascertainment.

Although the measures, of which I have just spoken, will tend to fill a gap in criminal legislation, their practical importance is necessarily limited to the case of solvent

offenders, individuals owning real property or at least some
personalty. But the majority of criminals is not recruited
in this class.

For measures against insolvent offenders, recourse must be
had to the *sentence itself and its execution.* To explain:
insolvency means the absence of property subject to seizure
on legal process: it does not signify absolute poverty or inability to earn money. Moreover, insolvency is very often
feigned. The greater number of offenders are insolvent, although they are capable of earning money and do in fact
acquire money, were it only by their crimes; or else they
feign insolvency by hiding the proceeds of their thefts or
swindling operations, or by investing these proceeds in in-
come-producing securities, depositing them in banks, etc.,
in another's name. Sometimes, indeed, it is even unnecessary
to take such precautions. Forms of property exist which are
exempt from legal seizure for whatever cause: in Italy, for
example, funds deposited in the Government savings bank. It
is by no means out of the question, therefore, to seek means
of compelling insolvent offenders to return what they have
misappropriated or to make compensation to the victim of
their crimes.

For this the ancient world had a very simple means, namely,
that of involuntary servitude. As a rule, the debtor who
either could not or would not pay, became the slave of his
creditor. And even at a later day when, under the influence
of more humane legislation, the "addictio" became in general
superseded, it was retained in cases where the debt was occasioned by a crime.[1] The last remains of the institution are
to be found in those restraints upon physical liberty, which
with numerous limitations are still recognized as applicable
to a defendant whose liability for damages is due to a felony
("crime") or misdemeanor ("délit"). But, owing to the in-
conveniences with which they are attended, these have now
fallen almost entirely into disuse.

[1] When the debtor had merited punishment: "qui noxam meruisset."
See Livy, VIII, 28.

It must nevertheless be conceded that the only means,
worth considering, of coping with feigned insolvency is to
deprive the debtor of his liberty.

Nor have I any fear, at this point, of objection on the score
that we have no right to do anything calculated to introduce
a lack of uniformity in the procedure governing the execution
of money judgments. I fail to see why an exceptional mode
of proceeding should not be admissible in dealing with a
debt founded on a crime. The obligation growing out of a
criminal delict ("obligation ex delicto") is altogether of too
different a nature from other obligations to justify the contention that it must be regulated by the same procedure.
Is this anything to be dwelt upon? Is it not sufficient to point
out that what the author of a criminal delict has violated is
not merely a rule of conduct agreed upon by two or more
individuals, but a rule of conduct adopted by society as a
whole? And to note that, resultingly, since in civil transactions a man may protect himself against fraud, may surround
himself with all sorts of legal precautions, civil injuries of a
fraudulent nature are, for the most part, to be attributed to
the creditor's want of care or his too implicit confidence in
the debtor? The defrauded person need not have dealt at
all with an insolvent. If he did not take the pains to assure
himself of his debtor's honesty or financial standing, then the
fault is his own.

Quite otherwise is the case of an obligation arising from a
criminal delict. No precautions are entirely adequate to
safeguard us from the aggressions of a malefactor. Moreover, there is a social interest requiring reparation of the damage occasioned by a criminal act; and this, in all cases, is
an interest of much more importance to society than that of
compelling a person to keep his promise. It is therefore perfectly logical, for the purpose of exacting such reparation,
to permit the use of much more stringent means than when
the question is simply one of compelling respect for contracts
freely entered into, for obligations "ex contractu" and "quasi

ex contractu." Since the origin of the two sorts of obligations is so diverse, why should not differences exist between the coercive measures respectively applicable?

Beyond this I do not go. I am not urging that a special system of corporal constraint for obligations "ex delicto" in general be introduced in civil procedure: too many practical difficulties stand in the way. But I do believe that where the obligation grows out of a crime, we can utilize the punishment itself as the means of insuring indemnification.

In the first place, brief terms of imprisonment — the inutility of which is today generally recognized — should be abolished. The minimum term should be extended to a sufficient length and the offender (unless he is a professional criminal or recidivist) allowed to exempt himself from this form of punishment by paying, besides the costs of prosecution, a sum to be fixed by the judge as a fine for the benefit of the person injured.

This is substantially equivalent to saying that the sentence should be *conditional.* Such is the form under which M. Prins has adopted these ideas. "If," he says, "the convicted person satisfies the total amount of the civil judgment, within the period fixed by the court, the prison sentence will not be put into effect." [1] It is apparent what far-reaching consequences would attend a legislative recognition of this very simple principle. A very large percentage of those convicted of the less serious offenses against the person (strikings, insults, defamation) or indeed of minor offenses against property (criminal breach of trust or obtaining money by false pretenses involving small amounts, simple theft, malicious mischief, and the like) or yet again, of offenses against decency unattended with scandal or serious consequences (the offering of indignities to a woman not in a public place, seduction of minors, abduction, adultery, and the like) would be eager to indemnify the person injured and pay the costs of prose-

---

[1] I have read somewhere that Norway passed a law of this character in 1894.

cution, rather than undergo a punishment whose minimum would be of considerable significance, say a term of one year in prison. There is room for hoping that this percentage would represent half, perhaps two-thirds of all the individuals found guilty of such offenses.

By the adoption of such a measure the drain upon the tax-payer would be materially lessened, for not only would the public treasury be saved the expense of maintaining thousands of prisoners, but it would also be reimbursed for all expenses of prosecution. For the offender, this would be a much more serious punishment than if he were merely obliged to undergo a few days' or weeks' imprisonment. And finally, the aggrieved person would have the satisfaction of being compensated for his injury, a result which today seldom comes to pass.

We turn now to crimes of a more serious character, to cases where the peace of the State demands that the offender shall be deprived of his liberty. Here we must note, however, the existence of an institution of comparatively recent date, which has found a place in the criminal laws of almost all the European countries: I refer to *conditional liberation*.

It is generally agreed that conditional liberation may be accorded to a prisoner serving a sentence of considerable length when there arises a presumption of his future good behavior. The difficulty lies in the test for determining this presumption. As is well known, expressions of regret and repentance on the part of the offender deserve but little attention, and the good conduct of a prisoner in his cell by no means warrants the belief that when set at liberty, he will not resume his former ways. When I had the honor, as a member of the Italian Ministry of Justice, to be in charge of matters of conditional liberation, I put in practice a test which for most cases is in my judgment the only means capable of determining the question of the prisoner's moral improvement. The individual usually sets store by money, especially money which he has earned. The convict sets greater store by it than the ordinary worker, for he is generally a peasant or laborer who has never succeeded in accumulating even the smallest sum. It is in the penitentiary that for the first time he is able to gather a little money. The case is not rare, in Italy, of convicts who, being in the prison or penitentiary for a long enough period, find themselves the owners of some hundreds of francs, — sometimes as much as eight hundred or a thousand. Laboriously earned, day by day, in the course of eight or ten years, this sum will be paid over to them upon their discharge.[1]

It therefore occurred to me that if a convict should show himself disposed to give up the larger part of his savings for the benefit of the injured person, this would furnish much stronger proof that he acknowledged his wrong-doing and of his wish to make amends than any number of professions of repentance or promises of good conduct. To all who applied for conditional liberation, it was therefore proposed, at my instance, that they should pay over to the aggrieved person, a considerable portion of their savings — a half or two-thirds according to circumstances. Many were eager to do it. Others refused, and in their cases liberation was likewise refused. I paid but little heed to the recommendations of the prison directors. These gentlemen are not required to concern themselves with the crimes of their prisoners; they are not interested in the injured person, whom they have never seen; they care only for the prisoner, and it seemed to them hard to deprive him of his little hoard. Hard, indeed, it may be, but repression is not accomplished by mildness, and when one considers the number of murders committed by discharged prisoners, he cannot but note the absence of sufficient guaranties for the prisoner's good conduct after release.

---

[1] Mr. Tallack, upon a visit to one of the Belgian prisons, found many inmates who had accumulated sums running into hundreds of francs. At the thought that on the expiration of sentence, this money would be placed at their absolute disposal, he could not help bringing to mind the plight of their victims, many of whom, robbed of everything they had in the world, must have been without even such food and shelter as is assured by the penitentiary.

In Mexico, one-fourth of the proceeds of the prisoner's labor must be paid over by the prison administration to the person injured.

In lieu of apings, of mummeries, of ostentatious application to work, of services rendered to the prison administration, the only thing I took into consideration as a positive sign of repentance on the part of the prisoner was the voluntary relinquishment of his money for the benefit of the victim or his family.

Thus it would be merely a question of putting in the form of law that which I was able to do as an administrative measure.

Here, again, I am gratified to find myself in agreement with M. Prins. The learned Belgian criminalist would go still further: he advances the view that "at the end of a certain period of detention, the prisoner might be conditionally liberated, subject to the requirement that, within a specified time, he pay to the injured person the amount due as reparation. Upon the satisfaction of the debt, his liberation would be made absolute. Failure to pay in pursuance of the condition would, on the other hand, impose the duty of serving out the whole or the unexpired portion of the term, and under a more rigorous form of penal discipline." And he adds: "Any bona fide offer of reparation, in whole or in part, it ought to be conceded, coming at any time whatever after conviction should have the effect of doing away with the punishment altogether or proportionately reducing its term."

It will, of course, be understood that these last proposals would have no application to recidivists or habitual criminals or to the authors of murder, culpable homicide, robbery, or arson, — in short, of any of those great crimes with respect to which the social interest requiring the offender's elimination must outweigh the interest of the injured person.

The only reasonable objection that can be urged against such a system is that it bears less heavily on the rich than on the poor. But this could be remedied by raising the amount of the indemnity in the case of rich offenders, while the poor offender would only be required to give up the amount of his savings. Moreover, it is impossible to establish absolute equality in repression. The prison itself, despite its outward uniformity, has all the difference in the world for different people. For persons accustomed to high standards of living, it is a continual torture; for others, it affords more comforts than their own homes and provides a life less fatiguing and more assured than that which was their portion when at liberty.

I come to the last question, — that of a State fund to insure at least a partial reparation to the person who has been unable otherwise to obtain compensation for his injury. This fund ought to be constituted from the fines paid by convicted offenders. At stated periods there should be a proportional allocation of its contents between the claims, allowed and outstanding, of persons injured by crime on the one hand, and, on the other, of persons who had suffered imprisonment for crimes of which they were afterwards shown to be innocent. A fund of this sort existed in the Kingdom of the Two Sicilies as well as in the Duchy of Tuscany, but it never appears to have been of much service to claimants, as the treasury always put it under contribution to defray the expenses of the courts. At the present day, the question is largely a financial one, since such a fund in taking over the fines now accruing from police offenses ("contraventions") and certain species of misdemeanors ("délits") would necessarily deprive the budget of one of its resources. I hardly think that the Ministers of Finance will yield a ready assent to the proposal. But their opposition must be overcome, the more so, as the item does not exceed a few millions a year.[1] The accomplishment of this will mark a definite gain for the principle of reparation. Moreover, — and it is this very thing that must be particularly impressed upon the law-makers, — we are dealing here

[1] So far, I have been unable to obtain figures as to the total collection of fines in Italy. Mr. Tallack is under the same handicap as to England, but informs us that in Scotland the annual revenue from this source is £40,000. In France, from 1896 to 1900, the average annual amount of fines collected was 2,831,102 francs ("Compte général de l'administration de la justice criminelle," p. cxii).

not with a question of private law, but with a matter of justice and social security.   It will be a long step in advance when the State comes to regard as a public function, the indemnification of the person injured by criminal delict.[1]

[1] At the same Congress, M. Prins again pronounced for these views, and brilliantly sustained them against attacks of the classical school.   M. du Mouceau, Procureur de la République at Beaune (Côte-d'Or), who read a very important paper upon the same question, proposed the creation of an Indemnity Fund, maintained, notably, by fines proportionate to the income of the law-breaker.   Every sentence of imprisonment should carry with it a fine, which, even in the case of extenuating circumstances, should not be less than the regular daily income of the convicted person for a period equal to the length of his sentence.   This system would possess the double advantage of being entirely equitable and, at the same time, of insuring the Treasury a source of revenue wherewith to repair all items of damage.   M. du Mouceau's paper also contained certain suggestions, similar to those set out in mine, as to measures for preventing the offender from disposing of his property.   He further urged (as I had done at previous Congresses) that remission of punishment should never be granted except upon condition of indemnification, total or partial, according to the means of the offender, unless the latter clearly establishes his inability to meet this obligation.

APPENDIX B

COMPARATIVE STATISTICS OF CRIME

IT would be of much interest to have at command a table exhibiting the number of different crimes periodically committed in each of the civilized countries. Unfortunately, the attainment of such comparative data is hedged about with all sorts of difficulties, principal among which are the diversities of police organization and the scope of police functions, the differences in the criminal laws, and the absence of any uniform statistical method. Attempts have nevertheless been made to institute some comparisons between certain groups of crimes, the inquiry, however, being limited to a few States whose administrative and judicial differences, with respect to the groups considered, are not such as to be altogether prohibitive.

Thus M. Bodio, Director General of Statistics in Italy, has, for crimes of homicide, strikings and woundings, and theft, succeeded in comparing Italy, France, Germany, Spain, Belgium, Austria, England, Scotland, and Ireland. These comparisons were subsequently brought down to 1899, by M. Bosco, Professor of Statistics at the University of Rome, to whose latest work ("La delinquenza in varii Stati d'Europa") I am indebted for the following table:

COUNTRIES	FELONIES AND MISDEMEANORS REPORTED TO THE AUTHORITIES		TRIALS		CONVICTIONS	
	AVERAGE ANNUAL NUMBER	AVERAGE PER 100,000 INHABITANTS	AVERAGE ANNUAL NUMBER	AVERAGE PER 100,000 INHABITANTS	AVERAGE ANNUAL NUMBER	AVERAGE PER 100,000 INHABITANTS
I. Homicides :						
Italy (1895–1899)	3,814	12.15	2,120	6.75	2,017	6.43
France (1895–1899)	1,251	3.27	617	1.61	475	1.24
Spain (1895–1899)	....	....	1,000	5.64	869	4.90
Austria (1894–1898)	....	....	....	....	429	1.72
Germany (1897–1899)	....	....	554	1.01	447	0.81
England (1895–1899)	415	1.34	....	....	131	0.42
Ireland (1895–1899)	112	2.46	....	....	44	0.97
Scotland (1897–1899)	46	1.08	....	....	15	0.35
					4,427	
II. (a) Strikings, woundings, acts of deliberate physical cruelty, ("coups, blessures, sévices")						
Italy	86,106	274.36	66,098	210.60	34,700	110.56
France	75,598	197.54	57,341	149.84	33,284	86.97
Austria	....	....	....	....	75,883	304.52
Germany	....	....	126,412	230.15	118,057	214.94
(b) Assaults						
England	....	....	....	....	31,248	101.46
Ireland	....	....	....	....	10,349	227.36
III. Thefts						
Italy	130,690	416.41	61,450	195.80	56,848	181.13
France	120,776	315.60	39,548	103.34	40,742	106.46
Austria	....	....	156,954	285.76	123,953	497.42
Germany	....	....	....	....	102,998	187.52
England	....	....	....	....	38,445	123.79

Homicides. — From the foregoing it appears that of the eight countries included, Italy and Spain head the list, as to homicides, exhibiting, for the period 1895–1899, a respective annual average of 6.43 and 4.90 convictions for each 100,000 inhabitants. Moreover, the figures for Spain would have been much higher were it not that in the Spanish statistics attempts to kill by means of fire-arms form a class apart, there being, in 1899, 1,633 convictions for this offense.

Next follow Austria with 1.72 and France with 1.24 as their annual averages per 100,000 inhabitants, the former, during 1894–1898 and the latter during 1895–1899.

Ireland (1895–1899) and Germany (1897–1899) take third place, each having less than 1 and more than .50 for the same quota of inhabitants.

England and Scotland come last, since the one, from 1895 to 1899, the other from 1897 to 1899, showed annually less than .50 convictions per 100,000 inhabitants. With reason, it may be said that in Great Britain the crime of murder tends to disappear.

Hungary is not included in this table, but statistics of a somewhat less recent date, require it to be assigned a prominent place. From 1885 to 1899, the annual average per 100,000 inhabitants of convictions for murder (exclusive of infanticide) was 7.50, the actual number being 1,262.

Holland, Denmark, Sweden, and Norway, according to statistics of the same period, rank with Ireland and Germany in that they give an annual average of less than 1 and more than .50 per 100,000.

Belgium falls in the second class, approaching Austria and France, with 1.48 per 100,000.

Still following M. Bosco's data, we find Russia in Europe given an annual average, from 1885 to 1889, of 3,266 convictions, or 3.71 per 100,000. It would thus occupy an intermediate position, below Hungary, Italy, and Spain and above Austria and France. But the figure mentioned is very different from that we would be led to fix by the official statistics of the

Russian government for 1901. According to this recent source of information, the number of homicides of every description reported to the judges of instruction in that year attained the enormous total of 15,326. The population being estimated at 113,629,270, it follows that the proportion per 100,000 inhabitants would be almost 13.5. These statistics, it is true, do not furnish us with the number of convictions, but assuming, on the one hand, that convictions ensue for two-thirds of the accused and, on the other, that two or more persons are often implicated in the same crime, it must be concluded that in respect of the number of its murders, Russia holds the foremost place in Europe, except, perhaps, for Greece and the Danubian and Balkan States, whose statistics we do not possess, but which we know must have a very high proportion of this species of crime.

It is important to notice, however, that there is a great difference between the proportions of the Russian, Little Russian, and German provinces on the one side, and those of Poland, the Caucasus, Georgia, and Armenia, on the other. The three last, grouped under the heading "Judicial Court of Tiflis," show especially high figures. In a population of 9,201,710, the number of homicides reported to the judges of instruction was 5,045 — about one-third of the whole number in the Russian Empire. These regions would therefore show almost 55 homicides per year for each 100,000 inhabitants. If we exclude the district of the Judicial Court of Tiflis, the average for Russia falls to 10 per 100,000. The case would be analogous to that of Italy if we left out of view the Southern provinces. Poland, also, with 1,172 murders for about nine and one-half millions of people, exhibits a higher amount of criminality of this sort than Russia proper (that is to say, the judicial districts of St. Petersburg, Moscow, Kharkoff, Odessa, Saratoff, Kasan, Kieff and Vilna), where out of a population of about 95 millions the number of homicides was 8,790.

Assaults, etc. — We turn now to those attacks upon physical integrity which the English law groups under the term "assaults" and which in other criminal systems are designated as "strikings, woundings and acts of physical violence" ("coups, blessures, voies de fait"). Here, at first glance, the proportions of the several countries appear to be very much changed. Austria, for every 100,000 inhabitants, has 304.52 convictions, Germany, 214.94, and Ireland, 227.36, while Italy shows but 110.56 and France, 86.97. Italy thus would approximate England in the present respect, since the latter's proportion is 101.46, whereas its convictions for murder represent less than one-twelfth the number of Italy. But the lack of statistical uniformity forbids any conclusion from this resemblance. In the first place, the class denominated as "assaults" is much more comprehensive than that of strikings and woundings and embraces cases of threats and minor attacks upon the person, which in France would be treated as mere police offenses ("contraventions"). In England, furthermore, the person aggrieved, however slight his injury, nearly always puts the matter in the hands of the police, with the result that prosecutions of this character are very frequent. Moreover, criminal justice is speedy, and the offender is almost certain to be convicted. And finally, the excessive use of intoxicating liquors, still very prevalent in the lower classes, accounts in a large measure for the frequency of this species of crime, which, however, is steadily decreasing.

As for Austria, although the proportion of strikings and woundings is comparatively high (almost three times that of Italy), it must be noted that prosecution in that country is always on official initiative, while in Italy and elsewhere, for the less serious (and, of course, the more numerous) offenses, it occurs only on complaint of the injured person; and very often in such cases no complaint is ever made. Then, again, racial differences have much to do with the offenses in question. Galicia and Bukowina (Poles and Ruthenians) and Carniola and Dalmatia (Slovenians and Serbo-Croatians) which together form scarcely a third of the Austrian Empire, contribute two-thirds of the total number of strikings and woundings.[1] On the contrary, the proportions are very low in the provinces where the German element predominates.

But how are we to explain the high number of such offenses occurring in Germany? The reason would seem to be that prosecution is there more rigorous and is generally concerned with minor acts of violence. Even for the class of serious woundings ("gefährliche Körperverletzungen"), the number committed with a knife or similar instrument is estimated at less than one-tenth of the whole number.[2]

Unfortunately, as much cannot be said of Italy, where the knife continually plays a part in the most trivial disputes, or of Spain, where the "navaja" is the inseparable companion of the peasant and laborer.[3] And yet, according to its official statistics, Spain would come last in respect to the offenses under discussion. This fact is principally due to habitual failure to make complaint, either because the injured person desires to take the law into his own hands, or because the results of a prosecution do not appear to him worth while.

Thefts. — With respect to the category of thefts, it is to be observed that the countries most favorably circumstanced appear to be England and France, the former having but 123 convictions per 100,000 inhabitants and the latter 106, as against 181 for Italy and 187 for Germany. The situation of Austria appears much more serious, since its proportion is 497 per 100,000 inhabitants. But here, again, we find that a large number of offenses considered as misdemeanors ("délits") in Austria would be treated as police offenses ("contraventions") under the laws of many other States. Moreover, the fact that three-fourths of the persons convicted were punished with less than eight days' imprisonment indicates the unimportance of most of these thefts. It is the opinion of M. Bodio, that the differences between the European countries in relation to this crime would be considerably

[1] *A. Bosco, op. cit.,* p. 86.   [2] *Ibid.,* p. 109.
[3] *Ibid.,* p. 71.

less if one could take into account the relative facility of complaint and prosecution.

Crime in General. — A word may be proper as to the tendency of crime in general. — Italy manifests a continual increase. The total number of felonies ("crimes") and misdemeanors ("délits") reported to the authorities, which was 357,430 in 1887, rose to 511,682 in 1899. This is an increase of 3½% per annum, while that of the population for the same period was only 1% per annum. In Germany, the number of convictions for the common offenses ascended from 309,720 in 1882 to 440,534 in 1899; the proportionate increase of crime during this period was nearly double that of the population. Austria, as against 18,154 convictions for felonies ("crimes") in 1865, had 31,000 in 1898; as against 202,193 convictions for misdemeanors ("délits") in 1875, 306,007 in 1898. In Spain, the progressive increase in the common crimes which continued up to 1890, appears since to have abated. Between the annual averages for the periods 1891–1895 and 1896–1899, the difference is not very marked, — the figures being 20,102 and 19,943, respectively. As for France, we have already noticed that the total number of offenses, on the increase from 1861 to 1895, has since begun to exhibit a perceptible diminution. In England and Ireland the decrease is constant. Scotland, however, showed a slight increase during the closing years of the 1800s.

INDICES

INDEX OF AUTHORS

[Square brackets indicate citation in translator's notes]

SUBJECT INDEX

(Numerals in bold type distinguish references to Part IV: "Outline of Principles Suggested as a Basis for an International Penal Code.")

A

Chastity, not an elementary altruistic instinct, 16, 17.
    violations of, without coercion or seduction, not natural crimes, 34, 35.
    offenses against, as influenced by temperature, 118.
Children, efficacy of religious and moral instruction limited to case of, 141, 256, 257.
    only intelligent study of reformative treatment in case of adolescents and, 256.
    Marro and Lombroso on criminality of, 291, 293.
    birth of, as tending to transform character of mother, 385, **411**.
    See also AGE; YOUTHFUL OFFENDERS.
Chile, commutation of death sentences in, 380, 381.
Chinese, cruelties of European armies to, 27.
    lack of vulnerability frequent among, 115.
Chrétien, 92.
Christianity, adoption of its ethics influenced by conquests of Rome, 11.
Chukchi, 6.
Cincinnati riot of 1884, 53, *note* 1.
"Circonstances personelles et matérielles," 321, *note* 2.
Civic degradation in French penal law, 59, *note* 1.
Civil party, in French and Italian criminal proceedings, 340, *note* 1.
    proposed modification of procedure concerning, 420.
Civil status, suppression of, 41, *note* 3, **408**.
Civilization, and racial character, 119, 120.
    in relation to crime, 135–137.
    what constitutes true, 135, 167.
    Poletti's theory of proportion between crime and. *See* PROSPERITY.
Civilized man, anatomically inferior to savage, 253, *note* 1.
Classes of criminals. *See* CLASSIFICATION.
Classical school, its notion of the criminal, 271, *note* 2.
    its view of justice as a regulator of punishment, 272.
    mentioned, 271, 290, 308.
    See also JURIDICAL SCHOOL.
Classification, of natural crimes, 40, 41.
    of offenses in French and Italian systems, 59, *note* 1.
    of offenders in author's system, 111–132, 134, 222, 223, **406**.
        (1) *Murderers*, 111, 112.
        (2) *Violent criminals*, 112–125.
        (3) *Criminals deficient in probity*, 125–130.
        (4) *Lascivious criminals*, 130, 131.
    of offenders according to Ferri, 132–134.
Clemency, executive, 368–371.
Climate, its influence on crime, 117, 118.
Coaction. *See* PSYCHOLOGIC COACTION.
Code. *See* LEGAL DISOBEDIENCES; PENAL CODE; POLICE OFFENSES.
Code Napoléon, 325, *note* 2, 330.
Coerciveness, its utilitarian origin, 241.
Collective crime, question of, 123–125.
Collectivism, and sentiment of probity, 31, *note* 2.
    according to socialists, an end of crime, 143, 144, *note* 1.
Commercial classes, their contribution to crime, 158.
Commercial crises. *See* ECONOMIC DISTURBANCES.
Communism, idea that it would mean cessation of crime, 143, *note* 1.
Compensation Fund, for benefit of injured persons and State, 390, **413**, 434.
    how to be constituted, 390, 434.
    allocation of its contents, 435.
    existed in Two Sicilies and Duchy of Tuscany, 434.

I

V

Vagabonds, and moral neurasthenia, 128.
    punishment of, 225, 390, **412.**
        in Tudor England, 247, 325, *note* 2.
    should not be granted provisional liberation, **347.**
Vagabondage, 165, 198.
Valjean, Jean, 145.
Vanity of criminals, 83, 103.
Vascular reaction, 92.
Vendetta, 49, 112.
Vengeance, the original basis of punishment, 230.
    punishment apparent expression of social, 232.
Vesanic heredity, 259, *note* 2.
Vesanic manifestations, 106.
Vicaria, a prison of Palermo, 206.
Vigilance, defects in, as causes of crime (Romagnosi), 180.
"Violation de domicile" explained, 42, *note* 1.
    mentioned, 42.
Violent criminal, a physiognomic type, 72.
Violent criminals (in author's classification), 112–130, 131, 134.
    punishment of, 382, 391.
        (*a*) homicidal offenders, 382–385.
        (*b*) offenders guilty of serious physical or moral cruelty, 386, 387.
        (*c*) youthful offenders, 387, 388.
        (*d*) offenders deficient only in moral training or restraint, 389–391.
Virtue, feminine, 16, 17, 36, 37.
"Vitium," 99.
Vitriol-throwing, 114, 196.
"Vitrioleuses," 196.
"Voies de fait," 440.
"Vol domestique," 245 and *note* 1.
"Vol qualifié," 151 and *note* 1, 198, 245 and *note* 1, 300.
"Vol simple," 151 and *note* 1, 202, 227.
Vulnerability, defective or lacking, 115.

W

Wages, increase of, in France, 159, 168.
War, may cause a political crime to become a natural crime, 39.
    and capital punishment compared, 51.
    effect upon crime in general. *See* ECONOMIC DISTURBANCES.
Warrant of arrest in French criminal procedure, 341, *note* 1.
Wealth, unequal distribution of, in relation to crime, 142–165.
Wheat, increase of its consumption in France, 159, 168.
Wheat crop, increase of, in France, 1825–1878, 168.
Will. *See* FREE WILL.
Wine, its consumption in France, 162, *note* 1.
    See also ALCOHOLIC LIQUORS.
Witchcraft, 5, 16, 113.
Wives, transfer of, 12.
Women criminals, differential treatment proper for, **408.**
Words, offensive. *See* INSULTS.
Work, in penitentiaries, data as to, in France and Italy, 394, *note* 1.
    State-provided, Romagnosi's plan for, 180, 181.